Society and Politics in Africa

Yakubu Saaka
General Editor

Vol. 1

PETER LANG
New York • Washington, D.C./Baltimore
Bern • Frankfurt am Main • Berlin • Vienna • Paris

Issues and Trends in
Contemporary African Politics

George Akeya Agbango, Editor

Issues and Trends in Contemporary African Politics

Stability, Development, and Democratization

PETER LANG
New York • Washington, D.C./Baltimore
Bern • Frankfurt am Main • Berlin • Vienna • Paris

Library of Congress Cataloging-in-Publication Data

Issues and trends in contemporary African politics: stability, development, and
democratization/ George Akeya Agbango, editor.
p. cm. — (Society and politics in Africa; v.1)
Includes bibliographical references.
1. Political stability—Africa, Sub-Saharan. 2. Political violence—Africa, Sub-
Saharan. 3. Democracy—Africa, Sub-Saharan. 4. Economic development—
Political aspects—Africa, Sub-Saharan. I. Agbango, George Akeya. II. Series.
JQ1879.A15I87   320.967—dc20   96-18452
ISBN 0-8204-3130-3
ISSN 1083-3323

Die Deutsche Bibliothek-CIP-Einheitsaufnahme

Issues and trends in contemporary African politics: stability, development, and
democratization/ George Akeya Agbango, ed. – New York; Washington,
D.C./Baltimore; Bern; Frankfurt am Main; Berlin; Vienna; Paris: Lang.
(Society and politics in Africa; v.1)
ISBN 0-8204-3130-3
NE: GT

Cover design by Wendy Lee

The paper in this book meets the guidelines for permanence and durability
of the Committee on Production Guidelines for Book Longevity
of the Council of Library Resources.

Printed in the United States of America.

Dedicated To:

Zurma, Zurti,
Georgina,
Avoka & Samiah

Acknowledgments

Putting together the scholarly works of colleagues is anything but easy. Through the hospitality, kindness and generosity of many friends in Bloomsburg University, a conducive climate was created for the successful completion of this work. I am truly grateful to these individuals who made my transitional experience in Bloomsburg worthwhile. They are too many for me to list here but special mention must be made of the following: Drs. Harry Ausprich, Betty Allamong, Curtis English, Carol Matteson, Tom Cooper, Hsien-Tung Liu, John Baird, Roosevelt Newson, Bonita Franks, Oliver Larmi, Roy Pointer, Larry Mack, Robert Rosholt, Scott Lowe, Robert Obutelewicz, Chang Shub Roh, Linda LeMura, and the late Tej Saini; Professors Tony Silvester, Irvin Wright, Kenneth Schnure, Martin Gildea and Richard Micheri. Secretarial support provided by the Political Science Department is greatly appreciated.

This work could not have materialized without the cooperation of the several authors of the articles in this volume. I must thank them for their support and cooperation. I am also indebted to Ms. Starlett Craig and Dr. Walter Brash for proofreading the initial drafts and offering useful suggestions. Mrs. Sue Whitman (my American mother) gave me encouragement and stood by me in stressful times during the completion of this work. I am forever grateful to Mrs. Whitman for her moral and material support.

Special thanks go to General Olusegun Obasanjo, Ms. Portia Scott, Charles Haruna Sumani, Mrs. Marte DiGiuseppe, Tony DiGiuseppe, and Frank Hingleton who in many ways, are a part of this work. To Frank Hingleton, I hope many of your concerns about Africa have been answered in this book. I am very much indebted to Owen Lancer (Acquisitions Editor of

Peter Lang Publishing), for his professionalism, trust and willingness to work with me and getting this book published. Similarly, I wish to acknowledge my indebtedness to Dr. Yakubu Saaka (the General Editor of Peter Lang's series on Society and Politics in Africa) for his help.

Drs. Earl Picard, Hashim Gibrill, and James T. Jones of Clark Atlanta University, and Dr. Fred Boadu of Texas A & M University deserve special mention for reviewing parts of this work and offering valuable suggestions. I also wish to acknowledge my indebtedness to the United States Institute of Peace for funding my research on "Political Instability and Economic Development in Sub-Saharan Africa."

Two chapters of this book have appeared in other publications. I am grateful to the original publishers for permitting us to use these works in this volume: "The Crises of Nation Building: The Liberian Experience," *Towson Journal of International Affairs* (Spring 1994); and "Ethiopia: The Pitfalls of Ethnic Federalism," *Africa Quarterly*, (Vol. 34, No. 2, 1993). I am also grateful to Cambridge University Press for permitting us to reproduce a map of Africa published in Roland Oliver and Anthony Atmore's *Africa Since 1800.*

I wish to thank my family for all the support extended to me during those long hours of work trying to meet publication deadlines. Finally, my students of African Politics in Bloomsburg University deserve special mention for motivating me to produce a book on Africa that they can relate to. To them, I say, "Enjoy it, this is what you asked for."

Contents

Chapter 1

Introduction

We prefer self-government with danger to servitude in tranquility . . .
Seek ye first the political kingdom and all things shall be added unto
you.[1]

Africa is the heart of the world. Archaeological findings confirm that Africa was the home of the early human. Africa provided vital resources (both human and material) which helped
build great civilizations in many parts of the world. Today, the
continent of Africa is still a vital supplier of many of the world's
needs. Africa has given a lot to the world but has received very
little in return. Consequently, a growing number of African
scholars are re-examining Africa's place in world politics and
are looking for solutions to the continent's problems. To these
scholars, the solution to Africa's problems does not lie with
always blaming the external enemies of Africa and their local
collaborators but in the realization that Africans have to rise
to the occasion and simply find solutions to the continent's
predicament. The strong economies of some South East Asian
countries are largely due to the will and industry of their people.
With Africa's enormous economic resources, it is capable of
reversing the current downward socioeconomic and political
trends. This requires good leadership, excellent economic planning and a sustained period of political stability.

Writing about Africa in the early 1970's, Basil Davidson said:

There are brief climatic periods in history when the destiny of whole
peoples seems to resolve itself for better or for worse. The old gives
way to the new; and the new goes forward with a force that is sudden
and mysterious.

Afterwards, peering back into moods and memories, historians explain this suddenness and mystery as an illusion, as the mere surface
shift from deep-down currents of social and collective change. But
those who were there at the time, who watched or played a part themselves, are none the less likely to recall their wonder and delight—or,
according to their condition, their trouble and dismay—as though these
emotions had really been the product of a kind of miracle. This is
how it appears to have happened to people at all times of great up-
heaval. And this is undoubtedly how it has happened to millions of
people in Africa these past years.
But even if the suddenness and mystery are an illusion, concealing
the long and deep growth of a new independence, the insistent fact of
change, and therefore the persistent fact of *choice*, are pressingly real.
Africa today may be in many ways remarkably the same as it was twenty
years ago: given the general groundwork of technological poverty,
nothing else could be expected. Potentially, though, everything of
importance in Africa has changed; and it has done so in a sense that
may be called irreversible. It has changed so far that everything now
seems possible where little or nothing seemed possible before. And
people of the most various kinds and loyalties up and down the continent, from peasants of war-shattered Algeria in the far north to the
harried populations of the distant south, and all the way between, are
repeatedly confronted with the questions of a great and often pas-
sionate debate, the questions of *change* and *choice*: what happens now?
where do we go from here? and by which means?[2]

Over two decades later, Africa is still confronted with the dilemma raised by Davidson in the early 1970's: Where do we go
from here and by which means? Admittedly, much change has
taken place in Africa, but the pace of development is not com-
mensurate with development in other parts of the world. Unfortunately, some African countries have degenerated into conglomeration of clan-territories where allegiance is not to the
nation-state but to the clan and/or the ethnic group to which
one belongs. Meanwhile, bogus and corrupt leaders who replaced the colonial masters, or who subverted the democratic
leadership of their countries through coups d'etat, suppress
the masses and cling on to political power.

Eduardo Mondlane, president of FRELIMO (the
Mozambique Liberation Front) who was assassinated in early
1969, rightly observed that "liberation does not consist of
merely driving out the Portuguese [colonial] authority, but also
of constructing a new country; and that this construction must
be undertaken even while the colonial state is in the process

of being destroyed."[3] But nowhere in Africa was the colonial state truly destroyed [Map 1 depicts independent Africa after 1990]. Change, in most cases, has been cosmetic. In other cases, the neocolonial state relied on foreign experts to provide plans and panaceas for their liberation from external domination and exploitation.

David Hapgood's observation about the African elite in control of the political machine is rather shocking but accurate:

> Any plan, national or corporate or personal, can go awry, but African economic plans all go awry in the same direction (if they do not vanish entirely, as did Guinea's plan): too much spending on administration, social overhead, showpieces; not enough on production, very little on agriculture. . . . The best way to illustrate the point is by comparison with France, whose postwar plans have been extremely successful and whose planners are authors of most existing African plans. A plan, in Africa or in France, is a series of choices: limited resources will be spent on this and therefore not on that; some people will benefit and others will be hurt. Planning is a political act. When the French plan is drawn, the various interest groups that have a stake in it—management, labor, farmers—use their political strength to push the planners to satisfy their interests as they see them. . . .
>
> Not so in Africa. African plans are drawn mainly by foreign experts invited by the African government; their work is therefore a foreign import. No domestic political struggle tests the plan against the interests of African power groups. Instead, the African government swallows in one lump a plan that is what a group of foreign experts think the Africans should do. But spending of the government funds is the most political of decisions, and when the African government actually decides how much it will spend on what, it is motivated by the realities of African politics, not by the advice of foreign experts. It is then, after the writing and adoption of the plan, that the real political decisions are made. The money goes where the power is, which, in Africa today, means it goes to satisfy the desires and interests of the elite, not the powerless peasantry.[4]

Hapgood was writing about Africa in the 1970's, but the story is not any different in the 1990's. Samuel Doe of Liberia imported the "apex-men" from the United States to assist him manage his ailing economy in the mid-1980's. His reliance on foreign experts is exemplary of the contempt that some self-imposed African leaders have against their intelligentsia. It is often wise and cheaper to use local think-tanks and the latter are better equipped to find solutions to Africa's perennial prob-

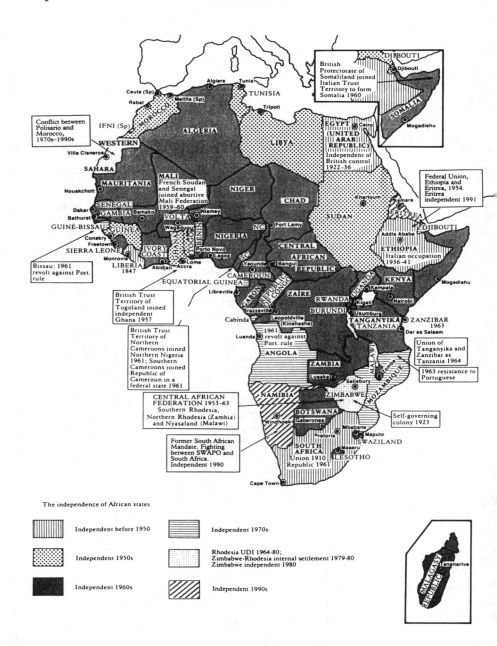

The independence of African states

▦ Independent before 1950	▤ Independent 1970s
▨ Independent 1950s	▦ Rhodesia UDI 1964-80; Zimbabwe-Rhodesia internal settlement 1979-80 Zimbabwe independent 1980
■ Independent 1960s	▨ Independent 1990s

British Protectorate of Somaliland joined Italian Trust Territory to form Somalia 1960

Conflict between Polisario and Morocco, 1970s–1990s

Independent of British control 1922–36

Federal Union, Ethiopia and Eritrea, 1954. Eritrea independent 1991

Italian occupation 1936–41

British Trust Territory of Togoland joined independent Ghana 1957

Bissau: 1961 revolt against Port. rule

British Trust Territory of Northern Cameroons joined Northern Nigeria 1961; Southern Cameroons joined Republic of Cameroon in a federal state 1961

French Soudan and Senegal joined abortive Mali Federation 1959–60

1961 revolt against Port. rule

Union of Tanganyika and Zanzibar as Tanzania 1964

1963 resistance to Portuguese

CENTRAL AFRICAN FEDERATION 1953–63 Southern Rhodesia, Northern Rhodesia (Zambia) and Nyasaland (Malawi)

Self-governing colony 1923

Former South African Mandate. Fighting between SWAPO and South Africa. Independent 1990

Union 1910 Republic 1961

Source: Roland Oliver and Anthony Atmore, Africa since 1800, *(Cambridge University Press, 1994), p. 203.*

lems than to rely on foreign experts who are often truly alien to our problems.

The impact of the failure of African countries to rely on local experts sometimes results in some African delegations going to loan negotiation conferences poorly prepared. In the end, they accept every condition.

In discussing the failure of the leadership in Africa in *Africa Betrayed*, George Ayittey contends:

> Competent leadership is vital for successful economic reform. African leaders cannot improve their countries' economic conditions without understanding how their economies run. Displaying such ignorance, many African leaders manage their economies by issuing decrees, orders, and threats.[5]

It is out of these common concerns about Africa that we were inspired to put together these essays to help explain the political developments that are taking place in the continent today. Readers will find in this collection works of some Africanists in the United States who have genuine concerns about the continent's future. While this volume does not pretend to cover all the nations of Africa, the countries studied and written about are, in our view, a representative sample of what pertains in Africa. There are a few success stories in Africa, such as Botswana, Lesotho, Mauritius, and Swaziland. Those will not be our principal focus in this book. Our main concern here is with the distressed countries of our continent.

The advent of the Second Russian Revolution, led by Mikhail Gorbachev, which ushered in the apparent end of the Cold War, has dramatically changed the political map of the world. As in Europe and Asia, Africa too is under tremendous pressure from both external and internal interests and forces to democratize. These "revolutionary" changes may present the continent with a second opportunity for genuine independence and economic solvency. The first struggle for, and attainment of, independence was a political one. But the second "independence" of Africa will be a socioeconomic one: leading to freedom from want, economic mismanagement, ethnic conflict, and despotic rule.

In Chapter 2, George Agbango examines the underlying theories of development and political instability. This is essen-

tial if we are to understand what led to the derailment of the
pre-independent dreams and post-independent development
plans/policies of the founding fathers of the emergent nation-
states of Africa. The chapter discusses the causes of political
instability and, using empirical evidence, illustrates the relationship between political instability and economic development in Africa.

Nigeria, the so-called giant of Africa, experienced a bloody
military coup in 1966. This was followed by a civil war in 1967.
In Chapter 3, Nchor Okorn traces the causes of political and
social violence in Nigeria. Using concrete examples, he draws
the readers attention to some of the setbacks that the country
has suffered as an outcome of the violence.

As in Nigeria, where political violence has marred and
scarred the country, many African countries have experienced
similar or worse predicaments. The 1994 Rwandan genocide
is the most recent example of this. However, Liberia, Somalia,
Ethiopia, Zaire, Angola, Algeria, Mozambique, Uganda, and
Chad have all had their share of violent political upheavals. In
Chapter 4, an in-depth analysis of the Liberian civil war is presented by George Agbango. A coup in 1980 led by Master-Sergeant Samuel Doe resulted in the assassination of President
William Tolbert and the subsequent execution of 13 of his cabinet ministers. The latter were tied to stakes and executed after
they were found guilty of corruption by secret military courts
established by Doe's ruling junta.

The alienation of some sectors of a population from participation in the political process sometimes lead to national crisis. In the case of Liberia the monopoly of political power since
1821 by the Americo-Liberians was resented by other elements
of the Liberian population. This partly explains Doe's coup
d'etat in 1980. After a decade of authoritarian and repressive
rule, Doe plunged Liberia into civil war. The adage that "what
goes around, comes around" was truly manifested in Doe's case
when he was tortured to death by a rebel force at the height of
the civil war.

In June 1994, the editor met Julius Ihonvbere at a conference organized by the Interfaith Hunger Appeal (New York)
and the Carter Center (Atlanta) at Spelman College in Atlanta,
Georgia, on "Governance, Equity, and the Global Poor." He

delivered a paper on "Beyond Governance, the State and Democratization in Sub-Saharan Africa." His logical analysis of Africa's ails captivated all participants. His ideas contrasted very sharply with another panelist, a "well-educated" African, who works for the World Bank and who came as an apologist for the Bank's poor performance in Africa. Ihonvbere's genuine concern for Africa and the relevance of his subject matter to Africa brought a few of the Africanists at the meeting to a mini-Organization of African Unity conference at the end of the day. It was amazing how similar the views about the future of Africa of all present were. Blunt as he was then, Ihonvbere is even more so today about developments in Africa. Hence in Chapter 5, he discusses the ramifications of the dismantling of multi-party political system in many African countries and the subsequent introduction of one-party political systems shortly after independence. There is now a new wave of multi-party political systems in Africa. In some African countries, keenly contested elections have been hurriedly organized. To give credibility to these democratic attempts, the leaders of these African countries have called upon international organizations to monitor and "give their blessings" to their "fair" elections. Using the 1991 Zambian elections as a case study, Julius Ihonvbere examines the role of foreign monitors in national elections in Africa in Chapter 5.

The political tide that is sweeping across Africa finds expression in Baffour Agyeman-Duah's article (Chapter 6) about Ghana. In this contribution, Agyeman-Duah examines the legitimacy of the post-colonial state in Africa and probes the prospects for democratic reforms in Africa.

In Chapter 7, Yakubu Saaka discusses election fraud in Ghana and the challenge facing the Rawlings' regime in its attempt to legitimize itself. Ghana has always been considered a pacesetter for Africa—particularly in the 1960's. Besides, Ghana's favorable standing among western donor nations as a showcase of International Monetary Fund and World Bank sponsored Economic Recovery Program "success" in Africa make her a relevant actor in the "Post-Cold War African Political Phenomenon." Saaka's paper analyzes how "Jerry Rawlings has succeeded in using party politics and constitutionalism to reinvent himself."[6]

For quite a while, Cameroon was considered one of the success stories in Africa because of its brief spell of economic buoyancy. In Chapter 8, Henry Elonge focuses on Cameroon's experiment with democracy. Cameroon's experience is very relevant here because, as Elonge suggests, "Mere sermons of democracy as it relates to America, France, Russia, or Britain are not necessarily the answer"[7] for Africa. To import wholesale western notions of democracy into Africa "detracts us from the real questions of our own plight."[8]

Unfortunately, the lack of substantive interest in Africa leads some in the developed nations to perceive Africa as one country inhabited by one ethnic group. One of the problems with nation building in Africa is the crisis of identity. The nationalism in the 1950's and 1960's that resolutely united Africans in their fight for independence disappeared in the post-independent era in many of these countries. In some instances, it is easier for some people to identify with their ethnic group first before identifying with the nation. Gregory S. Mahler suggests that identity crisis is a universal phenomenon. He points out:

> In the contemporary political world, one of the major hurdles faced by the new and developing nations is the need to help citizens develop a national identity. Failure to do so can result in national stress and possibly civil war: . . . Ibo "tribesmen" in Nigeria did not want to think of themselves as Nigerians, and attempted (unsuccessfully) to break away from Nigeria and form a new nation, Biafra . . . Similar situations exist for the Sikh population in India's Punjab region, the Eritreans in Somalia (sic), and the Tamil population in Sri Lanka, among others.[9]

In Chapter 9, Walle Engedayehu discusses the role played by ethnicism in the civil war in Ethiopia. Understanding the Ethiopian predicament may help us to appreciate why nations such as Somalia, Sudan, Liberia, Sierra Leone and Rwanda stand at the brink of annihilation today.

Margaret Lee's essay (Chapter 10) examines the long and arduous road to Black majority rule in South Africa. In her own words, "Between political violence, the seeming inability of the major actors to come to a consensus during negotiations, and the attempt by black and white right-wing elements to destabilize the transition, it often appeared that the country was moving toward an abyss. To the credit of the people of

South Africa, the April 1994 elections and the transition to democratic rule were peaceful and set an example for other countries," which are marred by civil strife, to emulate.[10]

Akwasi Osei makes the case, in Chapter 11, that "of the African nations, South Africa is the one best positioned to eradicate neo-colonialism as described by Amilcar Cabral."[11] Cabral is one of Africa's distinguished political philosophers who was at the forefront of the liberation war in Guinea Bissau.

In Chapter 12, Julius Ihonvbere discusses the challenges facing African nations as they initiate democratic reforms. Ihonvbere critically analyzes the democratic attempts being initiated in post-colonial Africa following the end of the Cold War. The intentions of both external and internal actors in the sudden democratization initiatives in Africa are exhaustively discussed and he suggests an African solution to the democratization agenda. Ihonvbere contends that, "Any serious effort at understanding the challenge or dilemmas of democracy in Africa, must, therefore, pay due attention to the region's historical experiences, the implications of that experience, and the contemporary inter-play of social and political forces."[12] He offers suggestions as panacea to problems that may hinder the democratization process.

George Ayittey presents a unique, but crucial, perspective on Africa's problems. He squarely lays the blame for the poor performance of the post-colonial state on the rather selfish political leadership. With concrete examples, he frankly discusses the "problem with Africa" in Chapter 13.

Julius Ihonvbere's article, "Pan Africanism: Agenda for African Unity in the 1990's?" was selected as the concluding chapter (Chapter 14) because of the constant relevance of the question of African unity in our discussions about Africa. The chapter is an edited version of a keynote address that Ihonvbere delivered at the All-Africa Student Conference held at the University of Guelph (Ontario) in May 1994. The conference theme was "African Unity." Thus, Ihonvbere tackles the problems which confront a continent that is not "only far from unity on any front, [but] it is today the most marginal, the most oppressed, the most exploited, the most poverty stricken, the most debt-ridden, the most unstable, and the most denigrated continent in the world."[13] He provides constructive suggestions for the continent's march to development.

The prospects for stability, development, and democratization in Africa are great. The forces opposed to progressive political and socioeconomic development of the continent will not prevail in the final analyses. From the discourses in this book, the reader will agree that any meaningful development programs must be initiated by Africans. Any form of external support should, therefore, aim at consolidating the gains of such African initiative. If these chapters stimulate further debates on Africa's future in a fast growing world, then our purpose for this work would have been fulfilled.

Notes

1   Party slogans and motto of the Convention Peoples Party under the leadership of Kwame Nkrumah in Ghana in the 1950's. See Kwame Nkrumah, *Autobiography of Kwame Nkrumah* (London: Panaf Books Limited, 1973), p. 135.

2   Basil Davidson, *Which Way Africa?* (Baltimore, Maryland: Penguin Books, Limited, 1973), pp. 11-12.

3   Eduardo Mondlane, *The Struggle for Mozambique* (Baltimore, Maryland: Penguin Books Limited, 1969), p. 163.

4   David Hapgood, *Africa: From Independence to Tomorrow* (New York: Atheneum, 1970) pp. 62-64.

5   George B.N. Ayittey, *Africa Betrayed* (New York: St. Martin's Press, 1992), p. 309.

6   Yakubu Saaka, "Legitimizing the Illegitimate: The 1992 Presidential Elections as a Prelude to Ghana's Fourth Republic," Chapter 7, page 145, of this book.

7   Henry Elonge, "Visions of Change in Cameroon within the Context of a New World Order," Chapter 8, page 186, of this book.

8   *Ibid*, page 187.

9   Gregory S. Mahler, *Comparative Politics: An Institutional Cross-National Approach*, (Englewood Cliff, New Jersey: Prentice Hall, 1995), p. 17.

10   Margaret Lee, "South Africa: The Long and Arduous Road to a New Dispensation," Chapter 10, page 237, of this book.

11   Akwasi Osei, "South Africa in the African Dilemma," Chapter 11, page 284, of this book.

12   Julius Ihonvbere, "Democratization in Africa: Challenges and Prospects," Chapter 12, pages 292-93, of this book.

13   Julius Ihonvbere, "Pan-Africanism: Agenda for African Unity in the 1990's?" Chapter 14, page 337, of this book.

Chapter 2

Political Instability and Economic Development in Sub-Saharan Africa*

George A. Agbango

INTRODUCTION

The impact of political instability on the development of Sub-Saharan Africa has generated intense scholarly debate. There are several reasons for this. First, the definition of economic development is itself debatable. Second, there is the problem of causality; that is, even if one settles the issue of what constitutes economic development, there are still problems of whether instability causes poor economic development or vice versa. Third, there is the problem of an appropriate theoretical framework to use in analyzing the relationship between economic development and political instability.

To shed some light on these issues it will be useful to briefly survey the literature on the subject. This is presented in three parts. The first part of the literature deals with definitions and theories of economic development. The second is a survey of the literature on the theories of political instability. The third part focuses on theories that have been developed to analyze the effects of political instability. The goal in each section is to identify those strategic factors that will be used in later sections of this chapter to construct and organize the author's analysis in an effort to explain the relationship between political instability and economic development.

* Research for this chapter was partially funded by the United States Institute of Peace, Washington, DC under the Jennings Randolph Peace Scholar fellowship program.

DEFINITIONS OF ECONOMIC DEVELOPMENT

The verb "to develop" is defined as "to cause to grow or expand."[1] Based on this definition, development is a relatively simple concept. Literally, therefore, economic development may be defined as the state in which an existing economy experiences advanced growth as a result of the application of "appropriate" economic policies. The word "appropriate" is used here very guardedly because what may be considered appropriate in one school of thought may not be appropriate in another. However, it is important to stress that the parameters of this study transcend the literal meaning of economic development.

The traditional conception of economic development has often referred to "the capacity of a national economy, whose initial economic condition has been more or less static for a long time, to *generate* and *sustain* an annual increase in its gross national product at rates of perhaps 5-7 percent or more."[2] Consequently, in the 1960's, most of the economic development policies of Sub-Saharan African countries were geared toward the attainment of these targeted growth rates. Unfortunately, the above definition failed to stand the test of time. For instance, during the 1960's and 1970's when the United Nations by resolution referred to this period as the "Development Decades," development was conceived largely as an attainment of six percent target growth rate of the Gross National Product (GNP). A larger number of Third World countries achieved this United Nations' target, but their standard of living remained for the most part unchanged. This proved the deficiency of the traditional approach in addressing the problems of the developing countries. Consequently, a new concept of development was propounded during the 1970's which redefined development as "the reduction or elimination of poverty, inequality, and unemployment within the context of a growing economy."[3] To Africa and its leaders, development means more than that. According to Claude Ake, in the eyes of Africans, development means the absence of poverty, a low incidence of disease, low levels of unemployment, absence of or low incidence of social disorganization and political instability, as well as the prevalence of military strength and technological advancement.[4] Thus, Ake's definition departs from the quantitative measures of growth in gross national product that paid little attention to the distributional and equity implications. Another important contributor to the development debate is Dudley Seers. Seers raised some important questions when he pointed out:

> The questions to ask about a country's development are, therefore: What has been happening to poverty? What has been happening to unemployment? What has been happening to inequality? If all three of these have declined from high levels, then beyond doubt this has been a period of development for the country. If one or two of these central problems have been growing worse, especially if all three have, it would be strange to call the result "development" even if per capita income doubled.[5]

Walter Rodney perceived economic development from a different angle. To Rodney:

> A society develops economically as its members increase jointly their capacity for dealing with the environment. This capacity for dealing with the environment is dependent on the extent to which they understand the laws of nature (science), on the extent to which they put that understanding into practice by devising tools (technology), and on the manner in which work is organized.[6]

However, there is one important area in which scholars agree, and that is that economic development must be seen as a multifaceted concept. Todaro, unlike Ake, provides an orthodox view of what should constitute development. He contends that economic development must be seen as a "multidimensional process involving major changes in social structures, popular attitudes, and national institutions, as well as the acceleration of economic growth, the reduction of inequality and the eradication of poverty."[7] The views of Ake, Seers, Rodney, and Todaro, despite their slight differences, address important concerns relevant to the debate on Sub-Saharan African development. Social structures, as well as popular attitudes, have largely determined the pace of development in Sub-Saharan Africa. It is not surprising, therefore, that most coup leaders in Sub-Saharan Africa often justify their actions by indicating that the need to reform socioeconomic and political structures, as well as national attitudes, for the better, motivated their rebellious actions. For instance, Colonel Acheampong of Ghana advanced those arguments in his "National Charter of Redemption" following the overthrow of the civilian government of Kofi Busia in 1972. Similarly, Thomas Sankara of Burkina Faso called for a social revolution in which there is equity in the distribution of the national wealth following his successful coup in 1983.

THEORIES OF ECONOMIC DEVELOPMENT

As in the case of the various definitions of economic development, there are equally varied opinions on the appropriate theory of economic development to be used in analyzing the performance of developing countries. In this section, we will examine several of the more popular theories on the subject. These include:

1. ... Classical Economic Theory;
2. ... Marxian Economic Theory;
3. ... Linear Stages of Economic Growth Models;
4. ... Neo-Classical Structural Change Models; and
5. ... International/Dependency Model/The World Systems Model/or Modern Development Theory.

Classical Economic Theory

Classical economic theory has its origins in the works of notable authorities such as Adam Smith, David Ricardo, and Thomas Malthus. The emphasis of the classical economic theory of development is in those factors that will generate and sustain an annual increase in the gross national product of a country. Because early classical economic theorists were concerned mainly with increases in gross national product they did not pay much attention to the distributional and equity implications of growth. Adam Smith, for instance, was concerned about the growth of the economy as a result of increase in production through the application of management science such as the division of labor and specialization. Smith's "invisible hand" referred to a free-market economic system that can boost economic production,[8] "whereby the private interests and passions of men are led in the direction which is most agreeable to the interest of the whole society."[9]

Thomas Malthus, unlike Adam Smith, was concerned about the relationship between the geometric growth in food production and population. He noted that there is a significant disparity between the growth in population and food production. The result of this disparity in growth over the long haul is to create a situation of overpopulation unmatched by adequate food supply. The end result is poverty, deprivation, and oppressive human conditions.[10] Some scholars and international development agencies still make references to the ideas of Malthus and have encouraged African governments to actively pursue policies aimed at reducing population while doubling efforts to increase food production. The family planning program in Ghana, for instance, was initiated by the government in the late 1960's with the hope that the reduction or control of population could ameliorate some of its economic problems.

David Ricardo, however, was concerned about the distribution of production among the various social classes and the impact of such distribution on the level of economic development.[11] Ricardo's views help to explain the socioeconomic problems created in Sub-Saharan Africa as a consequence of the unequal distribution of the "national pie." National policies often cater to the elite's interests rather than those of the broad masses. For example, one will question the rationale for building a multimillion dollar cathedral in the Ivory Coast by the late President Felix Houphouet-Boigny as his personal contribution to the growth and development of the Catholic Church when there are not enough clinics for the rural poor. Misplaced priorities such as the one in the Ivory Coast have led to political upheavals and, consequently, instability in many Sub-Saharan African countries.

Marxian Economic Theory
Karl Marx's analytical procedures and predictions differed from utopian socialists such as Robert Owen and John Stuart Mill, and liberal economic thinkers such as Adam Smith and David Ricardo. Karl Marx, using the historical experience of European countries, advanced five stages of economic development of nations. The last four of these progressive stages were "feudalism, capitalism, socialism under the dictatorship of the proletariat and, finally, utopian communism."[12] Marx predicted that capitalism, by its very oppressive nature, will destroy itself in that the exploitation of man by man will reach a stage when the masses will rebel against their oppressor because they can

no longer tolerate the naked exploitation and oppression. Such a rebellion may lead to a socialist revolution. Under socialism, Marx contends that economic equality will be restored.[13] However, Ronald Chilcote cautions that "the idea of development is firmly rooted in Marxist origins but that of underdevelopment is essentially non-Marxist in its original conceptions, and thus, recent Marxist attention to underdevelopment should be viewed as critically as bourgeois theory."[14]

Classical Marxian economic theories postulate that economic development is directly related to the process of production which involves the forces of production and the relations of production.[15] Marx argues that the origins of all historical changes may be in the conflict between the forces of production and the relations of production.[16] The forces of production refer to material conditions of production such as people and their skills, raw materials, and tools, whereas the relations of production refer to the relation between people during the processes of production, distribution, and exchange of society's material goods. Hence, the Marxist school maintains that conflict between the forces and relations of production results in a society's development being slowed down leading to radical changes to the extent that the absolute social relations are replaced by new and more advanced ones. Some of the revolutions that have occurred in some Sub-Saharan African countries have been largely due to the influence of Marxian theory of economic development. For instance, the revolutions in Angola, Mozambique, and Ethiopia have been claimed to be Marxian inspired.

Linear Stages of Economic Growth Models

The *Linear Stages Theory of Economic Growth* was the dominant paradigm in the 1950's and 1960's. During this era, development was considered as a series of successive stages through which all countries must pass. W. W. Rostow, a chief exponent of this model, argued that the advanced countries such as the United States, Britain, and Western European countries all passed through a "take-off" stage. During the "take-off" period, domestic and foreign savings were mobilized for investment and this accelerated these countries' economic growth. Rostow advanced the following argument:

. . . It is possible to identify **all** societies, in their economic dimensions, as lying within one of five categories: the traditional society, the pre-conditions for take-off into self-sustaining growth, the take-off, the drive to maturity, and the age of high mass consumption. . . . These stages are not merely descriptive. They are not merely a way of generalizing certain factual observations about the sequence of development of modern societies. They have an inner logic and continuity. . . . They constitute, in the end, both a theory about economic growth and a more general, if still highly partial, theory about modern history as a whole.[17]

Rostow's views were supported by the works of Roy Harrod and Evesey Domar. They used mathematical equations to justify the view that increases in national savings could trigger economic growth because "any net additions to the capital stock in the form of new investment will bring about corresponding increases in the 'flow' of national output (GNP)."[18]

The Linear Stages Theory, as expressed in the Harrod-Domar Growth Model, did not always work because more savings and investments, though a necessary condition for economic growth, were not a sufficient condition. According to Todaro, the Linear Stages Theory did not work because it ". . . failed to take into account the crucial fact that contemporary Third World nations are part of a highly integrated and complex international system in which even the best and most intelligent development strategies can be nullified by external forces beyond the countries' control."[19]

Andre Gundar Frank disagree with Rostow's view of the stages of development through which developing nations must necessarily pass. He argues:

It is generally held that economic development occurs in a succession of capitalist stages that today's underdeveloped countries are still in a stage, sometimes depicted as an original stage, of history through which the now-developed countries passed long ago. Yet even modest acquaintance with history shows that underdevelopment is not original or traditional and that neither the past nor the present of the underdeveloped countries resembles in any important respect the past of the now-developed countries. The now developed countries were never *under*developed, though they may have been *un*developed.[20]

It is obvious that colonization and imperialism played significant roles in the underdevelopment of most Third World countries—a system which the now-developed countries did not have to face. Thus, Frank postulates, "historical research demonstrates that contemporary underdevelopment is in large part the historical product of past and continuing economic and other relations between satellite underdeveloped and now-developed metropolitan countries."[21] Walter Rodney argues along the same lines when he declared that "Africa economies are integrated into the very structure of the developed capitalist economies: and they are integrated in a manner that is unfavorable to Africa and insures that Africa is dependent on big capitalist countries."[22] Rostow's approach to the development issues of less-developed countries, therefore, was unappealing to Sub-Saharan African countries which had to catch up with the developed world in the shortest possible time. Hence, as Gunnar Myrdal rightly noted, the less-developed countries must by-pass the historical stages of economic development if they are to catch up with the developed countries. To do otherwise, he maintains, will be disastrous for the less-developed countries.[23]

Neo-Classical Structural Change Models
Neo-Classical Structural Change Models dominated economic development theories in the mid-1950's and the 1960's. These models focused on the steps that the less-developed countries may take to transform their heavily dependent agrarian economies to more modern, urbanized, and industrially diversified manufacturing and service economies. Arthur Lewis and Hollis Chenery are renowned for their contributions to this theory.

Lewis advanced a two-sector surplus labor model which was later expanded and further developed by John Fei and Gustav Ranis. The assumption of Lewis' model was that there was surplus labor in the traditional, overpopulated rural subsistence sector which was characterized by zero marginal labor productivity. This surplus labor could be influenced, by high wages, to migrate to the high-productivity modern industrial sector. The model assumed that surplus labor from the agricultural sector will continue to be absorbed until it becomes uneconomical to do so. As economic activity shifts from traditional rural agriculture to modern urban industry, the economy expands and grows. In this way, the less-developed countries expand their economic base.[24] Lewis' model was very popular in the late 1950's and early 1960's. It was not surprising, therefore, that Lewis was appointed the chief economic adviser to President Nkrumah of Ghana in the early 1960's.[25]

Lewis' model failed to yield positive results because its key assumptions did not fit the institutional and economic realities of most contemporary Third World countries.[26] Hence, Todaro concludes:

> [W]hen one takes into account the labor-saving bias of most modern technological transfer, the existence of substantial capital flight, the widespread nonexistence of rural labor, the growing prevalence of urban surplus labor, and the tendency for modern sector wages to rise rapidly even where substantial open unemployment exists, then the Lewis two-sector model—while extremely valuable as an early conceptual portrayal of the development process of sector interaction and structural change—requires considerable modification in the assumptions and analysis to fit the reality of contemporary Third World Nations.[27]

Hollis Chenery has done some useful empirical analysis based on the *"patterns of development"* approach. Unlike the Lewis model, Chenery maintained that there are both domestic and international constraints on development. The domestic constraints include a country's resource endowment, its physical size, and the size of its population. Other constraints include access to external capital, technology, and international trade. Chenery who studied patterns of development in many Third World countries from 1950-1973, held that the differences among Third World countries *vis-a-vis* their level of development were largely due to the above constraints. Chenery's empirical findings concluded that "as per capita incomes rise, [there] was a significant shift from agricultural production to industrial production."[28] Those who subscribe to this view argue that the application of the right types of policies will yield positive dividends of self-sustaining growth.

International Dependency Model/The World Systems Model/or Modern Development Theory

The International Dependency Model is sometimes referred to as the World Systems Model or Modern Development Theory. The review of the literature on dependency reveals that there is no unified theory on the subject;[29] rather, individual scholars and institutions attempt to explain dependency based on their own experiences and conceptualizations. For instance, scholars at the United Nations Economic Commission for Latin America (ECLA) used underdevelopment as the underlying assumption for dependency theory.[30] Raul Prebisch, one of the ECLA scholars and pioneer of the dependency approach, postulated that persistent weakness in the prices of raw materials from the less-developed countries, negated the beneficial results expected from comparative advantage in international trade. Therefore, in a world of a developed center versus an underdeveloped periphery, the center nations exploit the periphery countries through "deteriorating terms of trade" mechanism.[31] The effect of this on the periphery nations is an "external dependency" that the latter must overcome.

Raul Prebisch and his colleagues at the ECLA, therefore, recommended three solutions for the development of the less-developed countries:

1. Industrialization through import-substitution;
2. The promotion of exports; and
3. Institutional changes in favor of underdeveloped countries at the international level.[32]

According to Michael Todaro, this model views Third World countries as beset by institutional, political, and economic rigidities. The model maintains that Third World countries are caught up in a dependence and dominance relationship to the rich and developed countries.[33] This approach provides two schools of thought on development—the *neocolonial dependence model* (continuous dependence of the poor and once colonized countries on their wealthy colonial masters) and the *false paradigm model* (continuous underdevelopment of Third World countries due to over reliance on flawed advise from experts in the developed countries and their donor institutions).

By the mid-1960's, a wave of scholars (including Paul Sweezy, Tomas Vasconi, Walter Rodney, Fernando H. Cardoso, Claire Savit Bacha, Andre Gundar Frank, Celso Furtado, Theotonio dos Santos and Osvaldo Sunkel) developed Raul Prebisch's views on dependency. To these scholars, any discussion on dependency must be linked to the capitalist mode of production. They argued there was a definite link between external forces, domestic factors, and transnational capitalism—the latter being a common denominator of the first two.[34] The unit of analysis of dependency, therefore, was to include nation-states, social groups, classes, and multinational corporations.

Hence, the neocolonial dependence model, which is neo-Marxist, theorizes that there is an international conspiracy by the advanced capitalist system to continue to exploit the less-developed countries. According to the model, the relationship between the less-developed countries and the advanced countries is one of unequal partnership by which local bourgeois elements protect the interest of the capitalist world for their own selfish needs. Theotonio Dos Santos is one of the leading advocates of the neocolonial dependence model. He argues that:

> Underdevelopment, far from constituting a state of backwardness prior to capitalism, is rather a consequence and a particular form of capitalist development known as dependent capitalism . . . dependence is a *conditioning* situation in which the economies of one group of countries are conditioned by the development and expansion of others. A relationship of interdependence between two or more economies or between such economies and the world trading system becomes a dependent relationship when some countries can expand through self-impulsion while others, being in a dependent position, can only expand as a reflection of the expansion of the dominant countries, which may have positive or negative effects on their immediate development. In either case, the basic situation of the dependence causes these countries to be both backward and exploited. Dominant countries are endowed with technological, commercial, capital, and sociopolitical predominance over dependent countries—the form of this predominance varying according to the particular historical moment—and can therefore exploit them and extract part of the locally produced surplus. Dependence, then, is based upon an international division of labor which allows industrial development to take place in some countries while restricting it in others, whose growth is conditioned by and subjected to the power centers of the world.[35]

Based on the above analysis, many Sub-Saharan African countries formulated national economic policies that were geared towards breaking their over-dependence on their former colonial metropoles. It became fashionable to condemn the capitalist market economy and to embrace the socialist mode of development. This accounts for the wave of so-called socialist governments that emerged in the continent between 1960 and 1980. The problem with this trend was that it constituted the rejection of one form of dependency (dependence on the West) and the embracement of another form of dependency (ideological dependence on the East).

Finally, the *"false paradigm"* model attributes the underdevelopment of the less-developed countries to faulty and inappropriate advice provided by misinformed (however well meaning) international experts who work for the developed countries' assistance agencies and multinational donor organizations (such as the International Monetary Fund). Their advice often leads to inappropriate policies which result in adverse economic outcomes in the less developed nations.

Studies conducted by several scholars, including Abdoulaye Bathily, Fantu Cheru, Zuwaghn A. Bonat, and Yahaya A. Abdullahi—on Senegal, Sudan, Tanzania, and Nigeria, have revealed that:

> The Fund-Bank [IMF and World Bank] stabilization programmes have become pervasive vehicles for negating hard-won national sovereignty through the anti-statist imposition of conditionality that has turned African countries into mere "adjustment states"—adjusting their countries and economies to the exploitative demands of world imperialism. Fund and Bank programmes also typically encourage repressive authoritarian regimes, the militarisation of politics and the negation of basic democratic and human rights. The basic point, therefore, is that all austerity programmes are basically measures of economies and political repression.[36]

The theories above have been discussed because they have a significant bearing on the economic development policies of political regimes in Sub-Saharan Africa. Succeeding regimes (both military and civilian) in the region have had to make policy choices out of a range of economic paradigms with the hope of finding panaceas for the economic decadence of their countries. A valid theory of economic development for Sub-Saharan Africa should address the continuous decline of the region's economy. It should provide solutions for arresting the abject poverty; create employment opportunities; ensure equity in the distribution of the national wealth; link economic development to political development as a means of tackling political instability; and more especially, provide an agenda for technological advancement.

WHAT CONSTITUTES AN
ECONOMIC DEVELOPMENT POLICY?

Public policy basically is the decision taken by a governing body aimed at accomplishing a specific goal or objective. According to Dennis Palumbo, "we define policy as the guiding principle behind regulations, laws, and programs; its visible manifestation is the strategy taken by government to solve public problems."[37] An economic policy is:

> [a] statement of objectives and the methods of achieving these objectives (policy instruments) by government, political party, business concern, etc. Some examples of government economic objectives are maintaining full employment, achieving a high rate of economic growth, reducing income and regional development inequalities, maintaining price stability. Policy instruments include fiscal policy, monetary and financial policy, and legislative controls (e.g., price and wage control, rent control).[38]

In most Sub-Saharan African countries, economic development policies are translated into development plans. An economic development plan is a written document outlining government policies on the allocation of resources with the objective of attaining "targeted rate of economic growth over a certain period of time."[39] Each plan-period is usually evaluated to determine the level of success of the plan. From such evaluations, appropriate measures are adopted to ensure a viable economic future for the country. Yearly budgets are, therefore, drawn around such plans. On the other hand, development plans are more inclusive and these deal with a large array of national needs such as the provision of quality education, increasing the transportation network, expanding quality health services, increasing food production/supply, and making housing affordable to a large section of the population.

Most Sub-Saharan African countries have been inspired by the relative success of the development plans of the developed nations. Examples of such development plans include the Marshall Plan which rebuilt war-torn Europe, the early post-

Great October Revolution development plans of the Soviet Union which catapulted that country into an industrialized nation, and the "Great Leap Forward" plan of China which made it a world power.

WHAT CONSTITUTES POLITICAL INSTABILITY?

The concept "political instability" may be defined as a condition in a political system in which institutionalized patterns of authority break down. During such situations, expected compliance to political authority is replaced by violence. Such violence is usually intended to change the political system through injury to person or property.[40] Wayne Nafziger, in expounding on Ted Gurr's "relative deprivation" model for explaining the courses of political violence, suggests:

> The probability of political violence is inversely related to the institutional mechanisms that permit nonviolent hostility to be expressed and is directly related to common experiences and beliefs that sanction violence, and the extent to which groups give normative support, protection from retribution, and cues for violence to the deprived. Political violence refers to all actual and threatened collective attacks within a political community against the political regime, its actors or its policies.[41]

Political violence also applies to attacks on citizens by a regime for the purpose of retaining political power as was the case of Iddi Amin's rule in Uganda.

Since the mid-1960's, Sub-Saharan African countries have experienced several levels of political violence and in some of these, such violence has been expressed in the form of military coups d'etat. Claude Ake has observed that high incidence of violence has a relationship to political instability in Africa and this consequently reduces "the prospects of overcoming underdevelopment."[42] Few will question Ake's conclusion; however, there is no consensus on the theoretical links between instability and underdevelopment. It is, therefore, necessary to examine some of these theoretical issues. In doing so, the approach used by Nafziger in his study of political instability in Nigeria is worthy of examination. Nafziger identified four models that have been used to study political instability. These are the Ethnic Model; the "Praetorian" Model; the "Relative

Deprivation" Model; the Marxist Model; and the Political Economy Model.[43]

Ethnic Model

The Ethnic Model approach to the study of political instability is expounded by authorities such as Rabushka and Shepsle. They maintain that ethnic cooperation before independence in the less-developed nations degenerated into inter-ethnic competition after independence. Consequently, post-independence ethnic chauvinism, hostility, and competition led to political violence and destabilization of democratic systems.[44] Nelson and Wolpe point out that where there is a significant difference in the rates of development between communal groups, attempts to narrow these differences could result in communal conflict leading to instability.[45] Nafziger's view is that in the "ethnic model" of internal political violence, "language, race, tribe, religion, national origin, or some other cultural sense of identity are considered the primary factors contributing to conflict."[46] Young has also indicated that political conflicts (instability) are due more to ethnic factors than class.[47] Pronouncements by coup leaders lend some support to the basic hypothesis posed by the ethnic model.

"Praetorian" Model

One advocate of the "Praetorian" Model is Samuel Huntington. The model suggests that the underdevelopment of political institutions in the less-developed countries is one of the principal causes of instability. Huntington argues that the inability of the political machinery to absorb popular participation creates dissatisfied groups who may resort to rioting, mob violence, guerrilla insurgence and military coups d'etat.[48] Hence, "political decay and instability," Huntington maintains, "depend on the level of political participation relative to political institutionalization."[49]

The "Praetorian" model maintains that primordial social forces (such as ethnic groups) contribute to instability because of conflicting interests. Although ethnic conflicts in countries such as Burundi, Nigeria, Uganda, and the Sudan tend to confirm the predictions of the model, countries such as Ghana, Burkina Faso, the Ivory Coast, and Benin are exceptions to the rule.

"Relative Deprivation" Model

Ted Gurr is the leading authority of the "Relative Deprivation" Model which is linked to the concept of "frustration-an-
ger-aggression syndrome." The model explains that frustration
and anger are accumulated in the masses as a result of the
inability of the state machinery to supply the goods and services that the masses expect. This inadvertently induces social
discontent and provides a basis for collective violence.[50] The
problem with this model is that Gurr does not consider the
state as a party to the resultant societal conflict and violence.
Rather, he considers the collective violence as attacks against
the political regime, its actors and policies. Most of the incidents of political violence in Sub-Saharan Africa since the
1960's are closely associated with the problem of unfair distribution of goods and services amongst the populace as well as
the inability of governments to satisfy the rising expectations
of the populace.

Marxist Model

The Marxist Model for the study of political instability attempts
to explain internal political strife as a condition for the alliance of the local bourgeoisie with foreign interest groups (foreign capitalists) purely because of their own economic interest
as against the interests of the general population (masses). The
latter class feels (and is) alienated and this pushes it to radical
revolt, uprising, violent strikes, guerrilla warfare, and various
forms of political violence. Such mass actions are usually led
by the lower classes. These, according to Baran, may result in
the establishment of a new regime based on the interest of the
broad mass of society over the interest of the selected few.[51]
Nafziger also contends that "divisions within the indigenous
bourgeoisie between allies and competitors of foreign businessmen can be a source of political instability."[52] The Marxist model
helps to explain the current political upheavals in Sub-Saharan
African countries such as Ethiopia, Angola and Mozambique
where pro-socialist governments are in control.

Political Economy Model

Economic factors interacting with political forces may also influence the incidence of political instability. This is the basic

proposition of the political economy explanation of instability. As Nafziger points out, economic factors such as "uneven economic modernization during the colonial period, transnational economic linkages, economic class discrepancies, changes in the relative incomes of class and occupational groups, communal economic competition, regional educational differences, and effects of differential regional economic development on the costs and benefits of political integration"[53] are critical in the study of political instability. In applying the political economy approach, one has to be careful in the selection of variables because the universe of relevant variables could be quite large.

We have discussed the various approaches that scholars have adopted in their attempts to explain why political instability has been a common feature in many nations. It is common for one/some/or all of the models discussed above to be instrumental in the instability of a given country. The following discourse further illustrates the above situations in Sub-Saharan Africa.

CONDITIONS LEADING TO POLITICAL INSTABILITY

Just as there have been several models offered to explain the relationship between instability and economic development, there have been various studies aimed at identifying the sources of instability in the first place. To put the discussion into perspective, our focus will be on aggregate factors rather than on minute details. Several scholars have indicated that political instability is created by phenomena such as political violence, corruption, conflict behavior, internal war (civil war), revolution, riots, and coups d'etat.[54] Although a coup d'etat could be a manifestation of political instability, it is in itself a perpetrator of instability.

We begin the discussion by first exploring the many faces of violence. As Sarkesian points out, there are difficulties in measuring order, violence and instability. Focusing on the issue of political instability, scholars have suggested two or three dimensions of the issue. Rummel, for example, identifies three—revolutions, subversions, and turmoils. Raymond Tanter and D.O. Bwy categorize them as internal war and turmoil, and organized and anomalous violence.[55] However, some political scientists criticize these categories of political instability as being too dependent on statistical explanation. According to Donald Morrison and his colleagues, the nature of political instability will vary according to the nature of groups involved in the political conflict.[56] This is particularly true about Sub-Saharan Africa where internal or civil wars, riots, guerrilla wars, revolutions, and coups d'etat have created significant levels of political instability. To analyze each of these causes and indicators of political instability is beyond the scope of this chapter. We will focus here on political instability conditioned by coups d'etat. We think this is essential because coups, as manifestations of political instability, have contributed considerably to the underdevelopment of Sub-Saharan Africa.

CAUSES OF COUPS D'ETAT IN AFRICA

The intervention of the military in government is not a new phenomenon in world history. "Coup" means "blow" in French. Hence, "coup d'etat" literally means "blow of state." According to Thomas Greene, its original meaning implied any sudden unconstitutional seizures of political power by individuals or groups already in a position of authority. However, Greene contends that in recent times a coup d'etat means "an alteration in policy-making personnel by using unconstitutional procedures, whether or not the coup conspirators enjoy prior political authority."[57]

According to Edward Luttwak, coups d'etat have been known for over three hundred years, but their development has been largely due to "the rise of the modern state with its professional bureaucracy and standing armed forces."[58] James Meise has argued that coups or revolts are as old as creation. To him the first recorded coup attempt was in heaven when Lucifer rebelled against God. He writes:

> The first revolt took place in heaven . . . the angel Satan-Lucifer rose up against his Lord to charge Him. . . . This was the first revolt against authority, with Satan, the first critic, arguing from reason. Because he belonged to the celestial family, they called him a traitor to his class. It was the first recorded split within a ruling group, and the arch rebel with his followers were penalized accordingly with expulsion from the party and exiled, in a vertical (downward) direction.[59]

Luttwak states that "a coup consists of the infiltration of a small but critical segment of the state apparatus, which is then used to displace the government from its control of the remainder.[60] He identifies three pre-conditions necessary to make a coup d'etat possible and successful:

. . . The country must be economically backward.

. . . The country must be politically independent.

. . . The source of political power in the country must be centralized.[61]

In Luttwak's view, economically backward countries have a population whose general condition is "characterized by disease, illiteracy, high birth and death rates and periodic hunger."[62] Under such conditions, the vast majority of the people are struggling to survive and are therefore politically inactive. Consequently, political participation is confined to the elite class who are well fed and better educated. In the event of a coup d'etat, the mass of the people do not resist because:

> All power, all participation is in the hands of the small educated elite. This elite is literate, educated, well fed and secure, and therefore radically different from the vast majority of their countrymen, practically a race apart. The masses recognize this and they also accept the elite's monopoly of power, and unless some unbearable exaction leads to desperate revolt, they will accept its policies. Equally they will accept a change of government, whether legal or otherwise. After all, it is merely another lot of "them" taking over.[63]

The above observations by Luttwak are accurate about many Sub-Saharan African countries. Ethiopia under Haile Selassie, for instance, was a country controlled by the aristocracy, and led by the royal family. The vast population lived in abject poverty, squalor, and hunger. Thus, when the Ethiopian revolution began in February 1974, there was no resistance from the populace. Rather, the soldiers who initiated the revolution were "cheered by the students and peasants of Ethiopia."[64]

Luttwak's second contention is that for a coup to be successful, "the target state must be substantially independent and the influence of foreign powers in its internal political life must be relatively limited."[65] This partly explains why most Sub-Saharan African countries have experienced so many instances of military coups. Those Sub-Saharan African countries that severed links with their former colonial masters are the most destabilized as compared to those countries with highly dependent relations. The Ivory Coast, Senegal, and Kenya are good examples of the latter. However, countries such as Ghana, Nigeria, Guinea, and Mali, which are relatively independent, are quite unstable. It has been suggested that French military presence in Senegal and Ivory Coast serves as a deterrent against any coup attempt. Similarly, the United States' military presence in Kenya helped derail a coup attempt against Daniel arap Moi's government in 1982.[66]

France is known to use its investment and assistance programs, as well as its military force, to influence domestic politics in Africa. For instance, France is on record for using its military operations to maintain "proteges in power (as in Gabon on behalf of President M'Ba in 1964. Zaire in 1977 and 1978, and Chad between 1968-72 and between 1975-80) as well as in the removal of discredited leaders such as Bokassa in the Central Africa Republic in 1979."[67] Similarly, Britain used its Special Air Services (SAS) to put "down a coup in the ex-British colony of the Gambia,"[68] while President Jawara was a guest of the Queen at a royal wedding in Britain.

Luttwak's third condition that favors successful military coups d'etat is that the governing machinery should be centralized. Events in Sub-Saharan Africa and Latin America support this contention. In centralized administrations, the capture of strategic buildings and positions in the national capital constitute sufficient power control to demand that other parts of the country comply with the orders of the new leadership.

Samuel Decalo has also advanced two arguments regarding the conditions which favor military intervention in countries. His first thesis is that countries with "social and structural weakness—institutional fragility, systematic flaws, and low levels of political culture—which act as a sort of magnet" tend to attract military intervention.[69] His second thesis is that African military hierarchies acquire certain traits from the grip of corrupt self-seeking political elites expound.[70]

Roger Tangri, while almost echoing this notion, says that there are more fundamental explanations for military intervention in Sub-Saharan Africa. He says:

Military intervention in Sub-Saharan Africa has often been seen as emanating from the inadequacies of civilian rule. Coups have occurred, it has been argued, as the military have sought to overthrow corrupt, inefficient or venal civilian elites, they ensue primarily from links between military and civilian elite groups. As Thomas Cox has demonstrated in his study of military takeovers in Sierra Leone, "it is within this rather complex spectrum of civilian and military intercourse that the actual preconditions for intervention are established."[71]

Tangri, using Sierra Leone as a case study, suggests that the politicization of the military by the civilian elites is an invitation for the military to intervene in politics. On the other hand, Decalo argued that coups d'etat are manifestations of the following prevailing conditions in the coup-prone country:

. . . Corruption by politicians or the ruling elite;

. . . Ethnicity (tribalism) and nepotism;

. . . The rise of despotic leaders;

. . . One-party state and one-man dictatorship;

. . . The ambition of soldiers to rule; and

. . . The influence of external forces through covert action.[72]

A critical study of the incidence of coup d'etat in Sub-Saharan Africa will reveal that some or all of the suggested conditions outlined by Decalo have been principal causes of military coups d'etat.

Ruth First has suggested that corporate army interest constitutes a predominant reason for military intervention.[73] The corporate army interest was a key factor that led to the overthrow of the government of Kofi Busia in January, 1972 in Ghana by Colonel Ignatius Acheampong. The first reason that Acheampong gave was that Busia's "austerity measures" eliminated even the few amenities that the army enjoyed under the previous regime of Kwame Nkrumah.[74]

Ali Mazrui provides very persuasive arguments for the frequency of coups in Africa. He writes:

A major reason is that the technology of destruction of Africa is ahead of the technology of production. And so ultimate power resides not in those who control the means of production, as Marxists would argue, but in those who control the means of destruction.

A related reason why Africa is coup-prone is that most other institution in Africa (such as labour unions, professional associations, religious leadership, universities, the judiciary, peasant associations, and

even the civil service) are relatively weak. In most cases they are unable to stand up to the military.

A third reason for coups in Africa is the low level of professionalism in the armed forces. Criteria of recruitment and promotion are
sometimes ethnic rather that based on merit; methods of professional
socialization are often haphazard: pay is often so low that it encourages corruption. Conditions do vary in different countries, but African soldiers in the streets of African capitals are more likely to display
petty arrogance towards civilians than professional pride.

Another reason for military intervention in Africa is boredom in
the barracks. Ultimately, what are African armies *for* anyhow? In the
majority of cases there are no likely wars with foreign powers on the
horizon. In most countries there are no major defense needs. Hero-
ism for African soldiers is therefore to be sought not on the battlefield but in the political arena, not in military command against the
enemy but in political command over one's own compatriots. African
armies are therefore tempted to proclaim themselves the political and
moral custodians of the national interest—rather than the military de-
fenders of the nation's security and sovereignty. It is of such material
that coups are made.[75]

However, Amos Perlmutter has tried to explain that the military intervenes in government because there is no "dichotomy
between 'civil' and 'military' [since] in a complex society, neither the military nor the civilian sector can be restricted to its
functional role."[76] Perlmutter argues that civilian groups such
as bureaucrats and politicians often perform functions which
otherwise are the responsibility of the army. Much as his asser-
tion is true, the military intervention in the overthrow of democratically elected government cannot be considered a proper
function of the former. The constitutional provisions by which
there is a smooth transfer of power from a less popular government to a more popular one after elections must be respected.

Perlmutter develops his case further by saying that the pro-
pensity to intervene is correlated with the increased influence
of the military and bureaucracy in government and that intra-
military conflict is connected with the evolution of organizational and managerial development of the army. Thus, he argues, military intervention takes place when the corporate
interest of the military is being threatened by fragmented social movements, interest groups, or political parties.[77]

William Thompson hypothesizes that relatively young regimes tend to be more prone to military coups. He draws this

analogy from the fact that most coups occur immediately after independence (for example, the Congo in 1960) or a short period of five to ten years after independence (for example, Ghana and Nigeria in 1966).[78]

Claude Welch, perhaps, provides the most comprehensive reasons why the military normally takes over a legitimate government in Sub-Saharan Africa. According to Welch, "the military seizures of control that rocked the Sub-Saharan area from the mid-1965 onwards cannot be attributed to a single factor . . . To assume that 'popular discontent' or 'economic stagnation' or 'neo-colonialist' interference brought about the coup d'etat does not do justice to each unique combination of circumstance." Welch advances the following as factors which help promote military intervention in any country:

> The declining prestige of the major political party, as exemplified by (a) an increased reliance upon force to achieve compliance, (b) a stress upon unanimity in the face of centrifugal force, and (c) a consequent denial of effective political choice.
>
> Schism among prominent politicians, weakening the broadly-based nationalist movement that had hastened the departure of the former colonial power.
>
> The lessened likelihood of external intervention in the event of military uprising.
>
> "Contagion" from seizures of control by the military in other African countries.
>
> Domestic social antagonism, most obviously manifested in countries where a minority exercises control (e.g., the Arabs in Zanzibar, the Watusi in Burundi).
>
> Economic malaise leading to "austerity" policies, which mostly affect articulate, organized sectors of the population (members of trade unions, civil servants).
>
> Corruption and inefficiency among government and party officials, a corruption especially noticeable under conditions of economic decline.
>
> A heightened awareness within the Army of its power to influence or displace political leaders.[79]

In the early 1960's when military intervention in the political administration of Sub-Saharan African countries was becoming a common occurrence, it was assumed that the military would become agents of modernization in the region. However, this perception was discarded when military rule in many countries was becoming a dismal experience. It was not surprising, therefore, when David Apter (a notable authority of the modernization school) admitted that:

> Despite the fact that military oligarchies appear to have modernizing values, and indeed, the nature of a military organization, with its command, planning, and technological biases, appears almost the prototype of modernity, they rarely serve as successful modernizers. The army may take peasants and make them into modern men, but it cannot rule effectively. Nor is it able to generalize its values into society.[80]

Similarly, Samuel Edward Finer dismissed any notion that military rule could contribute to modernization. Finer concludes that:

> . . . It is for the reader to make his own judgement; but in ours, in a vast number of cases this [military] intervention has been little or nothing more than an attempt upon feeble but nevertheless operative civilian institutions by a small group of willful men armed with lethal weapons, nurtured in arrogance, and pricked on by pride, ambition, self-interest, and revenge.[81]

CONCLUSION

The literature review, as presented above, is indicative of the diverse views on the concepts of "political instability" and "economic development" as they relate to the political and socio-economic conditions in Sub-Saharan Africa. It has been observed that "political instability" refers to the incidence of political violence and unstable political conditions created within a nation state as a result of the perpetuation of successful and/or unsuccessful military coups d'etat. "Economic development" refers to the ability of a nation state to implement policies which will help to reduce the rate of unemployment, eliminate poverty, and improve the quality of life of its citizens through the provision of goods and services (especially those services concerned with health, education, transportation, and communication). In short, economic development, as Todaro has indicated, involves major changes in the social structures, that enhance the growth of the national economy, and lead to the reduction of societal inequalities and the elimination of poverty.

It has also been established that several factors influence the incidence of military coups d'etat and instability in Sub-Saharan Africa. These causal factors range from the ineptness of the incumbent governments, to what Henry Bienen calls the "motives for military takeover" (that is, reason given by coup leaders justifying their action). Evidence of a government's ineptness in ruling is apparent when the government is unable to effectively utilize state resources and to mobilize the population to increase productivity. There are several motives for military takeovers and Bienen's statement here provides a good summary of the literature review:

> . . . the motives for military takeover continue: personal and corporate grievances; civilian pressures for the military to intervene; fear that someone else will act first or that counter-militaries will be created such as general service units, personal-bodyguard units, militarized polices forces; economic problems that force curtailment of defense spending and military privileges; general ethnic tensions that spill over into the armed forces, internal factionalism or dissolution of central authority within the armed forces, leading factions to think they must control the state in order to control the military.[82]

As previously noted, economic stagnation and underdevelopment have been prime causes of the chronic instability in Sub-Saharan Africa. Indeed, military coup leaders are always quick to use the "failing economy" as a prudent reason for their "timely intervention." Iddi Amin of Uganda in 1971, Mohammed Buhari of Nigeria in 1983, Jerry Rawlings of Ghana in 1979 and 1981, Jaafar al-Nimeiri of the Sudan in 1969, and Matthieu Kerekou of Benin in 1972 all used the ailing economy as a reason for their intervention. However, there are countries in Sub-Saharan Africa with poor economic performance and yet these have not generated political instability or motivated military intervention. Examples of such countries are Tanzania, Zambia, and Senegal. There are also countries which have relatively good economies but still are plagued with political violence and instability. A good example is Nigeria which had a civil war and military coups d'etat at the height of its oil boom.

The various authorities cited in the literature review have attempted to explain either what constitutes political instability or what causes it. Except for Nafziger who attempted to link the Biafran War in Nigeria as a consequence of instability, none of these authorities has made definite attempts to link political instability, caused by military coups, to the region's current level of economic development. It is this void that this discussion attempts to fill.

Nearly four decades after the attainment of independence, many African countries remain highly underdeveloped as measured by standard indices such as low life expectancy, low per capita Gross National Product (GNP), low per capita income, high infant mortality rate, stagnant economic growth, high unemployment rates, high illiteracy rates, and high poverty levels. Several African countries have also experienced considerable political instability in the period. Between 1960 and 1980, there were 43 violent changes in government and 42 attempted coups.[83] In addition to these, several incidence of ethnic conflicts and border disputes were reported. Coup leaders have been quick to provide a long list of reasons justifying the overthrow of legitimate governments. Among these are charges of corruption, nepotism, ethnicism, mismanagement of the state's economy, and abuse of political power. In some cases, these charges are legitimate, and it is not surprising when the masses jump into the streets spontaneously to express their support for the coup leaders. However, in many instances coups in Africa have served the selfish agenda of the coup leaders and the military body corporate.

In 1966, the military under General Aguiyi-Ironsi overthrew the government of Tafawa Balewa in Nigeria ostensibly "to prevent the disintegration of the nation-state." That same year the military in Ghana under Colonel Kotoka and Major Afrifa overthrew the government of Kwame Nkrumah to "rid the country of dictatorship." In the Congo (now Zaire), Mobotu seized power in 1965 to restore law and order. In 1974, General Aman Andom overthrew Haile Selassie and the historic monarchy of the Lion of Juda, in order "to establish popular democracy." Whatever reasons these military leaders had for initiating their coups we can now objectively judge their motives and determine if their actions served the best interest of their countries.

Several scholars have pointed to these unstable occurrences as the root-cause of the poor economic, political, and social development in Sub-Saharan Africa. For instance, the relationship between instability and economic development was succinctly stated by Dharan Ghai and Lawrence Smith when they observed that:

> Sub-Saharan Africa has been racked by political crisis and instability for over the past two decades . . . A number of countries, among them Ghana and Nigeria, have suffered from continuing political instability resulting in frequent coups and changes in administration. A tragic indicator of continuing turbulence is the existence of an estimated ten million refugees in Sub-Saharan Africa.
>
> Political instability naturally has a strong negative impact on economic growth. Not only are the limited financial and human resources diverted to military purposes but lack of security for life and property disrupts normal production and reduces productive investment. It is, therefore, not surprising to find countries that have been involved in prolonged conflicts among the worst economic performers in the region.[84]

Probably the most in-depth analysis of the subject is the recent study by Augustin Fosu in which he argued that political instability adversely affects economic development by reducing the availability of factors of production; encouraging capital flight; and inducing brain drain.[85]

Military rule has become a permanent phenomenon in most of Sub-Saharan Africa. Uganda, Ethiopia, Somalia, Liberia, Nigeria, Zaire, Benin, Togo, Chad, Mali, Guinea, and Burkina Faso have all had their share of military rulers. Military intervention in countries such as Ghana, Uganda, Sudan, Burkina Faso, Zaire, Sierra Leone, the Gambia, Ethiopia and Liberia has caused irreparable damage to the economy. The political turmoil in these relatively unstable countries has discouraged foreign investment and recent appeals for investment initiatives have only received lukewarm responses. The lack of confidence in the stability of coup-prone Sub-Saharan Africa is also a major cause of capital flight and the unwillingness to invest in these countries.

In several cases, military rule in Sub-Saharan Africa degenerated into personal dictatorships. In Ghana, the N.L.C. and the S.M.C. are examples of military regimes that degenerated into corrupt and dictatorial governments. Benin (under General Kerekou), Zaire (under General Mobotu), the Congo (under Colonel Sassou-Nguesso), Uganda (under Field Marshall Amin), and the Central African Republic (under Emperor Bokassa) are, perhaps, the best examples of this development. Unfortunately, military dictatorships cling to power by encouraging and exploiting ethnicism, usually relying heavily on the support of their own ethnic group. In Liberia, Samuel Doe clung to power until his murder due to the massive support he enjoyed from his Kran people. Similarly, Idi Amin's last source of political power was from his ethnic Kakwa compatriots in the Ugandan Army. Emperor Bokassa, like Amin, had to rely on the Mbaika forces which constituted his Imperial Guard. It is common knowledge that Rawlings' government in Ghana owes its survival to the Ewe ethnic factor in the Ghana Army.

In the wake of the 1966 coup in Nigeria, Prime Minister Tafawa Balewa was killed. His death and the assassinations of other prominent political leaders triggered the Nigerian Civil War of 1967. Other African leaders of international repute who were the pioneers of the struggle for self-rule such as Maurice Yamoego of Burkina Faso (1966), Hubert Maga of Benin (1963), Haile Selassie of Ethiopia (1974), William Tolbert of Liberia (1980), Modibo Keita of Mali (1968), Ould Daddah of Mauritania (1978), and Milton Obote of Uganda (1971) became victims of coups. Their disgraceful exits from the political scene, many would argue, were not only a loss to their countries, but to Africa as a whole. In the early 1980's Nigeria, under President Shehu Shagari, was beginning to earn respect as the Black Giant of Africa. Nigeria had played a decisive role in Zimbabwe's independence and was spearheading efforts for a peaceful resolution of the Namibian crisis. However, the fall of the Shagari's regime in December 1983 negatively impacted Nigeria's role in negotiating issues affecting the region.

It has often been argued that when a government fails to command the support of the people, then it ceases to be legitimate. The Shagari's regime could not have been unpopular when the country returned it to power in the summer of 1983 after national elections. Likewise, the Hilla Limann administration in Ghana (1979-1981) was voted into office for a four-year term in 1979. It had hardly served two years when it was overthrown by a military coup led by Jerry Rawlings in December 1981.

The implications of such erratic intervention in politics by the military is that present and future governments spend a great deal of time, energy, and the meager national resources on national security to the neglect of other sectors of the national economy. As Robert Jackson and Carl Rosberg have rightly observed, "The intervention of the military in African politics has . . .[often] led to the marked increase in the budgetary allocations for the armed forces."[86] Uganda provides one of the best illustrations of this. Between 1981 and 1984, the per capita military expenditure in that country was $58 while it was $9 for education.

Political instability will continue to haunt Sub-Saharan Africa for sometime to come unless appropriate measures are adopted to arrest the problem. The case against political instability has often been misconstrued to imply a quest for unconditional stability. As Dennis Austin has indicated:

> Stability is an ambiguous virtue. The regime of Papa Doc at one extreme, and that of Stalin at another, were both, in a sense, "stable." But that, too, is over-simple.[87]

Some countries in Sub-Saharan Africa have escaped the incidence of coups and have had fairly stable leadership transitions. The Ivory Coast, Malawi, Senegal, and Zambia have not experienced any coups, and yet, like most countries in the region, are debt-distressed. Have stability and continuity of development policies helped these nations? No. Therein lies the exception to the rule. Stability, though necessary, does not by itself ensure political or economic development. Stability must be supported by good and sound socioeconomic policies: policies aimed at the elimination of disease, hunger, poverty, unemployment, illiteracy, and the suppression of free speech.

The chaotic economic and/or political conditions in the Ivory Coast, Malawi, Somalia, and Zambia show that personal rule and dictatorship in the name of stability is not the answer to the regions's economic problems. Mauritius, a relatively small country with fewer resources, has been remarkably stable under numerous regimes since independence. Today, it has an economy with an enviable per capita income of $1,810 per annum, a life expectancy of 67 years, and the highest literacy rate (83 percent). These figures exceed by far the averages for Sub-Saharan Africa, which stand at $320, 51 years, and 47 percent, respectively.[88]

How, therefore, do we begin to seriously address this issue of Africa's political instability? Firstly, the political development of Sub-Saharan Africa is vital to any meaningful agenda towards economic emancipation. To achieve this, Sub-Saharan African states must, individually, establish democratic political institutions based on popular participation in the governance of their countries. The political leadership of each country must place the national interest beyond their own selfish and narrow interest. No leadership group should consider itself indispensable to the country. This recognition will leave room for leadership change if so demanded by the people.

Secondly, the Organization of African Unity should establish a monitoring council that will serve as an external observer unit for all political elections on the continent. Any member country found guilty of election fraud should be censored and, where necessary, sanctioned by the body with other penalties. As a prelude to this, the O.A.U. should consider amending Article III Clause 2 of the O.A.U. Charter which addresses the principle of "non-interference in the internal affairs of [member] States."[89] This clause was added to the O.A.U. charter as a compromise for those newly independent states that feared that more powerful nations may interfere with their sovereignty. At the 1963 O.A.U. Conference in Addis Ababa (Ethiopia), Nigeria's Prime Minister, Sir Abubakar Tafawa Balewa, voiced the opinion of a majority of the 32 African Heads of State and/or Governments when he declared in his speech, on the last day of the general debate, that:

> Nigeria's stand is that, if we want unity in Africa, we must first agree to certain essential things. The first is that African States must respect one another. There must be acceptance of the equality by all the states. No matter whether they are big or small, they are all sovereign and their sovereignty is sovereignty. . . . to my mind, we cannot achieve this unity as long as some African countries continue to carry on subversive activities in other African countries.[90]

That compromise was a necessity then. But in recent times, the recurrence of civil strife and violence in many countries in

Africa, necessitate intervention to preserve life and property. How many lives must be lost in Liberia, Somalia, Sudan, Burundi, and Rwanda before the O.A.U. intervenes to restore sanity into these countries?

Thirdly, to consolidate the individual efforts of Sub-Saharan African countries, there is the need to speed up regional economic integration as a precondition for future political unity. In this regard, the recent efforts of the Economic Commission of West African States (ECOWAS) must be applauded. The intervention of ECOWAS forces in Liberia to restore law and order, following the civil war, is a unique example, of what a strong regional group can do to foster political stability and economic growth. Although the decision to intervene in Liberia was not unanimous, it is my contention that the halting of the civil war by the ECOWAS forces justifies the intervention.

Fourthly, it is in the interest of Sub-Saharan African countries to pursue policies that will make them self-reliant. They should learn from the Chinese who, having successfully isolated themselves, were able to embark upon agricultural programs that helped feed that nation. In the area of technological advancement, China made a great leap forward while maintaining its political neutrality during the Cold War era.

Finally, Sub-Saharan African countries must take the necessary steps to attract the return of their nationals living in the developed countries so that they may contribute their talents towards nation building. That is, they must attempt to reverse the so-called "brain drain." Each country should adopt appropriate incentives to facilitate this. During the turbulent years of the Supreme Military Council rule in Ghana (October 1975-June 1979), for instance, many doctors, teachers, nurses, engineers, and architects left the country in search of greener pastures in Europe and the Americas. The same is true of Nigeria, Uganda, Ethiopia, the Sudan, Chad, and Liberia.

The Marxian dictum that the wealthy are not safe as long as poverty exists side by side with wealth is often generalized to take into account the disparities between nations of the world. In this latter sense, it implies that the developed countries are not safe as long as there is inequality and economic deprivation in the world. It is thus in their best interest to genuinely assist the less developed countries in their efforts to develop.

To this end, the developed countries should respond favorably to the demands of the Group of 77 and their quest for a new international economic order. It is hoped that, with the end of the cold war, Africa will cease to be the battlefield of the big powers and their covert activities.

In concluding this chapter, the following policy options are recommended for Sub-Saharan African countries:

. . . Initiate democratic processes through which political parties freely compete for the mandate to govern as is practiced in the United States of America, India, the United Kingdom, and other democratic countries.

. . . Include African traditional values in the search for a suitable and workable political system as much as possible.

. . . Acquire the appropriate technology for Africa's needs rather than re-inventing the wheel. Japan's economic and industrial success is evidence of the usefulness of technology (in national development) that it has managed to acquire from various sources.

. . . Give agriculture primary consideration in government planning because food is very vital to development. Of equal importance is health, education, and transportation.

. . . Reduce the size of the army without compromising its quality and military preparedness for national defense and for internal stability. The smaller the number of military personnel, the less the strain on the economy in terms of meeting their personnel needs (viz, salaries, fringe benefits, etc.).

. . . Sign military pacts with neighboring countries for speedy intervention in times of miliary uprisings.

. . . Establish Centers for Civil Education which should educate the populace on their rights against repressive and corrupt rulers as well as how to resist military intervention.

. . . Mobilize civilian groups (such as trade unions, professional associations and organizations, the clergy, students, and farmers) to renounce and resist despotic rule and any form of unwarranted military intervention.

. . . Initiate regional economic cooperation aimed at eventual political union of Sub-Saharan Africa.

. . . Continue progressive economic policies regardless of the change of government.

The one institution that has greatly influenced political development in Africa since the 1960's is the military. Like fire, the military in Africa, in many ways, is a "good servant but a bad master." The governments of Sub-Saharan Africa should explore further the military's role in the economic emancipation, as well as the political development of their various countries. That, in my view, constitutes the greatest challenge to the survival of democracy in the continent. With proper training and political re-education, the military can be a formidable asset to Africa.

Notes

1   *The New Lexicon Webster's Dictionary*, Encyclopedic edition (New York: Lexicon Publications, Inc., 1989), p. 261.

2   Michael Todaro, *Economic Development in the Third World*, (London: Longman, 1985), p. 83.

3   *Ibid.*, p. 84.

4   Claude Ake, *A Political Economy of Africa*, (New York: Longman, Inc., 1981), p. 141.

5   Dudley Seers, "The Meaning of Development," *Eleventh World Conference of the Society for International Development*, New Delhi (1969), p. 3.

6   Walter Rodney, *How Europe Underdeveloped Africa* (Washington, D.C.: Howard University Press, 1974), p. 4.

7   Todaro, *Economic Development in the Third World*, p. 85.

8   Adam Smith, *The Wealth of Nations* (New York: Modern Library, 1937) Book 4, p. 423.

9   Robert L. Heilbroner, *The Worldly Philosophers: The Lives, Times, and Ideas of the Great Economic Thinkers* (New York: Simon and Schuster, 1953), p. 45.

10 John M. Keynes, *Essays in Biography* (New York: Horizon Press, 1951).

11 Heilbroner, *The Worldly Philosophers: The Lives, Times, and Ideas of the Great Economic Thinkers*, p. 117.

12 Karl Marx, *Capital: A Critique of Political Economy*, edited by Frederick Engels (New York: International Publishers, 1967), 3 Vols. Also see Karl Marx and Frederick Engels, *Selected Works* (Moscow: Foreign Languages Publishing House, 1958), Vol. 1 & 2; and Martin Gerhard Giesbrecht, *The Evolution of Economic Society* (San Francisco: W. H. Freeman and Co., 1972), p. 290.

13 Heilbroner, *The Worldly Philosophers: The Lives, Times, and Ideas of the Great Economic Thinkers*, pp. 127-60.

14 Ronald H. Chilcote, *Theories of Comparative Politics: The Search for a Para digm* (Boulder, Colorado: Westview Press, 1981), pp. 288-89.

15 Magnus Blomstrom and Bjorn Hettne, *Development Theory in Transition* (London: Zed Books, Ltd., 1988), p. 9.

16 *Ibid.*

17 W.W. Rostow, *The Stages of Economic Growth, A Non-Communist Manifesto* (London: Cambridge University Press, 1960), pp. 1-4, 12.

18 Todaro, *Economic Development in the Third World*, p. 64.

19 *Ibid.*, p. 67.

20 Andre Gundar Frank, *Latin America: Underdevelopment or Revolution* (New York: Monthly Review Press, 1969), p. 4.

21 *Ibid.*

22 Walter Rodney, *How Europe Underdeveloped Africa*(Washington, D.C.: Howard University Press, 1974), p. 25.

23 Gunnar Myrdal, *Asian Drama: An Inquiry into the Poverty of Nations* (New York: Pantheon, 1968). Also see Giesbrecht, *The Evolution of Economic Society*, pp. 290-91.

24 *Ibid.*, pp. 67-68.

25 Chinweizu, *The West and the Rest of Us* (London: NOK Publishers, 1978), pp. 272-73.

26 Todaro, *Economic Development in the Third World*, p. 69.

27 *Ibid.*, p. 71.

28 *Ibid.*, p. 72

29 Chilcote, *Theories of Comparative Politics: The Search for a Paradigm*, p. 308.

30 Heraldo Munoz, ed., *From Dependency to Development* (Boulder, Colorado: Westview Press, 1981), pp. 2-3.

31 *Ibid.*, p. 2.

32 *Ibid.*, p. 2. Also see Raul Prebisch, *The Economic Development of Latin America and Its Problems* (New York: United Nations, Department of Social and Economic Affairs, 1950).

33 *Ibid.*, p. 78.

34 Munoz, editor, *From Dependency to Development*, p. 2.

35 Theotonio Dos Santos, "The Crisis of Development Theory and the Problem of Independence in Latin America," *Siglo* 21 (1969).

36   Bade Onimode, ed., *The IMF, The World Bank and the African Debt: The Social and Political Impact* (New Jersey: Zed Books Ltd., 1989), p. 2.

37   Dennis J. Palumbo, *Public Policy in America* (New York: Harcourt Brace Jovanovich Publishers, 1988), p. 10.

38   Todaro, *Economic Development in the Third World*, p. 582.

39   *Ibid.*

40   Donald George Morrison et al., *Black Africa: A Comparative Handbook* (New York: The Free Press, 1972), p. 122.

41   E. Wayne Nafziger, *The Economics of Political Instability: The Nigerian-Biafran War* (Boulder, Colorado: Westview Press, 1983), p. 9.

42   Claude Ake, *A Political Economy of Africa* (New York: Longman, Inc., 1981), p. 126.

43   Nafziger, *The Economics of Political Instability*, pp. 1-11.

44   Alvin Rabushka and Kenneth A. Shepsle, *Politics in Plural Societies: A Theory of Democratic Instability* (Columbus, Ohio: Charles E. Merrill, 1972), pp. 8, 20, 213.

45   Robert Nelson and Howard Hope, "Modernization and the Politics of Communalism: A Theoretical Perspective," *American Political Science Review* LXIV, pp. 1115-18.

46   Nafziger, *The Economics of Political Instability*, p. 2.

47   Crawford Young, *The Politics of Cultural Pluralism* (Madison: The University of Wisconsin Press, 1976), pp. 22, 213, 518.

48   Nafziger, *The Economics of Political Instability*, p. 8. Also see Samuel P. Huntington, *Political Order in Changing Societies* (New Haven, Connecticut: Yale University Press, 1972) pp. 3, 26, 28, 198; Donald Cruise O'Brien, "Modernization, Order and the Erosion of a Democratic Idea): American Political Science, 1960-1970," *The Journal of Development Studies* VIII (July 1973), p. 359; and Terry Nardin, "Violence and the State: A Critique of Empirical Political Theory," *Sage Professional Papers in Comparative Politics Series*, No. 01-020 (Beverly Hills, California: Sage Publications, 1971), p. 27.

49   Nafziger, *The Economics of Political Instability*, p. 2.

50   *Ibid.*, p.9. Also see Ted Gurr, *Why Men Rebel* (Princeton, New Jersey.: Princeton University Press, 1970), pp. 22-58, and "Psychological Factors in Civil Strife," *World Politics* (January 1968), pp. 245-78.

51 Paul A. Baran, "On the Political Economy of Backwardness," *The Manchester School*, XX (January 1952), pp. 66-84; also see Paul Baran, *The Political Economy of Growth* (New York: The Monthly Review Press, 1957).

52 Nafziger, *The Economics of Political Instability*, p. 11.

53 *Ibid.*, p. 18.

54 Edward Luttwak, *Coups d'Etat: A Practical Handbook* (New York: Alfred A. Knopf, Inc., 1969), pp. 12, 21; also see Samuel Decalo, *Coups and Army Rule in Africa* (New Haven: Yale University Press, 1976); Amos Perlmutter, *The Military and Politics in Modern Times* (New Haven: Yale University Press, 1976), p. 117; William Thompson, "Explanations of the Military Coup," (Ph.D. Dissertation, University of Washington, 1972); Samuel P. Huntington, *Political Orders in Changing Societies* (New Haven: Yale University Press, 1968), p. 86; Claude E. Welch, "Soldier and State in Africa," in Marian E. Doro and Newell M. Stulta, eds., *Governing in Black Africa: Perspectives in New States* (Englewood Cliffs, New Jersey: Prentice-Hall, 1970), pp. 163-64.

55 Raymond Tanter, "Dimensions of Conflict Behavior within and between Nations: 1951-1960," *Journal of Conflict Resolution* 10 (1966), pp. 41-66; D.O. Bwy, "Political Instability in Latin America: The Cross-Cultural Test of Causal Model," *Latin America Research Review* 3 (1968), pp.17-66.

56 Morrison et. al., *Black Africa*, p. 123.

57 Thomas H. Greene, *Comparative Revolutionary Movements* (Englewood Cliffs, New Jersey: Prentice-Hall, Inc., 1974), pp.87-88.

58 Luttwak, *Coups d'Etat*, p. 3.

59 James H. Meisel, *Counter-Revolutions: How Revolutions Die* (New York: Atherton Press, 1966), p. 4.

60 Luttwak, *Coups d'Etat*, p. 3.

61 *Ibid.*, pp. 13-46.

62 *Ibid.*, pp. 18-19.

63 *Ibid.*, p. 21.

64 Ali Mazrui, *The Africans*, pp. 269-70.

65 Luttwak, *Coups d'Etat*, p. 32.

66 William J. Foltz and Henry S. Bienen, eds., *Arms and the African*, (New Haven: Yale University Press, 1985), pp. 181-82

67   Tangri, *Politics in Sub-Saharan Africa*, (London: James Currey Ltd., 1985), p. 130.

68   *Ibid.*, p. 131.

69   Decalo, *Coups and Army Rule in Africa*, p. 7.

70   *Ibid.*, p. 12.

71   Tangri, *Politics in Sub-Saharan Africa*, p. 42.

72   Decalo, *Coups and Army Rule in Africa*, pp. 12-37.

73   Ruth First, *Power in Africa* (New York: Pantheon Books, 1970) p. 20.

74   Martin Meredith, *The First Dance of Freedom* (New York: Harper and Row Publishers, 1984), p. 283. Also see Harry A. Gailey, Jr., *History of Africa from 1800 to Present*, Vol. II (Huntington, New York: Robert E. Krieger Publishing Company, 1981), p. 400.

75   Mazrui, *The Africans*, pp. 182-83.

76   Amos Perlmutter, *The Military and Politics in Modern Times* (New Haven: Yale University Press, 1977), p. xiv.

77   *Ibid.*, p. 117.

78   William Thompson, "Explanations of the Military Coup" (Ph.D. Dissertation, University of Washington, 1972).

79   Claude E. Welch, "Soldier and State in Africa," in Mario E. Doro and Newell M. Stultz, eds., *Governing in Black Africa: Perspectives in New States*, (Englewood Cliffs, New Jersey: Prentice-Hall, Inc., 1970), pp. 163-164.

80   David E. Apter, *The Politics of Modernization* (Chicago: The University of Chicago Press, 1965), p. 135n.

81   Samuel Edward Finer, *The Man On Horseback: The Role of the Military in Politics* (New York: Frederick A. Praeger, Inc., Publisher, 1962), p. 141-42.

82   Henry Bienen, *Armed Forces, Conflict, and Change in Africa* (San Francisco: Westview Press, 1989), p. 40.

83   Figures tabulated from a chronology of incidents of instability in Africa compiled by Chris Cook and David Killingray, *African Political Facts Since 1945* (New York: Facts on File, Inc., 1984), pp. 182-94. Note that the figure for "attempted coups" does not necessarily reflect actual occurrences since most African governments prefer not to make public some coup attempts because of security and economic reasons.

84 Dahran Ghai and Lawrence D. Smith, *Agricultural Prices, Policy and Equity in Sub-Saharan Africa* (Boulder, Colorado: Lynne Rienner Publishers, Inc., 1987), pp. 48-49.

85 Augustin K. Fosu, "Political Instability and Economic Growth with Evidence from Sub-Saharan Africa"; a paper presented at the 32nd Annual Meeting of the African Studies Association in Atlanta, Georgia, November 3-5, 1989, pp. 3-4.

86 Robert H. Jackson and Carl G. Roseberg, *Personal Rule in Black Africa* (Los Angeles: University of California Press, 1982), p. 65.

87 Dennis Austin, "Prospero's Island," in W. Scott Thompson, ed., *The Third World: Premises of U.S. Policy* (San Francisco: ICS Press, 1983), p. 67.

88 World Bank, *Sub-Saharan Africa: From Crisis to Sustainable Growth* (Washington, D.C., 1989), Table 1, p. 221.

89 Zednedk Cerbenka, *The Organization of African Unity and Its Charter* (New York: Frederick A. Praeger, 1968), p. 232.

90 *Ibid.*, pp. 10-11.

Chapter 3

Violence: The Perennial Obstacle to Social, Economic and Political Development in Nigeria, 1960–1990

Nchor B. Okorn

INTRODUCTION

Nigeria is a multiethnic nation with many resources capable of making it one of the greatest centers of power in Africa. Since the attainment of its independence in 1960, Nigeria has experienced different types of violence which have disrupted political processes and socioeconomic development. Efforts are constantly being made to contain or eliminate sources of violence in the body politic of the country.

Some people have argued that "personal quest for power" and ethnicity are the key reasons for instability in Nigeria.[1] Others see class as the most important explanatory variable: viz, some classes seeking to control the economic and political apparati of power.[2] Clearly, all these factors are significant in any attempt to understand the nature of violence in Nigeria. This chapter will discuss the role of violence, as a whole, on the Nigerian polity. It will also examine the social, political and economic implications of the phenomenon.

THEORETICAL FOUNDATIONS OF VIOLENCE

Violence is an ubiquitous term because many shades of human behavior result in actions that can generally be classified as

acts of violence. Generally recognized incidents of violence
include the following: civil strife, war, riots, revolution, and
strikes. The global importance of violence makes its study aca-
demically relevant. In order to begin a detailed analysis of the
role of violence in Nigerian political development, it would be
appropriate to define violence and discuss some of the theories that explain its causation in human societies.

Webster defines violence as the use of physical force in a
way that harms a person or his property.[3] However, for the
purpose of this study, violence will be defined and
operationalized as the use of force by institutions, individuals, and groups in order to redress societal evils or to initiate
change in societal goals. The value expectation argument from
psychological theory contends that: "The more intensely people
are motivated toward a goal or committed to an attained level
of value, the more sharply is interference resented and the
greater is the consequent instigation to aggression"[4] which
leads to violence. Arguing from the biological perspective,
Lorenz contends that animals kill for food, but men and rats
kill their own kind in anger. He goes further to assert that:
"Human behavior . . . far from being determined by reason
and cultural tradition alone, is still subject to all the laws prevailing in all phylogenetically adapted instinctive behavior."[5]
The Anthropological school of thought posits that "discriminatory practices resulting from cultural variations often create inequities which are long lasting in their effects when regional norms are not held in common by the society as a whole.
In these cases, the legitimacy of such inequities may be strongly
questioned by the stigmatized groups." This generally creates
a feeling of injustice and is very likely to result in violence.[6]

Some sociological theories attempted to rationalize the use
of violence as an instrument of control vested in particular
institutions. For instance, Scarpitte endorses Weber's contention that the legitimate use of violence is vested in the state
and Durkheim's belief that "some degree of punishment is
necessary to integrate the conforming members of society by
defining the limits of acceptable behavior."[7] The implication
of the Weber and Durkheim argument is that the state has the
right to use the instrument of violence to serve its needs. This
proposition negates rational instruments of negotiations, com-

promise and bargaining as alternatives to violence. The sociological argument contends that the discriminatory application
of social norms can lead to the frustration of those who find
themselves as victims of injustice. This further aggravates these
victims and promotes violence.[8]

Eitzen points out that "economic deprivation leads to hope-
lessness, frustrations and violence." Governments of most states
can therefore attempt to learn from Eitzen's contention by trying to provide for their citizens' economic necessities and
employ policies of economic justice to avoid violent reaction
which leads to instability.[9]

These theoretical caveats give insights as to why violence
occurs in societies. However, it is impossible to completely
exhaust all possible theoretical assumptions and arguments
that explain violence, but this attempt serves as a guide and
hopefully will be useful for our understanding the forms of
violence that have taken place in Nigeria and the subsequent
reactions by individuals and the government. It should be noted
that throughout history, scholars and statesmen alike have advocated the use of violence as an instrument of public policy.

Karl Marx, a revolutionary theoretician, believed that human society is divided into two main classes: the masses and
the owners of the means of production. The owners of the
means of production, Marx asserts, have continuously exploited
the masses. He therefore advocated revolution by the masses
against the bourgeoisie as a means of emancipating the workers from poverty and exploitation. He foresaw a future in which
the society will become classless and the state will disappear.
Hence, he writes, "The classless society is the myth of the future which compensates for the disillusionment of the present
and the disappointment of the revolution itself."[10]

Another political theoretician who saw the use of force as a
necessary instrument in the solution of conflict is Niccolo
Machiavelli. In his work (*The Prince*), he contended that a certain level of "military valor required in actual warfare is also
required in situations of political crises for acquiring, maintaining and expanding power."[11] To him it is impolitic for rulers who want to remain in power not to employ instruments of
force against their recalcitrant citizens and disloyal subjects
or for the extension of political territory.

A more recent statesman and theoretician who also believed in the use and application of force was Mao Tse-tung of China. He believed that the peasantry should be the "vanguard" of the revolution in China as they represent about 70 percent of Chinese rural population. He argued that without these poor peasants there could be no revolution. Mao's strategy for seizing political power over the governing territory is depicted as, "Enemy advances, we retreat. Enemy camps, we harass; enemy fires, we attack; enemy retreats, we pursue."[12] This strategy is the strategy of guerilla warfare.

The universal application of violence as an instrument of political decisions and change led to the Prussian strategist, Karl Von Clausewit's maxim that war is "a continuation of diplomacy by other means."[13]

ANALYSES OF VIOLENCE IN NIGERIA

Violence in Nigeria can best be understood chronologically by beginning with an analysis of the Action Group riots of 1962 and how these events and other factors later created an atmosphere of hostility and violence in the country. Nigeria gained its independence from the British in 1960 with a three-prong party system. Each of the three represented one of the major ethnic groups in the country. The Northern People Congress (NPC) headed by Amadu Bello, was a northern-based political party. The National Council of Nigeria and Cameroon (NCNC), headed by Nnamdi Azikiwe, was an Ibo-based (eastern Nigeria) political party. The Action Group (AG), headed by Chief Obafemi Awolowo, was a Yoruba-based (western Nigeria) political party. This arrangement of parties in the country was to remain the source of ethnic conflict and violence for a long time.

Due to the Alliance between the NPC and the NCNC, the two political parties formed the government in 1960, leaving the Action Group headed by Awolowo as an opposition party. Within the Action Group there emerged ideological and philosophical differences between leading party members such as Chief Akintola and Chief Awolowo. Akintola preferred to cooperate with the NPC for the sake of national unity while Chief Obafemi Awolowo would not. This difference was to weaken the Action Group.[14]

According to Oyediran, when the Action Group members were meeting in 1962 in the Western House of Assembly on May 25, a riot broke out in the Legislative chamber. The meeting was reconvened again but this time with the presence of police in anti-riot uniforms. Violence erupted again with the eventual closure of the Legislative chambers. This led to a declaration of a state of emergency by the Federal government of Nigeria, the arrest of many leaders in the government of Western Nigeria, and the firing of the governor, the premier, ministers of State, president of the State House of Chiefs, Speaker of the State Assembly, and the Superintendent General of Local Government Police.

Another step taken to contain the situation was the formation of a commission of inquiry to look into the financial and investment policies of six regional statutory corporations and their relationship with political parties because of alleged financial impropriety and subversive activities. The commission in its report vindicated Chief Akintola who was one of the accused. However, Chief Obafemi Awolowo was found guilty of attempting to overthrow the federal government and was sentenced to ten years in prison. Many other high-ranking Action Group officials were also found guilty and imprisoned accordingly. At the recommendation of Majekodunmi (the government appointed sole administrator of the western region following the 1962 riots), and with the support of the federal government, the Western House reconvened on April 8, 1963 and Chief Akintola won a vote of confidence to continue as the premier of the region.[15]

Another significant episode in the history of Nigeria leading to violence was the 1965 election. During the election, conflict erupted between AG/NCNC alliance over nomination of candidates. The original agreement to divide the 94 seats equally between the members of the alliance broke down mostly in Ekiti and Ijebu areas where members of Action Group and NCNC contested for the same seats. Oyediran contends further that the election produced more violence than had ever been witnessed. As a result of the disruption, coming from all sides, a ban on all meetings and processions was announced on September 19, 1965. Thousands of Nigerian police officers were drafted to the region to maintain law and order. In many instances, particularly in the rural areas, the enforcement officers became the victims of political thuggery and murder. The electoral officers appeared to have suffered the most.[16]

This conflict and its disruptive consequences continued unabated, and on the actual election day serious rioting occurred in the western region; in some constituencies the police, in an attempt to contain the disruption, opened fire on civilians, thus resulting in deaths. After the election, representatives of Action Group as well as NCNC declared victory for their parties. This amounted to adding fuel to fire. Riots spread like wild fire in the country.[17]

In addition to the above factors that threatened the foundations of Nigeria's first republic was the boycott of the federal elections by Action Group in 1964 and the refusal of President Nnamdi Azikiwe to appoint a prime minister from the victorious party (NPC).[18] These were to engulf the country into serious crisis. It was this confused state of affairs that motivated Major E. K. Nzeogwu to conspire with Major E. A. Ifeajuna and others to overthrow the government of the first Republic of Nigeria. On January 15, 1966, their coup attempt resulted in the death of most of the northern and western political leaders. They killed the northern premier (Sir Amadu Bello, the Sarduana of Sokoto), the Federal Prime Minister (Sir Abubakar Tafewa Balewa who hailed from northern Nigeria), and the western premier Chief Akintola. Other high-ranking northerners and Yoruba senior officials were also killed. On the other hand, the premier for Eastern Nigeria and the midwest together with their senior executives survived unscathed. This invariably created a hostile atmosphere for the Ibo-dominated coup leaders. Their major goal was to destroy the authority of the old conservative government of Nigeria and to put an end to the northern political dominance.

The coup leader, Major Nzeogwu, in an attempt to avoid a military conflict, negotiated and surrendered the leadership of the country to Major J.T. Agugi Ironsi (who was incidentally an Ibo)—a more senior officer.[19] The coup illuminates the role of ethnicity in the political equation of instability and political development in Nigeria. At all times as seen from the discussion above, representatives of various ethnic groups want to be in control of the political apparatus of the country. Perpetuating the undulating political theater of Nigeria, was the northern Nigerian resentment of the coup. This gave cause for a counter coup. The reaction of the north following the coup was aggravated by the behavior of the Ibos in public places where they (the Ibos) constantly jeered and taunted the north for their losses (viz, the assassination of their political leaders).

Major General Agugi Ironsi was very insensitive to the mood in the country when he promoted 21 military officers (18 of whom were Ibo military officers) against the wishes of the Supreme Military Council. He surrounded himself with Ibo advisors and refused to put the January coup plotters on trial. Worst of all, he decided to convert Nigeria into a unitary state in place of the more feasible federal political structure. This action heightened the northern fear of an Ibo plot to dominate the country. Rumors of an Ibo plot to kill all northerners in key government positions also intensified the situation and degenerated into riots and attacks on the Ibos in many parts of northern Nigeria.

There were massive killings of the Ibos in July of 1966 in the north, as a consequence of which many of them fled to eastern Nigeria where they are in the majority. The atmosphere of general insecurity thus created so far led to a counter coup on July 29, 1966. In the process, the head of state, Major General Agugi Ironsi, was killed and Colonel Yakubu Gowon (a Northerner), emerged the new head of state. Once again, the north was in control of the country.

Gowon's position, however, defied military norms of seniority as Brigadier Babefemi Ogundipe was the most senior military officer at the time of the successful counter coup. He should have assumed command as the next head of state instead of Colonel Gowon.[20] The killings of the Ibos, the leadership question and many other factors discussed earlier were factors that eventually led to the civil war. The coming of Gowon to power was not acceptable to Lieutenant Colonel Odumegwu Ojukwu—the military Governor of the East Central State. He based his disagreement on the grounds that Gowon's ascension to power defied norms of seniority as mentioned earlier. He also felt that Colonel Gowon was merely a puppet for the northerners who were determined to regain political control of the country—a position which they lost in January of 1966.

Lieutenant Colonel Ojukwu saw the solution to this problem in the secession of the eastern region from the rest of the
country. However, this was not acceptable to Yakubu Gowon
and the rest of Nigeria. The attempt to find a solution resulted
in several conferences in the country. General Ankrah, then
head of state of Ghana, initiated a peace conference at Aburi
(Ghana) between Gowon and Ojukwu. At Aburi, an accord was
reached to stop the bickering and to work for the interest of
the country. However, when the feuding parties (Yakubu Gowon
and Odumegwu Ojukwu) returned to Nigeria from Aburi, they
interpreted the terms of the Aburi accord differently and thus
created further problems. Ojukwu understood the Aburi accord to mean the establishment of a confederation, while
Yakubu Gowon understood its terms to represent a federation.
This confusion over the interpretation of the terms of the Aburi
agreement led Ojukwu to promulgate the Revenue Collection
Edict, Legal Education Edict and the Court of Appeal Edict
which gave the eastern part of the country greater autonomy
from the federal government of Nigeria. The Federal government reacted with an embargo on communications and foreign exchange transaction on the east. The failure to resolve
the differences between the two sides led to the declaration of
the Biafran state.[21] The Federal government on May 27, 1967
responded by declaring a state of emergency and Yakubu
Gowon took direct control of the country and created 12 states
from the old regional political structure in the country. This
eventually led to the outbreak of the Nigerian Civil War on
July 6, 1967.[22] The strategy of using violence for decision-making in Nigeria leaves much to be desired. This is because increasingly, violence has become institutionalized in the political culture of Nigeria.

The Gowon administration pursued the civil war until it
ended in 1970 and proceeded with the tasks of nation-building. He created a constitutional review committee with the
duty of reconstructing the Nigerian constitution in preparation for handing over power to a civilian administration by
October 1, 1976. Unfortunately, problems of corruption in the
government, and disagreement within the military echelons
as to when to hand over power to the civilians, led to Gowon's
announcement on October 1, 1974 that the date for the re-

turn to civilian rule had been postponed indefinitely. This created dissatisfaction among the civilians and the military and consequently culminated in the overthrow of Gowon's regime on July 29, 1975 by General Murtala Mohammed.[23]

Murtala Mohammed had hardly kicked off his programs when he was assassinated six months after his assumption of office. However, General Olusegun Obasanjo (Mohammed's successor), carried out the political programs outlined after the July 1975 coup. General Obasanjo eventually returned the country to civilian rule in 1979. The elected civilian president (Shehu Shagari) took over office on October 1, 1979.[24]

The Shagari regime unfortunately lasted for only four years and three months. The military removed Shagari in a military coup on December 31, 1983 because of corruption, maladministration and for creating a general atmosphere of insecurity in Nigeria. General Sanni Abacha tried to explain why the 1983 coup was organized against the Shagari regime:

> Fellow countrymen and women—you are all living witnesses to the grave economic predicament and uncertainty which an inept and corrupt leadership has imposed on our beloved nation for the past four years. I am referring to the harsh, intolerable conditions under which we are now living. Our economy has been hopelessly mismanaged. We have become a debtor and a beggar nation.[25]

The coup brought Major General Mohammadu Buhari to power as the head of state of Nigeria. The Buhari administration on assuming office instituted draconian policies and tried to control public behavior with programs like "War Against Indiscipline" (W.A.I.) to the extent that there was total fear as public officials and citizens could not criticize the government. The suppressive nature of the government coupled with the high levels of unemployment in a recession led to the overthrow of the Buhari administration by Major General Ibrahim Babangida in 1985. The quest for power by military officers led to yet another attempted military coup. Just five months after the Babangida Administration assumed office, Maman Vasta led an abortive attempt against the new military government.[26]

Whatever the political and military justification for coups, it is my opinion that the rationale and reasons given demonstrate the personal ambition of the individuals who seize power. Most coup plotters give corruption, authoritarianism and mal-administration as causes for their intervention. Yet coups have not served as deterrents to willfully corrupt administrations. Of course, I do not dismiss the need for coups to remove entrenched dictatorships and corrupt regimes, but it is reasonable to advocate removal through the ballot box rather than through a contagion of coups and violence. As recently as April 22, 1990, a bloody aborted coup against the Babangida regime took place. This coup was organized by Major Gideon Ugwarzo Okah. In his radio broadcast to the Nigerian people, Major Okah declared:

> Fellow Nigerian citizens, on behalf of the patriotic and well meaning people of the Middle Belt and Southern part of this country, I Major Gideon Ugwarzo Okah wish to happily inform you of a successful ousting of the dictatorial, corrupt, drug-baronish, inhuman, sadistic, deceitful, homosexually-centered, oligarchistic and unpatriotic administration of General Ibrahim Babangida"[27]

It has been suggested in some circles that the 1983 elections triggered the coup which toppled the Shehu Shagari regime. Some suggest that Shehu Shagari's National Party of Nigeria (NPN) rigged the elections, and that was the last act which necessitated the military takeover of political power. Obviously, the traditional belief of ethno-political loyalty was defied when the NPN (a northern dominated political party) won elections in Ondo State and Oyo State which are all Yoruba states and were therefore expected to vote for late Chief Obafemi Awolowo's Unity Party of Nigeria (UNP). When this did not happen, an atmosphere of cynical anger was immediately created.

According to Andrew Apter, violence erupted throughout the Ondo State on August 16, 1983 due ostensibly to the gubernatorial election. The National Party of Nigeria was declared the winning party in an overwhelmingly Unity Party of Nigeria state. At the national level, the presidential contest between Shehu Shagari and late Chief Awolowo created the background for violence in other parts of the country. Shagari's NPN claimed victory in 12 of the 19 states (including even the UPN strongholds, Oyo State and Ondo State). In the west, the NPN won Anambra, stronghold state for the NPP. The overall election results were rather frustrating for chief Awolowo's supporters who saw the defeat in Awolowo's homeland as a personal insult to the chief. They concluded that the NPN rigged the elections. Since the NPN controlled the federal government, those aggrieved by the outcome of the elections could not guarantee justice if they petitioned the courts. Hence, in some cities, people took to the streets and rioted. Ondo state is considered one of the safe seats of the Unity Party. However, the Unity Party candidate lost the elections. The riots claimed dozens of lives in some cities. The gubernatorial election in Ondo State were reversed in favor of the Unity Party of Nigeria following the protest and legal petitions. Once again violence was used to solve a political problem. Andrew Apter recounts the events of the time as follows:

> "God is on our side," three young men said as they searched for an arrogant NPN girl to stab, beat and rape. As the crowd turned into a mob it broke into sections, burning and gutting NPN beer-parlors, compounds, cars and motorcycles, drinking plundered beer and smashing bottles. The atmosphere was sinister, festive and obviously threatening.[28]

The conclusion that an outsider can draw from this analysis is not necessarily that the elections were rigged but that election outcomes in most parts of Nigeria are always predetermined. Anything short of this calculated outcome becomes unacceptable to the group presuming it has superior members. Also being a member of a particular ethnic group implies one must always exercise one's democratic right to vote by voting only for a member of his ethnic group or risk being ostracized by members of one's community.

Other acts of violence beyond political violence in Nigeria include religious riots, student unrest and labor unrest. Unrest in the universities caused by student riots and faculty strikes remain crucial to understanding the problems associated with governmental policies in Nigeria. One illustration of this is the student unrest of April 1988 when university students demonstrated against increases in the prices of fuel. They also requested the restoration of the power to open and close universities to the university senate, the purpose of which was to avoid the unnecessary closures of universities by the federal government.

Another university unrest was caused by the non-implementation of a new salary structure in universities which the government approved for all Nigerian workers in January 1988. Workers in other areas within the country had already received their new salary scales. Efforts by the lecturers to reach an agreement on the issue failed and resulted in a nationwide strike by the Academic Staff Union of Universities (ASSU) and the Senior Staff Association of Universities Teaching Hospital Research Institute and Associated Institute (SSAUTRIAI) on July 2, 1988. The unrest was met with stiff government reaction.[29]

Educational institutions have certainly had their share of violence. One issue that led to a crisis in one of the Nigerian universities (Amadu Bello University) was a disagreement between Muslim students and Christian students on June 13, 1988 over an alleged rigging of a student union presidential election. In that election, a Christian candidate won. Again, on June 14, 1988, students protested in the University of Benin when about 10,000 of them decided to boycott classes over policy disagreement on the abolition of "re-sit" examination. The practice had been for students who failed specific courses to retake the examination in the failed subjects. This was a method inherited from the British educational system. The university had changed to the American semester. This made the old practice of retaking failed examinations obsolete.[30] The students were opposed to this change.

Religious fundamentalism has contributed in a major way to the Nigerian experience of violence and represents yet another dimension of the analysis. Nigeria is a secular society with a variety of religious groups including Christians and Muslims. This difference in religious beliefs, which occasionally explodes into violence, shows the role of religion in the Nigerian society.

In 1978 when the constituent Assembly was formed to draft a constitution which would guide civilian rule in 1979, the Muslim members of the Assembly argued for the introduction of a *Sharia* (Islamic) court system within the Nigerian judicial system. This was opposed by the Christian delegates and other members of the Assembly. The 1979 constitution, which was eventually promulgated, called for a secular state with all individuals entitled to freedom of worship. The Muslim Student Society and the Izala Movement rejected the constitution and advocated the establishment of an Islamic state.

While the traditional and conservative Emirs and their council had different approaches for dealing with this situation, the fanatical group (the Izala Movement) did not eschew violence as a means of establishing an Islamic state in Nigeria. The leader of this group was Alhaji Muhammadu Maroua. It was he who inspired the sect's religious uprising in Kano in 1980. Two years later (1982) the disciples of Maitatsine (another sect) were involved in another uprising in Maiduguri.[31]

Religious rioting has prevailed in all parts of the Nigerian society. On May 3, 1986, the University of Sokoto was in turmoil when members of the Muslim Student Society became embroiled in violence while protesting against the program of events prepared by the university student officials for the celebration of the achievement of Nana Asamau, the daughter of Othman dan Fodio.

Religious disturbances are not unique to northern Nigeria. In 1971, there were religious riots for three months in Calabar—the capital of Cross River State. There were violent disturbances between two warring factions of the Brotherhood Church of the Cross and Star.[32]

This discussion of violence in Nigeria will be incomplete without reference to violence associated with labor unrest. On April 11, 1988, due to a price increase of petroleum products in the country, Kano was in turmoil as civil servants, nurses, and other categories of workers went on strike. The unrest and strikes spread to Ilorin and Kwara States. On April 22 employees of some insurance and financial institutions joined the strike. As the situation continued unresolved, it affected all parts of the country. Kaduna and Bauchi States joined the national strike. In Bauchi, for instance, 18 industrial unions embarked on a sit-in action on April 25, 1988. The strike fever eventually reached Lagos when on April 28, 1988, the Murtala Mohammed international airport was deserted as air traffic controllers joined the strike. No planes could land or take off from the airport.

Nurses and other health workers in Lagos State refused to turn up for duty and the city general hospital in Ikeja, Lagos

Island, and the Lagos University Teaching Hospital shut their doors to patients while those already admitted were forcefully discharged.[33] These violent incidents had devastating effects on life and property.

CONSEQUENCES OF VIOLENCE IN NIGERIA

The cumulative impact of violence in Nigeria has far reaching political, economic, and social consequences as discussed below. Election riots in 1965 in the western region resulted in deadly confrontations between the police and civilians. The police fired on civilians. There were also killing of political opponents and massive looting in the region. The army unilaterally intervened. This military action without presidential authorization was to set a precedent for the military coup of 1966.[34]

As discussed earlier, the 1966 coup was executed by an Ibo clique in the army. This action presented the coup as an ethnic conflict designed by the Ibos to eliminate northern officials and their allies from political control of the country.[35] Northern retaliation led to the coup which ushered Gowon into power and the killing of Ibos in northern Nigeria.[36] The power struggle between the major ethnic groups has become part of the Nigerian political culture and consequently one of the explanations given frequently for political instability in the country.

The effects of the civil war in Nigeria cannot be exhausted in a chapter of this nature, but suffice it to say that it was bloody. Thousands of lives were lost and much property destroyed. According to Nafziger, the socioeconomic loss from the death and displacement caused by the civil war cannot be calculated. At least two million persons on both sides died of starvation alone between 1967 and 1969. As one would naturally expect, military expenditure increased tremendously during the civil war—diverting funds from socioeconomic activities. Ayida estimated that the total military expenditure by the Nigerian government during the war was 3,000 million pounds from September 1968 until March 1969; a cost of 270 million pounds above the normal peace time level and equal to more than one-tenth of the GDP for the period.[37]

Other negative consequences include loss of foreign exchange from export earnings, decrease in civilian production, and a consequent decrease in government revenue. The effect was delays in capital and human investment.[38] Other effects of the civil war included a slow economy with high unemployment rates, a high level of inflation, and a lower standard of living for Nigerians. Balance of payment deficits rose as export earnings from crude oil declined. On the other hand repatriation of earnings by foreign investors increased around the same time. There was, however, a drop in private capital flow into the country. Some problems also caused by the war include the derailment of the transportation infrastructure—especially those used to transport food to difficult parts of the country. Food shortages were common. The increase in import of mineral fuels, lubricants, and related materials because of the destruction of oil production facilities in Port Harcourt further depleted the Nigerian foreign exchange.[39] On the whole the economic effects were devastating. As would be expected, after the war, the government began to reconstruct and repair all damaged infrastructure and to move the economy to its pre-war level.

The consequences resulting from religious violence are also of special concern because of their disruptive nature, their frequency of occurrence and the difficulty in predicting their occurrence. According to Nwagboso, the religious riots that took place in Nigeria in 1980 resulted in the destruction of property worth millions of *naira* (Nigerian currency) and the death of about 6,000 people.[40]

The casualties recorded in the 1982 religious riot in Maiduguri were 400 killed. In Jimeta (Gongola State), in the month of February 1984, religious riots caused serious damage to property and subjected 5,913 people to near homelessness. Similar incidents occurred in Gombe (Bauchi State) when a group of individuals who believe in "the idea of history involving a continual conflict between oppressor and oppressed," with the eventual victory of the later rampaged in the city and killed about 100 within ten hours of fighting.[41]

The bloody clash between Muslim and Christian students in the University of Sokoto on May 3, 1986 occurred during celebrations honoring Nana Asamau (daughter of Othman dan

Fodio who was a renowned northern political and religious leader). The spill-over effect was the burning of the office of the university chancellor. Again at Amadu Bello University when the clash occurred between the Muslim Student Society and Christian students over an ill-fated student government election on June 14, 1988, about 100 students were injured. One student eventually died from the injuries suffered.[42] In 1978 Nigerian students protested against high food prices in universities and called for the removal of the then Federal Minister for Education (Colonel Ali) and in the clash that ensued between police and the students, six students died. The government banned the national union of students.[43]

Following the strike by university lecturers in the country in 1988, the then federal minister for education (Jibril Aminu) gave the Academic Staff Union of Universities, on July 5, 1988, an ultimatum to return to the classrooms or risk losing their jobs. He, however, announced that the federal government had allocated 75 million *naira* to Universities to enable them to pay faculty the new salary scales. Having satisfied the demands of the university lecturers, the government proscribed the teachers union because of its failure to comply fully with the order to return to the classroom. Alex Goboyega, the president of ASSU at the University of Ibadan branch and other members of his executive were seriously interrogated by security officials. The national president of ASSU, who was a lecturer at the university of Benin, was dismissed. His family was forcefully ejected from his official residence even though the case of his dismissal was still pending in court.[44]

Definitely, these problems facing universities impede the academic process in the country. The morale and enthusiasm of faculty can also be seriously hampered. The government therefore needs to re-evaluate its educational policies so as to avoid future conflict of this nature.

The labor unrest in Nigeria has periodically brought the country to near paralysis. During such times, vital service institutions such as hospitals are closed. Patients are often left unattended resulting in some deaths. In Murtala Mohammed Hospital in Kano, many pregnant women in labor died because they were not attended to. In Kwara State people had no drinking water as taps ran dry following a workers' strike. In Kaduna

State some owners of shops closed their stores, thus creating artificial scarcity at times of need. Truck drivers refused to haul oil from the Kaduna refinery in the north to the rest of the country—causing shortages of fuel and other petroleum products in the country. Consequently, transportation cost escalated and the spillover effect brought prices of consumer commodities to sky-rocket levels.[45]

CONCLUSION

In the analysis of violence conducted thus far, one thing remains obvious: the frequency of violence in Nigeria (from riots to military coups) has seriously affected the behavior pattern of Nigerians. The swift nature of military decisions (without consultation with the people) seem to have given Nigerians "speedy" personalities. They are always eager to accomplish their desired goals in record time. This aggressiveness is a result of the administrative and political culture experienced in the country since 1960. Also, because of the serious roles that the military has played in Nigerian politics, some Nigerians see the military as a short-cut to their ascendance to political power. This, certainly, is very destabilizing for the country as ambitious people instigate coups.

Frequent recurrence of political violence or instability poses a threat to the virtue associated with negotiation and compromise in decision-making processes within the Nigerian population. A polity preoccupied with violence is slow in developing politically.

Notes

1 William Tordoff, *Government and Politics of Africa*, (Bloomington: Indiana University Press, 1984).

2 Shehu Othman, "Classes, Crises, and Coup: The Demise of Shagari Re gime," *African Affairs*, Vol. 83 No. 333, October 1984, p. 441.

3 Merriam Webster, *Webster's Intermediate Dictionary* (Springfield, Massachusetts: Merriam-Webster Inc., 1977), p. 865.

4 Ivo K. Feierabend, *Anger, Violence and Politics* (Englewood Cliffs: Prentice Hall Inc., 1972), p. 41.

5 Knorad Lorenz, *On Aggression* (New York: Bantam Books 1971), p. 229.

6 Frank R. Scarpitte, *Social Problems* (New York: Holt, Rinehart and Winston Inc., 1974), p. 418.

7 *Ibid.*, p. 418.

8 *Ibid.*, p. 419.

9 Stanley D. Eitzen and Maxine Baka Zinn, *In Conflict and Order: Understanding Society* (Needham Heights, Massachusetts: Simon & Schuster Co., 1995), pp. 320-21.

10 George Sabine and Thomas Thorson, *A History of Political Theory* (Hinsdale: Dryden Press, 1983), p. 610.

11 *Ibid.*, p. 326.

12 *Ibid.*, p. 782.

13 Robert J. Lieber, *No Common Power: Understanding International Relations*, (Boston: Scott, Foreman and Company, 1988), p. 114.

14 Oyeleye Oyediran, *Nigerian Government and Politics Under Military Rule: 1966-1979*, (London: The Macmillan Press Ltd, 1979), p. 13.

15 *Ibid.*, pp. 14-15.

16 *Ibid.*, pp. 20-21.

17 *Ibid.*, pp. 21-22.

18 E. Wayne Nafziger, "Economic Impact of the Nigerian Civil War," *Journal of Modern African Studies*, 10.2 (1972), p. 224.

19 Tordoff, pp. 162-64.

20 Oyediran, pp. 27-29.

21 A.H.M. Kirk Greene, *Crisis and Conflict in Nigeria: A Documentary Source Book 1966-70*, (London: Oxford University Press, 1971), pp. 427-44.

22 Oyediran, pp. 30-31.

23 *Ibid.*, p. 243.

24 Peter Enahoro, "The Maturity of a Nation," *Africa Now*, (London: Pan African Publisher LTD 1981), pp. 139-142.

25 Shehu Othman, "Classes, Crisis and Coup: The Demise of Shagari's Regime", *African Affairs*, Vol. 83 No. 333 October, 1984, p. 441.

26 *African Concord*, 7 May 1990, p. 42.

27 *Newbreed*, May 14 1990, p. 4.

28 Andrew Apter, "Things Fall Apart? Yoruba Response to the 1983 Elections in Ondo State, Nigeria." *Journal of Modern African Studies*, 25, 3 (1987), pp. 489-501.

29 *West Africa*, July 18 1988, p. 1292.

30 *Ibid.*, p. 1293.

31 Raymond Hickey, "1982 Maitatsine Uprising in Nigeria: A Note," *African Affairs* Vol. 83 No. 331. April 1984, pp. 252-53.

32 Maxwell Nwagboso, "The Religious Dimension." *West Africa*, July 18, 1988, p. 1294.

33 *Newswatch*, May 16, "Uneasy Calm Returns." pp. 12-13.

34 Oyediran, p. 22.

35 Tordoff, p. 163.

36 Oyediran, pp. 22-29.

37 Nafziger, 10.2 (1972), p. 242.

38 *Ibid.*

39 *Ibid.*, pp. 232-38.

40   Newagboso, pp. 1294-295.

41   *Ibid.*

42   *Ibid.*

43   *Newswatch*, July 25, 1988, p. 16.

44   *Ibid.*, pp. 14-18.

45   *Newswatch*, May 16, 1988, pp. 12-18.

Chapter 4

The Crises of Nation Building: The Liberian Experience*

George A. Agbango

INTRODUCTION

Nation states aspire to develop a high standard of living for their citizens and to maintain such at all times. With the recent development of super communication systems, the world has become closer and smaller than before. Hence, economic, political, and social developments all over the world are quickly brought into the homes and offices of millions of people at every corner of the globe. The disparities between the developed and the less-developed countries become very apparent. And the less-developed countries are under tremendous pressure to catch up with the developed ones.

However, several factors mitigate against the less-developed countries in their efforts to develop. The attempts by governments to create conducive climates for the development of high standards of living have been seriously hindered by the *crises of nation building*. These crises, as identified in studies initiated by the Committee on Comparative Politics of the Social Science Research Center at the Center for Advanced Study in the Behavioral Studies at Palo Alto, California, in 1963 are: the Crises of Identity; Legitimacy; Penetration; Participation; and Distribution. A combination of some of these crises led to the military coup d'etat in Liberia in 1980 and the subsequent disintegration of the Liberian state.

* An abridged version of this chapter was published in the *Towson Journal of International Affairs*, Spring 1994, Vol.XXIX, No. 2

The crisis of identity is a major problem facing most developing countries—particularly in Africa. When citizens identify with their ethnic group and give tremendous loyalty to such a group rather than to their country, an identity crisis is bound to occur. The group effort of the Ibos in the then Eastern Nigeria in the creation of the secessionist Republic of Biafra was a manifestation of the crisis of identity. In Africa, it is not unusual for citizens to owe greater allegiance to their ethnic group than to their country. The disintegration of Somalia, and most recently Rwanda, bears testimony to what may happen if loyalty is not to the state but to one's ethnic group. Ethnic identity was exploited to the fullest during the "divide and rule"[1] era of the colonial period, and the problem has become a chronic one in the post-colonial era.

Associated with this identity crisis is the crisis of participation. In the latter case, some sectors of the population either by design or oversight, are denied access to the political system and are hindered from playing an active part in the political process. In many instances, minority ethnic groups are ignored in the political process because they "do not matter." Their minority vote is inconsequential because a reliance on the majority ethnic group assures leaders of political victory. However, in some instances, an affluent elite of a minority ethnic group may gain political power and may ignore the need to share power with the majority. The latter was the case of the minority white regime in apartheid South Africa. And prior to 1980, the minority Americo-Liberian population controlled political power in Liberia. The denial of the majority population of any access to the political system in both South Africa (prior to 1992) and in Liberia (prior to 1980) led to bloody struggles between factions in the two countries.

On the other hand, the crisis of penetration relates to the ability of a government to assert its authority in all parts of the country. Governments that have lost their legitimacy (the legal and moral right of a government to rule) are often unable to assert their authority over the entire country. This was what happened in Liberia in the last months of President Samuel Doe's regime.

The fair and equitable distribution of scarce resources (especially basic needs such as food, shelter, and health supplies) is a daily concern for many African countries. In Liberia for instance, educational facilities, housing, and health services were readily available in the Americo-Liberia dominated regions of the country. Unfortunately, other parts of the country remained in dire need of these services. It was, therefore, not surprising that the many anti-government demonstrations in Liberia conveyed the concerns of the masses about the unfair distribution of the national wealth.

In this chapter, we shall examine the causes and effects of the 1980 coup d'etat in Liberia that led to the rise of Master-Sergeant Doe. Doe ruled Liberia for nearly a decade. During this period, the political and socioeconomic climate in the country degenerated into one of Africa's disastrous experiences of military dictatorship.

In 1990, Doe was killed at the height of a civil war that had devastated his country. Whereas Doe's rise to power sends a lesson to African civilian regimes that fail to provide honest and democratic leadership, his fall also serves as a warning to African military dictators who ignore the wishes of the masses of their citizens.

CAUSES OF THE 1980 COUP IN LIBERIA

The circumstances leading to the 1980 coup in Liberia have their roots dating as far back as the 1820's when the state of Liberia was established. Founded as a colony for freed slaves from the United States, the country's code of arms has the inscription, "The Love of Liberty Brought Us Here." Ironically, "liberty" was not extended to all sectors of the Liberian population and this, in the last quarter of the 20th, escalated into civil strife.

In the first place, land was forcefully acquired from the indigenous people around the coastal lands of present day Liberia. Secondly, the settlers, comprising freed slaves from the Americas and slaves rescued from ships off the coast of Africa and elsewhere (referred to as "recaptives"), considered themselves superior to the indigenous people who were in the majority. Thirdly, among the settlers, the recaptives were discriminated against by the freed slaves from America who regarded their ethnicity to be "Americo-Liberian". The indigenous people were considered uncivilized, and a provision in the declaration of independence described the land as a "barbarous coast."[2] The Americo-Liberian sense of ethnic superiority was resented by the indigenous population and occasional feuds between the three groups reflected the mutual animosities that prevailed among them.

There were several motives underlying the repatriation of freed blacks from the Americas to Africa. Saigbey Boley has vividly analyzed the motives of the American Colonization Society in the repatriation of the group and slaves and suggests that the fundamental reasons were the following:

1. The desire to rid America of the care and danger of poor and disgruntled blacks who could repeat the rebellious terror of Nat Turner.
2. To create a shortage of black labor and hence stimulate white immigration to America from Europe.
3. To reduce the alarming growing rate of Blacks in America.
4. To use negro settlement in Liberia as a nucleus for the spread of Christianity in Africa.
5 The fear that America will lose its racial and cultural identity if the Negroes were allowed to mix with whites.[3]

Whatever the motives of the Colonization Society, it is reasonable to deduce that it was also in the self-interest of blacks to flee the racist climate in America—hence the notion that it was the "love of liberty" that brought them to Liberia. Yet those who were fleeing from discrimination in America were willing to discriminate against the indigenous peoples and the recaptives. The indigenous population was not only treated with contempt by the repatriates, but the indigenious peoples were recruited against their will and supplied as "laborers for Firestone and other foreign employers."[4] The indigenous population was also exported to Spanish plantations in places such as Fernando Po.[5] According to Raymond Buell, such practices led to complete "disorganization of the native village life, a high death rate in labor compounds, and depopulation of the villages."[6] It was not surprising, therefore, that Liberia was censored by the League of Nations for its slave practices following investigations. This led to the resignation of President

King and his Vice-President Allen Yancy, and other Liberian officials.[7]

However, the resignation of King and his accomplices did not end slavery in Liberia. As late as 1962, "one-fourth of the wage-earning labor force was recruited involuntarily."[8] This part of Liberia's history widened the rift between the indigenous population and the America-Liberians which succeeding political leaders ignored or did little to reconcile.

Economically, the national wealth of Liberia was never equitably distributed. Infrastructural development in Liberia was concentrated around Monrovia (where a large percentage of America-Liberians lived) whereas the hinterland (which is largely inhabited by the indigenous people) was left undeveloped. As socioeconomic disparities between the urban areas and the country-side widened, so also did the social class strata. As Dunn and Tarr put it:

> Wealth tended to be concentrated in the upper crust of repatriate society (broadly defined) which hardly exceeded one percent of the population. At the other extreme were the indigenous mass of rural poor and an ethnically mixed urban poor, underclass repatriates being included.[9]

Politically, a broad mass of the Liberian population was alienated from the political process. Since the founding of Liberia in 1821, until the 1980 coup, political power and the "authoritative allocation of values" were the exclusive preserve of the expatriate elites and the True Whig Party—the dominant political party in Liberia. The alienated groups resented this. As early as the 1930's, this resentment materialized in a coup plot. At the trial of the ring-leaders, it was revealed that "at the founding of their Youth Association in 1937, there had been a plan `to destroy the America-Liberian aristocracy, and to put all the aborigines in the government of the country.'"[10] Yet no efforts were made to defuse the tensions created through power sharing.

With the emergence of the continent-wide independence struggle in the post World War II era, it was hoped that the ruling elite in Liberia would progressively loosen up political controls and allow for the democratization of the political process. This did not happen. The ruling elite under President

William Tubman lost a unique opportunity to initiate reforms during this period. In addition, Tubman's repressive rule fueled the already volatile situation. As Wreh succinctly puts it:

> He [Tubman] surrounded himself with a network of security services and a plethora of agents to ensure that dissenters were silenced, being consigned to jail under the catch-all, nebulous crime of "security risk". The police, the army, the arms of the security service were all part of the apparatus used by Tubman to cow the people and make his regime seem faultless with himself as "god-king" who saw all and knew all. . .
>
> Not only were power and decision-making Tubman's exclusive preserve, but the means of redress and dissent open to the citizen were also restricted. Institutions which provided the constitutional checks and balances were never allowed to take an independent course unfavorable to his Administration.[11]

Personal greed crowned Tubman's repressive rule. For instance, in 1951, he purchased an expensive Presidential yacht for his exclusive use at the state's expense. Again in 1966, Tubman devoted large sums of money for the celebration of his 76th birthday.[12] This was at a time when the country needed better health and educational facilities. Tubman's national priorities were glaringly misplaced.

On July 23, 1971, William Tolbert succeeded Tubman following the death of the latter. Tolbert pledged to transform the Liberian society into one "which shall require the total dynamic involvement of every Liberian, and of all within our borders for an ever-spiraling advancement of productivity and achievement."[13]

The early years of Tolbert's administration witnessed a profound political climate which may be likened to a "Monrovia Spring." During this period, freedom of the press, speech and association flourished. It was during this period that several pressure groups were formed. The Movement for Justice in Africa (MOJA), and The Progressive Alliance of Liberia (PAL) were both founded in 1973. A year later, local chapters of Liberia welfare associations throughout the U.S.A. amalgamated to form the Union of Liberian Associations in the Americas (ULAA).

The "Monrovia Spring" was short-lived. The guarantees of freedom of the press, speech and association never material-

ized as corruption became the norm of the day. Although a
National Force for the Eradication of Corruption was formed,

> Dishonesty and corruption in government became widespread and
> uncontrollable . . . Friends and relatives of the President as well as
> those citizens well connected in dishonest or corrupt practices were
> seldom prosecuted. . . . Moral deterioration in society reached its
> lowest ebb.[14]

Several factors account for the incidence of coups d'etat in
Sub-Saharan Africa. These include greed, corruption, nepotism, moral decadence, ethnic strife, and the willingness of
the army (or a wing thereof) to stage a coup d'etat. The True
Whig Party under Tolbert, by 1980, was deeply entrenched in
these social evils. Tolbert's government was filled with rela-
tives and friends—only few of whom earned their positions by
merit. MOJA, PAL and other political associations exerted pressure on the Tolbert administration to rid the country of corruption and to democratize. The masses rallied around these
formidable groups with the sole objective of presenting their
grievances to the government in an organized manner. PAL
under Gabriel Baccus Matthews was at the forefront of the
organizations demanding reform. It successfully registered the
Peoples Progressive Party as an alternative to the True Whig
Party.

In the midst of these agitations, in April 1979, the Liberian
government raised the price of rice (the country's staple food).
This action was resisted by the populace. As organized labor
and the masses demonstrated against the government price
policy, the government mobilized the army and police to ruthlessly suppress the demonstrations. For instance, on April 15,
1979, about 100 people lost their lives and some 500 people
were injured during a demonstration.[15] As the popularity of
the Tolbert's regime continued to decline, the opposition
groups began to gain increased popular support.

The climax of Tolbert's political problems was the coup of
April 12, 1980. Tolbert was killed in the wake of the coup and
13 of his cabinet ministers were executed later. Master-Sergeant
Doe who led the coup declared himself the head of state. The
coup did not come as a surprise. Soldiers are first and foremost "people" and "soldiers" second. They are part of the so-

ciety which is a conglomeration of members of their family, ethnic group, fraternal and religious groups. They see the worsening plight of their people. They are not unaware of the contradictions of the society in which the wealth and splendor of the ruling elite contrast sharply with the poverty of the broad masses. Added to this concern is the usual ambition of soldiers to rule. Hence, the April 12, 1980 coup d'etat did not surprise political analysts. Nor was it surprising that a vast majority of Liberians welcomed the coup.

In his broadcast to the nation after the coup, Samuel Doe pledged to rid Liberia of all vices and to install a government that was to be responsive to people and in which justice, equality, and fairness would prevail. Doe's ascension to power ended the Americo-Liberian monopoly of political power in Liberia.

In the years that followed, the behavior of Doe and his ruling People's Redemption Council government revealed that Liberia in the post-coup era was "animal farm" revisited in which the pigs (as the rulers of Manor Farm) were no better than the men they replaced. Ruth First has rightly noted that no matter the noble intentions of the Army, they often seize power because of their own corporate interest.[16] The post-coup era in Liberia confirmed First's view. Dunn and Tarr recount:

Military spending became illustrative of this emerging pattern. While the immediate post-coup seizure of private property may be viewed as part of a revolutionary political change, their conversion to personal use in the visibly ostentatious living of leading military personnel quickly reversed the image of young soldiers committed to rectifying the evils of the past and working in the masses' interest. In 1980-81, the first full fiscal year after the coup, $144 million (80% of the recurrent budget) was spent on personnel services (wages, salaries, benefits, housing, etc.). The amount was double the $72 million spent on the same item in 1978-79, the year of Tolbert's benefits increase for the professional category of civil servants.

Overall spending on national security—defense and costs classed as "public order and safety"—increased from $17.8 million in 1978-79 to $44.6 million in 1980-81. The cost of national security as a percentage of total government expenditures also went up significantly after the coup. From security spending of 6.2% of the budget in 1978-79, the proportion of spending rose steadily from 10.1% in 1978-79 to 15% in 1980-81; in 1986, it is nearly one-third. At the same time, according to the World Bank's annual World Development Report, relative government spending on education and health fell from 30% of total government spending in 1977 to 23.6% in 1981.[17]

The history of military intervention in the politics of Sub-Saharan Africa reveals that the military upon seizing power clings to it until they are forced out of office. In Somalia, Siyad Barre clung on to power for over 20 years until his overthrow in early 1991. In Benin, Matthieu Kerekou was in power from 1972 to 1991 when he was defeated in a national election forced on him by pro-democracy movements. In Mali, Moussa Traore was in power from 1968 until February 1991 when pro-democracy forces necessitated a palace coup. In Togo, Gnassingbe Eyadema rode high on dictatorial rule until labor movements and democratic forces ended his "invincible" monopoly of power in mid-1991. In Zaire, Mobutu Sese Seko still clings to power he seized in 1965 despite the overwhelming national opposition to his rule.

THE FALL OF DOE

Samuel Doe, like the Machiavellian prince, out-maneuvered other members of the PRC. Five members of the PRC were executed in August 1981 for plotting to overthrow Doe. The elimination complied with the Machiavellian dictum that one way a prince can maintain political power is by getting rid of those who are capable of removing him from power.[18]

To legitimize his continuous hold on power, and partly due to external pressure from the United States, Doe made overtures towards a return to constitutional rule. He began with the appointment of a National Constitution Commission which drafted a new constitution. It was revised by a Constitutional Advisory Assembly and later submitted to the populace for ratification in a national referendum on July 3, 1984.

Following the lifting of the ban on party politics, Doe launched his National Democratic Party of Liberia (NDPL). Other political parties sprang up, but in the end, it was a contest between the NDPL and the Liberian Action Party (LAP).

In the ensuing elections, the NDPL emerged victorious by winning 50.9 percent of the votes. But it was widely acclaimed by observers that the LAP won by 62.8 percent of the votes cast.[19] Doe, as leader of the NDPL became President of the Second Republic of Liberia in 1985.

Meanwhile, the economy of Liberia continued to decline. In 1984, a "Report of the Committee to Review the Present Economic Situation in Liberia" had indicated that Liberia was at the brink of financial and economic collapse which could lead to social and political chaos.[20] By 1987, the Liberian economy was suffering from acute economic distress. Doe in desperation hired 17 operational experts—the apex men—from the United States to help control the Liberian government spending as well as minimize the chronic corruption.[21]

As the Liberian economy declined and Doe increased his grip over the country, Charles Taylor (a former ally of Doe) and Prince Yormie Johnson organized a guerilla campaign against Doe. Johnson and Taylor eventually split company due to ideological differences in February 1990. However, both factions continued to fight against forces loyal to Doe. In due course, a full-scale civil war developed, and several innocent civilians became victims. During the last Sunday of July, 1990, 600 people who had sought refuge in a church outside Monrovia were massacred by forces loyal to Doe.[22] As the civilian population continued to suffer great casualties, the number of refugees entering neighboring countries (Ivory Coast, Sierra Leone, and Guinea) escalated. It was no longer a Liberian problem. Hence the Economic Commission of West African States (ECOWAS), in the interest of the innocent lives lost daily in the civil war and in the interest of the member countries affected, commissioned some of its member states to deploy a peace-keeping force in Liberia.

Consequently, an ECOWAS peace-keeping force under the command of Lt. General Quainoo of Ghana was deployed to maintain law and order in Liberia. This intervention was resisted by the warring factions of Johnson and Taylor on the grounds that it might protect the interest of Doe.

In September 1990, Samuel Doe was abducted by forces loyal to Johnson from the grounds of ECOWAS peace-keeping headquarters in Monrovia. The captured and wounded Doe was taken to the Johnson camp were he was tortured, dismembered and allowed to bleed to death. However, the exit of Doe did not minimize the intensity of the civil war. And by December

1990, nearly 400,000 Liberians had fled the war, torn country and taken refuge in neighboring countries.[23] With the fall of Doe, both Johnson and Taylor claimed the Liberian presidency. However, Amos Sawyer, a relatively neutral party in the civil war was sworn in as interim president of Liberia pending general elections. Shuttle diplomacy, initiated by Ghana and Nigeria with the support of ECOWAS and the Organization of African Unity (OAU), seeking a lasting peace in Liberia yielded fruitful results. On September 1, 1995, a new governing council was inaugurated by President Jerry Rawlings of Ghana following the signing of a peace accord in August 1995, in the Nigerian capital of Abuja. Hopefully peace will at last be given a chance as Liberians regroup to build their country. But the legacy of the perils of the Doe administration looms over the country. It is doubtful that the many factional leaders who now form a coalition government will forgo their individual ambitions to rule Liberia for the sake of national unity.

LESSONS FROM THE LIBERIAN EXPERIENCE

Liberia in the 1990's is certainly worse off than the Liberia at the end of the 1970's. The Liberian experience clearly demonstrates the likely outcome of a nation state that fails to mobilize its people for national development. The Americo-Liberian dominance of Liberian politics was replaced by the personal rule of Doe with the support of his Krahn ethnic group. The gains envisaged under the military rule never materialized.

Samuel Doe would have remained a hero and a legend if he had handed over power to an elected government in the early 1980's. The demise of Doe is similar to the fate of General Ignatius Acheampong of Ghana who in 1972 was hailed for his coup—but by 1977, his repressive and corrupt rule led to his overthrow in a palace coup. In 1979, while he was tied to the stake and executed by a firing squad, the crowd cheered! Similarly in 1971 when Iddi Amin overthrew the government of Milton Obote in Uganda, he was well received by the people. However, by 1975, Amin had become the "butcher of Kampala" and presided over a reign of terror unprecedented in Uganda's history until his overthrow by the invading Tanzanian forces in 1979.

Unfortunately, these experiences fail to deter personal and dictatorial rule in Africa and many third world countries. Samuel Doe's sad end suggests that once political power has been seized, measures must be put in place for a popularly elected government to take control of affairs. Coups should not be avenues for personal gain. Coups should be patriotic and selfless acts. Once the corrupt political leaders have been removed from office, the task of national governance should not be the preserve of the coup plotters or leaders. The masses must have a voice in deciding their destiny. It is this lack of political foresight that has led to the demise of many coup stagers in the Third World. Perhaps the greatest lesson from the Liberian experience is that the military cannot be relied upon as an alternative instrument of social and political change.

The intervention of ECOWAS forces to maintain peace in Liberia is worthy of praise. It is a laudable African initiative at solving African problems without having to rely on foreign intervention. The ECOWAS experiment in Liberia lends credence to earlier calls for continental unity by the pioneers of African liberation such as Kwame Nkrumah. A united Africa with an African High Command could minimize regional conflicts.

The Liberian experience is a vivid depiction of the socio-economic and political problems created by military intervention in the politics of Sub-Saharan Africa and the developing countries in general. It is also a warning to African countries that refuse to democratize. The essential elements of democracy must be respected and preserved by all countries aspiring to build their political institutions. These elements amongst others being majority rule, free speech, freedom of association, freedom from want, and respect for the fundamental human rights of citizens as outlined in the United Nations Charter on Human Rights. Though "democracy has tended to lose its meaning in political debate,"[24] its vital qualities, such as those outlined above, still remain. To this end, former President Kaunda of Zambia deserves credit for gracefully leaving office following his defeat at the polls. After 26 years of personal rule he gave his people the longed for opportunity to vote him out of office. Doe's tragic fall serves as a warning to African military dictators who consider themselves indispensable to their countries. Civilian and military rulers must realize that the state, in the long run, will survive them. Their duty is to serve well and to bow out gracefully when they lose the support of the majority of the population.

Notes

1   The colonial powers in Africa entrenched their control by inciting conflict among the various ethnic groups in the colonies. The purpose was to keep the African population from uniting and, hence, delay nationalism. It was not until after World War II that African veterans of the war in alliance with few African elites spearheaded the struggle for independence in many of the colonial territories.

2   G. E. Saigbey Boley, *Liberia: The Rise and Fall of the First Republic* (New York: St. Martins Press, 1983), p. 29.

3   *Ibid.*, pp. 6-7.

4   *Ibid.*, pp. 43,45.

5   Martin Lowenkopf, *Politics in Liberia*, (Stanford, California: Hover Institution Press, 1976), p. 36.

6   Raymond Leslie Buell, *The Native Problem in Africa*, Vol. II (Frank Cass & Company, Ltd., 1965), p. 833; quoted in Boley, *Liberia: The Rise and Fall of the First Republic*, p. 45.

7   Lowenkopt, p. 36.

8   *Ibid.*

9   D. Elwood Dunn and S. Bryon Tarr, *Liberia: A National Polity in Transition* (Metuchen, New Jersey: The Scarecrow Press, Inc., 1988), p. 39.

10   *The African Nationalist*, December 7, 1940; quoted in Tuan Wreh, *The Love of Liberty...The Rule of William V.S. Tubman in Liberia, 1944-1971* (London: C. Hurst and Company, 1976), p. 62.

11   Tuan Wreh, p. 23.

12   *Ibid.*, pp. 25-26.

13   G. E. Saigbey Boley, p. 80.

14   *Ibid.*, p. 42.

15   Dunn and Tarr, p. 77.

16   Ruth First, *Power in Africa* (New York: Pantheon Books, 1970), p. 20

17 Dunn and Tarr, p. 96.

18 Niccolo Machiavelli, *The Prince and the Discourses* (New York: Random House, Inc., 1950), p. 34.

19 Dunn and Tarr, p. 120.

20 *Ibid.*, p. 127.

21 *The Economist,* November 28, 1987.

22 *African Events,* August/September, 1990, p. 8.

23 *African Business*, September, 1990, p. 13.

24 Jay M. Shafritz, *The Dorsey Dictionary of American Government and Politics,* (Chicago: The Dorsey Press, 1988), p. 162.

Chapter 5

Election Monitoring and the Democratization Agenda in Africa: The Case of the 1991 Zambian Elections*

Julius O. Ihonvbere

INTRODUCTION

The monitoring of elections in Africa by international organizations has become a major aspect of the current democratization agenda in the region. Samuel Huntington has noted that as developing countries became more involved in the "Third Wave," "democratization became a recognized phenomenon of global politics, the media paid more attention to it, and elections were increasingly subject to international monitoring."[1] Though the Western powers, in particular, had contributed significantly to shoring up despotic and corrupt leaders all over Africa especially in the era of the Cold War, the end of that era and the collapse of communist and socialist regimes around the world made a redirection of relations with Africa necessary. As Georg Sorensen has noted, "the end of the Cold War has had the good effect of reducing the tendency to protect corrupt and inefficient rulers in the South just because they were 'good friends' of the West . . . respect for human rights and the demand for political reform are receiving higher priority as preconditions for economic aid."[2] Foreign aid is now largely predicated on good governance,

*Research for this study was made possible by grants from the National Endowment for the Humanities and the American Philosophical Society.

multi-partism, accountability, and democracy. Douglas Hurd, the British Foreign Minister in mid-1990 declared that "Countries which tend towards pluralism, public accountability, respect for the rule of law and market principles should be encouraged. Governments which persist with repressive policies, corrupt management and wasteful, discredited economic systems should not expect us to support their folly with scarce aid resources which could be used better elsewhere."[3] This call was openly endorsed by Japan, Canada, the United States and France. President Mitterand of France declared that French aid "will be more tepid for regimes that behave in an authoritarian manner, without accepting the evolution toward democracy, and more enthusiastic for those who take this step bravely and go as far as they can."[4]

In its seminal report on sub-Saharan Africa in 1989, the World Bank not only acknowledged the *political* dimensions of the African crisis but also argued forcefully for the democratization of the political landscape, protection of vulnerable groups, decentralization of power, check on corruption and mismanagement, and the popular mobilization of the people for growth and development.[5] Of course, the World Bank came to realize that though authoritarian, particularly military juntas might be more capable of imposing harsh monetarist policies on their populace, an elected, accountable and democratic government was more capable of sustaining reform programs, involving the people in the process of adjustment, and that people, "tend to accept painful policies more readily from elected governments than from dictators."[6] Consequently, countries like Kenya were pressured to hold multiparty elections by the Western powers. In spite of his traditional opposition to political pluralism which he saw as an invitation to violence, unnecessary competition, hooliganism and "tribalism," Arap Moi was forced in December 1991, as a direct precipitate of pressures from donors and lenders, to concede to calls for multipartism in Kenya. Kamuzu Banda (Malawi's former President-for-Life) who had previously declared his country out of the range of the democracy drive was equally compelled by a drastic cut in British aid from 10 million pounds (sterling) to 5 million pounds (sterling) in 1992 to make concessions to prodemocracy agitators. Even Jerry Rawlings, who was a darling of the World Bank and the International Monetary Fund, was advised to carry out far-reaching democratization of Ghana's political landscape. Nigeria's former strongman, General Ibrahim Babangida was constantly reminded that only a disengagement of the military from politics could ensure continuing Western and donor support for the country's industrialization programs.

With the Western donors and lenders all clamoring for democracy and democratization, by the "late 1980s foreign observers had become a familiar and indispensable presence in almost all transition elections."[7] Without doubt, the activities of the non-profit international observers, supported by monitoring units from Western governments, the United Nations, and regional organizations, have "significantly enhanced the importance of elections in the democratization process."[8] In many instances, these bodies work with local human rights, pro-democracy, and other popular groups. In other instances, they work independently of all other organizations. It is not unusual to have 20 or more monitoring bodies in a small African country, from all regions of the world, all claiming to be interested in monitoring the election process to ensure that it would be free and fair. They are usually invited by the host government, opposition political parties, pro-democracy movements, and national electoral commissions. The fact that they often come at the invitation of local political authorities has not reduced conflicts and suspicions in any way. Indeed, the relationship between them and the foreign monitoring bodies characteristically deteriorates within a couple of weeks of their arrival in the state capital.

To be sure, international presence at the new wave of elections in developing countries (particularly African countries) is very important. In the first place, they help to prevent desperate and corrupt governments from openly "stealing" elections and abusing state power and resources in their bid to hold on to power. Of course, this function has not been made any easier with the confusion, opportunism, corruption, and factionalization among and within the opposition parties. Second, international observers contribute to the reduction of violence during elections. Their presence discourages the tendency of politicians to rely on thugs and other extra-legal methods of politics. It is common knowledge that the monitors or observers often arrive with journalists and sophisticated media equipment and acts of violence can easily be recorded. Third, international monitors, strengthen the legitimacy and work of domestic monitoring agencies. In several instances they work together and tend to put their facilities, connections, and resources at the disposal of local monitoring agencies. This increases the visibility, relevance, and influence of these local bodies. Fourth, coverage of elections by international monitors assists new governments to gain international legitimacy and acceptability. They are able to bring to the world at a very rapid rate clear information on the conduct of the elections and thus assist in the process of getting support and recognition from other nations. Investors and donors also base some of their responses to new regimes on reports from international monitors. Fifth, international monitors bring new ideas and at times "unbiased" information to researchers outside the specific and immediate area of political action. Their coverage, reports and materials obtained from the government, political parties, pro-democracy and human rights groups as well as local monitoring bodies contribute significantly to research and scholarship.

In spite of these advantages, it is doubtful if international monitors have made a far-reaching contribution to the democratization process in Africa. They have witnessed elections, written their reports and packed their bags and departed for their respective home countries leaving the new government (or the incumbent government) to work out its own contradictions. Specific complaints have been raised concerning the relevance of these bodies. Their "intervention" is seen as patronizing and paternalistic. As a respondent noted in Zambia, "who the hell do they think they are. Who told them we need them to tell us that we have done things right. This is another carry-over from the colonial days."[9] The point is that many politicians see the arrival of the observer groups as some sort of international condemnation, a verdict on the immaturity of African elites and politicians.

Additionally, many observer teams have tried to be too vocal, too visible and at times have intervened in national issues. This has created friction and eroded the support they enjoyed on arrival. Also, local monitoring bodies and electoral commissions see the observer groups as trying to relegate them to the background in their own countries. They "assume that we are illiterate. We do not understand democracy. We do not know how to educate our people about democracy. Yet, they cannot even communicate with the average voter in spite of their arrogant assumptions."[10] Journalists who accompany them prefer to interview the observers rather than local activists and it is the reports prepared by the observers that get into the international media.

The monitoring bodies have also been accused of being biased against incumbent regimes. They have a tendency to judge incumbent regimes on their past records and treat them with disrespect and suspicion. This puts the government in a no-win situation. As Huntington notes in this typical case, "If they manipulated timing and procedures in other than extreme fashion, they probably also were defeated. If they stole the election, they lost legitimacy rather than gaining it. The reasons that led them to holding elections—decreasing legitimacy and opposition pressure—were also the reasons they lost the elections."[11] While the fear of being accused of manipulating and stealing the elections have forced many African governments to invite foreign monitors or support calls by pro-democracy groups to invite foreign monitors, such governments have been placed at great disadvantage. In Kenya, Arap Moi faced such a dilemma culminating in conflicts not only with the observers but also with the U.S. Ambassador.

In Zambia, Kenneth Kaunda fell out with the observers within a month of their arrival in Lusaka. Foreign monitors have only a partial perception of the totality of the problem. They tended to focus on *elections* as the main problem. They monitored the election and passed their verdict. Yet, elections do not democracy make. In reality, as we have seen in Kenya and Ghana, the elections were the easiest part of the democratization agenda for African leaders. The real contradiction or problem was how the new regime could hold on to power and consolidate democracy. Monitors, who have since left the state capital, make no contributions in these areas. They give high hopes to the opposition parties and movements during the electioneering campaigns but do not provide them with an agenda for reconstruction, consolidation and survival.

Finally, the monitors do not appear to fully appreciate the importance of national pride and independence. Mistakes might be made, but foreign endorsement of elections do not change much. While their presence might reduce violence and blatant stealing of elections, it has not prevented violence, malpractices or military coups following the announcement of election results. It is not inconceivable that their actions probably generate more disaffection than otherwise. But they are tolerated because of Africa's vulnerable location and role in the international division of labor. After all, "we do not send monitors to their own countries, and even if they are more stable, they are not perfect. Why should they come here walking all over the place, giving press statements, interviewing people, and many of them behave like spies—they want to know everything and ask too many questions some of which have nothing to do with the election at hand."[12] The impact of foreign election monitoring, therefore, has been largely mixed.

In the Ghanaian presidential elections of November 1992 for instance, the presence of several foreign monitoring bodies including the Commonwealth Observer Group, the OAU Observer Group and the Carter Observer Group did not prevent the manipulation of the electoral process by Rawlings.[13] He had retired from the military but remained as head of state and chair of the Provisional National Defence Council (PNDC), and he contested in the presidential elections on the platform of the National Democratic Congress(NDC), exploited the privilege of incumbency, and used state resources to intimidate his opponents, attract support and fund his campaigns. This in itself was sufficient to cast some doubts on how "free and fair" the election was. In addition, Rawlings had, since his December 31, 1981 second return to power, actually plotted his civilianization project and set out an elaborate agenda to endear himself to the populace, discredit other political actors, and consolidate his control over the resources and institutions of state. His well known open distaste for democracy and disrespect for politicians did not attract the censure of observers and the international media as to the dangers which such an individual could pose to a genuine democratic agenda in Ghana. According to Prosper Bani, the observer groups all reached the conclusion that "the presidential election was conducted in a calm political atmosphere and was also a fair reflection of what really happened. They maintained that though there were some lapses which created tension and anxiety, the lapses did not distort the result of the election. The elections were conducted in a serene political atmosphere devoid of any political harassment and intimidation."[14] Bani notes that in spite of this verdict which was an obvious generalization, sophisticated modes and patterns of electoral fraud designed and put in place before the arrival of foreigners who did not speak local languages or understand the political terrain, could not have been "observed" by the groups. More importantly, the observers and opposition parties, while disagreeing on the extent of electoral malpractices, did agree on the inaccuracy of the voters' register used for the elections.

When the other political parties contended that the presidential election had been rigged and therefore decided to boycott the parliamentary elections, the observer groups did not think that this was a dangerous development which would further cast doubts on the quality of the political process or the overall value of the elections. The NDC, and two inconsequential political parties—the Eagle Party and the National Convention Party (NCP)—in an alliance went ahead with the parliamentary elections. The result was a full sweep for the NDC and the establishment of a largely rubber-stamp assembly. As Bani notes, "It is amazing how the international institutions concerned with democratization processes can endorse an election dominated by the ruling government without the participation of any meaningful opposition."[15] Consequently, Ghana today resembles a one-party state in several respects and the opposition remains very bitter about the ways in which state power had been used to carry out a pseudo-democratization program to entrench the interests of the incumbent government.

However, as we shall see in the case of Zambia, the fact that the World Bank and the IMF as well as donors were all in a "romance" with Rawlings and his commitment to the orthodox adjustment package in Ghana made it rather easy for the global community and observers to accept or tolerate all the deficiencies of the elections. Bani believes that these Western interest groups were determined to see "Rawlings back to power to ensure continuity of their policies as well as to maintain the status quo."[16] While there are sufficient grounds to accept this explanation, the division within the ranks of the opposition, poor leadership, poor financing, lack of innovative programs, and reliance on old bases of politicking made it impossible to challenge a charismatic leader, a darling of Western capital, with a record of achievements in the rural areas, and with all the powers of incumbency.

In Kenya the foreign monitoring bodies were certainly helpful to local pro-democracy groups and checked the blatant efforts of the ruling party to manipulate voters and the entire election process.[17] However, as in Ghana, the opposition presented several candidates and lacked a common front. The result was that opposition support was split, and Moi retained control of state power though the opposition snatched 100 of the 220 seats in parliament. The advantage of the ruling party in parliament was made possible only because the constitution allowed the government to appoint 20 members to parliament.

The Nigerian situation was equally intriguing. General Babangida had embarked on his long-drawn out transition to democracy and from his pronouncements and actions it became clear to Nigerians that he had a "hidden agenda," and did not want to relinquish power to an elected president.[18] In spite of the presence of foreign monitoring bodies—the Commonwealth Observer Team—and observers from the OAU, the Carter Center, Africa Watch and the International Observer Team, Babangida annulled the results of the June 12, 1993 presidential election precipitating a political stalemate which culminated eventually in the return of the Generals through Sani Abacha's coup of November 1993. The positive pronouncements of the local and foreign monitoring bodies on the June election did not in any way prevent the remilitarization of politics and the renewed suffocation of civil society in Nigeria.

The Zambian case is perhaps the most clear demonstration of the power and influence of foreign monitoring groups in African elections. This prominent role is largely due to the very negative publicity which Kenneth Kaunda had received internationally as a result of his failed economic policy and his frequent disagreements with the IMF and the World Bank. As well, he was one of the few surviving first generation leaders who had no intention of leaving office and had remained constant in his belief in the one-party state. Zambia was also a test case for a peaceful transition to democracy under the leadership of a pro-democracy movement made up of all sorts of interests—students, workers, the unemployed, businessmen and women and so on. Finally, the prominence of the foreign bodies was also a reflection of the weakness of local monitoring bodies prior to the arrival of the observer teams. Civil society under Kaunda had been suffocated and manipulated for 27 years. The country was still largely backward in every respect in spite of its prominence in African affairs. It was thus easy for the foreign observer teams to overwhelm the local bodies within a brief period.

BACKGROUND TO THE NOVEMBER 1991 ELECTIONS

A combination of unfavorable internal and external factors forced Kenneth Kaunda to concede to multi-party elections and to recognize the opposition in Zambia. Among these factors were: (a) the coup attempt in October 1980; (b) increasing opposition and riots against the failure of government economic policies; (c) several strikes, led by the Zambian Congress of Trade Unions (ZCTU), teachers, mine-workers, postal workers and students, which had virtually paralyzed the economy by the end of 1989; (d) another coup attempt led by Lieutenant Mwamba Luchembe in June of 1990 which received wide-spread support all over the country; and (e) the August 1990 National Assembly proposal on the introduction of multi-party politics and the need to amend the constitution in order to move Zambia away from the one-party system imposed in December 1972 which left Kaunda in no doubt as to the inevitability of change in the country.

Furthermore, challenges to Kaunda's power within the UNIP in combination with his failed economic policies contributed to the rapid erosion of his credibility as a political leader, thus weakening the ruling party, and strengthening the struggles of pro-democracy forces in Zambia. Of course, Kaunda had terribly offended the West (especially the United States) with his close relationship with Saddam Hussein of Iraq, and his refusal to support the allied forces during the Gulf War.[19]

The Movement for Multi-Party Democracy (MMD) itself had become the "unofficial government" in Zambia even before the elections. In May 1990, when Kaunda announced the date for a popular referendum on multi-party politics for October, he also announced that proponents of the system would be allowed to campaign, hold public meetings and set up organizations to propagate their ideas. In July, the MMD which had until then served as an unofficial opposition and vanguard of the movement to restructure the country's political terrain and get the UNIP government out of power constituted itself formally as an advocacy group. In December 1990, the MMD became a political party. On January 4, 1991 "the MMD transferred and registered itself as a political party . . . with the aim of winning the first free elections . . . under a Multi-party Constitution."[20] The Movement was led by Arthur Wina a former UNIP Finance Minister and Frederick Chiluba, the Chairman of the ZCTU.

In the MMD's fold were also prominent political heavyweights like Levy Mwanawasa former Solicitor-General, Robinson Nabulyato former speaker of the National Assembly, Humphrey Mulemba former Secretary-General of UNIP, Ludwig Sondashi former member of UNIP Central Committee, Andrew Kashita former Minister for Mines and Vernon Mwanga former Foreign Minister. As Munyonzwe Hamalengwa has noted, "This was an impressive collection of individuals who had at one time or another served UNIP very well."[21] The loose coalition which had become the MMD in several ways resembled the Janata Party in India, a coalition of all interest groups and persons opposed to the ruling government. It also resembled in several ways, the coalition of interests against Russian President Boris Yeltsin in October 1993; a coalition of people whose only common bond was Boris Yeltsin.

> The MMD in Zambia is a class alliance of the urbanized working class, a segment of the comprador bourgeoisie and former bureaucratic/ state bourgeoisie, urban petty bourgeoisie and the lumpen proletariat. This alliance has managed to win over the rural proletariat and its populist politics ensured that it captured the interests of the entire population, given the aggrandizement of the Kaunda regime.[22]

In its *Manifesto* the MMD argued that Zambians had become "disillusioned with the dictatorial excesses of the ONE Party System of Government imposed" on the people; that it was leading a Movement for the "restoration of the multiparty political system"; and that UNIP had "embraced political and economic programmes without reference to the people, programmes which resulted in the total collapse of the country's economy" which had been "exceptionally sound and strong at the time of political independence." It warned the people of Zambia that "if left unchallenged, UNIP would be re-elected (even under a multi-party system)" and that it would simply "revert to its bad old ways of dictating to the people." The Movement declared that it was "determined and committed to ensuring that basic and universally recognized human rights are enshrined in the Constitution—the right to life; privacy of property; freedom under the law; the right of movement in and out of the country; freedom of conscience and freedoms of expression, association and worship." Declaring its economic philosophy, the *MMD Manifesto* stated that:

> MMD believes that economic prosperity for all can best be created by free men and women through free enterprise; by economic and social justice involving all the productive resources—human, material and financial, and by liberalising industry, trade and commerce, with the government only creating an enabling environment whereby economic growth must follow as it has done in all the world's successful countries.[23]

In spite of its commitment to freedom, equality and free enterprise, the MMD was conscious of the fact that:

> when it comes to power it shall inherit a totally bankrupt economy and a crippling foreign debt. . . . MMD shall inherit an exhausted public treasury due mainly to the fact that the UNIP government during its 27 years in office wasted the national wealth, it voted itself public funds to support its own political organization, it neglected all social and economic infrastructures such as roads, schools and hospitals and reduced the nation to a starving, beggar state barely surviving on donor finance.[24]

The Movement believed that political, infrastructural and economic recovery and rehabilitation can take place in a new Zambia with a "renewed spirit of hard work, entrepreneurship, public commitment, honesty, integrity and public accountability." It was prepared to take "bold but painful measures in order to arrest" the current decline and decay and "make a fresh start towards rebuilding a more reliable and sustainable infrastructure to promote growth."

Finally, the MMD seemed to have swallowed hook line and sinker the monetarist economic prescriptions of the IMF and the World Bank. There is no doubting the fact that Zambia, like most African states needs a comprehensive structural adjustment program. It is contestable, however, to assume that just by reducing the role of the state, opening up the economy, privatizing public enterprises, imposing new fees and taxes, devaluing the currency and introducing other painful economic policies on a poor population unprotected by any welfare measures, growth and development will follow. The failure of structural adjustment programs all over the continent, the terrible impoverishment of non-bourgeois forces, and the tensions, violence, coups, instability and economic and social deterioration it has generated all over Africa were ignored by the MMD in drafting its manifesto. It had somehow overlooked the fact that even a popularly elected government would have to deal with the problem of what to do with a frustrated, hungry, unemployed, poverty-stricken, and very alienated populace when it gets into power. Of course, the open commitment to the market and to policies dictated by the International Monetary Fund and the World Bank endeared the Movement to donors, Western powers, the Scandinavian countries, and other global capitalist interests.

THE MMD: THE ROAD TO VICTORY AND POWER

Early 1991 witnessed the resignation of very prominent members of the UNIP who immediately declared their support for the MMD.[25] In the same period, the Zambian Congress of Trade Unions (ZCTU) officially transferred its support and allegiance to the MMD. Trade union offices all over the country immediately became recruiting centers for the Movement, while trade union leaders openly campaigned for public support to defeat Kaunda and the UNIP. Violent clashes between UNIP and MMD supporters became rampant in 1991, and this trend led to charges and counter-charges on both sides. The already jittery Kaunda government carried out several last minute cabinet changes in the hope of demonstrating a stronger resolve to provide a democratic, credible, and accountable leadership. June 1991 witnessed a major struggle between the UNIP and the MMD over constitutional proposals made by the Constitutional Commission (CC). Among other recommendations, the CC had proposed the creation of the post of Vice-President, expansion of the National Assembly from 135 seats to 150 seats, and the establishment of a constitutional court. Though Kaunda had accepted most of the CC's proposals and had them submitted to the National Assembly for ratification, the MMD opposed them because the proposed changes vested too much authority in the Presidency rather than the National Assembly. It also opposed the recommendation which allowed ministers to be appointed outside the National Assembly. The MMD threatened to boycott the elections if the Assembly ratified it, and to demonstrate its resolve on this matter, it refused to attend an inter-party conference chaired by Kaunda in July 1991 to discuss the draft constitution.

Representatives of UNIP, MMD and seven other political associations were later to meet on the issue under the chairmanship of Zambia's Deputy Chief Justice, Matthew Ngulube. Following this meeting, Kaunda suspended the draft constitution and agreed to further negotiations. With the intervention of church leaders, a joint commission was set up to review the constitutional proposals, and in July, Kaunda agreed to MMD demands to abandon the idea of a constitutional court and not to appoint ministers from outside the National Assembly. The power to impose martial law previously recommended for the president was abandoned, and any imposition of a state of emergency beyond seven days was to be approved by the National Assembly. The new proposals were approved by the National Assembly on August 2, 1991.

This was a major victory for the MMD. It signaled the end of the UNIP government even before the elections. The powerful Kaunda had been forced to give in once again to the opposition on practically all its demands. This was followed in quick succession by an agreement to allow international observers into the country to monitor the elections, a position which Kaunda had previously opposed. The government also agreed to grant state subsidies to all registered political parties. As noted earlier, Kaunda's leadership of UNIP was challenged partly as a result of frustration over his declining political credibility and influence in the country. As far back as September 1990, Kaunda had urged so-called UNIP Militants to revamp the party and, "to rejuvenate" it "into a formidable political organ if it is to win the 1991 elections."[26] Of course, he managed to retain control and get nominated to lead UNIP into the struggle for the presidency. He tried as much as possible to convince the opposition that the election would be free and fair. He disassociated the armed forces from UNIP, and senior officers were required to retire from the UNIP Central Committee to ensure the neutrality of the armed forces.

It was obvious to all observers that the electoral battle was going to be between UNIP and MMD. The few fringe political parties that emerged on the political scene lacked the organizational structure, resources, credible leadership and programs, as well as the ability to mount effective political campaigns. Yet, they were part of the growing civil society and evidence of the demise of the one-party state. They signified the emergence of multi-party politics. The Movement for Democratic Process (MDP) paid the K20,000 registration fee but "failed to raise the 200 registered voters in support" of Chama Chakonmmoka's presidential ambitions. The Christian Alliance for the Kingdom of Africa (CHAKA), led by Jairus Kalisirila withdrew from the electoral race for the presidency on "technical grounds." Emmanuel Mubanbga Mwamba of the Democratic Process (DP) "never even pitched up to file his nomination" to run for the presidency.[27] Early efforts by the DP to organize a rally in April 1991 flopped very badly as "only 15 children aged between 5 and 10 gathered at Kampenba Welfare Hall in Twapia township" to listen to what the party had to say.[28] There were other fringe parties like the Multi-Racial Party of Zambia (MP), The Theoretical Spiritual Political Party (TSPP), the Peoples Liberation Party (PLP), and the National Democratic Alliance (NADA).[29]

Following the dissolution of the National Assembly in September 1991 in preparation for the October elections, Kaunda tried to demonstrate that a new UNIP would emerge from the election to lead a reinvigorated and more democratic government: UNIP was disassociated from the state, and workers in the public sector were banned from participating in political activity. Of course, Kaunda knew that it would take more than one month for people to unlearn what it had taken them 27 years to learn. In any case, the state-controlled media houses continued to campaign for UNIP and Kaunda and discriminate openly against the MMD. Kaunda directed the *Zambia Daily Mail*, the *Times of Zambia* and the Zambia National Broadcasting Corporation (ZNBC) not to cover the activities of the MMD. Even without such directives, some over-zealous bureaucrats went beyond the call of duty to discriminate against the MMD in their news coverage and to play up the popularity of Kaunda and the UNIP. The MMD challenged this order in court and won a victory over the government. However, the state of emergency which had allowed Kaunda to suppress the opposition was still very much in force. Kaunda made threats against "anarchists" and warned the nation that he would "brook no nonsense from opposition elements who might try to disrupt" the political system. He then ordered the police to "arrest multiparty advocates who might have issued insulting utterances to the leadership."[30] Certainly, support for UNIP and Kaunda was not in short supply, mostly "out of loyalty to the old man rather than to any serious commitment to the party which was already withering away."[31] Area Governors like Imasiku Lyamunga campaigned for Kaunda. District Governors like Shiyenge Kapriri supported Kaunda, and traditional rulers from Luampula Province and several chiefs who had actually been maintained in office by Kaunda threw their weight behind him and UNIP.[32] With this, the reports from his security forces and the scores of sycophants surrounding him, and his personal confidence that there was no way in which a person like him could lose an election in Zambia, Kaunda predicted several times, even on election day that UNIP would not only sweep the polls, but "Will continue winning any polls."[33]

There were several reports of violence especially against MMD supporters by ardent UNIP supporters. The MMD revealed that UNIP members, probably in anticipation of losing the election, were looting state treasuries and property. In January 1991, the UNIP Parliament granted "1.3 billion *Kwacha* to members for various party schemes" while government properties "were being taken over locally and abroad."[34] The MMD urged their supporters to "expose the cash grabbers." Vernon Mwanga accused UNIP of using the Government Printer to print party membership cards and of misusing public funds. Kaunda himself was very direct in his threats against the MMD and warned Zambians that a vote for the opposition was a vote for anarchy. This, according to him, was because the MMD was bound to sink the economy further into crisis:

> The campaign against our party was terrible. Zambians were told that we lacked experience, that we had no international support, that we were going to destroy the economy and make life unbearable for all. In fact, the picture that was painted was one of total disaster without the UNIP and KK.[35]

The MMD was of the view that only foreign observers could keep Kaunda in check. It mounted a major campaign to get the electoral commission to invite foreign observers.

Kaunda accused the international observers of meddling in Zambian affairs by trying to influence the content and direction of politics in favor of the MMD. According to Hamalengwa, and this was confirmed in several interviews in Zambia, Kaunda "repeatedly accused the MMD advocates of inciting the army and mine-workers to disrupt the country in order to weaken the power of UNIP. He also accused them of soliciting military support from the rebel leader in neighboring Angola."[36] In addition, Chiluba, the presidential candidate of the MMD, accused Kaunda of amassing troops on the Malawi border to fight the MMD if the UNIP lost the election. Chiluba called on the Organization of African Unity (OAU) to send peace-keeping forces to Zambia because a plot to assassinate him had been hatched by the UNIP.

The October 31st election in Zambia witnessed an monumental routing of UNIP. Zambians flocked to the polls. Courts and businesses were closed, and acts of violence and intimidation were few and far between.[37] Chiluba received 75.79 percent of the votes cast in the presidential election defeating Kaunda who received a mere 24.21 percent. In the election to the National Assembly, the MMD won 125 seats leaving the remaining 25 to UNIP. It was a crushing defeat for UNIP, and many reached the conclusion that the party had been "wiped out."[38] All but four of the members of the previous government were defeated in the election. A UNIP candidate for Nkana Constituency, Noel Mvila, was crushed by an unknown MMD candidate Barney Bungoni with a "big margin." Mvila quickly announced that the polls had been rigged because his opponent was "so old."[39] In Livingstone Constituency, MMD candidate Peter Muunga defeated two former Members of Parliament, Kebby Musokotwane (the incumbent) and Daniel Lisulo who ran as an independent.[40]

Many members of UNIP put the blame for the party's humiliation on Kenneth Kaunda. Enoch Kavindele a former member of the UNIP Central Committee argued that Kaunda was "responsible for the party's humiliating defeat in (the) elections because by clinging to leadership despite apparent unpopularity from the masses," he made it easy for alienated and disaffected supporters to switch to the MMD.[41] A loyal UNIP activist interviewed in Lusaka supported this view when he noted that, "KK (viz, Kenneth Kaunda) was just stubborn. You see, he is a very stubborn man. He did not want to believe that the people were fed up with him, that his government (had) failed and that the MMD was popular. If he had stepped aside, the defeat might have been less."[42] The parliamentary election had been contested by 330 candidates from six political parties. It was indeed a new dawn in Zambian politics as Frederick Chiluba, former Chairman of the ZCTU, leading an amalgam of political interests known as the MMD was inaugurated as President on November 2, 1991.[43] What role did local and foreign monitoring organizations, as well as foreign governments play in this somewhat unique transition from a one-party authoritarian regime to a popularly elected government?

BEYOND KK: THE POLITICS AND ROLE OF MONITORING BODIES IN THE ZAMBIAN ELECTION

It is true that Kenneth Kaunda, the UNIP and the deepening crisis of the economy, as well as unfavorable global conditions combined to enable the MMD to snatch power from the UNIP government. Yet, the story is not as straight forward as it is often presented: a multi-party democracy movement, led by a trade unionist defeated one of the early nationalists in Africa who had bestrode the political landscape of Zambia for almost three decades like a colossus. It is important to go beyond the factors above, the disillusionment of the people which had a bandwagon effect during the election, and the new desire for freedom and democracy. It is important to see the role of Western nations, donors, and other external interests in the establishment of liberal democratic politics, institutions, and relations of power in Zambia.

The Polish experience was perhaps the very first recent experiment in which foreign (Western) interests joined hands and resources with opposition elements in order to defeat an incumbent regime. In the case of Poland, President Ronald Reagan and Pope John Paul forged a so-called "Holy Alliance" to "keep the Solidarity union alive" in the hope "not only to pressure Warsaw but to free all of Eastern Europe."[44] Both leaders agreed at a June 7, 1982 meeting at the Vatican to "undertake a clandestine campaign to hasten the dissolution of the communist empire," and they "committed their resources to destabilizing the Polish government and keeping the outlawed Solidarity movement alive after the declaration of martial law in 1981."[45] As part of the support for this project of forcing Poland onto the path of capitalism for which Solidarity stood, Solidarity "flourished underground, supplied, nurtured and advised largely by the network established under the auspices of Reagan and Pope John Paul II. Tons of equipment—fax machines (the first in Poland), printing presses, transmitters, telephones, shortwave radios, video cameras, photocopiers, telex machines, computers, word processors—were smuggled into Poland via channels established by priests and American agents and representatives of the AFL-CIO and European labor movements. Money for the banned union came from CIA funds, the National Endowment for Democracy, secret accounts in the Vatican and Western trade unions."[46] As well, spies were recruited from within the Polish government including a Deputy Minister of Defense "who was secretly reporting to the CIA."[47] The Zambian experience was not as elaborate only because Zambia was a smaller prize, and the transition to multiparty politics in Zambia would not have the sort of impact that the "fall" of Poland was to have in Eastern Europe.

Though Kaunda dropped his opposition to having international observer groups monitor the 1991 elections, he remained suspicious of their role.[48] This fear was not unfounded as the general feeling, especially among UNIP members at that time, was that these monitoring bodies tended to favor pro-democracy movements and had been known to dislike sit-tight lead-ers in developing countries. To allay such fears though, the Commonwealth Secretariat set broad guidelines on its elec-tion monitoring activities: "missions are undertaken only at the invitation of a member government and if all contesting political parties agree; observers have no executive or super-visory role in the election process; though appointed by the Secretary-General, observers are independent individuals rep-resenting only themselves; and their task generally is to ob-serve all aspects of the organization and conduct of an elec-tion according to that country's law and to come to judgement as to whether that process has been free and fair."[49] The Com-monwealth also has what it describes as the "essentials" for the "practical expression of democracy": "the participation of the adult population in the selection of government through free and fair elections; . . . freedom of association and expres-sion, including freedom of the press; . . . the transparency of the process of government, and . . . the rule of law, with guar-antees for equality under the law."[50] Not all monitoring bodies have laid down conditions for participation, and some repre-sentatives have been carried away with their personal views or biases. That happened in the Zambian situation though not to a degree capable of marring the contribution of these bodies to effective monitoring of the elections.

Fears existed within both parties that the election would be rigged. The UNIP was of the view that the MMD was so des-perate to unseat it from power, that the MMD would do any-thing to rig the elections. At that point in the competition, it was difficult for the UNIP to determine how many of its re-maining supporters actually sympathized with the MMD though they had held on to their UNIP membership cards. The MMD on the other hand, believed that UNIP was so used to power and had an over-blown image of its continuing influence that it would do anything to remain in power. It was only natural therefore, that monitoring groups from within and outside the country be allowed to observe the conduct of the election in order to promote an environment of fair play, tolerance and democracy.[51] Both parties tried to assure the nation that the election would not be rigged. UNIP also declared its opposi-tion to calls for an early poll. According to Joseph Mutale,

UNIP Chairman for Publicity and Elections, the "MMD statements were the usual rubbish which should be dismissed with
the contempt it deserves."[52] It was felt that the calls for an
early poll by some MMD leaders was an attempt to capitalize
or maximize the widespread support and enthusiasm which
the party was enjoying and a "sign of fear that by election day,
UNIP would have regained all lost ground."[53] In June, Kanyama
MP, Donald Chilutya, "hoisted a small black coffin with `MMD
is Dead' written on it in white in a mock burial" to demonstrate how UNIP was going to destroy the opposition.[54] Such
open display of hostility towards the MMD convinced the party
of the need to have neutral actors on the scene especially as
Kaunda still had control of the state, its resources, and coercive power.

The MMD benefitted extensively from foreign support at a
level which might not be replicated in any other African country. In fact, information available shows that no other African
pro-democracy movement or political party in the Post-Cold
war era has enjoyed such extensive logistical, political, moral,
and financial support as the MMD. In June 1991, the Governments of Denmark, Finland, Norway and Sweden offered to
"help run the elections" in Zambia. They announced that the
Zambian government had made a request for "transport, publicity and provision of stationery for the government printer,"
but the request was turned down.[55] This meant that the offer
to help was not aimed at helping the government remain in
power as only materials that could not help the government
consolidate its control over the political process were to be
provided. In the same month, Kaunda himself surprised the
opposition by personally inviting the Carter Center of Emory
University in Atlanta and the Ford Foundation to Zambia to
monitor the elections.[56] UNIP itself started seeking "international aid to help it to organize (the) . . . presidential and parliamentary elections."[57] This was a public demonstration of
financial weakness and vulnerability by the party which had
dominated Zambian politics and had control of the national
wealth for 27 years.

Within a short time, several independent monitoring organizations emerged in Zambia. The Zambian Independent Poll
Monitoring Team (ZIMT) led by former Bank of Zambia Gov-

ernor, David Phiri was created in July 1991.[58] It received support from the American National Democratic Institute and other prominent Zambians like former Law Association of Zambia Chairman Ali Hamir and Chaloka Beyani a prominent legal figure. With the increasing enthusiasm for foreign observers and the growing prominence which foreign NGOs and ambassadors accredited to Zambia were having on the election process, Kaunda began to have second thoughts about their presence in Zambia. In August he alleged that "foreign and local agents were working to disrupt the polls." He specifically alleged that three ambassadors "from otherwise friendly countries" were working with the opposition to subvert the polls in favor of the MMD.[59] Such allegations did not discourage Zambians from going ahead to form new monitoring bodies. In August the Zambian Voter Observation Team (Z-Vote) was formed by the Carter Center and the National Democratic Institute for International Affairs with Karen Jenkins as its Director. Z-Vote also included "experts from Europe, America, and Benin. Part of its mission in Zambia was to advise ZIMT on a non-partisan basis and independently monitor the electoral process." In the same month, the Canadian Government donated $50 million to ZIMT. With this money, ZIMT (which had emerged as the most credible independent Zambian monitoring agency) embarked on a mass training program for volunteers who were mostly students from the University of Zambia. The National Democratic Institute and Z-Vote assisted with the training of the volunteers. By the end of August other monitoring bodies had joined Z-Vote and ZIMT: Elections Canada represented by Ronald Gould; Namibian Council of Churches represented by Vero Mbahuurua; Philippines National Movement for Free Elections represented by Maritino Queseda; the British Council; University of Zambia Students; the National Women's Lobby Group of Zambia; and a monitoring group from Chile.[60] In less than a month, over 150 volunteers had been trained by ZIMT.[61] Based on recommendations from other international bodies active in Zambia, the ZIMT received more donations from foreign governments. The British government donated 7,000 pounds (sterling) in vehicles and 3,000 pounds (sterling) in communication equipment.[62] Denmark donated 1 million *Kwacha* which was used to pay the rent for ZIMT's Headquarters on Lumumba Road in Lusaka. Sweden pledged $40,000 while the United States and Norway promised further assistance. Former American President Jimmy Carter also arrived in Zambia accompanied by the Senior Political Officer of the Organization of African Unity (OAU), Chriss Bak Wesegha; Michelle Kourouma of the National Conference of Black Mayors; and a top member of Nigeria's National Electoral Commission (NEC) Dr. Adele Jinadu. It was as if a miracle was about to take place in Zambia, and the whole world had descended on the country to watch every move made by both parties, but more fascinatingly, to watch the MMD snatch political power from Kenneth Kaunda and UNIP.

With this sort of support, ZIMT was able to intensify its campaign, set up a 20-member Board of Directors and recruit an additional 1,500 University of Zambia (UNZA) students as volunteers.[63] Though the ZIMT had started out forging a strong alliance with the churches and church premises had been used for some of the training programs, the heavy presence of UNZA students in ZIMT began to cast shadows on its neutrality. Students at the UNZA have traditionally been opposed to the Kaunda government. Many of the young MMD candidates like Samuel Miyanda had been victims of Kaunda's high-handedness when they were students at UNZA. Throughout the 1970's and 1980's, the university had been closed several times in response to its opposition to government policies, and hundreds of students had been rusticated or suspended for speaking out against Kaunda and his policies.[64]

The Church began to accuse ZIMT of being partial and that UNZA students were clearly partisan towards the MMD.[65] In protest against ZIMT, representatives of the church pulled out of ZIMT "after they voiced strong opposition to the presence of officials with `links' to the state in the group."[66] Father Ives Bantungwa, Secretary General of the Catholic Secretariat, and Bishop John Mambo, Overseer of the Church of God, announced that they were starting their own independent monitoring team. The churches eventually set up a new monitoring group, the Christian Churches Monitoring Group (CCMG), to educate Christians on the electoral process. The CCMG had representatives from the Christian Council of Zambia (CCZ),

Evangelical Fellowship of Zambia, and Zambia Episcopal Conference. Its 12-member board was Chaired by Reverend Foston Sakala of the Reformed Church of Zambia and they pledged to work with Z-Vote and ZIMT.[67] UNIP seized the opportunity of this disagreement to accuse ZIMT of being "70 per cent MMD." Ironically, the UNZA Students Union (UNZASU) also called for a "new look at ZIMT" arguing that it was a partial body which had co-opted two students, Edward Sefuke and James Lungu without clearance or consultation with the union. The two students were disowned by the students' union and accused of representing themselves and not the students of the university.

With the developments above, ZIMT came under heavy pressure. It was "clear that anti-democratic forces were at work. They had succeeded in sponsoring confusionists and trouble makers into ZIMT. The plan was to weaken it, discredit it, and harass the foreign observers who would now be left open without any indigenous group to work with."[68] The media in Zambia orchestrated the crisis and pronounced the ZIMT dead. The *Times of Zambia* reminded its readers that the ZIMT was actually conceived by Africa Bar Association Chairman Roger Chongwe who was a member of the MMD.[69] Towards the end of September the paper gleefully announced that ZIMT was no more and that it had "been dismantled and a new coordinating body formed in its place."[70] At a meeting of some NGOs, churches, the Law Association of Zambia, and UNZASU, a new monitoring body—Zambia Elections Monitoring Coordinating Committee (ZEMCC)—was created with representatives from each group and with a commitment to go beyond the limitations which had plagued ZIMT.

What happened in ZIMT was actually a very deep ideological and power struggle between those who wanted to use the group to support either the MMD or UNIP. Additionally, as "soon as money started coming in, especially in foreign exchange, some people got greedy. They wanted to lay their hands on the money for personal use. When they could not do so, they decided to destroy the group. There were also those who saw that money could be made by networking with the foreign observers. To create their own monitoring group and gain some legitimacy, they had to first, discredit and destroy, or at the very least weaken ZIMT. They did just that."[71] ZIMT continued to exist in Zambia although the political attacks were now shifted to ZEMCC. In fact, donor agencies which had supported ZIMT from the beginning reaffirmed their support for and confidence in the body when Peter Faxell, representing the Scandinavian countries and donors "expressed displeasure at the mudslinging levelled against ZIMT and declared their support for the body by donating $1.7 million to be shared with Z-Vote and the electoral commission."[72]

ZEMCC began its foray into the political terrain by setting up a 14-member executive and dedicating itself to its motto: "Setting Standards for Africa. Free and Fair Elections." It advocated: the need to count votes at the polls rather than moving them to other locations in order to avoid switching and stuffing of ballot boxes; the need to provide tilley lamps at polling stations to avoid irregularities in the dark; that those who had lost their voter registration cards should be allowed to vote with their national registration cards; that Kaunda should lift the state of emergency immediately; security forces who were obviously loyal to UNIP should not be deployed to polling stations; and that continuing acts of intimidation and harassment of ordinary people was creating fear among the people and threatening possibilities for a free and fair election. ZEMCC declared that its operations would be completely non-partisan and went on to attack the composition of the national electoral commission arguing that it was incomplete. The organization contended that having a Chairman and one other person did not leave room for checks and balances, that a third member was needed.[73] ZEMCC also condemned what it described as "the use of scares of violence and civil strife in TV campaign advertisements" and advised donor countries not to "decide which monitoring group was right for Zambia."[74] This statement was directed at the intensification of negative and dirty campaigns especially by UNIP members warning Zambians not to tolerate or vote for the MMD because it would plunge the nation into "war and untold pain." It was also a response to the statements by Peter Faxell above reaffirming the confidence of the donors in ZIMT. UNIP interpreted this action as an unnecessary attempt by foreigners to influence the direction of Zambian politics.

Within a week of being registered, ZEMCC had set up monitoring centers across the country using several church buildings; trained 250 monitors "from all parts of the country who were asked to recruit 3000 to be stationed at polling booths;" provided bicycles to its monitors and de-emphasized the use of money; had attracted over 700 UNZASU members; and emphasized free and fair elections as "intimidation, coercion, corruption, violence and anything intended to subvert the will of the people" will be resisted.[75] ZEMCC announced, a day before the elections through its Provincial Chairman Pastor Kabila that it had uncovered a plot in Livingstone where UNIP supporters were misleading the people that "voting symbol `X' was meant for candidates they did not favour."[76]

Meanwhile, UNIP and other opponents of the MMD intensified their attacks against foreign and local observer groups. The out-going UNIP Chairman for Social and Cultural Committee, Joshua Manuwele described ZEMCC as a "body of stooges allegedly designed to cause confusion to the electorates" and pointed out that the bodies which make up ZEMCC, including students, the law association, and churches were actually pro-MMD and opposed to UNIP.[77] According to Hon. Samuel Miyanda, MMD MP for Matero and Chairman MMD Lusaka Central District, "the renewed attacks convinced us that it was good to have them here. They were disturbing no one. In fact, they brought in a lot of foreign exchange to the cash starved government. The UNIP was just scared that it could not go all out to intimidate the opposition without international condemnation."[78] For instance, the Minister for Mines, Mulondwe Muzungu contended that the groups "appeared to have come to dictate election policy to Zambia."[79] According to the Minister, "They give the impression that they are not here to observe but to dictate to us what should be done as if we do not have election procedures."[80]

Kenneth Kaunda himself showed a lot of anger and disillusionment with the alleged activities of the observers. He alleged that a foreign observer questioned a Mazabuka UNIP businessman why he had not defected to the MMD like others had done. He reached the conclusion that "all these things are showing that there is a plan somewhere to get Zambia into turmoil."[81] Finally, a group calling itself Lusaka Concerned Citizens also launched an attack against the observers:

> It is very sad to note that we have invited outside countries to observe, our first plural presidential and party elections. Sad in that Zambian tax payers money is so good to waste to entertain Americans, Nigerians, Europeans etc to come and tell us that we have voted correctly. . . . No body came to verify the fairness of colonial elections in 1964. . . . We have our professional lawyers and judges in this country to do the job. . . . Most of the observers who have been invited come from countries with bad reputations and also countries where assassinations take place during elections. Who decides the fairness of an election in America? How democratic are American elections?[82]

Such nationalistic positions cannot be dismissed as signs of "frustration." Foreign election monitoring bodies give the impression that Africans are incapable of conducting elections and behaving themselves. They give the impression that even an issue like conducting elections can only be carried out with the support and direction of foreigners without whose pronouncement as to the fairness of the exercise, it would not receive recognition from abroad. Another group which called itself Concerned Zambians Abroad also warned Zambians to beware of observer groups from other countries. In a letter to all media houses, it argued that the ultimate objective of these observer groups is to replace governments with puppets "that will pledge allegiance to western ideals."[83] In spite of these attacks on the foreign and domestic observer groups, donors and Western governments continued to provide support to the NGOs to enable them monitor the elections and contain acts of violence and fraud. In early october, just a few weeks to the election day, the Canadian government donated office equipment worth 2.8 million *Kwacha* to ZIMT. The Acting Canadian High Commissioner, Bob Pim announced that the equipments included fax machines, hard disk computers, Rank Xerox copier with accessories and a desk computer. The Government of Denmark also pledged to give additional support to ZIMT.

While these donations might have been well intentioned, they certainly invoked in the minds of many Zambians a feeling of loss of autonomy. Many of the donors and ambassadors actually behaved like "god fathers" appearing on television regularly and often making press statements and commenting on local politics; an action African ambassadors to Western nations will never contemplate. Also, by giving them these monies and materials, they "discouraged indigenous bodies from raising resources locally, an effort which would have brought them closer to the people and forced them to educate the people was easily subverted and replaced with dependence on the outside world."[84]

Finally, one critical question which many Zambians asked was "will these countries and organizations continue to give us money any time we have elections? Will they invite us to monitor elections in their home countries if **we** feel that their elections will not be free and fair?"[85] These questions might sound simplistic or rhetorical, but they reflect a genuine concern for the way and manner in which foreign observers, donors and western governments invade African countries as if their presence is enough to encourage, and sustain the democratic process long after they depart. Pronouncing an election as "free and fair" does not in any way guarantee the survival and strengthening of the democratic process. It might buy some foreign recognition, demonstrate growing political maturity and sophistication, but it does not guarantee that the contradictions which inhibit democracy and democratization will disappear.[86] The Nigerian experience after the annulment of the June 12, 1993 presidential election and the Sani Abacha coup of November 1993 is clear evidence of the limitations of foreign election monitoring which is not part of a broader strategy to consolidate and sustain democracy. There is no doubt that foreign observers make substantial inputs into the political process by emphasizing Western liberal ideological and political models and traditions which might have in reality been overtaken or rendered irrelevant by concrete objective conditions on ground. Conditions which seek to go beyond the mere procedural features of democracy to emphasize the issues of empowerment and *democratization* through the gradual strengthening of the people and their communities and organizations on terms determined and dictated by the people themselves. In other instances, the observer groups tend to be very domineering, patronizing, even dictatorial in their pronouncements. For instance, the Commonwealth Observer Group led by Justice Telford Georges arrived in Zambia only on October 23, about a week to election day, and immediately called for the lifting of the state of emergency and proclaimed that the police must not deny political parties permits to hold rallies.[87] Yet, the Commonwealth Observer Group had very limited experience in the monitoring of elections in Africa. Prior to the 1991 Zambian elections, it had only monitored elections in Zimbabwe and Uganda in 1980, Namibia in 1989 and Malaysia in 1990.[88]

Another interesting development was Frederick Chiluba's trip overseas in April 1991 at the heat of the campaigns. The MMD National Convention was February 27 to March 5, 1991. Following his election at the Convention as MMD flag bearer in the presidential election, Chiluba declared that the Movement was a "shadow cabinet."[89] Rather than stay to put the party together, he embarked on an overseas trip to the United States and the United Kingdom to honor "invitations from organizations" in these countries. He was to meet with officials of the National Endowment for Democracy (NED) because the NED was honoring Violeta Chamorro of Nicaragua and Vaclav Havel of Czechoslovakia; meet with Herman Cohen at the State Department; meet with the Foreign Affairs Committee of the U.S. Senate; and meet with Lynda Chalker in the United Kingdom.[90] It is possible to question the necessity for such a trip at a critical moment in the history of the MMD and of Zambia. It is precisely such "inability to determine priorities that will preserve the dignity of our leaders that have turned them into errand boys of the West."[91] Whatever our opinion may be, Chiluba certainly made an error of judgment and opened his relations to Western interests to question. UNIP leaders and the opposition saw the trip as an effort to consolidate the MMD's subservience to Western dictates as well as to seek support for the elections.

CONSOLIDATING DEMOCRACY IN AFRICA: BEYOND OBSERVER GROUPS

The new MMD government in Zambia has been confronted with countless problems and contradictions. For the MMD, the real problem is as posed by Robert Pinkney, "How far can it control its own destiny, independently of the forces that brought it into being? And what sort of governmental performances, and public responses to them, are most likely to enable the democratic system to survive or to acquire greater strength."[92] It has had problems with organizing itself as a real political *party* rather than a *movement* of all sorts of interest groups. It has not been able to effectively build its own cadres. It continues to face challenges from the opposition whose long-standing supporters dominate the security services and the bureaucracy. The economic crisis has not subsided and it has continued to inflict much pain on the people through its policies of desubsidization, deregulation, retrenchment and privatization. The cabinet has been reshuffled so many times that people are beginning to recall such activities which were rampant in the Kaunda days. Corruption, waste, mismanagement, and drug trafficking continue to characterize the cabinet. Donors have warned the Chiluba government several times to check drug trafficking among its ministers and several have resigned due to these allegations. The provinces appear to be largely out of the control of the party. In the Southern Province for example, complaints of neglect and victimization are loud and clear. Some party leaders have no respect for the president, the MMD hierarchy or its programs. Crime, AIDS, and drought continue to challenge well thought-out programs of the government. In spite of the commitment to market reforms, foreign investors are not coming in and the anticipated inflow of foreign aid has not kept pace with pledges. Infrastructure remains poor as pot-holes dot the main highways, and hospitals remain without drugs and doctors while schools remain without basic facilities and qualified teachers. Finally, the frustration is so high that there is a new nostalgia for the Kaunda days: "It seems we made a mistake. Can you believe that I lost my job under Chiluba. He promised us a better life, now, look at me. Life has become unbearable."[93]

These problems and contradictions challenge the process of consolidating democracy in Zambia. The Chiluba government has to move decisively and rapidly in these areas to check the forces of disintegration. As Pinkney has noted, democracy in developing formations cannot survive without "a period of sustained social and economic development in which stable institutions . . . that enjoyed widespread legitimacy and could be adapted to a world of universal suffrage and mass partici-pation," is evolved.[94] The MMD's moral image, in spite of Chiluba's "born again" Christian declarations, has been badly hurt by allegations of corruption, drug trafficking, nepotism and gross inefficiency. Zambia now has about 34 opposition parties all attacking the Chiluba government from one end or the other. Add to these attacks, increasing disillusionment and withdrawal by the populace; and inability to revive the economy, the net result will be democratic decay, or at the very best a democratic deadlock. While economic decay has made it easy for opposition groups to delegitimize authoritar-ian regimes and to crush such regimes in popular elections, they can also easily pave the way for the defeat of the new democratic regime. If decay occurs, the MMD will be seen out of power and a coalition of opposition parties will take over.[95] Either way, it is ordinary Zambians that will suffer, and for-eign monitoring bodies will be of no use at that stage.

Notes

1   Samuel P. Huntington, *The Third Wave-Democratization in the Late Twentieth Century*, (Norman and London: University of Oklahoma Press, 1991), p. 184.

2   Georg Sorensen, *Democracy and Democratization*, (Boulder, Colorado: Westview Press, 1993), p. 129.

3   Douglas Hurd quoted in "Democracy in Africa—Lighter Continent," *The Economist* (February 22, 1992).

4   Francois Mitterand quoted, *ibid*.

5   See World Bank, *Sub-Saharan Africa- From Crisis to Sustainable Growth* (Washington, D.C.: The World Bank, 1989).

6   "Democracy in Africa . . . ," op. cit.

7   Huntington, p. 184.

8   *Ibid.*, p. 185.

9   Interview with an MMD activist, Lusaka, Zambia, June 1993.

10   Interview with a pro-democracy activist, Lagos, Nigeria, December, 1993.

11   Huntington, op. cit., p. 185.

12   Interview with a UNIP Activist, Lusaka, Zambia, July, 1993.

13   See Ruby Ofori, "Ghana: The Elections Controversy," *Africa Report* (July-August, 1993).

14   Prosper Bani, "Politics of Structural Adjustment in Ghana: From Revolution to Democracy." Unpublished paper, Department of Government, The University of Texas at Austin, April, 1994.

15   *Ibid.*

16   *Ibid.*

17   See Russell Geekie, "America's Maverick Ambassador," *Africa Report* (March-April, 1993) and Binaifer Nowrojee, "Kenya: Pressure for Change," *Africa Report* (January-February, 1994).

18   See Karl Maifer, "Nigeria: Voodoo Democracy?" *Africa Report* (January-February, 1992); Paul Adams, "Babangida's Boondoggle," *Africa Report* (July-August, 1993); and Peter da Costa, "The Politics of 'Settlement'" *Africa Report* (November-December, 1993).

19   In fact, Kaunda had made a trip to Iraq during the crisis to express his support for the Iraqi leader. This convinced Western leaders that, contrary to some of his pronouncements, he was not in any way a democrat.

20   Movement for Multi-Party Democracy, *Manifesto* (Campaign Committee: MMD, Lusaka, n.d.), p. 2. Hereafter cited as MMD Manifesto.

21   Hamalengwa, *Class Struggles in Zambia 1889–1989 and the Fall of Kenneth Kaunda 1990–1991* (Lanham: University Press of America, 1992), p. 149.

22   *Ibid.*, p. 160.

23   *Ibid.*

24   MMD Manifesto.

25   See Melinda Ham, "An Outspoken Opposition," *Africa Report* (November-December 1993).

26   "Revamp UNIP, Militants Prodded," *Times of Zambia* (September 25, 1990).

27   Isaac Malambo, Agnes Banda and Victor Kayira, "Three Bow Out of Presidential Race—Its Now KK vs Chiluba," *Times of Zambia* (October 2, 1991).

28   "DP Ndola Rally Flops." *Times of Zambia* (April 8, 1991).

29   When NADA tried to organize a rally at Kamanga Township in March 1991, not a single person showed up. See "NADA Rally Flops," *Times of Zambia* (April 1, 1991).

30   "Don't Spare Anarchists," *Times of Zambia* (September 28, 1990).

31   Interview with Hon. Samuel Miyanda, MMD MP for Matero, Lusaka, May 1993.

32   See "Campaign for Kaunda—DG," *Times of Zambia* (November 16, 1990); "Campaign for Kaunda," *Times of Zambia* (December 4, 1990); and "Chiefs Throw Weight Behind Kaunda," *Times of Zambia* (September 28, 1990).

33   "UNIP to Sweep Polls—KK Tells Press," *Times of Zambia* (October 5, 1990).

34   "Leaders Scramble for Wealth." *Times of Zambia* (January 13, 1991).

35   Interview, Lusaka June 1993.

36   Hamalengwa, op. cit., p.149.

37   See "Courts Shut as Workers Vote," *Times of Zambia* (November 1, 1991); and "Zambians Flock to Polls," *Times of Zambia* (November 1, 1991).

38   Hicks Sikazwe and Davis Mulenga, "UNIP Wiped Out- Zambians Reject Kaunda's Rule as MMD Heads for Landslide," *Times of Zambia* (November 2, 1991); and Kondwani Chirambo, "Zambia Goes Agog," *Times of Zambia* (November 3, 1991)

39   "Polls Rigged Says Mvila," *Times of Zambia* (November 2, 1991).

40   "Ex-Premiers Routed," *Times of Zambia* (November 3, 1991). While Muunga received 14,711 votes, Musokotwane received a mere 3,246 votes and Lisulo got only 881 votes.

41   Davis Mulenga and Victor Kayora, "KK was a big liability," *Times of Zambia* (November 4, 1991).

42   Interview, Lusaka May 1993.

43   At the formal swearing in of Chiluba as President, the Zambian National Broadcasting Corporation blacked out the event probably as their last demonstration of support for Kaunda. See "TV Blackout Shocks Nation," *Times of Zambia* (November 3, 1991).

44   See Carl Bernstein, "The Holy Alliance," *TIME* (February 24, 1992).

45   *Ibid.*

46   *Ibid.*

47   *Ibid.*

48   "Observers Welcome," *Times of Zambia* (April 24, 1991).

49   "Breathing New Life Into Democratic Hopes," *Commonwealth Currents* (December 1992-January 1993), p. 2.

50   *Ibid.*

51   See "Election Rigging Danger Exists," *Times of Zambia* (April 27, 1991); and "Ngulube Dispels Vote Rigging," *Times of Zambia* (May 15, 1991).

52   "UNIP Dismisses Early Polls Call," *Times of Zambia* (May 21, 1991).

53   Interview with a UNIP Member, Lusaka, Zambia, May 1993.

54 John Phiri, "Campaign Drive in Top Gear," *Times of Zambia* (June 16, 1991).

55 "October Polls: Nordic States Offer Help," *Times of Zambia* (June 12, 1991).

56 Geoffrey Zulu, "Foreign Observers Coming," *Times of Zambia* (June 16, 1991).

57 "UNIP seeks foreign aid," *Times of Zambia* (June 19, 1991).

58 "Phiri Heads Watchdog," *Times of Zambia* (July 27, 1991).

59 "Poll Plot Laid Bare," *Times of Zambia* (August 7, 1991).

60 "Polls Monitors Under Training," *Times of Zambia* (August 25, 1991).

61 See "Election Volunteers Trained," *Times of Zambia* (August 26, 1991); "Get ZIMT Moving–Mambo," *Times of Zambia* (September 1, 1991); and "Have Observers at Booths- Expert," *Times of Zambia* (August 29, 1991).

62 "ZIMT Gets Shot in the Arm," *Times of Zambia* (september 6, 1991).

63 It should be noted that all donations to ZIMT were received by the accounting firm of Peak Marwick and Co. in Lusaka.

64 See Hamalengwa, *Class Struggles in Zambia* op. cit. and *Thoughts Are Free: Prison Experience and Reflections on Law and Politics in General*, (Don Mills, Ontario: Africa in Canada Press, 1991).

65 "Church Doubts ZIMT Fairness," *Times of Zambia* (September 15, 1991).

66 "Church Quits Monitoring Group," *Times of Zambia* (September 20, 1991).

67 See "Churches Set up Own Polls Watchdog," *Times of Zambia* (September 21, 1991); and "Church to Monitor October Election," *Times of Zambia* (September 21, 1991).

68 Interview with Hon. Samuel Miyanda, Lusaka, June 1993.

69 "ZIMT Under Fire," *Times of Zambia* (September 23, 1991).

70 "ZIMT is no More," *Times of Zambia* (September 24, 1991).

71 Interview with a former ZIMT official, Lusaka, June 1993.

72 "Squabbling Irks Donor Agencies," *Times of Zambia* (October 10, 1991).

73 See "ZEMCC Pledges Fight for Fair Polls," *Times of Zambia* (October 3, 1991); and "Elections Body Not Complete," *Times of Zambia* (October 3,

1991). The Chairman of the electoral commission was Deputy Chief Justice of Zambia Matthew Ngulube.

74   "Monitors Slam Scary Ads," *Times of Zambia* (October 11, 1991).

75   Sam Phiri, "Is ZEMCC Mature Enough to Judge Polls?" *Times of Zambia* (October 12, 1991).

76   "Voters Misled," *Times of Zambia* (October 30, 1991).

77   "Manuwele Ticks Off ZEMCC," *Times of Zambia* (October 21, 1991).

78   Interview with Hon. Samuel Miyanda, Lusaka, May 1991.

79   "Observers Off Mark, Says Muzungu," *Times of Zambia* (September 26, 1991).

80   *Ibid.*

81   "Observer Irks Kaunda." *Times of Zambia* (September 27, 1991).

82   Lusaka Concerned Citizens, "We Don't Need Americans to Monitor Elections," *Times of Zambia* (September 29, 1991).

83   Concerned Zambians Abroad, "Beware of Observer Groups—Zambians Warned," *Times of Zambia* (October 12, 1991).

84   Interview with Mr. Johnson Kanduza, Mamba Collieries Guest House, Lusaka, June 1993.

85   *Ibid.*

86   For a discussion of these constraints see Julius O. Ihonvbere, "From Movement to Government: The Crisis of Democratic Consolidation in Zambia," *Canadian Journal of African Studies*, Vol. 29 (1), (1995) pp. 1-25 and Richard Sandbrook, *The Politics of Africa's Economic Recovery*, (Cambridge: Cambridge University Press, 1993).

87   "Ban Must Go—Commonwealth Observer Group," *Times of Zambia* (October 26, 1991). This group was in existence all the while when UNIP had the state of emergency in place. It did not work for sanctions against Zambia for that reason. It is equally doubtful if it had sufficient information and ground experience to understand how and why the Zambian police denied permits to some political parties.

88   "Breathing New Life into Democratic Hopes," *Commonwealth Currents* (1993), pp. 2-3.

89   "We are a Shadow Cabinet," *Times of Zambia* (April 4, 1991).

90   "Chiluba Off on Overseas Trips," *Times of Zambia* (April 10, 1991).

91 Interview with a UNIP official, Lusaka, June 1993.

92 Robert Pinkney, *Democracy in the Third World* (Boulder, Colorado: Lynne Rienner, 1993), p. 163.

93 Interview with an unemployed youth, Lusaka, Zambia, July 1993.

94 Robert Pinkney, op. cit., p. 169.

95 For a more detailed discussion of these contradictions and possibilities see Julius O. Ihonvbere, *Democratization and Civil Society in Africa: The Zambian Experience.* (Forthcoming).

Chapter 6

Global Transformation and Political Reforms in Africa: The Case of Ghana

Baffour Agyeman-Duah

INTRODUCTION

The potential for political reforms in Africa has aroused much academic and practical interest since former Soviet president, Mikhail Gorbachev, bounced onto the world stage in 1985 and introduced *glasnost* and *perestroika* to transform the correlation of forces in international relations. The transformation affected not only superpower relations, but it also excited a global movement for political liberalism and pressured undemocratic states to reform. Several African states responded, albeit reluctantly, by announcing measures to liberalize their political systems. But how veritable are these responses? Would the processes for reforms ensure fair and just governance? Considering that African societies are pregnant with socioeconomic contradictions, are democratic reforms feasible and even practicable? These and similar questions pertaining to the debate help to set the tone and provide guidance for the discussion.

The primary objective of this chapter is to probe the prospects for democratic reforms in Africa, with a focus on Ghana where the Provisional National Defense Council regime ruled the country between 1982 and 1993 was most responsive to the vicissitudes of our time. The main thesis is that the legitimacy of the post-colonial state in Africa is obfuscated mainly because of the state's inability to master the accumulation process and ensure reasonable access to economic surplus.[1] And, considering the symbiotic relationship between economics and politics, it will be argued further that the dereliction of the economy is correlated with the dilemma of political efficacy which has, subsequently, provoked intense disputation over governance. The incapacity of the state in these two critical areas of performance—economic and political—has seemingly alienated the relevant social classes on whose support the state depends for its legitimacy. Hence, the paper takes the position that for African states to achieve any development and register any measure of legitimacy and credibility, it is imperative that there be a progressive transformation of the structures and processes of governance and the system of accumulation and distribution of wealth and resources.

The probe will proceed in three main parts. First, the nature of the global transformation will be explored in order to demonstrate its impact on the politics of African states. Next, there will be a discussion on why the early attempts at political reforms in Ghana under the PNDC regime were unsuccessful. The final part of the paper will focus on the efforts by the regime to reintroduce electoral politics into the country as a consequence of both internal and external pressures.

COLLAPSE OF THE COLD WAR ORDER: IMPACT ON AFRICA

A new world order is said to have emerged following the collapse of communism and the apparent rise of pluralism in Eastern Europe, the unification of Germany, and the radical shift in domestic and international political values of the former Soviet Union. These dramatic phenomena were facilitated by the politics of "new thinking" that was inherent in the Soviet policy of *glasnost* and *perestroika*[2] and which led Britain's Margaret Thatcher to declare that the West could do business with Gorbachev.

Based on the communist dogma, the Soviets had seen the world as divided into two camps (West and East), and that the struggle between these camps will determine history. This theoretical perception pitched the East against the West in a relentless ideological battle following the Second World War. The ideological bifurcation created a bipolar world where even so-called non-aligned nations had to be patronized by one or the other superpower. In the 1980's, however, the Soviets retracted this position and regarded the world as "a unitary whole" where despite the contradictions and complications, "all parts of it are mutually interdependent."[3] More emphatic was Gorbachev's own position:

> Today, the preservation of any kind of "closed" society is virtually impossible. . . The world economy is becoming a single organism, and no state, whatever its social system or economic status, can develop normally outside it.[4]

Ostensibly, the Soviet desire for change was influenced in no small measure by economic necessities, but more importantly, they recognized the futility of pursuing economic progress in a "closed" political system. Considering the severe limitations imposed by the Cold War system on their development capacities, the Soviets had to demonstrate, by word and deed, the revocation of their traditional positions and a commitment to a mutation in the status quo of East-West relations. With communism, the nemesis of capitalist democracy, rendered defunct by its own purveyors, the United States considered the Cold War over and sought to reshape its strategic goals. A White House document acknowledged the transformation by stating that:

> Our goal is to move beyond containment, to seek the integration of the Soviet Union into the international system as a constructive partner. For the first time in the postwar period, this goal appears within reach.[5]

The fundamental shift in the mutual perceptions of threat by the Soviets and Americans, and the repudiation of communism in the former Soviet Union and most of its satellite states, had tremendous impact on the politics of Africa where the superpowers had played out much of their Cold War rivalries.[6] Economic or military aid to African countries had been provided generally on the basis of the recipient's ideological affiliation to the East or West. Several rulers became surrogates for the powers and manipulated the resultant patronage for their self-aggrandizement. With the demise of the Cold War, "Africa would be less of a pawn and also has less of a choice of moving across the ideological divide," as noted by one eminent statesman.[7]

Furthermore, development in several African states was inspired by the Marxist model. The collapse of the model in the Soviet Union where it originated and in Eastern Europe where it was forcibly imposed, belied its credibility and strongly suggested, at the minimum, rectification in countries where it had excited development practices. Also, the pluralistic thrust in the former communist countries weakened the legitimacy of dictators who thrived on the socialist principle of democratic centralism which justified the centralization of state power in the ruling party. African leaders who most often clothed their totalitarianism in the socialist garb were stripped bare by the upswing of democratic ideals.

Coinciding expediently with the demise of communism and adding to the momentum of pressure on African rulers was the demand for democratic governance as a condition for continued assistance by Western international financial institutions and donor nations. Attributing Africa's development problems to such phenomena as the extensive personalization of power, the denial of fundamental human rights, widespread corruption, and the prevalence of unelected and unaccountable government, the World Bank resolved that development could take place only if political leaders abandon their authoritarian practices.[8] The major donor nations, the United States and Britain in particular, cautioned their clients to liberalize or lose much of their support.[9] Hence, the now ubiquitous "structural adjustment program" (SAP) of the World Bank/International Monetary Fund has explicit requirement for political liberalization. The linkage of economic progress to democracy presented yet another challenge to the persistent notion that new nations need "strong leaderships" (euphemism for dictatorships) to develop.

Notably, 37 countries had signed SAP agreements by 1989; several others including Zaire, Benin, Cote d'Ivoire, Sierra Leone, Gabon, Zambia, Togo, Burkina Faso, and Kenya inched away from one-party and/or military-controlled states to allow political pluralism. Since 1989 not less than eight states have held multi-party elections; several others have held national conferences with the objective of creating democratic structures.[10] In fact, Benin in 1990 and Zambia in 1991 changed their long-entrenched hegemonic regimes through the ballot-

box. Ghana and Nigeria had plans to usher in elected governments by the end of 1992. The program of reforms in Ghanaian politics and whether or not these reforms and the plan to
return the country to civilian rule will facilitate democratic
governance are the subject of discussion in the following
sections.

POLITICAL REFORMS OF THE PNDC

The attempt by the PNDC to change the political logic that
had guided post-colonial politics in Ghana has undergone three
main phases: populist (1982-83), adjustment (1983-87), and
consolidation (1987-present).[11] The regime burst onto the Ghanaian political scene on the last day of 1981, by means of a
military coup, and declared unequivocally its intention to radically transform Ghana's political and economic terrain. Populist in his appeal, the charismatic leader, Flt. Lt. Jerry J.
Rawlings, spared no rhetoric in denouncing the exploiters and
oppressors of the masses who had used state power to enrich
themselves.[12] Because the regime initially appeared to lack
popular support, the proclamation to give "power back to the
people" through popular participation, to introduce a new system of "people's justice" and social accountability was regarded
by many as a facade to consolidate its hold on power.

However, the immediate establishment of new institutions
and guidelines for political participation, the administration
of justice and accountability, and the acceptance in 1983 of
the Bank/IMF conditionalities (at the time fiscal rather than
political) for its economic recovery program,[13] validated the
regime's determination to transform the Ghanaian political
economy. It must be noted, therefore, that before Gorbachev
came to the scene and introduced his *perestroika*, and before
the debate over SAP gained academic currency, the Ghanaian
authorities had already begun to reform the country's political and economic order.

The PNDC heralded the new political order with the creation of popular defense committees which were instituted in
local communities and working places (People's Defense Committees, PDCs, and Workers Defense Committees, WDCs). At
the same time, national investigation and citizens vetting com-

mittees (NIC and CVC) were instituted to ensure probity in public and private life. The two defense bodies were merged in 1985 and redesignated Committees for the Defense of the Revolution (CDRs) with the charge to serve as the "operating centers for the revolution." Their duty was to "defend the rights of the ordinary people, expose and deal with corruption and other counter-revolutionary activities . . ."[14] As if by design rather than default, the functions of these committees were left ambiguous to allow both officials and opportunists a free hand to pursue the objectives of the regime. Reminiscent of the Red Guards during the cultural revolution in Mao's China, the PDCs/WDCs terrorized those perceived to be enemies of the revolution and, in the process, alienated sizeable segments of the population, particularly those in high social and economic standing. It was primarily due to the excesses of the committees and their negative political impact that the PNDC restructured and refocused their energies in 1985. Until then, it was obvious that the committees were empowered for watchdogship rather than as effective instruments for political participation, the additional charge to choose delegates to a "constituent assembly of the popular masses"[15] notwithstanding. Not surprisingly, they were perceived by many as promoters of the regime's parochial interests.

Although the new order might have been enacted with a genuine intent for Ghana's progress, it appeared equally to have promoted the self-aggrandizement of the PNDC. This point is crucial because, unlike Gorbachev, Rawlings' *perestroika* did not include a *glasnost*, a contradiction in such a process which the Soviets were quick to recognize and address in their own situation. Moreover, the PNDC devoted much of the country's resources to develop and maintain paramilitary/security outfits—the Civil Defense Organization, People's Militia, Commandos, Bureau of National Investigation and Castle Security Unit—that were meant purposely to ensure the regime's security. Thus, the PNDC appeared to be more solicitous about its own impregnability than creating structures that would allow the germination of credible alternative political forces.

Such a political agenda seemed to have been influenced by Libya's *jamahiriyya* model of popular government which, according to Muammar Khadafy's so-called *Green Book*, posits a

"Third Theory" in which the "state of the masses" is the only alternative to the communist-capitalist dichotomy. In this model, the masses are said to be empowered through their membership of grassroot committees. Apparently, Khadafy and Rawlings shared some common interests: the latter moved swiftly to restore diplomatic relations with Libya which had been severed by the erstwhile Limann regime in 1980. Khadafy, on his part, was quick to respond to the needs of the new regime by shipping food, drugs, crude oil (and, some say, arms) to shore up the badly depressed Ghanaian economy.

Whether or not the Libyan aid was a *quid pro quo* for adopting the *jamahiriyya*-style politics is another matter, but it was clear that just as Khadafy dominated Libyan politics in spite of the supposed empowerment of popular committees, so did Rawlings in Ghana despite the cant about "power to the people." Like Ayyub Khan of Pakistan in the 1960's and Khadafy, Rawlings used the PDCs/CDRs to diffuse political opposition and to legitimize military rule. Even though the committees allowed the incorporation of the masses into the prevailing power relations, the power of the state itself was not restructured and remained at the center. Indeed, the practices of the regime became capricious and coercive and led, later, to a strange citizen aloofness which Rawlings bemoaned as a "culture of silence."

Ultimately, these early attempts at political transformation could not be said to have laid a lasting foundation for democratic governance. Rawlings did not come across as a true democrat who was willing to subject his regime to public scrutiny in instilling a new sense of social equity, accountability and responsibility. The inability to plant these attributes firmly in politically acceptable structures and practices meant that they would be of no lasting consequence.

REFORMING (ADJUSTING?) THE ECONOMY

The decision to restructure the economy on the basis of the Bank/IMF prescriptions must also be seen within the context of the internal dynamics of the PNDC itself. The regime was earlier dominated by self-proclaimed Marxist-Leninists who were eager to transform the country into a scientific socialist state. But the economic condition in 1982 was precarious: inflation ran in three digits; industrial production recorded negative growth; food was in short supply; cocoa production, the main export commodity, was in abeyance; and, to make matters worse, nearly a million Ghanaians were repatriated from Nigeria. What strategy for economic resuscitation was best under these conditions? With the dominance of Marxists, the obvious solution was to turn to the Soviet Union for patronage, but as Onyema Ogochukwu reported:

> The Russians had pointed to their own problems which they said made it difficult for them to offer much help, and advised Ghana to go to the IMF but try at the same time to hold on to the revolution. It was impractical advice. The government has had to compromise its ideology in order to get help.[16]

The failure of the Soviets to redeem a fledgling revolution might have accounted for the regime's swing to the West for assistance. However, it is important to note that Rawlings, as the leader, was less inclined toward the Marxist proclivities of most of his colleagues at the time. He was a nationalist with the primary interest to create a just and equitable society, not necessarily a socialist one. For instance, during his brief interregnum in 1979 as the leader of the Armed Forces Revolutionary Council (AFRC), he resisted pressure from his associates to transform Ghana into a scientific socialist state; the main motivation for his rule that year was to "punish corruption and redress economic inequalities."[17]

Again, in the early years of the PNDC, Rawlings rebuked the Marxists for their "empty theories"[18] and accused them of failing "to offer solutions, let alone realistic ones, to the problems that confronted the country in 1982."[19] We can surmise, therefore, that the adoption of the Bank/IMF package in 1983 was consistent with Rawlings' vision of pragmatic solutions to the deranged economy. Or, perhaps, he was quick to realize that the prevailing economic conditions did not lend themselves to Marxist fixations.

Because of the fiscal stabilization policies adopted in 1983 under the SAP, Ghana's economic growth and development saw a new surge by 1990: cocoa and mineral production shot up dramatically; export earnings grew; and most of the deteriorated infrastructure were restored.[20] Hence, free-market economists point out, expediently and expeditiously, the impressive statistics which show positive economic growth since the reforms were introduced. The Ghanaian SAP has even been considered as offering "transferable lessons which policy makers in negative-performing Third World countries may learn."[21] Evidently, the economy has partially "recovered" albeit with massive foreign aid, but the distribution of the benefits of the growth, the other half of the development package, cannot be easily measured.

The problem of distribution inequity remains grave: few people are said to have benefitted from the seeming economic growth. Urban unemployment rose because of retrenchment policies of the PNDC and mass impoverishment prevailed because of the withdrawal of subsidies from public services.[22] Consequently, the feeling of alienation and disenchantment became widespread among people who earlier had supported the regime. The problem of legitimacy which bedeviled the regime was, consequently, "rooted in the weakness of the Ghanaian economy," as pointed out by Kwame Ninsin.[23] Because of the exacerbated inequities in the accumulation of and access to wealth, the PNDC simply could not turn the high economic growth to political advantage. No wonder then that the country's continued underdevelopment was blamed on the recurring external intervention, particularly from the World Bank/International Monetary Fund.[24]

It is obvious that the recovery program has stopped the economic hemorrhage in Ghana where conditions today are far better than they were in 1983; in terms of the availability of goods in the stores the country today is a paradise. However, most people cannot afford the items because SAP benefits have yet to trickle down to the masses for whom the "revolution" was said to have been undertaken and restiveness is widespread. The verdict on the reforms, therefore, remains a matter of diverse interpretation and appreciation. But for the regime, the adjustment program was most instrumental for gaining respect and legitimacy in international circles, and for consolidating itself in power for over ten years.

CONSOLIDATION AND CHALLENGES

As the foregoing analysis shows, the populist and adjustment phases were triggered essentially by the regime's own internal logic and dynamics. The phase of consolidation, where the regime became fully committed to constitutional rule, however, came as a direct response to pressures from internal opposition forces who were by now emboldened by widespread disaffection because of rising adverse effects of the SAP, and the global movement for liberalization. These developments coincided with the new World Bank/International Monetary Fund politics of aid which required liberal governance. It became incumbent on Rawlings to embark upon a "political structural adjustment,"[25] which, from his vantage point, would grant his rule the much needed legitimacy.

Increasingly, the PNDC had become irascible on the issue of political pluralism and intolerant of open dissent. It claimed to be a "people's government" and was irritated by those who questioned its legitimacy. Not only did the regime retain and add to the colonial legacy of preventive custody laws under which anyone could be held without trial, there were more political executions than at any other time. In addition to silencing outspoken newspapers, the regime even attempted to regulate religious organizations, for the first time in the country, through a licensing law. Political opponents were intimidated, arrested, and detained, and political fora could be organized only at the pleasure of the PNDC. As the regime became more and more arbitrary and capricious in the exercise of state power, this behavior fueled the fear of an emergent dictatorship. Such repressive methods were largely responsible for the emergence of the "culture of silence" that gripped the nation by 1986 and undermined the regime's political efficacy.

The official assault, however, could scarcely stifle opposition which had begun in 1986, to call publicly for open national politics. Even though the leaders of dissent were detained routinely, for instance in May 1987,[26] the highly alert Ghanaian polity proved resilient and sophisticated and persisted in challenging the legitimacy of the "provisional" regime. No one was startled when the PNDC announced in July 1987 a schedule for the creation of District Assemblies and proceeded, in the following year, to institute these bodies through elections. The assemblies were presented as evidence of the regime's commitment to "true" democratic rule and as a major effort to decentralize state structures. However, the bodies were made to operate under the direct control of Accra, and a third of the membership and the District Secretaries were appointed by the PNDC.[27] In essence, these bodies did not reflect a strong sense of autonomous local politics and many perceived them, just as they did the CDRs, as mere tools to serve the regime's interests.

Though the assemblies provided a much needed break from the political pressure and a semblance of stability for the PNDC, they did not "supply an adequate response either to the regime's need to attract backing in the urban areas or, more vitally, to the problems of state legitimacy and regime author-ity."[28] The elections indicated a miserable lack of regime sup-port in the urban centers, particularly, among the intelligen-tsia: turnout was high in rural areas, but very low in Accra and Kumasi where just around 45 percent was recorded; Legon, the university center had a turnout of a mere 11 percent.[29]

In August 1990, the Movement for Freedom and Justice was formed as the first formal opposition group, to demand the lifting of the ban on politics, a timetable for constitutional rule, release of political detainees, and amnesty to all exiles. Five months later, the Movement and 12 other groups formed the coordinating Committee of Democratic Forces to pose a greater challenge to the PNDC. As the demand for more po-litical liberalization gathered momentum, the regime could not help but find political space to accommodate the increas-ing agitation for elective government.

Responding to the political turbulence, Rawlings announced in his 1991 New Year's Eve address that the PNDC's "eyes (were) now firmly set on the final phase of our journey as a provi-sional government and on the road toward establishing for Ghana a new constitutional order."[30] On May 10, a government White Paper was issued establishing a Committee of Experts to draft constitutional proposals which were subsequently placed before a Consultative Assembly in August for a final draft. Proclaiming that Presidential and Parliamentary elec-tions would be held in late 1992, the regime suppressed previous prevarications and set in motion the transitional process toward elective politics.

QUESTIONABLE PROCESS OF TRANSITION?

Ultimately, the legitimacy of the next elected government in Ghana will be judged not only by its ability to improve the economic conditions and ensure social equity but, more importantly, by the credibility of the process by which it came to power. Though this issue has seldom been a factor in African politics, it has become salient because of the widespread suspicion among Ghanaians that the PNDC was engineering the transitional process to its advantage. The regime's disposition toward the process and the methods for managing the transition raised poignant concerns.

Unlike Ibrahim Babaginda in Nigeria where a similar transition was in progress, Rawlings refused to renounce any personal pretence as a presidential candidate nor did the PNDC, as a group, rule against competing in the coming elections. Rawlings, his wife and close associates clearly were campaigning in all corners of the country[31] though he claimed not to know about his political future which, according to him, "will be decided by the people."[32] The dubiousness of such political shenanigans confused the political observers, particularly the opposition groups whose weaknesses were further exacerbated by the continued ban on legal political activities.

The political atmosphere was further unsettled by Rawlings' known drain for democracy in the nominal sense of multi-party politics and constitutionalism. He reportedly boasted in November 1991 that Ghanaians, under his regime, have had the extraordinary opportunity to participate in decision making "because of the absence of outward forms of democracy like a formal constitution, national elections and a parliament."[33] Earlier, he had strangely described the notion to exclude the military from politics as "a colonial legacy."[34] With such a state of mind, how could Rawlings be trusted to allow the process of transition to proceed on its natural course? As the incumbent head of state, would his distaste for constitutionalism affect his decision to hand over the reigns of power? And, if he became the elected president, to what extent would he feel bound by the constitution?

Another concern related to the composition of the Consultative Assembly (CA) and attempts by the PNDC to shape its outcome. The 260-member body was made up of 117 delegates from the District and Metropolitan Assemblies, 121 from various "recognized associations and organizations, and 22 PNDC appointees. Unlike the NLC transition in 1969 where the constituent assembly appeared to be nonpartisan, the CA was loaded with individuals known to be highly sympathetic to the PNDC.[35] Considering that members of the district/metropolitan assemblies were "revolutionary" cadres, their delegates together with the PNDC appointees gave a clear majority on the CA to the regime. Would such a majority be used to shape the final outcome of the CA's deliberations? As issues of critical interest to the PNDC come for debate—for example, the proposal that the military be given a political role, that the controversial Public Tribunals and CDRs be given constitutional protection, that the regime render account for its national stewardship, and that members of the PNDC be granted immunity from any form of prosecution—this CA majority, it was feared, would provide a useful mechanism for the regime to swing the outcomes to its favor.

The seeming measured management of the transition process and the regime's continued monopoly of the national media, proscription of the more redoubtable newspapers, retention of repressive decrees, execution of political offenders, and limitations of habeas corpus, did not suggest a sincere commitment to the evolution of a democratic government. The managed process rather suggested a determination to prevent the CA from snowballing into a "national conference" to put the PNDC on trial as had happened elsewhere in Africa.[36] Even so, this behavior did not support any interest in pursuing the democratization process to its logical conclusion; at best, the regime appeared not to want to relinquish power, but to create a semblance of democracy to provide itself the much needed aura of legitimacy.

CONCLUSION

The problem of political transformation in Ghana reflects the macrocosmic African dilemma of development. Across the continent, post-colonial politics have dissipated the civic public realm and created states where rulership is personalized, violation of human rights abound, power is centralized in authorities, and individuals tend to withdraw from politics.[37] The persistence of the primordial and hegemonic traditions make political reforms difficult because incumbents, generally, do not preside over their own demise. In the former Soviet Union, for instance, Gorbachev's major problem as a reformer was his lingering communist proclivities and reliance on the Communist Party of the Soviet Union (CPSU) for change. It was hard for him to accept that his reforms could succeed only by dismantling his own rule. For true transformation to occur, he and the party had to be toppled by an alternative force which found expression through Boris Yeltsin.

In Ghana, as elsewhere in Africa, political liberalization is not being "granted" out of the kindheartedness, goodwill, or the genuine interest in democratic governance of rulers. The elites have reluctantly obliged to the persistent pressure from within and without because of their own sense of lack of legitimacy. Though the PNDC appeared to have improved the national economy in term of achieving significant economic growth, the regime was unsuccessful in claiming a national mandate to rule primarily because it came to power through the barrel of the gun.

The collapse of the Cold War order has spurred the movement for political reforms, but it remains very unclear how the new world order would support the democratization process, and whether or not the process would yield veritable transformation. While the outcome of the transformation should be of a prime interest, we should also consider that any transition from non-constitutional, military, or one-party state to political pluralism and consititutionalism represents important steps towards democracy. After decades of authoritarian rule, any measure taken by the elites to increase political competition and allow for mass political rights such as the freedom of expression and association should be a welcome relief.

Though it would be illusive to believe that the democratic outcomes achieved recently in Eastern Europe could readily diffuse to Africa, there is hope that the tidal wave of change cannot easily be stopped. Even if incumbent dictators metamorphose overnight into democrats for the sake of retaining power, their political options would be limited by the sustained pressure to accommodate the global and continental yearning for democratic governance. As observed by Gyimah-Boadi, "the fall of authoritarian regimes and rulers in eastern Europe and elsewhere removes a major nondemocratic role model and sources to whom Ghanaian [and African] authoritarian rulers and factions have appealed for moral and logistical support in the past."[38] In this sense alone, the Gorbachev Revolution has impacted positively on African states and has provided another opportunity for reconstructing the political space.

Notes

1 Samir Amin, "Democracy and National Security in the Periphery," *Third World Quarterly* 9, 4 (October 1987), p. 1130.

2 Robert J. Kigston, ed., *Perestroika Papers* (Dubuque, IA: Kendall/Hunt, 1988). Though these policies could be said to have failed with the forced resignation of Gorbachev in December 1991, they provided the basis for the reforms that led ultimately to the demise of communism and the disintegration of the Soviet Union.

3 Georgi Arbatov, "Beginning with Perestroika." In Kingston, p. 18.

4 Mikhail Gorbachev, *A Road to the Future: Complete Text of the December 7, 1988 United Nations Address* (Santa Fe, New Mexico: Ocean Tree Press, 1990), p. 13.

5 The White House, *National Security Strategy of the United States* (Washington, D.C.), March 1990, 9.

6 Zaki Laidi, *The Superpowers and Africa: The Constraints of a Rivalry, 1960-1990.*

7 Olusegun Obasanjo, former Nigerian head of state, at the African Leadership Forum, Paris. Reported in *West Africa*, 7-13 May, 1990, pp. 762-63.

8 World Bank, *Sub Saharan Africa: From Crisis to Sustainable Growth* (Washington, D.C.: The World Bank, 1989).

9 The U.S. Assistant Secretary of State for Africa, Herman Cohen, for instance, warned that African states that did not respond to "popular demands for democratization will find themselves in an increasingly disadvantageous position" in competition for donor assistance resources. See "Imposing Conditions," *West Africa* 21-27 May, 1990, p. 830.

10 Robert Press, "Africa's Turn." *World Monitor* (February 1992), pp. 37-43.

11 Naomi Chazan, The Political Transformation of Ghana Under the PNDC. In Rothchild, ed., *Ghana: The Political Economy of Recovery.*

12 Donald Rothchild and E. Gyimah-Broadi, "Populism and the 'Thermidorian Reaction' in Ghana and Burkina Faso." A paper pre-

sented at the 31st Annual Meeting of the African Studies Association, Chicago, Illinios, October 1988.

13 Baffour Agyeman-Duah, "Ghana, 1982-86: The Politics of the PNDC," *Journal of Modern African Studies* 25, 4 (1987), pp. 613-42.

14 PNDC Initial Proclamation, *Daily Graphic* (Accra), 12 January, 1982.

15 *Ibid.*

16 *West Africa* 25 February 1985, quoted in Agyeman-Duah, "Ghana, 1982-86: The Politics of the PNDC."

17 James C. W. Ahiakpor, "Rawlings Economic Reforms and the Poor: Consistency or Betrayal?" *Journal of Modern African Studies,* 29, 4 (1991).

18 See *West Africa* 12 September 1983: 2103.

19 See *West Africa* 18 January 1988, p. 72.

20 Jon Kraus, "The Political Economy of Stability and Structural Adjustment in Ghana." In Donald Rothchild, ed., *Ghana: The Political Economy of Recovery* (Boulder, Colorado: Lynn Rienner, 1991).

21 James C. W. Ahiakpor, "Economic Policy Reform in Ghana: 1983-90: Some Transferable Lessons." A paper presented at the 66th Annual Conference of the Western Economic Association, Washington, D.C.

22 Kraus, "The Political Economy of Stability."

23 Kwame Ninsin, "The PNDC and the Problem of Legitimacy." In *ibid.*

24 Emmanuel Hansen and Kwame Ninsin, eds., *The State, Development and Politics in Ghana* (London: CODESRIA, Books, 1989).

25 *Amnesty International 1984* (London, 1984), pp. 48-53, cited in Agyeman-Duah, "Ghana, 1982-86."

26 See "Ghana: Political Ferment" *West Africa* 25 May 1987, p. 99. Those detained were leaders of the African Youth Command, the Kwame Nkrumah Revolutionary Guards, and the National Democratic Movement.

27 Agyeman-Duah, "Ghana, 1982-86."

28 Naomi Chazan, "Liberalization, Governance and Political Space in Ghana." In Goran Hyden and Michael Bratton, *Governance and Politics in Africa* (Boulder, Colorado: Lynn Rienner, 1992) p. 137.

29 *Ibid.*

30   See *People's Daily Graphic* (Accra) 2 January 1991: 1, 8, 9.

31   E. Gyimah-Boadi, "Notes on Ghana's Current Transition to Constitutional Rule." *Africa Today* 38, 4 (1991): 5-18.

32   Rawlings' BBC interview broadcast. Cited in Ben Ephson, "The Rawlings Factor." *West Africa* 23 December 1991-5 January 1992: 2138.

33   Ben Ephson, "The Rawlings' Factor."

34   Rawlings' address to security forces on 31 December 1990, reported in *Peoples Daily Graphic* (Accra) 2 January 1991, cited in Gyimah-Boadi, "Notes on Ghana's Current Transition."

35   Gyimah-Boadi, "Notes on Ghana's Current Transition."

36   See: "Waves of Independence." *West Africa* 12-18 August 1991: 1314-1315.

37   Goran Hyden, Governance and the Study of Politics. In Hyden and Bratton, *Governance and Politics in Africa*: 23-25.

38   Gyimah-Boadi, op. cit.: 17.

Chapter 7

Legitimizing the Illegitimate: The 1992 Presidential Election As a Prelude to Ghana's Fourth Republic*

Yakubu Saaka

INTRODUCTION

After the remarkable success the Provisional National Defence Council (PNDC) had with the non-partisan District Assemblies elections in 1988, a number of delegations came from some African countries to see what lessons they could draw from the Ghana experiment.[1] The probability was quite high that there would be a similar stampede following the even more spectacular coup the regime engineered with the 1992 presidential and parliamentary elections. Flight Lieutenant Jerry Rawlings (Chairman of the PNDC) and his cohorts, it would seem, had succeeded in developing the kind of winning formula[2] many other nations clearly thought was worth emulating.

It is acknowledged that after the PNDC adopted the International Monetary Fund (IMF)/World Bank sponsored Economic Recovery Program (ERP) in 1983, the regime became a favorite of many Western governments and international donor agencies. An important consequence of this was the generous treatment it consistently received from the Paris Club.[3] What is, perhaps, less well known is the equally sympathetic attention it generally attracted in the usually cynical western

*This paper was originally prepared for the 24th Annual Meeting of the National Conference of Black Political Scientists, held in Oakland, California, March 1993.

scholarly community. All of this "good press" notwithstanding, and in spite of an abundance of revolutionary gestures and rhetoric within the government, there was always an appreciation by informed observers that the regime's governance was rooted in coercion and repression. Characterized as such, the PNDC was not unlike many authoritarian African regimes; hence these other governments' interests in Ghana's singularly successful disengagement process.

In January 1982, following the coup that brought him to power the second time, Flight Lieutenant Rawlings was asked by reporters about his plans for a return of power to civilians. His rhetorical quip was "to whom?"[4] As far back as then he seemed to have been anticipating the events of January 7, 1993.[5] Even though Rawlings and his colleagues in the PNDC had, on numerous occasions, declared their willingness to be made redundant, it was difficult to say what this really meant. But going by experience in Ghana, it would certainly have been unique if their concept of redundancy turned out to be anything, as one perceptive observer put it, "significantly beyond a retirement of structures and forms."[6]

A fundamental problem all authoritarian regimes have to face in one degree or another is the inevitable crisis over legitimacy. This is an issue that seems to have lately become acute in Africa. What is euphemistically referred to by Africanists as "the second revolution"[7] and seen by Samuel Huntington as an extension of the "third wave" in the world-wide democratization process,[8] appears to have taken many African authoritarian regimes by surprise. Beginning in the late 1980's, many of these governments have been forced by the changing tide not only to come to terms with their illegitimacy but, more importantly, to deal with the even more problematic issue of disengaging from an authoritarian order. For most, the ideal route has been to put in place processes that would ensure either their continuation in power or the transfer of power to groups sympathetic to them.[9] In spite of the massive coercive power at their disposal, however, the record shows that it has generally not been easy for these regimes to achieve their desired goals. In fact, many have become causalities en route.[10] Successful ones like Ghana's under Rawlings are the exception.

The purpose of this chapter is to analyze how, in spite of his personal aversion for them, Jerry Rawlings has succeeded in using party politics and constitutionalism to reinvent himself. It argues that by manipulating structures and forms to enable him to hand power over to himself, he has not only reintrenched personal rulership but has, in effect, reversed (in the case of Ghana) the "winds of change" now blowing across the African continent.[11]

ELECTIONS AND AUTHORITARIAN REGIMES IN AFRICA

In the 1970's and 1980's, conventional wisdom about the meaning and future of elections in Africa among many decision-makers and scholars was extremely negative and pessimistic. During that period elections, perhaps, deserved to be widely regarded as irrelevant. For as Fred Hayward points out, "[t]here was growing evidence of elections which did not reflect democratic values; that those responsible followed neither the electoral procedures set out in the institutions bequeathed at independence nor other requirements of free and fair competition."[12]

Commenting on the particular situation of Ghana, Naomi Chazan linked the diminished significance of electoral politics to the generalized waning of interest in national politics in the 1970's.[13] According to her, by 1979 the relationship between elections and the socioeconomic and political realities in the country had become so tenuous that when candidates and voters participated in electoral processes they were merely going through the motions.[14] If this picture is correct, then Rawlings' reticence about—or, on occasion, his overtly stated distaste for—electoral politics was understandable. Why then did he eventually submit himself as a candidate for the presidential election of November 1992? It would appear that he did so because, contrary to the misgivings of experts, and in spite of whatever personal prejudices leaders such as he may have about them, elections continue to play a very significant role in contemporary African politics, for good or ill.

The evidence indicates that authoritarian regimes have been the most resistant governments to popular elections in Africa.

And when they have permitted the vote to take place, it has not been because of a newly discovered love for democratic principles. Rather, elections in such cases have essentially been attempts by these regimes to respond to the crises of legitimacy. Ruling elites in authoritarian regimes like all others relish the idea of a demonstrated public approval of their policies and/or existence. Elections may provide such endorsements. In some situations they may also function as means of recruiting new talent or rewarding loyal members with higher profile sinecures or, conversely, easing out or demoting individuals considered detrimental to the well-being of leadership.[15]

Most authoritarian regimes, be they personal rulerships or military oligarchies, upon coming into power tend to base their legitimacy on performance criteria. In the African case the promise was always of economic growth and development. The unspecified transitional period was when, it was hoped, a serious attempt would be made to fix the problems the country faced. Competitive politics, accountability, transparency, openness, predictability and the rule of law, principles by which a system's legitimacy are generally evaluated, tend to be on a hiatus during this period. But it is only for so long that the regime will be able to sustain this kind of legitimacy. Sooner or later, internal or external exigencies or a combination of both will lead to an erosion of whatever legitimacy it may have. In the 1970's, for instance, the dramatic increases in oil price undermined the ability of many authoritarian governments to derive legitimacy from economic growth.[16]

The most common reason for the decline of legitimacy in authoritarian regimes is the sheer weight of time. As the provisional period begins to look more like a "perpetual transition," the population or certain portions of it begins to agitate for greater access to decision-making processes and greater transparency and accountability. In short, the very basis of the regime's legitimacy begins to be questioned. A country's previous experience with democracy, even when it has not been terribly successful, has often been an additional incentive for this challenge of the system's legitimacy. In such situations, Huntington asserts, the belief remains that, a truly legitimate government is the one that is based on democratic principles.[17]

As their awareness of the intensity of the problem has become even more critical, authoritarian regimes in Africa have had to confront the deepening crises of legitimacy in a variety of ways. The first reaction to the crisis, especially if it occurs early in the lives of these regimes, is one of denial. They simply refuse to admit there is a problem. A second and, perhaps, more common approach used by authoritarian governments to contain sagging legitimacy is increased repression. Sometimes they are deluded into believing that the use of firmer and more aggressive disciplinary tactics in the society will enhance the system's effectiveness. As the experience in Ghana demonstrates, a greater and more efficient use of the coercive machinery of state may, indeed, in the short run, foster a "culture of silence."[18]

An option that is always available to these regimes, but which they seldom willingly follow, is an open admission that the time has come for the reintroduction of democratic processes. Ironically, this change of heart tends to happen a lot, although it invariably is preceded by a change of leadership or orientation.[19]

The typical response of African authoritarian regimes, once they have concede that a return to constitutionalism is inevitable, is to be disingenuous. At this point, for most of them, the main idea is to endeavor to create structures with semblances of democratic legitimacy while simultaneously maintaining the essential authoritarian character of the system. This balancing act, simply put, is an attempt to legitimize the patently illegitimate.

In the attempt to restore constitutional order, the regime has to deal with a whole range of problematic issues, the most pressing of which (because of its significance for regime legitimacy) is the holding of "free and fair" elections. The vulnerability inherent in this proposition, for such regimes, forces them to answer some rather difficult questions before the process even begins. In the Ghana case under review here, the regime had to face questions such as: Is it safe even to sponsor an election? If it proceeds with the election, should it form its own political party or be in coalition with other groups? Is there a guarantee it will win, freely and fairly? If it is not certain about this, should it ensure victory by rigging the election? What will the implication of the choices it makes be on the legitimacy of the regime to be installed at the end of the process? Clearly, holding elections was going to be a monumental challenge for the PNDC.

FOREGROUND TO THE ELECTION

The military coup that brought Rawlings back to power in December 1981 came at a time when, by every indication, Dr. Hilla Limann's Peoples National Party (PNP) government was committed to constitutionally mandated elections in 1983.[20] The provisional government that was subsequently set up was thus, by intent and action, subversive of traditional democratic processes. Indeed, for some analysts, the coup seemed to have been conceived "as a social revolution aimed at the complete and radical change of both the existing socio-political and economic structures."[21] The allusion to an "Ethiopian-type" revolutionary solution for the country's problems implied a clear departure from the democratic principles that the previous regime was struggling to maintain.

According to its architects, this social revolution was to be based on a new form of grassroots "participatory democracy." The idea was to use Cuban-style Workers and Peoples Defence Committees (WDCs and PDCs) to form the basis for the social and economic mobilizing of the population. As vanguards for the defense of the "revolution" the committees were also to act as vigilantes against social ills like corruption, exploitation and abuse of power. In the early days of the "revolution" the actions and especially the rhetoric of the regime were decidedly ideological. There was a marked distinction between the "people" (masses) and "citizens" (privileged classes). The tables were turned against "citizens," and ordinary folks were now to be directly involved in making and implementing decisions affecting their lives. The political orientation of the most vociferous elements of the ruling group was unmistakably socialist. Less than two years later, however, while the regime's rhetoric was still sometimes stridently anti-imperialist and populist, its most significant policy decisions were anything but socialist.[22] By 1983 all of the radical left-wing members in the top hierarchy had been ousted,[23] and the committees, now rechristened Committees for the Defense of the Revolution (CDRs), had begun to be transformed into a new kind of privileged group.

For all the misgivings we may have about the democratic intent of the new structures introduced into Ghana by Rawlings, some give him tremendous credit for attempting to provide realistic solutions for Africa's endemic political and economic problems,[24] problems which presumably have remained immune to the old approaches. Colin Legum, for instance, cites Rawlings together with Sankara and Mengistu, as the only African leaders in recent years to have made serious attempts "to create new institutions with political and economic programs that differed radically form those of their predecessors."[25] This may well be true. On the other hand, it is also important to point out that as exciting and original as these leaders were in their attempts to restructure their respective societies, it is also true that the extreme authoritarianism that their regimes exhibited was detested and resisted by many of their compatriots. It is, perhaps, not by accident that the only one of the three so credited by Legum, who has survived (Rawlings) has done so through the use of those very same due processes they all initially thought were irrelevant and hence condemned.

THE IMPETUS FOR CHANGE IN GHANA

There is a definite wind of change currently blowing over Africa. Regardless of whether this change is inspired by external or internal forces, at the moment, it corresponds to a growing grassroots movement against existing authoritarian leadership reminiscent of the nationalism in the 1950's.[26] The impulse might be stronger in some parts than in others, but in all regions, well-heeled megalomaniacs are being challenged to put their purported popularity to the test in free and, hopefully, fair elections. In the 1970's and 1980's, politics in Africa seemed to have been hijacked by a variety of authoritarian regimes ranging from personal dictatorships to military oligarchies. The struggle now is to win back the rights and privileges many Africans thought the first independence had assured them. In spite of the attempts by endangered regimes and paranoid presidents to derail the efforts, there is already in many countries a fresh openness of expression and in some cases even a tolerance of pluralism.[27]

The pressure for change in Ghana was as much induced by external developments as it was by internal agitation. Domestic pressures were huge, but I would argue that, on a comparative level, external considerations had by far the greater impact on the PNDC.

As stated above, it is not by accident that Ghana usually scores high marks with the IMF and the World Bank and all the Western countries with which it has economic dealings. Arguably it is the one African country that has religiously followed the economic prescriptions of the West. Since adopting the ERP in 1983 it has been consistent in the applications of all proposed remedies, critics would say, regardless of their impact on Ghanaians. And, in macro-economic terms, there seems to be a lot to show, statistically, for the effort. Between 1985 and 1989, for instance, Ghana's economy posted a regular yearly rate of growth of about 5 to 6 percent.[28] For a regime that was not noted for its openness and competitiveness, the amount of economic liberalization it was willing to tolerate was phenomenal. But as Richard Sandbrook points out, when this level of liberalization is accompanied by austerity measures, as the case was in Ghana, "repression, not democratization, is the outcome."[29]

For Western democracies to continue supporting Ghana's economic recovery program, it became necessary for the regime to show clear signs of its commitment to a return to some form of constitutionalism. The turn of events in Eastern Europe made this demand even more imperative. By the late 1980's, the pressure from the West, particularly Britain and the United States, was becoming intense. The US Assistant Secretary for African Affairs even went to the extent of accusing Rawlings and his colleagues of being allergic to democratic reforms.[30] It was especially this kind of prodding coupled with the incessant demands of internal opposition groups that finally convinced the PNDC of the need to return the country to democratic civilian rule.

Recent commentaries on the nature of the state in contemporary Africa have suggested that the state's weakness and fragility have forced many citizens to retreat from participation in national politics.[31] People now tend to focus a lot more on non-formal and local communitarian politics.[32] With the demise of the Convention Peoples Party (CPP) government in 1966, non-formal political participation has been on the ascendancy in Ghana. As opportunities for participation in legitimate political action drastically declined during the periods of military rule, the only serious political outlet available to citizens was in the non-formal sector.

Naomi Chazan identifies two main categories of non-formal political structures. They are: (a) voluntary organizations of the interest group variety ranging from trade unions to women's and professional associations; and (b) primary associations based on local and ascriptive loyalties like ethnic, hometown and kinship groups and associations.[33] The net impact of the intense politicization of these groups has been an escalation of pressure and interest group politics. In all of the three major periods of military rule in Ghana, the greatest confrontations the regimes had were with groups like the Bar Association, the National Union of Ghana Students, the Churches and Professional associations. In a sense, these groups have had to act as surrogates for the non-existent party structures.

By the very name the Rawlings military regime chose when it came into power, Provisional National Defence Council (PNDC), the tacit understanding was that it was a transitional government. But getting the Chairman (of the PNDC) and his colleagues to agree on the appropriate procedures for disengaging proved to be rather difficult. It took over a decade for them to arrive at that point. After the radical coalition,[34] which was the initial driving force of the "revolution" fell apart, the true nature of the regime began to emerge. As Kwame Ninsin points out, it was clear by this time that the "military action which brought the PNDC to power was an ordinary coup d'etat. It merely transferred the existing state apparatus from one group of the political elite to another. It neither destroyed the state machine nor put a new class in a position of political dominance . . ."[35] Shorn of the ideological posturing and rhetoric of the early days, the PNDC had become, in political terms, just another authoritarian regime committed to using populist strategies to hold on to power for as long as possible.

Ghana under Rawlings and the PNDC was an amazing repli-
cation of the ideal model of the patrimonial state Thomas
Callaghy discusses in his essay on "Politics and Vision in Africa."[36] In the first place, in spite of the incessant talk within
the government about the desirability of decentralization, the
significance of the process was only noticeable in the periphery. At the core, executive authority was not only centralized
but extremely personalized. Everyone knew that ultimate power
resided in Chairman Rawlings, the "presidential monarch" and
controller of the state. Secondly, the chairman's position was,
indeed, "legitimated by complex and shifting blends of charismatic . . . and legal-rational doctrines and beliefs, in an attempt to 'routinize' power."[37] The third characteristic of the
model is, perhaps, the one that provides the best fit for the
Ghana case. Rawlings, as the personal ruler, maintained his
grip on the country by appointing personal officials and state
and para-statal cadres whose positions rested mainly on their
personal loyalty to him. The support he received from these
officials had its basis in the complex of ethnic, familial and
patron-client networks the regime maintained all through. The
most powerful officials were the ones in the closest proximity
to the chairman. Finally, as far removed as the regime was
from the era of colonialism, it bore a remarkable resemblance
to the administrative-traditional system that the colonial authorities operated.[38] The power and authority that Rawlings
and his associates wielded reminded one very much of the
absolutism of colonial Governors and Commissioners.

Going by the definition provided by Kenneth Jowitt, it seems
appropriate to characterize Rawlings essentially as a populist
rather than a revolutionary leader.[39] Let me briefly discuss
three aspects of his populism. The element of populism that
has been most prevalent in his political career is charisma.
Arguably, apart from Nkrumah, Rawlings has been the only
other truly charismatic national leader Ghana has ever had.[40]
He is very much aware that he possesses the quality and again,
like Nkrumah, has rightly sought consciously to use it to his
political advantage. He has engendered in his followers a sincere belief that he is the only guarantee for the continued success of the "revolution." This is, perhaps, why he was the only
presidential candidate who, in many ways, was "anointed"
rather than elected or selected in the 1992 party primaries.

The second characteristic of populism that has been evident in his political career is the emphasis he has consistently put on the ethical dimensions of leadership. He seems to think that leadership, above else, should be about moral imperatives (as he defines them). When he first surfaced in June 1979, he warned the country not to think of his intervention as a coup but as a house-cleaning exercise, aimed principally at the hierarchy of the military. He blamed them for the moral degeneration that was so rampant in the country. His "second coming" in December 1981, was again characterized by him as a "jihad," a holy war, presumably against the deformed "democratic state." Couched in these terms it was easy for him to justify the draconian sanctions he and his colleagues imposed on the people judged to have violated on the moral codes of the society.[41]

The third aspect of his populism has to do with his tendency to be inflexibly insistent about the absolute virtue of *the people*. This amorphous concept which sometimes refers to those at the grassroots or to rural folks is elevated and extolled as the primary referent of the "revolution." For him, the only authentic politics is grassroots politics, the kind that allows ordinary folk (people) to become significant participants in the decision-making processes that affect their lives. Rawlings' initial rejection of party politics came out of his belief that, as a rule, parties have always worked to enhance the exploitation of ordinary people. In this view, the immediate beneficiaries are usually the educated middle class and the rich because often they control party apparati.[42]

Some critics have suggested that Rawlings' notion of the supremacy of the people is more symbolic than real. As one bluntly puts it, "politics [in Ghana] since 1981 may be regarded as an attempt to construct a new political framework that will in-corporate the sentiments, values, ideas, and myths of rural society without actually mobilizing the so-called people to attain political and social liberation. The aim is the realization of a new legitimacy for essentially modern authoritative structures by giving the People an illusory sense of political power, participation, and worth."[43]

If the PNDC had had its way, the transition to a constitutional Fourth Republic would have been accomplished without the benefit of an electoral system based on political parties. The model that the regime initially contemplated using bore an uncomfortable resemblance to the discredited Acheampong "Union Government" idea.[44] The government's preference for this option was quite audacious considering that it was the confusion generated by Acheampong's proposal (which many believed was an attempt to "re-legitimize" his dictatorship) that caused his ouster in 1978.

Compared to Acheampong, Rawlings and his colleagues were more successful with their plan even if it did not run its full course either. The way they envisaged it, much of this "politics without parties" was to be played out at the local level, starting with district legislative units. Two thirds of the members of each of the 110 District Assemblies they created in 1987 were to be elected on a non-partisan basis, that is, on their own individual merits. It was hoped that when the National Assembly (the premier legislative body in the country) came into being, the majority of its members would come as electoral college nominees of the District Assemblies.

Over the objections of such well-organized pressure groups as the Trade Union Congress (TUC), National Union of Ghana Students (NUGS), the Ghana Bar Association and the Catholic Bishops' Conference, the government did implement the first phase of the program. The elections to the District Assemblies were held between December 1988 and February 1989, ushering in what the regime termed the era of grassroots democracy. The stage, it seemed, had been set for a new kind of politics.

History, it is said, really never repeats itself, but a lot of times it comes pretty close. The Ghanaian situation is a case in point. Just as it happened during the run-up to the third republic, in the eleventh hour the government changed its mind and reluctantly accepted, late in 1990, that the elections leading into the Fourth Republic would be based on the regular multi-party model. What brought about this dramatic reversal? In its attempt to validate its preference for a no-party model, the government authorized the National Commission for Democracy (NCD) to organize regional debates on the constitutional future of the country. To the regime's surprise by the end of the exercise, the overwhelming consensus among the citizens was for a reintroduction of the multi-party electoral system.[45] The PNDC, thus, had not much of a choice but to acquiesce.

HOW TO TAILOR-MAKE A CONSTITUTION

Once it was decided to return the country to a multi-party constitutional democracy, the immediate problem the government faced was how to draw up a constitution that furthered its goals. Rather than go the open and representative "national conference" route adopted by francophonic African states like Benin and Congo (Brazaville), the regime chose to follow a process in which all the significant aspects of the transition would be under its direct control or influence. It resisted the attempts of opposition parties and some civic groups to make it relinquish power to an impartial interim government and, with very little consultation outside of government circles, drew up the time-table and procedures for the transition.

A committee of experts was set up in May 1991 to formulate proposals for the new constitution. The proposals were then deliberated upon by a Consultative Assembly which submitted a completed draft constitution to the PNDC early in 1992. It seemed, however, that every aspect of the process was problematic. In the first place, many people took exception to the title of the Assembly. Because it was called a Consultative (rather than the usual Constituent) Assembly, the technical implication was that its recommendations would essentially be advisory. That, indeed, was how events eventually played out. The Constitution was promulgated solely by the government, at which time a number of highly questionable transitional provisions were inserted, none of which had been debated by the Assembly. The most controversial of these was the clause indemnifying PNDC members and officials against future prosecutions for any acts of commission or omission during their time in office. Many Ghanaians were upset about this. They thought it was a deliberate attempt to legitimize some inherently illegitimate acts of the regime.[46]

The composition of the Assembly also gave rise to controversy. Of its 260 members, 121 came from the District Assemblies, most of which had strongly argued against multi-partyism during the regional debates. Another 22 were direct government nominees, and several more represented the Armed Forces and other official agencies. Presumably, to validate his populist credentials, Rawlings insisted on the inclusion of representatives from such *peoples'* organizations as the Hairdressers' Association, Farmers' Association, Fishermen's Association, and Market-Women's Association. With so many Assembly members having such obvious ideological ties to the government, many opposition groups charged that the Consultative Assembly had been deliberately put together to produce a tailor-made constitution for the PNDC. To register their protest, two of the most influential pressure groups in the country, the Ghana Bar Association (GBA) and the National Union of Ghana Students (NUGS), refused to take part in the Assembly's work.

It was hard to tell from the way members of the Consultative Assembly conducted themselves (in the Assembly) whether they were conscious of the government's hidden agendas. However, many Ghanaians were encouraged to see the Assembly them make bold decisions on some weighty issues. Two examples of this are their rejection of the idea of dual citizenship and their proscription of chiefs from running as candidates in national elections. On the other hand, the Assembly members tended to avoid positions that negatively impacted on Rawlings' viability as a presidential candidate. For instance, they watered down the citizenship requirement for the presidency to ensure that he qualified. In the previous constitution, one was disqualified if either parent was an alien. Rawlings' father is a Scottish national.

The major provisions of the constitution were: An executive presidency with a limit of two four-year terms; a vice-president to be elected on the same slate; a cabinet to be appointed by the president and approved by parliament; a unicameral legislature with a membership of 200, directly elected through a multi-party system; a traditional judicial system similar to what existed in the previous constitution, with a Court of Appeals as the highest court in the land; and a Council of State.[47] One of the strangest aspects of the transitional program was the government's insistence on subjecting the Constitution to a national referendum. It seemed pointless to require an entire country to vote "yes" or "no" on a document as complex as a constitution. But that was exactly what they did. With the vast majority of the population never having seen it, not to mention understanding its basic principles, the constitution was overwhelmingly (92% majority) endorsed in a referendum held on April 28, 1992. Regardless of the interpretation one put on these results, for the government, the whole exercise was a win/win proposition. Either vote was for some form of continuity for the PNDC. By the end of the entire process it was clear that the government had succeeded in creating the conditions necessary for the constitution to be molded in the regime's own image. But, to be fair, it should be pointed out that this was not unusual. As someone has observed elsewhere: "No matter how carefully prepared, meticulously drawn up, legally elegant, or imbued with liberal concerns, Ghanaian [or for that matter most] constitutions have, first and foremost, served the interests of their molders."[48]

CHANGE VERSUS CONTINUITY:
THE STRUGGLE FOR POWER

The responsibility for organizing the presidential and parliamentary elections, scheduled for November 3 and December 8, 1992 respectively, was given to a government appointed Interim National Electoral Commission (INEC). In the meantime, the ban on party political activities remained in force till May 18. As late as July, most opposition parties were still unable to start organizing seriously because of the restrictive laws governing party registration. It was not until early August that they were in a position to begin campaigning openly.[49]

Approximately ten political groups registered as parties or at least received provisional certification, three of which—the US-based Ghana Democratic Republican Party (GDRP), the New Generation Alliance (NGA), and the radical-left, Popular Party for Democracy and Development (PPDD)—for a variety of reasons, were unable to field candidates. The remaining seven could be grouped into three categories: the center-right, represented by the New Patriotic Party (NPP); the center-left, a bloc of four parties—National Independence Party (NIP), National Convention Party (NCP), Peoples National Convention (PNC) and Peoples Heritage Party (PHP), and, finally, the pro-government Egle and National Democratic Convention (NDC) parties.

Within the opposition, the center-right bloc was the most cohesive. Made up of a coalition which traditionally takes its inspiration from the conservative politics of early nationalists like J.B. Danquah and K.A. Busia, the group (NPP) took the elephant as its symbol and selected the well-known historian, Professor Adu Boahen, as its presidential candidate. The center-left, made up of groups claiming to be followers of Ghana's radical first president, Kwame Nkrumah, was the most fractured of the three blocs. Differences over issues of ideology and leadership and, some would add, the exploiting of these problems by the government, resulted in their registering five separate parties, of which the PNC, the party led by ex-president Hilla Limann was, perhaps, the best organized. The basis of unity for the pro-government groups was their implicit belief in the leadership of Jerry Rawlings. The vast majority of followers of the two parties in this bloc were members of government sponsored "revolutionary organs," para-military bodies and the District Assemblies.

The politicians and parties, especially those in the opposition, encountered considerable criticism during the campaign for concentrating too much on issues of personality rather than policy. The concern over this may be more academic than real. The fact is, all of the major parties tried, and, for the most part, succeeded in putting together elegant documents that spoke eloquently to the goals they hoped to pursue when they came to power.[50] But were people really interested in analyzing these documents? One would have to say most were not, and for a good reason. The elections were essentially about personality or more pointedly, who should occupy Christiansborg Castle[51] (the seat of political power) on January 7, 1993. The fundamental argument was over continuity and change in the leadership of the country.

As November 3 (election day) drew near, two grand coalitions had formed around these polar positions. The pro-government bloc, which had been enlarged by the addition of NCP, a defector from the opposition fold, was, of course, for continuity. In the view of the group which had now been christened "Progressive Alliance," the only way political and economic stability could be maintained in the country was if the incumbent head of state were allowed to continue ruling. Their opposite number, the "Democratic Alliance," made up of the remaining parties and dominated by the NPP, on their part, argued that only a change of leadership could assure Ghana of the re-emergence of democracy and a rejection of authoritarianism and dictatorship.

It was obvious from the start of the campaign that the advantages the government parties enjoyed were enormous. Long before political parties were legalized the government had been using state resources and its general power of incumbency to get a headstart on other political groups. Under the "informal" Eagle Club, para-statals and revolutionary organs like the CDRs and the 31st December Women's Organization were being mobilized in preparation for when the ban on parties would be lifted. During the campaign, government vehicles and other resources like meeting places and rental equipment were all openly used, at taxpayer's expense, for the benefit of the PNDC sponsored parties. About 18 Cabinet and Sub-Cabinet Secretaries and several District Secretaries ran for parliament while still at their posts. Since no distinction was made between state and party activity, the incumbents were, in a sense, able to use the state to underwrite their electoral expenses. Opposition parties and other concerned groups complained in vain about what, according to them, was a patently unfair situation.[52] As Carl Mutt the humorist opined, the whole exercise looked uncomfortably like "Kokofu Football".[53]

Another thing that, some say, strengthened the hand of the government was the ability it had to sow confusion in the Nkrumaist camp (i.e., the center-left bloc). Of the two broad social constellations that have dominated electoral politics in Ghana since the 1950's, the Nkrumaists and the supporters of Busia, it is the former that has traditionally had the broadest base. In fact, much of the support Rawlings and his regime has enjoyed throughout the years has been from that group. With the impending elections, the regime feared many of these people would return to the original group. To forestall that, it succeeded in cultivating its own sub-groups within the bloc. This tactic, together with other internal problems, led to the fragmentation in the Nkrumaists' camp.

LOSERS AND WINNERS

If the odds were so stacked in favor of the PNDC and its incarnation, NDC, then why did the opposition parties agree to participate in the process they now condemn as a sham? In the first place, even if they were initially suspicious of the motives of the regime, they had to recognize that their's was a true case of "Hobson's Choice." The choice was between two evils, to participate or not to participate, and agreeing to do the former was clearly the lesser of the two. Besides, there was always the outside chance the government would be as interested in fairness as, presumably, they were. On the other hand, if they rejected the offer, then they were doomed to a continuation of the system they considered intolerable.

But in fact, when it came to the presidential election, their apprehension of the situation was less sanguine. Conventional wisdom among the opposition parties was that, all things being equal, even with his ability to manipulate certain aspects of the process Rawlings still could not win the election because of the immense unpopularity of his regime. Partisan considerations aside, most objective observers believed that the best he could garner in the first round would be a third of the votes. The expectation was that he would be in a run-off with either Professor Adu Boahen or ex-president Hilla Limann. As it turned out, he not only won convincingly in the first round with about 58.3 per cent of the votes but defeated his competition in all of the regions of the country, except for Ashanti where he came in second (see Tables I and II).

Let us now examine the breakdown of the results and see if there is any merit to the opposition's claim that the elections were fraudulent. From the aggregates and percentages for the regions identified it seems that in all cases the election results defy the actual population figures.[54]

According to the figures released by INEC, the voter turnout was a respectable 48.3% (3,989,020 out of 8,255,056). Based on the actual figure of 12,205,575 for 1984 and projected at an annual growth rate of 2.6, the population of Ghana for 1992 probably was 15,136,118. Even a conservative estimate of 50% of under 18 year olds, would put the projected eligible voter population at 7,569,559 suggesting an overestimation of some

TABLE 1   1992 Ghana Presidential Election Results(by region and party).

NPP	PNC	NIP	NDC	PHP	TOTALS
	WESTERN REGION				
89,830	33,760	21,924	239,477	9,335	394,326
	CENTRAL REGION				
83,982	5,808	11,630	222,092	7,312	330,824
	UPPER EAST REGION				
67,114	67,027	3,944	140,327	3,894	282,306
	EASTERN REGION				
198,744	9,754	11,730	294,783	3,693	518,704
	BRONG AHAFO REGION				
119,551	20,668	9,332	252,805	3,735	406,091
	VOLTA REGION				
17,295	7,427	3,430	446,346	4,105	478,603
	ASHANTI REGION				
347,112	17,607	20,088	176,508	2,954	564,269
	UPPER WEST REGION				
11,535	48,075	2,329	66,049	1,612	129,600
	NORTHERN REGION				
52,540	35,452	4,702	203,004	26,715	322,413
	GREATER ACCRA REGION				
175,401	21,382	18,445	258,046	5,700	478,974
	TOTALS				
1,163,104	266,960	107,554	2,299,437	69,055	3,906,110

Source: *Ghanaian Times*, November 11, 1992 and *The Statesman* (Ghana), December 13, 1992.

685,497. (This figure does not discount for the huge number of people who were unable to register in 1987 when the last national voter register was compiled mainly because they were under-age then.) But, in fact, based on the projections of the "Preliminary Report, 1984 Population Census of Ghana," the maximum percentage of eligible voters in 1992 could definitely have been under 50%. Taking this into consideration and allowing for the discount referred to above, it is not surprising that, for every region cited, the turn-out was higher than the national average (see Table II). The cause of this disparity is traceable to the gross inflation of the base INEC figure to over 8 million for eligible voters.

An evaluation of the actual figures in certain constituencies reveals even more disturbing patterns. In several of them

TABLE II   Election Results by Select Regions
(percentages of eligible voters).

Region	Projected Pop. of 1992	Aggregate/ % of Pop. Age Group 18+	Election Results	Results as % of 18+
Brong Ahafo	1,546,222	728,271/47.1%	406,086	55.8%
Ashanti	2,552,857	1,215,160/47.6%	714,584	58.6%
Central Region	1,319,266	639,844/48.5%	330,824	51.7%
Northern Region	1,528,619	655,578/46.4%	320,973	49%
Eastern Region	2,036,688	1,002,050/49.2%	518,704	51.8%
Western Region	1,436,959	708,421/49.3%	394,326	55.7%
Greater Accra	1,863,478	977,735/52.2%	507,445	52.2%
Volta Region	1,388,461	684,511/49.3%	478,445	69.9%

Source: *Ghanaian Times*, November 11, 1992 and *The Statesman* (Ghana), December 13, 1992.

the turn-out was not only suspiciously high but in some cases exceeded the eligible population, a clearly inexplicable outcome when, officially, no new names could be added to the register after 1987. The most glaring of these inconsistencies occurred in the Volta region. In at least four constituencies there, the turn-out was over 100%. The figures for the four are shown in Table III. Figures in Ashanti and Greater Accra also indicated unexpectedly high trends. In areas like Kwabre and Obausi even the bloated INEC figures suggest that nearly 100% of eligible voters participated, while in the eight Accra constituencies an above national average of 71.6% was recorded.

Thus, on the basis of the figures alone there was good reason to complain about the authenticity of the elections. Clearly, the country will need a more honest register for future elections to be considered truly fair.

The problems about the voters' register aside, what the PNDC seems to have done is simply play the authoritarian elections game to perfection. As Huntington points out, authoritarian regimes have often succeeded in rigging elections by crafting electoral practices and procedures that were favorable to them or their clients, making life difficult for their opponents through intimidation and harassment and finally by openly expending state resources for their campaign.[55] All these tactics were, indeed, employed by the PNDC. But perhaps the

TABLE III   Voting Irregularities in the November 3, 1994 Elections.

Constituency	Population, 18+ years	Election Results	Percentage Eligible
Keta	14,697	24,108	164%
Avenor	26,671	28,742	108%
Dayi N/South	39,144	40,060	102%
Ho Central	31,285	35,918	115%

Source: *The Statesman* (Ghana), December 13, 1992.

regime was not convinced such manipulation alone was suffi-cient because it seemed to have resorted to the ultimate ploy—that of "outright fraud and theft." That too, going by Hunting-ton again, should not be considered all that unusual. According to him, "Authoritarian rulers can steal elections if they want to. Often in the past they were able to steal elections quietly, in unobvious ways, so that although everyone knew the elec-tions were stolen, no one could prove it."[56] That exactly was the dilemma the opposition parties in Ghana faced in the af-termath of the November 3 election. It was, indeed, difficult for them to show exactly how the theft was done. In any case, whatever feeble attempt they made to explain the nature of the fraudulence was, invariably, dismissed by the state-con-trolled media (the *Daily Graphic,* the *Ghanaian Times,* and the Ghana Broadcasting Corporation), the government and its supporters as "sour grapes."

Have there been any real winners in these elections? Super-ficially it would appear that President Rawlings and his follow-ers were the big winners. And in many ways, they really were. The evidence suggests, however, that there was not much jubi-lation in Ghana following the announcement of the results. Even the pro-government media recognized that, more than anything else, the results were noteworthy for the enormous tension they generated in the country. There was sporadic vio-lence in several of the major cities, forcing the government to put the army on full alert. A dusk to dawn curfew was imposed on Kumasi, the capital of Ashanti, where the turmoil was se-verest. This contrasts very sharply with the reactions to previ-ous presidential elections. In 1979, for instance, as disappointed as the losing parties were, they were gracious enough to allow the winners to celebrate their victory because they knew they had lost, fair and square. The fact that there was so much tension in the country this time around was indicative of some deep-seated problems with the entire process. The PNDC may have used all the tricks in the book to ensure Rawlings' victory, but in the end all it did was make a mockery of the process, which in turn has, in the eyes of many Ghanaians, damaged the credibility of the new "civilian" government.

Although the center-right bloc may technically be counted among the losers in the elections, there is a good chance that, in the long run, it will be the real winner. The NPP is now seen as the credible alternative to a new Rawlings regime which is not very different from the illegitimate authoritarian one many in Ghana wanted to get rid of. The NPP took the lead in organizing a boycott of the parliamentary elections by the opposition parties, forcing the Fourth Republic to commence life as a virtual one-party state, a situation that does not bode well for the future political and economic stability of the country.

One of the groups that has emerged as a definite loser in the debacle is the center-left bloc, the Nkrumaists. By allowing its ranks to be infiltrated by the Rawlings camp, it seems to have lost all of the advantages it previously had. A close reading of the results of the elections suggests that the PNDC committed its worst fraud in regions that were the strongholds of the Nkrumaists. The "favorite son" theory for instance, should have enabled ex-president Limann to do well in the three northern regions, but the determination of the government to win, by all means necessary, ensured his defeat even in his native Upper West region. The way things stand in Ghanaian politics now, it will be exceedingly difficult for the traditional Nkrumaist coalition to reemerge as a viable alternative to the current government.

An aspect of Ghanaian life which, paradoxically, will be negatively impacted by the unfolding political events in Ghana is the economy. If western countries and donor agencies have been encouraged by the continuity implied by Rawlings' "election" as president, they could not be too pleased with the manner in which it was done. The zero sum game that was adopted by the PNDC has resulted in a "constitutional" NDC-dominated government which, compared to its predecessor, may be different in form but certainly not in key personnel and policy orientation.

As has been pointed out above, the ERP has enabled Ghana's macro-economic environment to improve considerably. But for the economy as a whole to reach the threshold for a meaningful take-off, the level of direct private investment must be substantial. Under the PNDC, foreign private investment was very limited. Between 1979 and 1989 the total was a paltry $90 million, with the bulk of it going into the mining sector.[57] Indigenous entrepreneurs have also, for a variety of reasons, been consistently cautious about investing in the country. In spite of the enormous economic liberalization that has been fostered under the ERP, Ghanaian businessmen have generally been suspicious about the PNDC's interest in and support for the private sector. Many of them did not forget the humiliations they were subjected to, particularly in the early days of the "revolution." For the most part, it was the authoritarian and arbitrary character of the regime that created the justifiable fears among local, as well as foreign, private entrepreneurs regarding the security of their investments. If the essential nature of the regime is not going to change, then it is likely the political and legal preconditions desired by private investors will remain unmet.[58]

FUTURE PORTENTS

The verdict of the international observer teams on the presidential elections became the butt of cynical jokes in the major cities of the country.[59] Following the introduction of the last PNDC budget (January 5, 1993), complaints to vendors about the high prices of commodities, were often greeted with the wry comment that the new prices were "free and fair."[60] The obvious implication being that both the election results and the new budget were a farce. And yet, soon after the results were declared, the British Foreign Secretary, Douglas Hurd and his minister of Overseas Development, Baroness Lynda Chalker both visited Ghana, ostensibly to lend international credibility to the new Rawlings government. The congratulations that came from several Western countries were also quite warm. To many Ghanaians, these events, overtures and "interventions" taken together, pointed to some form of international conspiracy. They were perceived as a betrayal of the West's oft touted "genuine" interest in the creation of democratic order in a third world dominated by authoritarian regimes.

It was easy to see that the composition of the "new" government and the general structure of the "new" state do not augur well for democratic praxis. The key personnel in the executive branch were the same ones who worked the authoritarian PNDC system to perfection. The economic, foreign and military policy-making bodies were still in the same hands and so were the security agencies. As many people in Ghana suspected, it was, indeed, too much to expect these officials to start acting as the good democrats the constitution wants them to be.

The first parliament of the Fourth Republic has, in terms of composition, inadvertently turned out to be an even better bargain than the government anticipated. Except for two independent representatives, (both of whom happen to be female) the remaining 198 members belong to the NDC-dominated "Progressive Alliance". And for a speaker, the regime selected the former Deputy Chairman of the PNDC, Justice D.F. Annan. With this make-up, it is difficult to disagree with the correspondent who suggests that, "[p]arliament will surprise everyone if it turned out to be more than a rubber stamp for the executive."[61] There is no escaping the fact that Ghana today is all but a one-party state. And judging from the past performance of the judicial branch, the chance of that institution doing anything significant to prevent the reemergence—some would say continuation—of totalitarianism in the country is quite minimal. Even when the constitution has placed considerable trust in judges and the courts as guardians of democratic order (as both the 1969 and 1979 ones did), they could not be counted on to sanction the most serious subverters of the fundamental laws of the land, i.e., successful coup makers. On the contrary, in all cases, the initial legitimacy such usurpers have enjoyed has come from being sworn in by these same judges.[62]

The nomenclature of political structures in Ghana may have changed, but in essence the system is still the same. Rawlings as president rather than chairman is, perhaps, even now better equipped to exploit the patrimonialism that has always characterized his leadership. Just as in the PNDC era, the military leaders and heads of the state security agencies are all an integral part of the government. The civilianization of politics notwithstanding, it seems the potential for these state organs to use the coercive and repressive methods that Ghanaians have grown accustomed to is still great. The totalitarian nature of the regime is fortified by the fact that key appointments in the state system, including the print and electronic media, are still dominated by individuals chosen through the ethnic and clientelistic networks Rawlings has depended on throughout his years in office. When all of these factors are combined with the prospects of a weak judiciary and a rubber-stamp legislature, it can only point to one thing: Authoritarianism is very much alive and well in Ghana.

Notes

1 Countries reported to have sent delegations include Sierra Leone under Momoh, Uganda, and Tanzania. See Maxwell Owusu, "Democracy and Africa: A View from the Village," *Journal of Modern African Studies*, 30, 3, 1992, p. 390.

2 The phrase, "a winning formula," is borrowed from Richard Joseph's characterization of the 1992 elections in *Africa Report*, January-February 1993, p. 44.

3 At its annual meetings in Paris, the Consultative Group on Ghana, has consistently showed its appreciation for the country's economic performance by agreeing to fund most of Ghana's aid requests. In some years pledges were a good deal higher than requested. In 1987, for instance, the $818.6 million provided by the Club was a good $250 million above the requested amount. See *Colliers Year Book*, 1988, p. 239.

4 Rawlings is again reported to have said at a public meeting in Takoradi (January 1982) that he had no intention of handing over. Radio Ghana quoted in *West Africa*, February 1st-7th, 1982, p. 333.

5 The date marks the beginning of the Fourth Republic when Rawlings was sworn in as President of Ghana.

6 Sefa Mohamed, "Questions of Democracy," *West Africa*, August 13th-19th, 1990, p. 2271.

7 Timothy M. Shaw, "Reformism, Revisionism, Radicalism in African Political Economy during the 1990's," *Journal of Modern African Studies*, 29, 2 1991, p. 194.

8 Samuel Huntington provides an excellent discussion of the on-going democratization process in his, *Third Wave: Democratization in the late 20th Century*, Norman, Oklahoma, 1991.

9 Naomi Chazan, "The Anomalies of Continuity: Perspectives on Ghanaian Elections since Independence" in Fred M. Hayward, ed. *Elections in Independent Africa*, Westview, 1987, p. 63.

10 Notably the regimes of Kerekou in Benin, Nguesso in Congo and Kaunda in Zambia.

11 Shaw, p. 194.

12 Hayward, p. 1.

13 Chazan (1987), p. 62.

14 *Loc. cit.*

15 Fred Hayward, p. 13. This, clearly, seems to have been the case with the recent elections in both Ghana and Kenya.

16 Huntington, p. 51.

17 *Ibid.,* p. 47.

18 The repressive nature of the PNDC regime fostered a "culture of silence" which lasted form 1982 to about 1990. The following comment by the well-known historian, Professor Adu Boahen, captures the essence of the public sentiment in the country on the issue: "We have not protested or staged riots, not because we trust the PNDC. We are afraid of being detained, liquidated, or . . .subjected to all forms of molestation." *Colliers Year Book*, 1989, p. 258.

19 An example of this was the June Fourth, 1979 coup against the Supreme Military Council regime of General F. W. Akuffo.

20 Opoku Agyeman, "Setbacks to Political Institutionalization by Praetorianism in Africa," *Journal of Modern African Studies*, 26, 3, 1988, p. 91.

21 Maxwell Owusu, "Customs and Coups: A Juridical Interpretation of Civil Disorder." *Journal of Modern African Studies*, 22, 1, 1986. p. 86.

22 Kwame A. Ninsin, "Ghanaian Politics after 1981: Revolution or Evolution?" *Canadian Journal of African Studies*, 21, 1, 1987, p. 30. Ninsin argues here that the PNDC's actual ideological position was pro-imperialist.

23 Zaya Yeebo's, *Ghana: The Struggle for Popular Power*, (London: New Beacon), 1991, is a candid account of how the "Left" fell out with Rawlings in the early years of the "revolution."

24 Owusu (1992), p. 388.

25 Colin Legum, "The Coming of Africa's 2nd Independence," *Washington Quarterly*, Winter, 1990, p. 129.

26 Commentary in, *West Africa*, May 7th-13th, 1990, p. 751.

27 Shaw, p. 194.

28 For a positive evaluation of the PNDC's macro-economic performance see, James C. W. Ahiakpor, "Rawlings, Economic Policy Reform and

the Poor: Consistency or Betrayal?" *Journal of Modern African Studies*, 29, 4, 1991, p. 583.

29   Richard Sandbrook, "Liberal Democracy in Africa: A Socialist-Revisionist Perspective," *Canadian Journal of African Studies*, 29, 4, 1991, p. 583.

30   Secretary Herman Cohen, on the June 25th, 1990 edition of Channel 4 (British TV) program, "The World This Week." Quoted in *West Africa*, June 25th-July 1st, 1990, p. 1087.

31   Jackson and Rosberg's essay, "Why Africa's Weak States Persist: The Imperical and Juridical in Statehood," (*World Politics*, 27, 1982), sets the tone for this discussion. The more recent volume edited by Donald Rothchild and Naomi Chazan, *The Precarious Balance: State and Society in Africa*, (Westview, 1988) carries the debate a little further.

32   Naomi Chazan, "The New Politics of Participation in Tropical Africa," *Comparative Politics*, 14, 2, 1982, p. 169.

33   *Ibid.*, p. 172.

34   This coalition was made up of militant groups like, the June 4th Movement, the Peoples Revolutionary League of Ghana, the National Democratic Movement, the Kwame Nkrumah Revolutionary Guards and the African Youth Command.

35   Ninsin (1987), p. 26.

36   Thomas M. Callaghy, "Politics and Vision in Africa: The Interplay of Domination, Equality and Liberty," in Patrick Chabal, ed., *Political Domination in Africa: Reflection on the Limit of Power*, Cambridge U. Press, 1986, pp. 30-51.

37   *Ibid.*, p. 36.

38   For a discussion of the administrative-traditional model adopted by military regimes in Africa, see Edward Feit, "Military Coups and Political Development: Some Lessons from Ghana and Nigeria," *World Politics*, 20, 2, 1968, pp. 179-93.

39   Kenneth Howitt, "Scientific Socialist Regimes in Africa: Political Differentiation, Avoidance and Unawareness," in Carl G. Rosberg and Thomas Callaghy, eds., *Socialism in Sub-Saharan Africa: A Reassessment*, Berkeley, 1979. For a critique of Jowitt, see the introduction by Edmond J. Keller in Edmond J. Keller and Donald Rothchild, eds., *Afro-Marxist Regimes*, Lynne Rienner, 1989.

40   Yakubu Saaka, "Recurrent Themes in Ghanaian Politics," *Journal of Black Studies*, Vol. 24 No. 3, March 1994, p. 277.

41 During his "first coming" (June-September, 1979) eight senior military officers, including three former heads of state, Afrifa, Acheampong and Akuffo, were executed by firing-squad, as part of the house-cleaning exercise.

42 Owusu (1992), p. 384.

43 Ninsin (1987), p. 35.

44 Maxwell Owusu presents a less critical view of the "union government" idea in "Political Without Parties: Reflections on the Union Government Idea in Ghana," *African Studies Review*, 22, 1, 1979, pp. 89-108.

45 *Colliers Year Book*, 1992, p. 266.

46 Owusu (1992), p. 371. Contrary to our view, Owusu argues here that these controversial provisions are a sensible effort to prevent the possibility of the politics of vengeance in the Fourth Republic.

47 *The Constitution of the 4th Republic*, Accra: Government Printers, 1992.

48 Chazan (1987), p. 65.

49 *West Africa*, June 1st-7th, 1992, p. 917.

50 An example of this was the PNC pamphlet, "Twenty-Four Months of Peoples National Party Rule," a well-written piece which outlined the essential elements of the policies of the Limann administration and how aspects of it would be adopted in the Fourth Republic.

51 Ironically it is this old Danish colonial castle which has become the seat of government in Ghana.

52 *West Africa*, January 13th-19th, 1992. p. 1102, carries the report of two memoranda from the Christian Churches of Ghana to the government expressing their disquiet over aspects of the arrangements for the return to constitutionalism.

53 Carl Mutt, a humorist in *The Mirror* (Ghana), November 28th, 1992, p. 5. "Kokofu Football" refers to a soccer match in which the referee is also a key player on one of the teams.

54 For an excellent analysis of the election results, see Kwaku Gyimah's article in *The Statesman* (Ghana), of December 13th, 1992.

55 Huntington (1991), pp. 55-57.

56 *Ibid.*, p. 184.

57 Roger Tangri, "The Politics of Government-Business Relations in Ghana," *Journal of Modern African Studies*, 30, 1992, p. 103.

58 See *ibid.*, p. 109 for a discussion of these preconditions.

59 *West Africa*, February 1st-7th, 1993. pp. 140, 164.

60 Of the three foreign observer teams, the Commonwealth group was quickest in declaring the elections "free and fair and free from fear." This position was generally supported by the small Organization of African Unity (OAU) team. It was only the larger Carter Center team's endorsement that came with some qualifications. Joseph (1993), p. 44.

61 *West Africa*, January 25th-31st, 1993, p. 100.

62 For a most perceptive commentary on the ineptitude of the Ghanaian judiciary, see the statement by Mr. Justice Robert Hayfron-Benjamin quoted in *West Africa*, June 29th-July 5th, 1992, p. 1102.

Chapter 8

Visions of Change in Cameroon Within the Context of a New World Order

Henry A. Elonge

INTRODUCTION

The "New World Order" proclaimed by the major western states in the early 1990's has socioeconomic, military and political implications for the rest of the world. Economically, it represents the coming together of these states to properly define their economic interests vis-a-vis the rest of the world. Militarily, it emphasized the need to use force to protect perceived economic and political interests of the powerful states. Politically, with the collapse of the former Soviet Union and the subsequent rise of a multitude of autonomous states in its place, the democratic ideal of governance has become a dominant force globally.

African states have not escaped these new developments, especially the political realities they entailed. The implication of the demise of the Soviet Union on African states is a hotly debated issue. On the one hand, it is argued that the precipitous events that led to the collapse of communism sparked similar protests throughout the continent. But, on the other hand it has also been argued that what happened in the Soviet Union occurred in Africa in the 1960's, when several of the states in the region gained their independence.

The spread of the political ideal of democracy all over the African continent has led to a growing awareness and commitment by mainly Western powers to ensure its success. But the experiment seems to have failed to deal with the realities of these states. In effect, the utility of democracy in these societies depends on how far these societies have integrated their own experiences of governance within the new democratic processes and practices they have adopted.

This chapter focuses on Cameroon's experiment with democracy. It attempts to show how the concept of democracy is undergoing a political metamorphosis in a way that is not necessarily dysfunctional as often perceived. These developments represent, in my opinion, Cameroon's efforts to enrich the concept of democracy.

CAMEROON'S EXPERIENCE IN NATION BUILDING

Nation-building and State-building have historically been processes involving the interaction of ideas and actual deeds. While the two processes may usually compliment each other, they are often separate, far apart, but at times dangerously connected.

The marriage between ideas and actual deeds has great relevance for Cameroon today, because, the "essence" or *raison d'etre* of the nation-state is presently being questioned on the basis of the ideas and concepts upon which they have been built since independence.

Cameroon, which has survived over 30 years of uninterrupted "nationhood" or "statehood" under the labels of "Republic of Cameroon" (1960-1961), Federal Republic of Cameroon (1961-1966), United Republic of Cameroon (1972-1985), and Republic of Cameroon (1985-present), is presently facing a crisis of confidence in terms of the legitimacy of the state. This crisis raises several unanswered questions which must be examined and explained if Cameroon wants to exist as a united country in the years to come.

It is instructive to begin this discussion by posing some fundamental philosophical questions essential to an understanding Cameroon's political democratic efforts. The questions are as follows: (1) "how do we know anything?" (2) "how do we know that we know it?" and (3) "how do we choose among competing claims about what we know?"[1]

If these questions are paraphrased with regards to Cameroon, they will read like this: (1) how do we know anything about Cameroonian democracy? (2) how do we know that we know it? and (3) how do we choose among the competing claims about what Cameroonian democracy is and what it is not? These questions constitute the frame of reference and point of departure in this paper.

Essentially, what Cameroonians are debating about involves their "will" to continue to live together in a single state called Cameroon, and to call such an entity a "democratic" state or whatever. The form that this new entity takes depends on the outcome of this debate. That is why it is important, at this juncture, to examine the philosophical premises of this discourse.

Cameroon's existence and evolution has been influenced by two major factors: (1) the European factor; and (2) the indigenous factor.

On the one hand, there are those who consider Cameroon's history to have begun with the expansion of Europeans. They argue that historically, the name "Cameroon" is a derivative of the Portuguese word *Rio dos Cameroes* (bay of prawns). In the 15th century, the Portuguese found an abundance of prawns at the estuary of the river Wouri (viz, where it emptied its contents into the Atlantic ocean). On the other hand, there are others like me who contend that prior to this period, various societies/ethnicities inhabited this region with different levels of socioeconomic and political organization. The residual aspects of this political culture continue to influence the development of Cameroon. Whichever frame of reference one takes informs his/her analysis and conclusions about the nature and future of the Cameroon state.[2]

The former argument places much emphasis on the European factor in Cameroon's subsequent development while the latter view considers Cameroon's development as representing a conflict between the European and the African cultural heritages, and the struggle of the latter to become dominant.

The point must be made here that between the two views, the European factor has remained dominant and has influenced to a considerable extent what we have come to know about Cameroon and its nature of government. Simply stated, knowledge of and about Cameroon has emanated from this dominant premise, and although it cannot be discounted, it no doubt suffers from the biases and misperceptions inherent in the thinking of those who subscribe to it.

This dominant frame of reference has also involved a deliberate and systematic attempt by its proponents to suppress, distort, and/or destroy indigenous socioeconomic and political "realities" of Cameroon's landscape which are in opposition to their ideas and ideals.

THE "PORGEFRAB" vs. THE TRADITIONAL THESIS

The PORGEFRAB thesis represents Cameroon as a creation of Portuguese, German, French and British colonialism. After the Portuguese discovered and named the country, the Germans, French and British followed this by formally colonizing the country. Germany took control of Cameroon in 1885. Following the defeat of Germany in World War I (1918), Cameroon was partitioned into two (French-Cameroon and British-Cameroon) and governed by France and Britain under the mandate of the League of Nations. After World War II (1945), French-Cameroon and British Cameroon became United Nations trust territories under French and British rule. In 1960, French-Cameroon was granted its independence and a year later, following a United Nations plebiscite, British Cameroon was annexed by the former French-Cameroon and Nigeria (the northern part of the country chose to be with Nigeria and the Southern part elected to join the former French-Cameroon). Thus, from 1885 to 1961, Cameroon was under colonial rule. This period saw the beginnings of the formation of the modern Cameroonian state, founded on imposed European concepts of state development. This process continued after independence.

The predominantly French-speaking "Republic of Cameroon," gained political independence in 1960 and was formally amalgamated with the smaller British-ruled section in 1961, to form a new structure called the Federal Republic of Cameroon. In 1966, this structure was transformed into a Unitary Republic, following a so-called integration of the administrative systems of governance of both parts of the Federation. The United Republic survived until 1985 when it was remodified into its present form, the Republic of Cameroon.

The traditionalists contend that Cameroon's pre-European political structures did not completely disappear as a result of the European onslaught. These political institutions survived colonialism and constitute a major part of Cameroon's political legacy to this date. This thesis is supported by P.M. Kale who has observed that:

> A notable fact is that when the white men came to Cameroon as far back as 1472, they actually met organized states and kingdoms and Cameroonian rulers were addressed as Kings; they signed treaties of amity and of commerce on terms of equality with the representatives of Kings and rulers of other nations.[4]

He later went on to conclude that:

> The advent of Europeans with its concomitant effects disrupted the indigenous system of government and halted the political growth, so much so that today some of the descendants of those pristine monarchs, who are still wearing the crowns and sitting on the stools of their ancestors, are styled and addressed "Chiefs", a nomenclature which has no equivalent in any Cameroon language—Bakweri, Banyangi, Bali, Bakossi, or Duala. This is the baneful result of "Kulture Klash"—Clash of Culture.[5]

The consequences of European influence on the development of the Cameroon state were that: (1) Cameroon developed authoritarian institutions of governance patterned after German, French, and British systems; (2) the structure and constitution of these institutions of governance were inspired by the ideas and ideals of European countries; (3) the development of these institutions was also accompanied by attempts to systematically destroy and efface indigenous practices of governance; and (4) institutions for socialization (schools, churches, and other non-formal organizations) were developed to uphold the virtues and advantages of these new political institutions and forms of governance. More importantly, this process bequeathed to Cameroonians and other Africans a lexicon of terms, including democracy, which have today become the center of debate on what Cameroon should or should not be.

According to the traditional thesis, the basis of existence and evolution of the Cameroon state is faulty because it has been fashioned more by the European factors than by indigenous factors, therefore such visions or debates about the country centered solely around this premise are partially faulty and misleading. This view raises the following questions: (1) if the traditionalists are right, why should Cameroonians continue in this direction? (2) how relevant then are the present terms used in the political discourse about Cameroonian democracy? and (3) what can be done to ensure that Cameroon's experiences correspond to its realities?

A response to these questions will partially answer the remaining two questions posed at the beginning of this essay— "how do we know that we know anything?" and "how can we decide on competing claims of what we know?" Also, it will correct the perceived visions of what Cameroonians think and/or claim to know about the future of their country. Finally, new or enhanced meanings of the terms of the current debate would be sought to influence the restructuring of the state.

THE AFRICAN CONTEXT OF CAMEROON'S DEMOCRATIC EXPERIENCE

A cursory review of the newspapers, magazines, memoranda and other position papers on the state in Cameroon and the shape it should take in the future features the following terms and concepts: democracy; the constitution; federalism; regional autonomy; pluralism; state accountability; ethnicity; legitimacy of the state; state leadership; role of women and the younger generation; economic control of Cameroonians by foreign governments; and national conference, etc., etc. These issues can be categorized into three major groups: (1) ideas/ideals upon which the state is founded; (2) issues dealing with the structure of the polity; and (3) the terms and conditions of group coexistence within the state structure.

Definitions of the concept and practice of democracy abound. But the relevance of these definitions to any particular political situation depends on how people in that society define the concept, its utility and how adaptable it is to their specific realities. An idea or concept could be lofty for one society but mean something different in another society.

Since independence, African states have been grappling with making governance relevant to their societies. As previously stated, most of these states have ended up with governmental models structured on European examples with the unfortunate result that these borrowed models have proved irrelevant to the realities of governance in their countries. Although some of these states, such as the single-party state of Cameroon, have called themselves democracies, the governing mechanisms have not been representative of the population and thus not given citizens the benefits of good government; hence, the present crisis of confidence in the legitimacy of the state.

Claude Ake has argued that democracy represents "the introduction of standards, institutional norms and constraints," that "will guide behavior."[6] In addition, he sees democracy as representing "a dialectical negation of . . . barbaric conditions and the introduction of standards, institutional norms and constraints that will make that kind of behavior . . . impossible." More importantly, he also finds African traditional societies to be inconsistent with authoritarian rule. In other words, he contends that the pre-European African institutions of governance were more representative than present ones.[7] Therefore, although modern democratic institutions may be good for the continent, they must be seriously adapted to reflect attributes of pre-European institutions.

For Richard Joseph, a democratic system is one which both appointive and elective state offices are competed for and utilized not for personal and limited group benefit but transformed in such a way that the "legal-rational, bureaucratic constitutional facade becomes something much closer to a reality."[8]

These arguments in favor of a "democratic" system of governance in Africa represent but the beginning of the debate on the essence of the modern institutions of governance in Africa. With respect to Cameroon, the quest for democracy can be examined on two levels. The first is at the society/system level. That is, should the system of government in Cameroon be democratic? The second level is that of governance. Is democracy just a form of governmental structure? Finally, are the two levels of inquiry complimentary, or can one exist independently of the other?

Bearing in mind that the concept of democracy as discussed in Africa today has more of a Western-European origin, connotation and bias, the question of what truly constitutes a democratic society or system in Cameroon becomes even more paramount.

Cameroon may obviously not be a democracy by any of the standardized definitions (regardless of the guarantees in the constitution and the practices of the governmental system). However, the question is whether the society should attempt to be a democracy at all? Or should it devise a system of governance which is relevant to the needs of its people? The simple answer to both questions is: Yes, Cameroon should become a democracy because it is an ideal and a basis for good government. But this answer is only a partial one. To respond to the question fully requires a greater understanding of the current political dynamics of Cameroon.

POLARIZATION OF CAMEROONIAN SOCIETY

What is clearly evident is that Cameroon is presently a society of two worlds—one European-created and elitist, and the other traditionally-oriented.[9] Political and government leadership assumed since colonial days, that these two societies could coexist without any difficulty. Based on this premise, a selected few were educated and trained to transmit acquired socioeconomic, political, and cultural European values to the traditional majority.[10] This European system was superimposed on a strong ethnically divided country with over 200 distinct groups and about a hundred different languages.

Colonialism and subsequent western-styled post-independent Cameroon governments developed systems of education and socialization to integrate the traditional masses into the mainstream of the modernized Cameroon society not as participants but as spectators. It was erroneously conceived that ethnicity and "tribalism" would "wither away" and make way for a strong nation or state. The chief agents of this new era were the educated elites.

In addition, the basis of colonial society was *de jure* and *de facto* authoritarian. Any institutions that challenged the power and authority of the colonizers were systematically destroyed.

Consequently, many societies not only lost their boundaries but, in addition, had to acquiesce to a system of governance imposed from outside and which in all likelihood was brutal. Government, which by definition had to be, **"of the people, by the people, and for the people,"** became government **"by foreigners (Europeans), through their Cameroonian agents, for European interests."** This form of government never intended to take the wishes of the indigenous masses into consideration. Again it was intended to relegate them into passive obscurity.

The kind of society and government which Cameroon inherited at independence was one with little consensus on anything other than expelling the colonial powers. The government also represented the elite, most of whom had been groomed in the ways of their predecessors to preform the role of mediators and buffers between the "two societies."

As a result, the gap between the two societies continued to widen as the educated elite gravitated more towards European forms of governance and political behavior and practices, with no buffer between them and the masses, while, the other "society" developed internal mechanisms to resist the pressure imposed on them from within. Consequently, the Cameroon that the elites came to "know" was not the same Cameroon the masses "knew."

Despite the fact that the political system has variously styled itself democratic-socialist, planned-liberal and the "New Deal" Democracy, it was indeed alien in the eyes of many Cameroonians. Presently, both the elites and masses in Cameroon have come to the realization that the Cameroon state is in crisis, and remedies must be sought to address that. To paraphrase the words of the political scientist Henry Ejembi, the crisis confronting Cameroon is in some measure moral, intellectual, and institutional; a crisis which is affirmed by all Cameroonian newspapers. It is manifested by moral bankruptcy, ideological poverty and undiscipline among the enlightened publics.[11]

Several years ago, the late Cameroonian philosopher Bernard Fonlon warned in his numerous writings such as "The Task of Today," "Will We Make War or Mar," "Idea of Culture: Culture As Fruit And Harvest," and "Under the Sign of the

Rising Sun", about these impending dangers to the Cameroon state if nothing was done to address the problems confronting the country. Fonlon's prophetic words in these articles were not heeded by the governing elite.[12]

THE NATURE OF THE CAMEROON STATE

Let us examine critically, Harold Laski and Max Weber's (both of whom are authorities in the conceptualization of the modern western state) views on the modern western state. Max Weber considers the state as "a human community that (successfully) claims the monopoly of the legitimate use of physical force within a given territory."[13] Laski on the other hand defines it as "a society . . . which is integrated by possessing coercive authority legally supreme over any individual or group which is part of the society." The state's power which is called *sovereignty*, is used to "organize the collective will of a given society through a body of men and women in its name as the supreme coercive authority which the state disposes; that is, the government of the state." The state is different from the government in that the government is "simply a mechanism of administration which gives purposes to state power." Government is not sovereign in the sense in which the state is sovereign.[14]

Given the European tradition of state development, these two authors may be right to consider legitimate force as the primary characteristic of the state. Many, if not all European states owed their existence to war or some form of violence. But this opinion may not necessarily apply to all societies. And since modern African states can trace their existence to European influence it is not difficult to understand why some of these states are essentially violent in nature.

To understand the nature of any state it is first and foremost necessary to understand the nature of the people who make up that society. Cheikh Anta Diop presents an interesting point of departure on the nature of the African state structure. Diop posits that:

> Africans thus never experienced a lay republic, even though the regimes were almost everywhere democratic, with a balance of powers.

That is why every African is at heart a hidden aristocrat. . . . The deeper reflexes of the present-day African are more closely tied to a monarchic regime than to a republican one. Rich or poor, peasant or urbanite, all dream of being a small or great lord rather than a small or great bourgeois. The quality of their gestures and attitudes, their manner of seeing things, whatever their caste, is lordly and aristocratic in contrast to bourgeois "pettiness." There is still one revolution's distance between African and Western consciences, in terms of instinctive behavior. These aftereffects of aristocrasm would have been extirpated only if the African, in the course of history, had become responsible for his own destiny within the framework of a republican regime. Western colonization, even when republican, could not change these facts. . . . It is hard to trace to this factor a certain aesthetic approach of the Black, although it does seem to be an important trait of the African character.[15]

Herein lies the core contradiction in the vision of the Cameroonian state as perceived by the educated elites and that perceived by the traditional-oriented masses. The educated elite argue for a redrafting of the state constitution to form a western-style democratic, unitary or federated, republican form of government, while the latter perceive and argue for a modern state centered around their traditional visions and forms of governance—a state founded on elements of aristocracy.

THE CASE FOR A MODERN CAMEROON CONSTITUTIONAL STATE

The case for constitutionalism in Cameroon is popular, strong and emotional, especially given the systematic abuse of authority and power by governmental leadership. It is also more of an African problem than one restricted only to Cameroon. This debate on the state has been evident in the academic discussions carried out by the Carter Center African Governance program.[16] With regards to Cameroon, Bernard Fonlon had two decades ago in a treatise titled, "The Task of Today," made a case for a modern constitutional state, while H.N.A. Enonchong had also attempted to describe Cameroon's Constitutional Law in a Mixed Common law and Civil law system,[17] as constitutional arrangements upon which a modern state of Cameroon could be founded.

Recently strong calls have been made for a new constitution for Cameroon, while some have called for a National Conference to accomplish this task. In his "Proposition for the Agenda of a National Conference," C.N. Etinge in the Cameroon Daily *Le Messager* sees the constitution as the "nucleus of the national conference." Ndiva Kofele-Kale also makes a strong case for a national conference to draft a new constitution aimed at restoration—a process of constitutional change whereby the political system resumes an earlier structure to evolve into a viable vehicle that adequately addresses the pressing needs of that society.[18] He suggested a 21-point program to the government for this constitutional conference.

Both Etinge and Kale, jurists by profession, consider the federal constitution of 1961 as a useful baseline. Understandably both of these viewpoints represent the feelings of English-speaking Cameroonians who believe that their region has been "colonized" by the larger French-speaking section.

The call for a National Conference was also made by the Conference of Cameroon Bishops who, in their message of appeal for peace, insisted that:

> It is absolutely necessary that all parties in our national life accept to sit down together, and to talk to one another, as sons and daughters of the same fatherland. Such discussions should be carried out in an appropriate framework with a realistic approach, devoid of any hardening of attitudes. This will ensure that the present situation does not get out of hand, and that we avoid all recourse to extremist solutions, as well as acts of provocation and of repression. In this way we will be able to offer fair and equal opportunities to all those who desire to contribute towards the orderly development of our country.[19]

Finally, within the context of the 1961 constitution, Ebako Mutanga calls for a Ten States Federal Structure.

The call for a new constitution and for a national conference is popular and attractive indeed. But what claim does such an option have against other competing options, such as the government's option for gradual constitutional reforms and change, and the option of working within the unitary state structure or a grassroots approach for a new Cameroon? The attractiveness of the above options should not prevent a thorough analysis of the basis of other options. This is where James Heaphey's thinking becomes relevant as a guide and a basis for any discussion on the future of Cameroon.[20]

According to Heaphey, it would be possible to relate the study of the Cameroon state, society or government to any cosmology, in this case the African/Cameroonian cosmology, and relate its existence to social truths and values. More bluntly, Heaphey would argue that "Cameroon is what it is and that's what it is," and no more. What you see is what you get. It is pointless then to argue or debate whether Cameroon should be a democratic state, socialist state, liberal state, *per se* "Cameroon is Cameroon," no more no less. At one point it can be totalitarian, at other times it can be democratic or socialist. What is important is for Cameroon not to be viewed in terms of fixed or static reality, but in terms of a dynamic reality in a state of "constant flux,"[21] For Heaphey:

> A process approach to reality begins with assemblage rather than system; it is primarily an attempt to understand what is happening rather than with the formulation of a system of concepts and models which we purport to capture the essences of things.[22]

Following the preceding arguments many of the ideas advanced recently in favor of a so-called "democratic system" for Cameroon based on the British/American or European experiences have to be viewed with great skepticism because, those who strongly advocate these ideas are also the same ones who condemn the socioeconomic and political evolution of the country, under especially the Ahidjo and Biya regimes. On the contrary, simply stated, over the past 34 years, Cameroon has had its successes and failures and these should not be denied. The country is just passing through stages of development. What is important to note here is that Cameroon like any other state is in the process of constantly becoming rather than being and should be understood as such.

Such thinking should guide the debate on the democratic nature of the Cameroonian state and refine many of the ideas and ideals proposed for a new Cameroon. It brings out unique aspects of Cameroon's democratic process which must be examined closely before they are discarded as dysfunctional.

The question of form and process remains at the core of Cameroon's democratic debate. Several transitional forms of government have been suggested: (1) limited national conference; (2) "Etats generaux" on specific aspects; (3) non-sovereign national conference; (4) government of national unity;

and (5) the government option of planned democratic reform. What is interesting in these options is that they are all slanted towards Western-European experiences and hardly towards any traditional forms and processes of governance in pre-European Africa.

It is important to note here that the republican constitutional form of government continues to be popular with the elite even though it has blatantly failed to gain the popular approval of the masses. How is this form of government consistent with Diop's "nature of the African" and the kind of government they prefer? To the extent that the values described by Diop are made to shape the former forms of government, Cameroon's democratic experience will be thus uniquely Cameroonian.

The process of instituting any form of democratic change is as significant as the change itself. And the success of any process depends on contextual variables. For example, the electoral code is not just a mere process of conducting elections, it entails (among other attributes), the people's traditions of leadership and rules and procedure of selecting those to be elected. Therefore all new processes of democratization should be instituted against a backdrop of environmental characteristics inherent in Cameroon's internal development and evolution.

Democratic change in Cameroon is occurring within the context of highly polarized ethnic cleavages. The success of these changes will depend on how the system accommodates these ethnic differences. If the form and processes of governance succeeds in doing so, this will be Cameroon's greatest contribution to the concept of democracy. Such a government would actually reflect Diop's wish.

CONCLUSION

The questions raised in this discourse for a national political identity for the Cameroon state should help us to understand where Cameroon is, and where it is going. Mere sermons of democracy as it pertains to America, France, Russia, or Britain are not necessarily the answer. The forms of government in the developed countries are specific to the historical and contextual realities of these countries. They may help shape and inform our vision but they do not necessarily constitute the vision itself. Focusing the debate on the traditional notion of Western democracy would not direct our efforts to devise a system or government unique to Cameroon. In fact, it detracts us from the real questions of our own plight.

Notes

1 Robert Formani, *The Myth of Scientific Public Policy* (New Brunswick, Transaction Publishers, 1990), p. 33.

2 The full extent of this debate can be found in the works of Engelbert Mveng, *Histoire du Cameroun*, (Paris: Presence Africaine, 1963).

3 The German colonial period in Cameroon is typical in the attempt to destroy African institutions of governance. See Harry R. Rudin, *Germans in the Cameroons 1884-1914: A Case Study of Imperialism* (New Haven, Connecticut: Yale University Press, 1938).

4 P.M. Kale, *Political Evolution in the Cameroons* (Buea, Cameroon, August 1967), p. 2.

5 *Ibid.*, p. 3.

6 Claude Ake, "The Case for Democracy," *African Governance in the 1990's*, Working Papers from the Second Annual Seminar of the African Governance Program (Atlanta: The Carter University Center of Emory University, 1990), pp. 2-6.

7 *Ibid.*

8 Larry Diamond, "Beyond Autocracy: Prospects for Democracy in Africa," *Beyond Autocracy in Africa*, Working Papers for the Inaugural Seminal for Governance in Africa Program (Atlanta, Georgia: The Carter University Center of Emory University, 1989), pp. 24-27.

9 Contributions in the local Cameroonian Press such as *Cameroon Press, Le Messager*, reveal the magnitude of the problem.

10 Ahmadou Ahidjo, *The Political Philosophy of Ahmadou Ahidjo* (Yaounde, Cameroun: Paul Bory Publishers, 1968); Paul Biya, *The New Deal: Two Years After* (Bamenda, Cameroon: 1985).

11 Henry I. Ejembi, "Science vs. Philosophy: The Search for a Relevant Political Science," in Yolamu Barongo, *Political Science in Africa*, (London: Zed Books, 1983), p. 20-21.

12 The following publications by late Dr. Bernard Fonlon discussed many of the problems facing Cameroon as a young state. His writings included "The Task Of Today," "Will We Make or Mar," "Idea of Culture: Culture as a Fruit and Harvest" and "Under the Sign of the Rising Sun."

13   H. H. Gerth and C. Wright Mills *From Max Weber: Essays in Sociology,* (New York: Oxford University Press), pp. 77-79.

14   Harold J. Laski, *The State in Theory and Practice* (London: George Allen and Unwin, Ltd, 1936), pp. 15-23.

15   Cheikh Anta Diop, *Pre-Colonial Black Africa* (Westport, Connecticut: Lawrence Hill and Co., 1987), pp. 72-3.

16   *Beyond Autocracy in Africa* (1989) and *African Governance in the 1900's* (1990) Working Papers from the First and Second Annual Seminars of the African Governance Program, (Atlanta, Georgia: The Carter University Center of the Emory University).

17   H.N.A. Enonchong, *Cameroon Constitutional Law in a Mixed Common Law and Civil Law System,* (Yaounde, Cameroon: C.E.P.M.A.E., 1976).

18   Ndiva Kofele-Kale, "Memorandum on An All Party Constitutional Conference: A Proposal in Response to President Biya's Call for a Dialogue with Cameroonians," (Dallas, Texas, July 13, 1991), pp. 1-7.

19   *Cameroon Panorama,* No. 353, May 1991, p. 1.

20   James J. Heaphey, "Legislative Staffing: Organizational and Philosophical Considerations," in James Heaphey and Alan P. Balutis, *Legislative Staffing: A Comparative Perspective* (New York: Sage Publications, 1975), pp. 17-20.

21   *Ibid.,* p. 17.

22   *Ibid.,* p. 19.

Chapter 9

Ethiopia: The Pitfalls of Ethnic Federalism*

Walle Engedayehu

INTRODUCTION

One of the most heralded political developments in Africa after the end of the Cold War was the overwhelming drive towards democracy in countries where authoritarianism had reigned for decades. Africa's trek to political liberalization was aided by events favorable to political democratization at both the domestic and international levels. The cessation of Soviet hegemony over Eastern Europe was followed in 1991 by the breakup of the Soviet Union itself, which also closed the final chapter of the ideological schism that had plagued East-West relations for more than four decades. In the light of the new realities of post-Cold War global politics, coupled with the growing socioeconomic crises plaguing much of Africa, the stage was set for profound political changes to take place in many of the African countries, forcing military dictators and their civilian counterparts to ride with the wind of democracy sweeping much of the continent.[1] While genuine political reforms have since been implemented in a few of the African states,[2] in others, however, the hopes raised by initial political liberalization have been dashed. Perhaps nowhere in Africa has this been more evident than in Ethiopia.

This chapter critically analyzes Ethiopia's experiment with "ethnic federalism" and seeks to understand why the democrati-

* This is an edited version of an article of the same title published in *Africa Quarterly* Vol. 34, No. 2, 150-192.

zation process is currently facing a difficult hurdle under the transitional regime dominated by the Tigrean People's Liberation Front (TPLF). It is argued that the policies of the current regime, especially in respect of ethnic federalism, are likely to lead the country to ethnic disintegration rather than political pluralism. The scope of this chapter is limited to the first three years of transitional rule under the TPLF regime.

BACKGROUND TO CHANGE IN GOVERNMENT

Ethiopia's political history spans over centuries of monarchical rule that was brought to an end in 1974 and a 17-year dictatorship that followed under a military-dominated, Marxist-Leninist regime, led by Mengistu Haile Mariam, who was ousted from power in 1991. It was during Mengistu's reign that the country saw the worst of its civil wars, pitting his government and the well-armed guerrilla fighters of the country's foremost ethnic-based armed movements: the Eritrean People's Liberation Front (EPLF), the group that declared Eritrea's independence from Ethiopia in 1993, and the TPLF, a movement that originated from its ethnic power base in the Tigray province and whose leaders at present are running the government in Addis Ababa. Both the EPLF and TPLF received outside support mainly from Arab governments[3] that have historically had strategic interests in the Horn of Africa.

The EPLF has its beginning in a movement that started in the early 1960's when Eritrea's federal union with Ethiopia was dissolved by Emperor Haile Selassie, the Ethiopian monarch who was overthrown by Mengistu in a 1974 military coup. The TPLF, on the other hand, emerged, along with more than a dozen or so anti-Derg[4] opposition groups[5] in the mid-1970's, as a guerrilla movement that was at first committed to winning autonomous rule for the Tigray province. Having seized the province by force in 1988, however, the TPLF changed its strategy and took on a broader military campaign that ultimately drove out Mengistu from Addis Ababa. In doing so, first it forged a military alliance with the EPLF, whose interest in training and lending support to TPLF fighters against Mengistu was prompted by its own desire to weaken government forces militarily and then win the war of independence it had been waging for almost three decades for the northern province.

TPLF leaders, who belong to an ethnic group that constitutes no more than six percent of Ethiopia's total population and some of whom are also known to be of Eritrean origin, went further by organizing non-Tigrean opposition groups that were all united in their determination to overthrow the Mengistu regime. Thus, the emergence of three other groups— the Ethiopian People's Democratic Movement (EPDM) in 1989, the Ethiopian Democratic Officers' Revolutionary Movement (EDORM) and the Oromo People's Democratic Organization (OPDO), both formed in 1990—did not only add muscle to the TPLF-EPLF military alliance but also gave an added dimension to the multi-ethnic character of the opposition to the Addis Ababa government. In the end, the TPLF, OPDO, EDORM and EPDM together formed what became known as the Ethiopian People's Revolutionary Democratic Front (EPRDF), now the ruling group in the country. The TPLF touted the EPDM as a representative of the Amhara, one of the country's major ethnic groups, while designating the OPDO as an Oromo component of its multi-ethnic alliance. Recruits to the OPDO came from captured government soldiers of Oromo origin, the ethnic group believed to be the largest in Ethiopia. Members of EDORM were government officers who were either captured or who defected to the opposition during the course of the Ethiopian civil war. The EPDM had as its members guerrilla fighters, some of whom were among the remnants of an older armed group known as the Ethiopian Peoples' Revolutionary Party (EPRP), founded by civilian opponents of the Derg regime.

A multi-ethnic Marxist movement, the EPRP first took up arms against the Derg in 1976, when Mengistu and his cohorts reneged on their promise to hand over power to a civilian, popularly elected government. The EPRP then launched its urban based guerrilla war against the Derg during which thousands of Ethiopian intellectuals and youths lost their lives in a campaign of terror and counter-terror carried out between EPRP forces and the government. Having failed to dislodge Mengistu from power, however, the EPRP was finally forced to move from the cities to the countryside, where it attempted

unsuccessfully to relaunch a peasant-based revolutionary movement that would drive out the military from power. But this
campaign in the northern provinces, particularly in Tigray,
brought it in conflict with the TPLF, which was then committed to liberating the province from centralized control by Addis
Ababa. Thus, the rivalry between the two over ideology, territory, and over a number of other political and nationality issues made them bitter enemies. As a single-ethnic-based movement, the TPLF was regarded by the multi-ethnic movement
of the EPRP as too narrowly nationalist.

However by 1980, the EPRP was dealt a severe blow militarily when the government successfully crippled its operations
in the northern provinces of Gondar and Wollo, forcing most
of the movement's rank and file to flee to neighboring Sudan.
In contrast, the TPLF had steadily grown in both manpower
and military strength throughout the decade by virtue of its
association with the EPLF. During that period, the animosity
between the TPLF and EPRP had continued, although the latter had by then lost much of its fighting strength to either the
Derg or the TPLF. While the TPLF expanded its influence
from Tigray to the adjacent northern provinces, the EPRP, on
the other hand, was forced to move what was left of its forces
to Gojjam, where it boasts to be active in guerrilla activities
against the current TPLF-dominated regime in Addis Ababa.

As EPRDF forces, along with those of the EPLF, were fighting their way into the capital in May 1991, the EPRP was in no
military position to bargain for political power-sharing in Addis
Ababa. This realization prompted it to form the Coalition of
Ethiopian Democratic Forces (COEDF) in 1991 with the All-
Ethiopian Socialist Movement (Meison), another civilian group
that first collaborated with the Mengistu regime in the early
stage of the 1974 Ethiopian revolution but was driven shortly
after into opposition along with the EPRP. Although once bitter enemies because of differences in ideology, the EPRP and
Meison, both currently operating in exile from the U.S., are
leading the opposition to the EPRDF government. The COEDF
initially was also joined by such groups as: the Ethiopian Democratic Union (EDU), a movement formed shortly after the overthrow of Haile Selassie and was known to favor the return of
monarchy in Ethiopia; the Ethiopian People's Democratic Al-

liance (EPDA); and the Tigray People's Democratic Movement (TPDM). However, the trio withdrew their membership from COEDF and joined the EPRDF shortly after the latter's seizure of power in Addis Ababa. Their withdrawal stemmed mainly from differences with both the EPRP and Meison over issues concerning the makeup and direction of Ethiopia's post-Mengistu government.

In addition to the COEDF, the exile opposition to the EPRDF also includes the Ethiopian Medhin Democratic Party (Medhin), which is headed by Colonel Goshu Wolde, former minister of foreign affairs under the Mengistu government and who later defected to the U.S. Medhin was formed in the U.S. in early 1992, as the EPRDF ascended to political power in Addis Ababa following Mengistu's ouster. A pro-unity party, Medhin vehemently opposes the right of nations or nationalities in Ethiopia to "self determination, including secession," a right to which the EPRDF, and even to some degree the COEDF, has given full support. As Ethiopia is known to have more than 70 ethnic groups, Medhine's position is that the country's political unity and territorial integrity are inviolable and therefore must transcend rights to which any one ethnic group may be entitled. The philosophical differences between COEDF and Medhin over this issue, however, appears to be superficial in that both favor the preservation of Ethiopia as a united political entity. By contrast, the EPRDF has made the right of self-determination the cornerstone of its policy, a policy that made Eritrea's secession from Ethiopia a reality two years after EPRDF-EPLF forces seized Addis Ababa.

Also included in the alliance against Mengistu was the Oromo Liberation Front (OLF), another one of the ethnic based groups formed in mid-1970's by Oromo nationalists who, like the EPLF leaders, had a vested interest in weakening the central government. An adamant supporter of self-determination for the Oromo people, OLF's ultimate objective ". . . has remained more ambivalent from those of the Eriteans, alternating among increased influence at the centre, greater centralization, regional autonomy and independence."[6] Yet, the movement's underlying motives have always been to carve out a distinctively Oromo territory it calls Oromia from the rest of Ethiopia, which could embrace almost 11 of the 13 provinces, and to develop a cultural identity and pride based on a newly-found nation. According to this brand of Oromo nationalism, being identified with Ethiopia therefore is not only rejected but also loathed, as this would mean the acceptance of the historical domination of the Oromo-inhabited areas by non-Oromo people from other parts of the country. This belief, of course, can be explained partly by the historical development of the Ethiopian state itself and the pattern of exploitative relationship between the north and south that once marked the country's feudal past. The problem was rooted mainly in the land tenure system[7] created and in the manner in which Amhara absentee landlords from the north exploited Oromo tenants in the south. Furthermore, it is generally believed that two-thirds or more of the people and territory of southern Ethiopia were incorporated in the latter part of the 19th century into the state structure dominated by the north, although historical facts also indicate that the integration between the peoples of the two regions had begun four centuries earlier. This started when the heart of the Abyssinian empire of the north was invaded by Oromo warriors, who not only settled in the territories they conquered but also became part and parcel of the ruling elite, thereby influencing Ethiopia's history and politics for more than 300 years. Says Edmond J. Keller, a well-known observer of Ethiopian politics:

> But in certain instances where they [Oromos] penetrated Abyssinian strongholds . . . they were fully integrated into Amhara society, often intermarrying with the Amhara and accepting the Christian religion. There was a good deal of intermarrying between Amhara royalty and people of Oromo origins, and this eventuality resulted in the emergence of nobility and even emperors who were not of a purely Abyssinian stock.[8]

It was, however, against this backdrop that the OLF had been waging a guerrilla war against Addis Ababa for more than a decade and a half, since it saw its armed struggle as one of "liberating" the Oromos from Ethiopian "colonization." With this in mind, the OLF, like the TPLF, allied itself with the EPLF, which used both movements as proxies in its war of independence against Ethiopia. But at no time did the OLF on its own ever pose any serious threat to the regime in Addis Ababa during the course of the Ethiopian civil war. This was partly because OLF's forces were too small, loosely organized and, even more importantly, the movement lacked both legitimacy and mass following among the Oromos whom it claims to represent.[9]

Thus, given its limited military capability, it became strategically expedient for the movement to forge an alliance with the EPRDF and EPLF forces, whose ultimate goal was to topple a nationalist government in Addis Ababa that was determined not only to keep Eritrea from breaking away from Ethiopia but also to prevent the further disintegration of the country; the Mengistu regime saw the growing separatist tendencies promoted by the leaders of these ethnic-based armed insurgencies as a major threat to Ethiopia's unity and territorial integrity.

Therefore, the threat of ethnic and political fragmentation was used by the government as a rallying point behind its policy toward the various ethnic-based insurgencies. Particularly worthy of note is the 1978 Ogaden war in eastern Ethiopia at which time many Ethiopians responded willingly to the "call of the Motherland" as Mengistu harped on the need to repulse Somali invasion behind the cover of the Western Somalia Liberation Front (WSLF). An Ogaden-based movement that came on the scene in 1960, the WSLF's aim was to separate that region from Ethiopia and unite it with neighboring Somalia. The threat ended when the government was able to rally the Ethiopian people behind its military campaign against the ethnic-based invasion in which Somalia played a major part and was defeated decisively.

Nevertheless, the military pressure brought to bear by the aforementioned guerrilla forces on the Derg was undoubtedly responsible for the fall of the Mengistu regime in the end. And yet there were other factors that contributed measurably to the regime's demise such as the debilitating socio-economic conditions in the country and the external political forces that undermined the government in Addis Ababa.

While the Ethiopian economy stagnated throughout the 1980's under the pressure of recurring droughts and armed conflicts, the country's population growth shot up, for example, from an estimated 25 million in the early 1970's to more than 50 million at the beginning of 1990.[10] This meant that the centrally planned economy, which was reflective of the socialist policy the Derg adopted after the 1974 revolution, was unable to meet the hopes and aspirations of many Ethiopians. As unemployment became a chronic problem, particularly for the youth and working-age groups, the regime's ability to govern the country became more tenuous, causing a growing uncertainty throughout the nation.

The unsettling political and economic conditions in the country thus became the major driving force behind the continual migration of thousands of Ethiopians from their homeland to North America and Western Europe, seeking both political freedom and better economic opportunities. First, thousands trekked to the neighboring states of Sudan, Kenya and Djibouti for fear of being forced to join the ongoing civil war in the north of the country. From there, many ultimately were admitted as refugees to the U.S., Canada, Germany, Great Britain, Italy, France, Sweden and to a number of other European countries, where some became active opponents of the Derg, exposing its undemocratic, repressive methods to foreign governments. They held occasional rallies and demonstrations and demanded a democratically-elected civilian government that would replace the Derg. Their actions would become a source of major embarrassment for Mengistu's dictatorial rule, prompting Western governments, the U.S. in particular, to disapprove of Western development loans to Ethiopia. The regime's human rights violations were often used as the reason for denial.

Inside Ethiopia itself, opposition to the Derg, though officially suppressed, continued to manifest at times in some surreptitious ways, and on rare occasions openly, amongst some members of the military, the bureaucracy, and the general population, in the countryside and cities. The regime was regarded with contempt by many in the country for placing military-turned-civilian officials[11] in top political positions throughout the bureaucracy.

To facilitate direct control, the administration of each government ministry and agency was made subservient to the whims of political cadres belonging to the ruling Marxist party.[12] At all government-run-service-oriented facilities such as schools, hospitals and hotels, managers and administrators that were not members of the Workers Party of Ethiopia discharged their official functions and responsibilities under the watchful eye of party representatives. At times, the party representatives and non-party bureaucrats, who were primarily responsible for much of the administrative and managerial work at the various government agencies, constantly bickered over questions, ranging from policy formulation to dispensing orders to mid-level officials and workers.[13]

The steadfast interference of political cadres with the day-to-day functions of the bureaucrats in the major cities reared, over time, a great deal of resentment, causing a hostile atmosphere at the work-place and even a belligerent attitude towards the regime and its civilian allies. This sort of tension gradually bred further a feeling of indifference toward government policies and directives, chronic tardiness by workers, and endemic corruption amongst officials and administrators at each level of the bureaucracy.

Likewise, the public posture toward the government in cities and the countryside appeared to be one of antipathy during most of the 1980's. Farmers in some parts of the country became non-receptive to the twin Derg policies of villagization and resettlement and to farmers' cooperatives established in many parts of Ethiopia. These were strategies borne out of the belief in agrarian socialism for which Ethiopia was being readied by its Marxist politicians and economists. These policies perhaps caused the most revulsion and resentment among farmers towards the Derg.

While much of the development effort in rural areas went into effect to alleviate the famine, the policy in large measure turned out to be a failure. First, the government was unable to carry it out vigorously for lack of funding, and, second, a stern opposition inside and outside the country to a scheme that was uprooting villagers from their traditional homelands and moving them to distant villages under the guise of socialism proved a difficult hurdle to overcome. Many opponents saw the policy as politically-motivated rather than development-oriented.[14] Consequently, the Derg's support in the countryside was extremely minuscule at worst and non-existent at best.

In the cities, on the other hand, where the Derg had a much more effective control over the lives of residents, opposition to the government was more restrained. Public demonstrations against the regime were not permitted. The experiences of the Red Terror Campaign,[15] launched by the Derg in the latter part of the 1970's against demonstrations and the EPRP during which thousands of students and civilian sympathizers were gunned down by the revolutionary guards in Addis Ababa and other cities, had not gone unnoticed; it made an open defiance against the government an unworthy venture.

However, throughout the decade and a half, city residents in Addis Ababa and elsewhere privately expressed their abhorrence of the government in ways that appeared at least to foreign observers to suggest nonchalance or total resignation from political life. Of course, the fear of being persecuted by the government must have played a key part in this culture of silence.

In the same vein, a deep-rooted repugnancy to the way in which the war against the guerrilla forces in the north was conducted was evident within some army divisions stationed in the region. At the forefront of their grievance was the fact that their material needs were not well provided for and their personal and family welfare was not adequately protected. It was common, for example, for members of an army division stationed near a battlefront in the northern region to serve in the frontline for a great number of years without either a vacation or being rotated with members of other divisions stationed in less stressful areas. Further, the troops were aggrieved over the inadequacy of uniforms, meals, and pension and health benefits.

What was even more troubling to the soldiers and their commanding officers in the north was that their efforts were not being appreciated by the higher-ups in Addis Ababa. They envied their superiors and military-turned-civilian colleagues, who, under the provisional military administration earlier on and under the republican form of government established in 1984, were enjoying the comforts of leadership positions in the capital city. But the soldiers had to endure the daily threats of guerrilla ambushes in their camps and all the discomforts of fighting a seemingly never-ending civil war. That thousands of Ethiopian troops were discontented with their political leaders and therefore fought the guerrillas with a subdued spirit, halfhearted determination, and fading enthusiasm for the war was never in doubt.

Thus, from 1988 until May 1991, it was clearly evident that the guerrillas' offensive campaign against the Derg in the northern fronts was significantly aided by continuing troop desertions on the other side, stemming from the aforementioned conditions, and by weapons that fell into their hands either taken from deserters or recovered from government warehouses. These events made the major difference in their ultimate victory over government forces.

However, the internal problems of the Ethiopian government were not by themselves the cause of the Derg's downfall. Some dramatic events that had taken place in the international arena also added to the political misfortune of the regime in Addis Ababa. These events were in large measure precipitated by the end of the Cold War, and more specifically, by political events in the former Soviet Union and the rest of the Eastern bloc.

The structural reforms initiated by Mikhail Gorbachev, the ex-president of the Soviet Union, in the second half of the 1980's through his policy of perestroika, "not only revolutionized the dynamics of numerous international relationships but it has also altered the course of domestic events in a dozen or more countries."[16] One of such countries was Ethiopia. Strategically located in the Horn of Africa, the country had been a close ally of Moscow and of the socialist countries of Eastern Europe. Thus it was a political pawn in the East-West struggle for a sphere of influence. However, with the ending of that struggle and the further lessening of the ideological, military and diplomatic wanderlust between the two superpowers, came the dispensability of some Third World countries that were once objects of superpower rivalry. Ethiopia, thus, became inconsequential strategically for Moscow. Not only did Mengistu lose his ideological ties with Moscow and Eastern Europe, but he was also deprived of the Soviet military support and diplomatic cover that were crucial to the survival of his regime.

As the largest recipient of Soviet arms in sub-Saharan Africa for a decade and a half, Ethiopia had acquired more than

$12 billion worth of sophisticated military hardware that made its armed forces one of the most powerful in the continent. Some of these arms were initially shipped to Addis Ababa when the country was threatened by secession in the north and by Somalia's irredentism in the east, beginning in the late 1970's. Soviet arms shipments continued until the latter part of the 1980's. Moscow also provided the Addis Ababa government with most of its petroleum needs at a price lower than the world market, which was reciprocated by Ethiopia with coffee, hides and other non-industrial products. However, as the Soviet Union embraced a revitalization scheme designed to bolster "an infusion of large amounts of capital into the production of consumer goods for both domestic consumption and exports,"[17] economic priorities thus took precedence over ideological compatibilities when dealing with its Third World allies. The Soviets reasoned that neither Ethiopia's financial position nor its military campaign in the north at the time made a rational sense to continue supporting a crumbling, dictatorial regime in Addis Ababa. Even then, Moscow did not abandon Mengistu abruptly.

In accord with the new Soviet foreign policy objectives, Gorbachev and his advisers pressed Addis Ababa to follow the Soviet path in terms of reforming its economic and political structure. They encouraged the regime to adopt a policy that would steer the economy away from socialism. Noting the futility of continuing the costly war against the EPLF and TPLF, the Soviets also advised the Ethiopian government to seek a political solution to the decades-old conflicts. However, the Derg, with or without Soviet support, seemed content with the pursuit of both its socialist policies and the war efforts against the rebels.

With Soviet military and diplomatic support gradually waning by the end of 1990, however, the Derg made a desperate attempt to seek alternative arms supplies, courting the governments of China, North Korea and Israel. But none of these countries replaced the Soviet Union as a major supplier of arms to the Addis Ababa regime.

The end of Ethiopia's dependence on the Soviet Union promoted the need for a renewed effort by the Derg to reach out to other countries for friendship and diplomatic support. Therefore, the government's rapprochement with the West, particularly the U.S. during the latter part of the 1980s. As U.S.-Soviet ideological confrontation ebbed by the end of the decade, American attitude toward Marxist Ethiopia also tempered. In 1989, the first serious attempt to find a diplomatic solution to the Eritrean crisis was initiated by former U.S. President Carter, with the blessing of the U.S. State Department. As a result, two meetings—the first in Atlanta, Georgia, and the second in Nairobi, Kenya—were held under his chairmanship, but both failed to produce a breakthrough because of disagreements between the representatives of the government and the EPLF over procedural and substantive matters.[18]

By 1990, the Derg, officially shunned by the Soviets and generally viewed unfavorably by the West, continued to impress upon the Americans that it was casting off its leftist orientations and even ready to adopt Western-prescribed reforms in the once centrally-planned Ethiopian economy. As part of this effort, Mengistu announced on May 5, 1990 the end of socialism in the hope that it would quicken Western development assistance and interest in the areas of capital investments and tourism, both of which had come to a halt after the 1974 revolution. By the end of 1990, the Ethiopian government made yet another friendly gesture toward the U.S. and its allies in the diplomatic front. As an alternate member of the U.N. Security Council for 1990, Ethiopia cast its vote in support of the U.S.-led military campaign against Iraq, which had occupied Kuwait since August 1990. Yet neither his diplomatic gesture toward the U.S. nor his announcement of doing away with socialism won Mengistu any friends in the West.

At the close of 1990 and the first half of 1991, the Ethiopian regime was at a historic crossroads, visibly shaken by events resulting from the end of the Cold War and also deeply overtaken by a series of domestic crises that made its downfall much more inevitable. Not only was the regime's ability to govern the country increasingly undermined by all the events described, but also severely hampered by immediate domestic problems such as shortages of fuel, which had devastating effects on the economy overall. In the end, these events provided a major lift to the military campaign waged by the EPRDF-EPLF forces against the Derg and facilitate their ultimate success in driving Mengistu from power in May 1991.

ETHNIC POWER CONSOLIDATION

While the fall of the Mengistu regime was seen largely as welcome news throughout Ethiopia, it was greeted with a subdued emotion in many parts of the nation since it came at a time of extreme public apprehension and about an unknown political future. Public anxiety in Addis Ababa and elsewhere in the country had been fueled by concerns about the political objectives of the two northern-based rebel movements.

Particularly worrisome to many was EPRDF's position on the question of Eritrea. The Front, as indicated in the earlier discussion, had taken a position that would recognize the rights of self-determination, that is, independent of the northern province, thereby incurring the wrath of many Ethiopians who are religiously protective of the unity of their country.

The Eritrean issue therefore had caused such a sharpened political and ethnic polarization between Eritreans and non-Eritreans, and in some cases between Tigreans who supported the EPRDF's position and non-Tigreans who opposed it, that no one knew for certain what the change in government would bring. Because of political and ethnic cleavages borne out of this and other issues, a dominant view had begun to emerge, with an expression that the coming to power of the EPRDF in the Ethiopian capital would not only lead to Eritrea's secession, but also trigger an inter-ethnic conflict of major proportions. It was also feared that in the battle for control of Addis Ababa between the remnants of the Derg forces and the rebel armies, many lives would be lost and properties destroyed.[19] All of this, of course, did not occur in the way it had been feared, except for the secession of Eritrea. This came to the open as the EPRDF took power in the capital and announced, as expected, its support for Eritrea's independence.

EPRDF's ascension to political power was first sanctioned at a U.S.-brokered peace parley held in London on May 27, 1991 among representatives of the EPLF, EPRDF and OLF. Thus, there was no doubt that a major turning point in Ethiopia's political history was in the making when it was disclosed after the meeting that EPRDF forces would enter Addis Ababa to maintain law and order and establish a provisional, broad-based government responsible for introducing a democratic system based on political pluralism.

The collapse of the Derg and its replacement by the EPRDF set in motion at least four major political developments, the social, economic and geo-political consequences of which are already being felt in Ethiopia and will be felt in the years to come. First, the ultimate control of Eritrea by the ERDF, after having defeated 120,000 Ethiopian troops around Asmara and captured all the weapons left behind by the Second Army Division and the naval facilities on the coast of the Red Sea, brought to an end one of the long-running liberation struggles ever seen since the post-colonial era in Africa. This was a significant event in Ethiopia's political history in that the country's territorial integrity, which both the governments of Haile Selassie and Mengistu Haile Mariam had made the cornerstone of their national policy, was, for the first time, dealt a fatal blow as the province won its independence, with the blessing of a new government in Addis Ababa.

Second, in the eyes of many observers, it was also the end of Amhara "domination" over other ethnic groups in Ethiopia. However, this was a perceived rather than actual domination and therefore the subject of heated debate. This issue will be treated at some length later. Third, the predominant view among observers was that the change in government offered Ethiopia the best prospects ever for transforming its traditionally authoritarian political system to a system based on an open and free political competition, respect for human rights and civil liberties, freedom of the press, and other democratic rights intrinsic to any society committed to the highest principles of democracy. Finally, the events of 1991 also produced more than just the ouster of an unpopular regime in Addis Ababa. In its aftermath, the new social and political order that was introduced aggravated inadvertently—though many may say intentionally—inter-ethnic animosities among Ethiopia's numerous nationality groups in ways that the country had never known before. I will explore each of these points throughout this segment. But first a brief discussion about the formation of the transitional government in Addis Ababa and the ethnic oligarchy that has developed during the transition.

The one-month interim administration in Addis Ababa under the EPRDF was followed by a national conference, which was held in the capital city from July 1-5, 1991, among a number of political organizations and social groups, as stipulated by the U.S.-brokered peace talks in London. The conference was "organized and carefully stage-managed"[20] by the EPRDF which took upon itself the task of spearheading a major drive to assemble as many diverse ethnic and political organizations as it could within a one-month period. As a result, 20 different political organizations and groups participated in the presence of foreign delegations invited by the EPRDF as observers. The participant organizations and groups were:

> The Ethiopian People's Revolutionary Democratic Front (EPRDF).
> The Benshangual People's Liberation Movement (BPLPM).
> The Ethiopian Democratic Union (EDU).
> The Ethiopian Democratic Coalition (EDC).
> The Ethiopian National Democratic Organization (ENDO).
> The Gambella People's Liberation Movement (GPLM).
> The Western Somalia Liberation Front (WSLF).
> The Sidama Liberation Movement (SLM).
> The Somalia Abbo Liberation Front (SALF).
> The Islamic Front for the Liberation of Oromoia (IFLO).
> The Oromo People's Liberation Front (OPLF).
> The Oromo Liberation Front (OLF).
> The Afar Liberation Front (ALF).
> The Isa and Gedebursi People's Movement (IGPM).
> Representatives of the Guraghe nationality.
> Representatives of the Hadiya nationality.
> Worker's Representatives.
> Representatives of the Addis Ababa University instructors.
> Representatives of the Ometic People.
> Representatives of the Adere People.

The foreign observers included representatives from the U.S., the former U.S.S.R., Great Britain and ten other nations, as well as delegates from the U.N. and the Organization of African Unity (OAU).[21]

The meeting adopted EPRDF's national Charter, which was to serve for the two-year transitional period as the legal document by which Ethiopia's government would be run and its future political, social and economic system decided. The participants agreed to set up an election commission that would prepare the country for local and regional elections within the two years, after which a permanent national constitution would be drafted by a constituent assembly and approved by popular vote.

The Charter, which outlines the structure and principles of the transitional government, provided not only for the freedom of expression, association and peaceful assembly, but also for the "right of nations, nationalities and peoples to self-determination." It created a government consisting of a Council of Representatives of national liberation movement, political group and prominent individuals, all preemptively hand-picked by the EPRDF to make up a total of 87 members. Neither the political party of the former government nor any of its members were allowed to take part.

As a legislative body and one empowered to exercise ". . . all legal and political responsibility for the governance of Ethiopia until it hands over power to a government popularly elected on the basis of a new constitution,"[22] the Council was also to elect its chairperson, who would become the head of state. Participants agreed to all the provisions of the Charter, with the sole abstention coming from the representative of the Addis Ababa University (AAU) instructors, who objected to the deal worked out in advance by the EPRDF and EPLF on the latter's independence. At the conclusion of the five-day conference and the adoption of the Charter, the EPRDF came out, as expected, the big winner, having secured the presidency, premiership and the defense, foreign affairs and interior portfolios of the newly created provisional government.[23]

In accord with the Charter, the appropriation of legislative seats in the Council was voted on by conference participants. Of the 87 Council seats created, six were left unfilled as they were reserved for groups that did not make the conference because of the short time between "liberation and the convening of the conference."[24] The seat assignments to the 20 organizations and groups were approved by a majority of the conferees, with abstentions cast by the IOLF, EDU, ENDO and the AAU representatives, and one opposing vote registered by the EDC. Each of these groups may have been displeased by the number of seats awarded to their organization. Seat allocations were as shown on Table 1.

Despite its accomplishment in creating a democratic forum for a debate on Ethiopia's political future, the EPRDF confer-

Table 1   Seat Allocation in the Ethiopian Council of Representatives

Organization/Group	Assigned Council Seat(s)
EPRDF	32
OLF	12
IFLO	3
ALF	3
Worker's Representatives	3
WSLF	2
GPLM	2
BPLM	2
SLM	2
Guraghe Nationality	2
Hadiya Nationality	2
Kembata People	2
Wolaita Nationality	2
Ometic Group	2
Adre Nationality	1
EDO	1
EDC	1
EDU	1
ENDO	1
IGLM	1
OALM	1
Ogaden Liberation Front	1
OPLF	1
AAU Instructors	1
–	6 (vacant)
Total	87

Source: *EPRDF News Bulletin*, 1, 9, 8 July, 1991.

ence was faulted for a least three major deficiencies. First, it failed to have the EPLF participate in the process, along with all the other organizations, in a spirit of national reconciliation and within the framework of a united Ethiopia, both of which could have been vital to a permanent political stability and peace in the region. The EPLF was accorded rather uncharacteristically an observer status in the same diplomatic stature as the delegates from the O.A.U., the U.N. and the ten countries in attendance. The fact that the EPLF's presence took the character of an independent state prior to any formal declaration as such and a recognition of the same by a popularly elected Ethiopian government removed the chances of bringing the Eritrean-Ethiopian conflict to an amicable conclusion. A negotiated settlement acceptable to both the peoples of Eritrea and Ethiopia would have been the desired outcome.

On the contrary, the meeting made Eritrea a non-issue; thus, it would not be difficult to imagine the extent to which this may affect adversely the nature of politics in the Horn of Africa in the years to come. Lacking the resolution of this issue to the satisfaction of all concerned, the conference to many Ethiopians, particularly those whose interests were not represented by any of the participant organizations and groups, appeared to be a sinister effort by the EPRDF to gain credibility in the eyes of the international observers in attendance. This was at least the prevailing view among members of the COEDF, Medhin, and a few other political groups that were formed after the change in government such as the United Democratic Movement (UDM), a multiethnic political organization created immediately after the conference and the All-Amhara People's Organization (AAPO), established in January 1992 to protect the rights of Amharas and to promote the unity of Ethiopia.

In retrospect, members of the COEDF, Medhin, UDM, AAPO, and others not associated with these groups may have never fully embraced the outcome of the conference because of the Eritrean issue in general and, more specifically, because of the Charter's provision for the right of nationalities to self-determination. Many Ethiopians consider this right as an invitation to political fragmentation at best and self-destruction at worst. The implications of this issue will be discussed further. Moreover, the fact that the COEDF and Medhin were not part of the national conference meant that two of the most recognized exiled opposition groups that would have challenged the deliberations at the conference were excluded. This was a major setback for a conference, touted by observers in the West as the epitome of Ethiopia's path to national reconciliation and political democratization.

According to the COEDF, its representatives to the conference were denied entry permits to Addis Ababa by EPRDF's Washington office, adding that political differences between its group and the EPRDF made it difficult for the coalition to function as a legal political opposition in Addis Ababa. In an open letter, a few months after the formation of the EPRDF dominated provisional government, the coalition wrote, criticizing the government's policy of exclusion, as follows:

> . . . in a demonstration of our unrelenting commitment to ensuring peace, national unity, and civil liberty, the Coalition of Ethiopian Democratic Forces (COEDF) requested the Ethiopian Embassy to issue passports to its delegation. The purpose of the request was to enable us to initiate peaceful and legal political activities in Ethiopia by organizing a headquarter there. The Ethiopian transitional government, which portrays itself as the promoter of democratic transition in Ethiopia, has yet to prove its sincerity and commitment. Barring COEDF from functioning as a legal and democratic opposition force in Ethiopia, is in and of itself, a blatantly undemocratic act.[25]

The EPRDF's response to this and similar accusations was that the COEDF had in fact excluded itself from becoming part of the national government. According to numerous statements put out by the government, members of the COEDF did not attend the conference because its leaders had been insistent not only on having the conference held outside Ethiopia, but also having it chaired by a team of impartial mediators from Canada, the U.S., the O.A.U., and the European Economic Community (EEC),[26] conditions which were unacceptable to the EPRDF.

Aside from the absence of the exiled opposition groups, questions were raised with respect to the participant organizations themselves. It was revealed that of the twenty political organizations and social groups present at the conference, no more than six[27] were known to have ever existed in Ethiopia as organized opposition to the Derg. Therefore, critics argued that their participation was either orchestrated or coerced by the EPRDF to gain credibility in the eyes of the international delegates it invited as observers.

Some of the conferees who supposedly represented ethnic groups, such as the Hadiya, Guraghe, Omotic and Adere, for instance, were created instantly by the EPRDF when it took power shortly after the collapse of the Derg. Reports also indicated that representatives such as the WSLF's had their legitimacy questioned by others in their organization, while groups like the BPLM and GPLM were seen as no more than just "shadowy" organizations unknown to many Ethiopians.[28]

Finally, the Charter itself came into question since it had been put together by the EPRDF itself, perhaps with the help of the EPLF. Although having the Charter during the transitional period was a good idea, the fact was that the document had been prepared well in advance by a group that was already in power on account of its military victory and had not contained inputs by the other participants. This was confirmed, for instance, in the ways the allocation of legislative seats in the 87-member Council was made. The problem with the seat allocation was that it showed no evidence as to the type of criteria used for determining the number of seats each group received, nor did it provide a hint to whether or not population count of each ethnic group or any other factors played a role in the allocation of seats to each nationality. Was the seat assignment correlated with the strength of the guerrilla army each front fielded against the Derg? What was, for example, the rationale for appropriating 32 Council seats for the EPRDF and 12 for the OLF? Was the EDU, a movement that began in 1975 and a recipient of one seat, less important than the BPLM, which no one knew or heard of until the conference and yet was awarded two seats in the Council? Were all Ethiopian nationalities represented in the Council? If not, what was the **basis** for including some and excluding others? Were the selection of these groups and their seat allocation based exclusively on ethnic considerations? If that was the case, what justified the absence of Amhara representation? These and many other similar questions remained unanswered.

On the positive side, however, the Charter's provisions for freedom of expression and peaceful assembly were hailed by many as a major victory for Ethiopians, who had been silenced for 17 years under the Derg's authoritarian rule. Providing an unprecedented freedom, the provisions made it easy at first for opposition groups to voice their objections to the policies of the EPRD government. To test this newly-found freedom, political groups such as the United Democratic Nationals (UDN) and AAPO organized mass rallies in Addis Ababa against the EPRDF's position on Eritrea, as well as against the reconstitution of a new ethnic-based map for the rest of Ethiopia. Legal political demonstrations, though unprecedented in that country's history and therefore a good measure of freedom of assembly, did very little, however, to influence the policies of the Transitional Government of Ethiopia (TGE). As officials of the government were not popularly elected, they were simply not accountable for their actions.

Besides, EPRDF's tolerance of peaceful assembly, freedom of association and the right to engage in unrestricted political activity in Ethiopia quickly evaporated, as the opposition to its policies increased in both numbers and intensity. Therefore, throughout most of 1992 and 1993, the TGE, used social and economic pressures, existing statutes, and outright harassment against opposition parties and groups critical of its policies. Says, Makau wa Mutua, Project director of the Human Rights Program at Harvard Law School, who visited Ethiopia in 1993:

> The first main sign that the EPRDF does not intend to compete politically for power with its rivals came during the 1992 elections. EPRDF security and armed forces, which also serve as government forces, engaged in the widespread harassment, intimidation and arrest of non EPRDF political actors and individuls . . . Since the election, the TGE has become increasingly intolerant of dissent.[29]

The authoritarian character of Tigrean leadership came to light even more sharply in three major actions the government took against its critics. In January 1993, EPRDF security forces reportedly killed in Addis Ababa at least seven university students and wounded more than 100 during a demonstration protesting the role of the United Nations in the Eritrean independence referendum.[30] Following that incident, the TGE took over the administration of the Addis Ababa University, dismissing 42 professors and instructors and adopting increased security surveillance of the campus. Among the dismissed faculty were some of the country's most distinguished scholars. They were dismissed not only for their opposition to the government's highly controversial ethnic map but also for being Amhara, the ethnic group that has been targeted by the Tigrean leaders since they came to power.[31] A more violent government action against the opposition occurred in September 1993, when more than two dozen Christian worshippers in the city of Gondar were killed and wounded by EPRDF security forces under the pretext of arresting a religious leader that the government considered a threat to its rule in that Amhara region. Following that incident, more than 2,600 followers of the popular clergyman were arrested; most of whom were released early in 1994.[32] EPRDF's repression of its opposition in Ethiopia was not limited to these incidents, however. As an organization representing the interests of the Amharas, the AAPO, along with the OLF, was seen by the TGE as a major threat and thus was subjected to frequent political harassment. The organization's headquarters in the capital was occasionally broken into, and its leaders were subjected to constant security surveillance and even to unwarranted arrests. Some members of the organization became victims of government-sanctioned kidnapping, and a few were reported to have disappeared.

As the Amharas were the only ethnic group not represented in the Council, the Tigrean-led government seemed determined to stifle the political activities of the AAPO, as the latter endeavored to open branch offices in the various regions of the country to promote solidarity among members of the ethnic group. Describing the plight of the Amhara under Tigrean rule, Worku Aberra states:

> Historically, the Amharas, who constitute about a third of the population have been politically and culturally dominant. The present government is shamefully exploiting this fact for its own short term objectives. . . . The government is still conducting a propaganda campaign through the government owned media against the Amharas, brandishing them as exploiters, colonialists and oppressors. It has outlawed the election of Amharas in southern regions. Its' cadres continue to seize with impunity the property of Amharas, especially vehicles. It continues to lay off Amharas from civil service and government-owned companies, a process described as "ethnic cleansing" by its political opponents.[33]

In the face of growing opposition, the TGE has showed increasing intolerance of others as well. For example, following the departure of the OLF from the Council in 1992, the government in 1993 expelled five non-EPRDF parties from the Southern Peoples' Democratic Coalition (SEPDC) after which the groups reported harassment of their staffs by security forces and permanent closure of their offices. Two others—EDU and the Agaw People Democratic Movement (APDM)—were also kicked out from the quasi-legislative body in January 1994 because of their participation in a peace and reconciliation conference held in Addis Ababa in December 1993.[34] In a related development, members of the Moa Anbessa Society, a pro-monarchy advocate group founded in June 1991, also reported early in 1994 that their supporters in Gondar and Wollo provinces were arrested, adding that their offices in both provinces were closed down for no apparent reason. The Society is known, along with the EDU, to favor the return of the Ethiopian monarchy to its centuries-old sovereignty in a model patterned after Great Britain or Japan.

The new ethnic oligarchy thus developed during the transitional period has come largely with the help of ethnic satellite organizations created from time to time by the government and whose loyalty to Tigrean leadership was never questioned. EPRDF's domination of the government, the military, and the transitional process provided the impetus for controlling the major social, political and economic institutions of the country, hence the authority to punish opponents and reward supporters. This "divide and rule" policy was further promoted by government control of the public media which, in effect, has become the principal mouthpiece of the TGE.

Although as many as 65 private publications were sold on the streets of Addis Ababa by 1993, a controversial Press Law has since curtailed press freedom. In the same year, EPRDF authorities seized and destroyed selected magazines for being critical of the government's actions against the opposition. In January 1994, editors of 18 privately-owned magazines were rounded up for questioning, and a few were reportedly in prison without formal charges for articles critical of the government. Since the broadcasting media and major newspapers were controlled by the regime, the content of news, opinions and viewpoints therefore continued to promote the government's position. No attempt has been made to make them free from any government control and ownership.

With respect to fairness within the judicial system the record of the EPRDF has been dismal. *Africa Watch*, the Washington-based human rights group, observed in its May 8, 1992 report that serious abuses of human rights were occurring in Ethiopia, adding that "Sadly, in Ethiopia today, obtaining justice remains a privilege, not a right."[35] Citing a resurgence of politicized and militarized ethnic problems throughout the country, the organization called for: the immediate halting of arbitrary killings and arrests of political opponents of the government; a reestablishment of the rule of law under a functioning police force; and the creation of an independent judiciary. While commending the EPRDF for making the Universal Declaration of Human Rights as supreme law in its Charter, it pointed out, however, that in many areas the actions of the government did not match the promises stated in the document.

Particularly troubling to the human rights watch group was the lack of civil rights for members of the previous government. Following EPRDF's seizure of power, Ethiopia's army of more than 400,000 men was demobilized, causing a severe unemployment problem in the country, particularly in the capital, where 27,000 ex-servicemen found themselves without jobs and unable to support their families. Consequently, many soldiers were forced to sell their weapons to buy food, thus making firearms readily available in Addis Ababa, and increasing the frequency of robbery and other types of crime in the city.

Meanwhile, former top members of the dissolved Workers Party of Ethiopia remained in prison, awaiting trial since June 1991. Party functionaires of the former government were not only denied certain civil rights, but also were barred from running for political office. While the government claimed that this denial was a temporary measure to ensure that former government supporters would not undermine the effort to democratize the society, *Africa Watch* condemned this measure, saying ". . . the denial of civil rights to a category to people on the sole basis of their membership of the WPE is not justifiable. For WPE members should be held accountable solely on the basis of individual criminal acts."[36] Throughout the first and the second year of transitional rule, close to 2,400 political prisoners were held awaiting their days in court, among whom were members of the politburo of the WPE and hundreds of high-ranking officials of the former government. Since the *Africa Watch* report, the government has released 1,300 of the detainees held for crimes committed under the previous government. At the beginning of 1993, the TGE held more than 20,000 OLF soldiers, most of whom were released in early 1994.

OVER-EMPHASIS ON ETHNICITY

In retrospect, though, the EPRDF's effort to convene the national conference and adopt a charter that would create conditions for political democratization in Ethiopia was very much in tune with what the majority of Ethiopians had wanted. However, the popular sentiment foresaw very little of the major problems discussed so far. Besides helping bring about the secession of Eritrea, which is likely to alter the future character of the Ethiopian state, EPRDF's monopoly of power has had an even greater impact on the nature of ethnic relations in the rest of the country. Whereas previous Ethiopian governments had discouraged the overt expression of ethnic differences as the basis of governance, which in their view, would have amounted to social disharmony and political fragmentation, the new regime by contrast is striving to promote a new social order in which ethnic identity with the right to self-determination would define the national character of the Ethiopian state. Under the new order, the "political unity" of Ethiopia thus would be based on the degree to which "ethnic assertiveness" at all levels of political and social institutions is promoted and accepted. The state, as the prime agent of the new order, would not only encourage but also execute policies, which would ensure the right of each nation to preserve its nationalist identity, promote its culture and history, use and develop its language, and administer its own affairs within its own defined territory.[37]

In contrast, it had been the national goal of both the Haile Selassie and Mengistu governments to uphold a social myth, based on accepted historical justifications, that Ethiopia's national strength rested on the inviolability of its territorial boundaries, as well as on the inseparableness and/or "oneness" of its people. Though ethnicity had always been recognized as a major feature of the Ethiopian society, both governments, nonetheless, never considered it to be a significant element in the formulation of national policy, let alone creating conditions in which each ethnic group would feel "separate and different" from one another. In the past, each group, at least officially, was made to feel and have a place in the cultural milieu of the larger Ethiopian society, as defined, of course, by the ruling class. And this class consisted of members from each of the major ethnic groups (including the Oromos, Amharas, Eritreans, Tigreans, Guraghes) and of the minority segments of the population.

Although no data was available to show the exact ethnic distribution relative to political, economic and social positions held by members of each group, it would not be far from the truth to contend that no one nationality group ever had the exclusive control of national political life in Ethiopia. Contrary to the perception that the Amharas had been the dominant group in Ethiopia, a close evaluation of the past and present political and socio-economic status of each of the country's ethnic groups may prove otherwise.

The perception about Amhara domination militates against the fact that the most underdeveloped parts of Ethiopia's provinces are predominately inhabited by this group and that Amharas had been subjected to political repression under previous Ethiopian governments like members of any other ethnic group. Therefore, anti-Amhara hysteria whipped up by the TPLF, OLF and EPLF over the years was brought about because of the continued use of Amharic as an official language of the state, beginning with the reign of Emperor Tewodros (1855-1872), and its use in a limited way as a language of instruction in schools until the change in government. Both of these facts, however, gave neither a political privilege nor any economic advantage to the majority of the Amhara group. In sum, one can argue that the Amharas had no better economic, political and social standing under previous governments than the rest of the population groups in Ethiopia. To the contrary, many of the poorest peasants in the countryside,[38] the larger segment of the unemployed in Addis Ababa and that city's non-skilled workers—maids, servants, guards, and prostitutes—and the poor, all come historically from this group. In the view of Patrick Gilkes, the belief that the Amharas were the privileged group in Ethiopia was more imaginary than real:

The Amharas are widely, if inaccurately, perceived as the ruling elite of Ethiopia, in part because of the simplistic equation caused by the use of Amharic as a national language.[39]

However, to the OLF, TPLF, and EPLF, Amhara domination had been more real than imagined. Both the Haile Selassie and Mengistu governments were regarded by these organizations and others as Amhara-dominated, although all the major ethnic groups were represented in the highest positions of government.[40] Had the Amharas been the sole beneficiaries under these regimes, one may argue, they would not have helped, along with all other ethnic groups, in bringing down both governments. It was not a coincidence then that the fall of the Derg and its replacement by the Tigrean-dominated EPRDF brought no armed resistance from the Amharas as no privilege, be it political or economic, was lost by them.

The fluidity upon which the "Amhara domination" argument is based, therefore, has prompted one observer to ask the following hard questions:

If the [Ethiopian] state is simply an Amhara conspiracy against the rest of the people who inhabit it, why have the inhabitants of Wag, Lasta, Saynt, Gaynt, Semyen, Manz and Juru [all Amhara-inhibited districts] remained at such a low level of economic and political development? Why [were] they such strong opponents of [the Derg] that [was often characterized as Amhara-dominated? If the vast southern regions brought into the Empire by Menelik ll suffered such deep alienation from it, why have they generated so little resistance. . .] If Northerners find Amhara and Oromo so unappealing. why have so many Eritreans and Tigreans migrated southward. and why do they continue to take advantage of opportunities to participate in government professions and trade throughout the country?[41]

However, the ethnic-based policy being promoted by the new government is targeted primarily at the Amharas and is further justified in large measure to overcome economic, social and political inequalities among nationalities that, for all practical purposes, had been nonexistent. According to this policy, each group is to utilize its own manpower and natural resources found in its own respective region and embark on a "separate" development. The means by which to accomplish this is the creation first of an "ethnic map," consisting of 14 newly-drawn mini-states based, for the most part, on linguistic and ethnic considerations.

THE NEW "ETHNIC MAP"

Following an agreement between the OLF and the EPRDF on October 18, 1991, the newly made national map was presented a few months later to the Council and got approved. However, the idea of the ethnic enclaves the provisional government attempted to create was met with stiff opposition, both inside and outside the country. The new ethnic map would give a big chunk of the fertile lands of Gondar to Tigray—home of the Tigrean-dominated EPRDF—and benefit the OLF, which "draws most of its strength from areas firmly within the new Oromo region."[42] Regardless of the rationale behind the new map, any policy that would create ethnic enclaves in Ethiopia would be tantamount to forcing people to believe in "nationhood," other than Ethiopian nationhood, that, whether in real or imagined terms, does not exist in the minds of the majority of Ethiopians, irrespective of their ethnic backgrounds. Critics of the government saw the map as a way of dividing up Ethiopia to weaken its potential strength in the face of Eritrean independence and to lessen the likelihood of its reemergence as a strong state. They said that the objective was to prevent Ethiopia from reasserting its leading role in the Horn of Africa. One opponent of the government saw the consequences of EPRDF's policy as follows:

> According to EPRDF's new map of Ethiopia, there will be two states. To the north is Eritrea as a united one people state; and in the south, what remains of Ethiopia will be a South African apartheid system where people are divided into tribal homelands. This will secure a viable, independent Eritrean state and also guarantees the EPRDF a strong position within the remaining pieces of Ethiopia.[43]

The problems of remarking Ethiopia's map based on ethnic particularities and the danger such an undertaking could pose to certain regions of the country have been accurately described by another critic as follows:

> The leadership of TPLF does not understand that the problem of ethnic identity is one which is fraught with many complexities. A person-

can be defined as a member of an ethnic group in one of three ways: by history, by choice and by opposition. Historically no evidence exists for the proposition that the people of Gondar, Welo, Gojam and Shewa have ever sought to define themselves as Amharas. On the contrary, they along with others have always sought to define themselves as Ethiopians. Nor is there any evidence that they have ever consciously made the choice to define themselves in terms that exclude others. Thus, the only way in which they can be regarded as Amharas, in a non-religious sense, is by imposing such a definition on them, whether they like it or not—that is, by opposition. As a matter of choice or history, however, identities such as Gondar'e and Shew'e do have a good deal of validity. Remember that Shewa, Gondar, Gojam and Welo do not just describe real estates. Rather, the histories of these regions may be sources of particular identities for the inhabitants of these regions. It is these particularities, no less real than Tigrean particularism, that the new map maker.seeks to destroy and supplant with an inarticulate and nonexistent Amhara identity. Finally, the decision to reconstitute Ethiopia along ethnic lines, even assuming such identities have clear-cut boundaries, will face further difficulties. Dividing Ethiopians along ethnic lines runs the risk of accentuating and freezing ethnic identities in ways that may undermine the meaning and value of Ethiopian citizenship. The more ethnic groups turn upon themselves and concentrate on what divides them from others, the more it costs their members in terms of their chances/opportunities in the larger system. Also, to freeze ethnic identities runs the risk of inter-ethnic friction and conflict, a risk that has already materialized in much of southern Ethiopia.[44]

Despite the problem cited above, the policy of "ethnic federalism," as the EPRDF government prefers to call its policy, was perhaps an idea borne out of a belief by its proponents that the decentralization of power from the center to regional units in Ethiopia would not only be democratic, but also efficient in terms of decision-making at all levels of government. A sharing of constitutional powers between a national government and its regional constituent parts is indeed a form of federalism and thus a major feature of a democratic political system. And it is this democratic principle that may have prompted the proposed rearrangement of Ethiopia's administrative regions. According to the government and its supporters, ethnic federalism would provide for an equal development of nationalities in their own defined territories that would lead, in the long term, to a peaceful, stable united Ethiopia. The assumption is that when social and political equality is achieved among historically "unequal" nationalities in the totality of Ethiopian life, the chances of political unity and stability among them could be much greater in the future. The principle of self-determination therefore would be the foundation upon which this could begin. A supporter of the EPRDF's policy of self-determination and its formula of ethnic federalism argues that Ethiopia's more than 70 ethnic groups of which ten are major national groups must have the right to determine their own future, adding that:

> As a Somali-Ethiopian, self-determination means a lot more to me than a mere secession from Addis Ababa: It is an integrated political principle which promotes the Somali culture, language and history at no one's expense. It is a doctrine of coexistence.[45]

An opposing view to the policy of ethnicization, however, paints a different picture:

> We should all remember that people who are divided along ethnic lines and do not dream of national greatness cannot survive as a state. That is the lesson of Yugoslavia.[46]

While admiring in principle the idea of self-determination, another critic of the government's policy makes a convincing argument against its application to Ethiopia:

> Self-determination is a noble idea which basically entails the principle of government by consent. It does not mean balkanization of a nation to exact vengeance on a group that has been oppressive.[47]

"Oppressive" is a reference used by the EPRDF to describe Amhara's role in previous governments and therefore the major reason for invoking the principle of self-determination. However, this very principle and the problems it has created in multi-ethnic states prompted the following comments by Arthur Schlesinger, the noted American historian and Pulitzer prize winner:

> . . . Ethnic conflict is tearing nations apart.. The virus of tribalism risks becoming the AIDS of international politics, lying dormant for years then flaring up to destroy countries. The time had come to reconsider the doctrine of self-determination and to incorporate the limitations. . . . The objective should not be to give every people the

right to choose the sovereignty under which it shall live It should rather be to seek ways by which people of diverse ethnic, religious and racial background can be brought to live together in harmony under the same sovereignty.[48]

The immediate result of this new policy of ethnicity in Ethiopia has been the proliferation of more than 100 political organizations—both multi-ethnic and single-ethnic—that are pro or against the policy. As ethnicity became the overriding factor in the dispensation of social services, in the area of political appointments, in the distribution of limited resources for regional development, and in many other government decisions, the pace of ethnic polarization has quickened, and political polarization has reached its highest point.

One of the immediate fallouts of the new policy was the intensification of inter-ethnic rivalry on the political front between the two major political actors in Ethiopia—the EPRDF and OLF. As a junior partner in the provisional coalition government, the OLF discovered about a year later that the EPRDF had violated "the letter and spirit of the Charter,"[49] of which both were the main signatories. Calling the Tigrean-dominated EPRDF "dictatorial," the OLF accused that:

> . . . the EPRDF has put all the legislative, executive and judicial powers under its total grip and conducts everything as it wills and wishes. There is no police force to maintain law and order; no independent courts and EPRDF armed forces are dictating their will at gunpoint everywhere in the country . . . .[50]

The two former rebel movements became at odds as the EPRDF began gradually asserting its power in areas controlled by the OLF. In the southern provinces, where the OLF claims to have a large following among the Oromos, EPRDF encroachments into OLF's strongholds brought the two into military confrontations. Hundreds of deaths were reported to have resulted from periodic clashes between the two rival forces throughout the first half of 1992 and after. Mediation efforts by outside parties failed to produce a negotiated settlement of their political differences.

Massacres by the EPRDF's Oromo followers of Amharas and other Christians in the provinces of Arsi and Harrar were frequently reported. This came about as a detailed account of the killings of more than 300 Christian Amhara inhabitants reached the international community and became an embarrassment to the EPRDF government in Addis Ababa. One version of the events in the South, however, alleged that the EPRDF itself may have been responsible for the massacre to incite ethnic clashes between the Oromos and the Amharas in the region, who are the two largest ethnic blocs in Ethiopia. In any case, the government's inability to protect civilians against ethnically-inspired killings in the region contributed in large measure to the deterioration of relations between ethnic rival forces.

Critics of the EPRDF government charged that the politics of ethnicization were largely to blame for what happened in central and southern Ethiopia, where inter-ethnic conflict had reached alarming proportions, involving not only the Amhara, but also the Afar, Adere, and Isa population groups. According to a report prepared in Amharic by the surviving victims of the Arsi violence, the EPRDF government:

> . . . deliberately wanted not to publicize.. the massacre of innocent Ethiopians in Arsi, let alone taking action to protect them as any one sensible and ethnic-blind government would have done to protect its innocent, unarmed citizens . . .[51]

REACTION TO ETHNIC OLIGARCHY

In the light of the growing dictatorial tendencies of the Tigrean dominated regime in Addis Ababa, a sense of urgency—fuelled by revived nationalist sentiments—has stirred up the opposition. Though still divided and scattered, Ethiopian opposition forces have reacted to the emergent ethnic oligarchy on two major fronts, one involving a peaceful approach and the other an armed struggle.

The first and foremost of the response has been a sustained non-violent struggle in which both well-organized groups and loosely-organized masses of concerned Ethiopians have protested occasionally against the policies of the TGE, both inside and outside the country. However, freedom of assembly—although guaranteed in the Charter—was met with brute force in Ethiopia as evidenced by the incidents regarding the student demonstrators at the Addis Ababa University and the

Amhara Christian worshippers in Gondar city. In both cases, peaceful protestors were shot and killed. Public demonstrations also have been held throughout the transitional period in many parts of the country, usually targeted against the government's policy of dividing up the country into ethnic enclaves. This policy is seen by many as a disaster waiting to happen, citing the recent Yugoslavian crisis.

More often than not, Ethiopians who live in North America and Europe have made their anger known to Western governments through peaceful protests against EPRDF's monolithic political domination, urging them to half diplomatic and financial support for the Tigrean regime. In the U.S., in particular, supporters of domestic Ethiopian political organizations, such as the AAPO, have continued to plead with American authorities to use diplomatic pressure so that the Addis Ababa regime could be forced to negotiate with the opposition.

As part of the peaceful approach, a few opposition parties also have served notice on the EPRDF by simply withdrawing from the executive and quasi-legislative bodies of the transitional government itself. For example, seeing its power base being undermined by the EPRDF, the OLF withdrew from the coalition government in June 1992. The OLF justified its withdrawal by citing EPRDF's intolerance to its political activities in the central and southern provinces. This was supported by the reports of an international observer team, organized by the African American Institute to monitor the balloting in Ethiopia's 1992 regional elections. The team concluded that voting irregularities and manipulations by the ruling EPRDF party prevented fair, open and democratic competition.[52] The OLF boycotted the elections after its candidates had been arrested and its party offices shut down by the government. It was also joined by the AAPO, the Ethiopian Democratic Action Group (EDAG), IFLO, and the Gideo People's Democratic Organization (GPDO). The OLF further claimed that the EPRDF had violated the electoral laws passed by the Council, adding that ". . . at each instance the [EPRDF] honored only those provisions . . ." that favored their strategy of domination.[53]

The AAPO's withdrawal from the elections came in the wake of reports of OPDO's massacre of Amharas in the south and in response to the continuous harassment of its members by government security forces. AAPO president Professor Asrat Woldeyes gave a detailed account of the atrocities perpetrated against Amharas by the EPRDF-created Oromo organization, indicating further the inability of his organization to operate freely—as guaranteed in the Charter—in Addis Ababa and elsewhere in the country. His office in the capital was reportedly ransacked by armed government agents in an effort to intimidate him and other leaders of the organization and prevent the group from protecting the rights of the Amharas through political and legal means. His statements painted a bleak future regarding the peaceful participation of his organization in the democratic process, predicting that he may be forced by the government to close altogether the offices of his organization.[54] Woldeyes was jailed after he was allegedly found guilty of crimes against the state.

However, the AAPO still continues to wage its non-violent struggle primarily by sponsoring public rallies against the government. The organization has even pleaded its case before the United Nations, the United States Congress, the European Parliament and before other multi-national and human rights' organizations believed to have some influence on Ethiopia's transitional government. For instance, in one of the letters sent by the AAPO to the Carter Center in Atlanta, Georgia, the president of that organization wrote:

> AAPO has been managing its activity peacefully and its main task has been to open branches all over the country for the purpose of gathering information and to preach harmony between various ethnic and religious groups. The information so gathered are used for pleading to the TGE to have gruesome and extensive atrocities that have been carried against Amharas be stopped. However, the TGE, from the outset has seen the organization with disfavor and every conceivable way of stifling the activity of this organization has been used, disregarding all the claims of democracy and respect of human rights.[55]

Also worthy of mention in the peaceful struggle against the EPRDF is the withdrawal of the five southern ethnic minority parties[56] in 1993 and their recognition of the need for a non-violent approach to effect desired political change in Ethiopia. However, the action of each of the opposition groups cited above was met with either indifference or outright condemnation by the EPRDF of both the group's motives and of the legitimate demands it put forth to reverse Ethiopia's slide into a dictatorship.

More recently, the search for a peaceful resolution of the political crisis in Ethiopia took a dramatic turn when the previously divided opposition came together for the first time for an open and democratic dialogue on Ethiopia's political future. First, the COEDF, the most vocal of the opposition, organized a conference in Paris in March 1993 on "peace and reconciliation" in Ethiopia, which was attended by Medhin, the SEPDC, the Tigray-Tigrigny Ethiopia (TTE), the Afar Revolutionary Democratic Union (ARDU), the Multinational Congress Party of Ethiopia (MNCPE) and the OLF. Though invited to attend the parley, the AAPO was unable to participate because the government denied exit visas to its delegation. The EPRDF and its ethnic satellite organizations simply refused to attend.

The Paris conference passed a resolution, demanding the inclusion of all political organizations in the transition to democracy in Ethiopia and the suspension of the results of the regional elections that were held in the summer of 1992.[57] Noting that the TGE was headed toward dictatorship, the participants called for a national peace and reconciliation conference to be held in Addis Ababa, involving all political groups and including the EPRDF and its satellite organizations. The conference, in effect, demanded the suspension of the transitional process that has been underway under the tutelage of the EPRDF.

In accord with the Paris resolution, the National Peace and Reconciliation Conference (NPRC) was held in Addis Ababa from December 18 to 22, 1993. Though dubbed by the EPRDF as a "propaganda exercise,"[58] it brought together a wide range of political organizations and was attended by labor activists, elders, scholars, professionals, religious leaders and civic organizations. In the presence of 31 foreign diplomats and 20 non-governmental agencies, 45 domestic political organizations and six opposition groups from outside the country were assembled. Having succumbed to U.S. pressure, the TGE allowed the Conference to be in Addis Ababa, but the TGE neither attended the Conference nor was it impressed by the resolutions passed by the participants. In fact, the government had attempted to gag the Conference by arresting seven of the participants, who were to represent the COEDF, OLF and Medhin, on their arrival in Addis Ababa. They were accused of "the murder of hundreds of thousands of Ethiopians" under Mengistu, of having "waged war on the transitional government" or of having "conducted terrorist activities inside the country." Six were let go after the Conference while one still remained in jail after having been formally charged with an alleged crime.[59]

Among many other resolutions, the Conference declared that there was no democracy under the TGE and thus demanded that the government step down by January 1994. The participants concluded with a resolution, stating the need for a new transitional government, which would also include the EPRDF. It established a new body known as the Council of Alternative Forces for Peace and Democracy in Ethiopia (CAFPDE). In theory, the CAFPDE consists of all political groups and would function as an alternative government body but with no formal powers to enforce or execute its decision. Among the tasks assigned to it are: the formation of a new transitional government; the establishment of a police force that is diverse and reflective of the ethnic makeup of the nation; the institutionalization of an independent press that is free from government control; and to "organize itself and create various working committees, sub-committees etc. to address and help resolve issues and problems in the areas of foreign policy, internal affairs and other relevant issues."[60]

In reality, though, the mandates given to the CAFPDE by the participants are not accomplishable, given EPRDF's entrenchment throughout Ethiopia and its total control of the country's military, social, political and financial institutions. The TGE has neither recognized the CAFPDE nor expressed the desire to abide by the resolutions passed by the NPRC. While recognizing the need for national reconciliation, the Tigrean leaders have rejected the possible establishment of a new transitional government. They have demanded, however, that every political organization be committed to the renunciation of violence before being permitted to negotiate the political future of Ethiopia with the government.

The search for peace in Ethiopia was continued again in a formal setting on February 7-8, 1994 at the Carter Center. This time the gathering under the chairmanship of the former U.S. President involved selected opposition groups, including the COEDF, CAFPDE, Medhin, SEPDC and the OLF. AAPO declined to send representatives to Atlanta because "To come to the issue of the meeting that is envisaged for the opposing groups, we note that the EPRDF is not included."[61] The purpose of the meeting, according to Mr. Carter, "was to give the groups full opportunity to express their specific concerns about conditions in Ethiopia."[62] After meeting individually and collectively with the first four groups and separately with the last, Mr. Carter reported that "There seemed to be a consensus among the participants that the government of Ethiopia had moved substantially toward a one-party domination of governmental processes . . ."[63]

Having concluded thus from his discussions with the opposition groups, Mr. Carter recommended that the election of representatives to a constituent assembly, scheduled for June 1994, be extended and also encouraged the participation of all political parties "for a future of harmony and democracy in Ethiopia."[64] He was to share the views expressed in the Atlanta meeting with the EPRDF leaders and with officials of the U.N., the U.S. and other interested governments. The former president was expected to sponsor a second conference, perhaps with the EPRDF in attendance this time. Unfortunately, Carter's initiative proved futile.

While the majority of the opposition has chosen the peace route to reverse the ethnic dictatorship that has evolved under the guise of democracy in Ethiopia, a low-key armed struggle was also being waged by others at a different level. However, those who chose this route received the least publicity in the international media, since the EPRDF continued to deny the existence of any armed groups within the country. The denial came in spite of occasional armed clashes that were reported between EPRDF forces and the Kefagne Patriotic Front (Kefagne), and others as well.

Operating mainly out of Gondar province, Kefagne began its movement in 1982 in protest against the Derg and the destruction its military operations caused in the province in late 1970's. Derg forces were then fighting the EDU, EPRP and TPLF in the region, which has suffered disproportionally from repeated devastations of war, both economically and socially. Reacting to the continued battles (among these guerrilla forces and between them and the Derg) to which the province was subjected, a small group of people founded the movement without any ideology and a clearly defined political agenda. Yet, the founders had these general objectives in mind: "the struggle for the establishment of a democratic system of government; the defense of Ethiopia's international boundary along the Sudan; and the struggle against organization inimical to the unity of Ethiopia."[65]

With almost no formal organization and leadership structure at its inception, Kefagne grew from a localized resistance in north Gondar to an effective rural guerrilla force operating freely in other parts of the province. Since 1993, the movement reported that it was expanding its operations to the predominantly Amhara regions of Gojjam, Wollo and Shoa.[66]

Kefagne's opposition to the current regime stemmed from the problems created by the new ethnic map. This being the root of the problem, Kefagne also saw itself "as being in the forefront of protecting Ethiopia from its internal and external enemies and working toward the political empowerment of the Ethiopian people through democracy."[67] With no known foreign backing, Kefagne frequently ambushed EPRDF forces in the Gondar region that were overseeing the forceful incorporation of the fertile lands of Tselemit, Tsegede, Humera and Armachiho into the adjacent province of Tigray, home of the leaders of the EPRDF. According to Amharic reports received by this writer, several hundreds of elders and prominent persons from districts incorporated into Tigray were executed publicly by government forces, when they resisted their incorporation and refused to renounce their Amhara identity in favor of Tigray. Kefagne, through its representatives in the U.S., publicized occasionally its military victories against the EPRDF. For instance, in one of its battlefield reports in 1993, the movement claimed to have shot down two government helicopters engaged in bombing missions in the Woldayet-Tsegede area. In that report, it identified the pilot and the five military personnel who lost their lives in the crash.[68] However, the government continued to refuse to even recognize the existence of the movement.

Armed operations against the EPRDF have were also reported throughout the transitional period by the ARDU in the Red Sea Afar region; by the OLF in Wollega province; by the IFLO in Harrar; by the SPLM in Sidamo; and by a few unknown small armed bands scattered throughout the northern, southern, and eastern provinces. Periodic clashes with each of these armed groups had become dangerous to EPRDF forces, who were increasingly finding themselves fighting back numerous isolated guerrilla attacks in the various parts of the country. Support from EPLF forces was lacking at that time, as the Eritrean government is having its own security problems with an armed insurgency, which receives its support from Islamic groups in Sudan, Morocco, Tunisia and Algeria.[69] Early that year (1993), Eritrea expelled a Sudanese diplomat in retaliation for supporting the group of Islamic insurgents, who reportedly had taken control of "six districts and (were) poised to attack Massawa, according to witnesses who came from the region."[70] However, security problems in either country would be neither encouraging to peace and stability, nor conducive to any efforts of democratization in both countries.

CONCLUSION

One aspect of the "transition to democracy" in Ethiopia, which outside observers may unknowingly lose sight of, is the high ethnic content of all the political decisions made by the EPRDF during the last three years of its traditional rule. Beginning with the dividing up of the country into ethnic enclaves, and the gradual elimination of public sectors jobs, and even the government's interference in the running of the country's premier university all have come at costs to some targeted ethnic groups but with gains to some others. Of course, those belonging to the same ethnic background as the rulers are likely the major beneficiaries. Even the most routine application for public services in Ethiopia now require ethnic identity declaration, thus making it the chief criterion for social and political mobility and even personal economic advancement. In a country where nepotism has been endemic to the system and political power has been monopolized rather than shared, one's ethnicity therefore could become an object of reward or punishment.

Today in Ethiopia, persons born and raised in one ethnic enclave but who do not speak the official language of that region are denied job opportunities; they are simply pressured to move to the region of their ancestral background. This has been at least the experience in southern and eastern parts of Ethiopia of those whose ethnic origins happen to be from other parts of the country.

Democracy and nation-building can hardly prosper under the conditions described in this paper. The ethnic political baggage employed by the ruling EPRDF party serves only one purpose: the perpetuation of political dominance under the cover of democracy. But this can only be accomplished at the expense of peace and stability and at the loss of an opportunity to build a democratic future in the country.

Notes

1   As of August 1993, for example, a large number of sub-Saharan African countries were showing encouraging signs of movement toward democracy, with a few still on shaky grounds, and only Sudan actively resisting free political competition; see list in "The Scoreboard for Sub-Saharan Africa," *The Houston Chronicle*, August 1993, p. 24A.

2   For example, Zambia, Benin, Burundi, Togo, Cape Verde, Lesotho, Madagascar, Ghana, Mauritius, Namibia and Sao Tome and Principle.

3   Support to the rebel movements came from Sudan, Iraq, Syria, Egypt, Saudi Arabia and the Gulf States.

4   Derg is a term used to refer to the military officers that launched the 1974 Ethiopian revolution and who ruled Ethiopia under the leadership of Mengistu until 1991; the literal meaning of Derg is committee. It is an Amharic word.

5   List of rebel movements is found in Harold D. Nelson and Irvin Kaplan, eds., *Ethiopia: A Country Study* (Washington, D.C.: The U.S. Government Press, 1981), pp. 310-11.

6   John Harbeson, "The Future of the Ethiopian State After Mengistu," *Current History*, 92, May 1993, p. 211.

7   One of the major causes of the 1974 revolution in Ethiopia and of the student protests prior to that was the feudal land tenure system founding the southern regions; the Oromos were the immediate beneficiaries of that revolution.

8   Edmond J. Keller, *Revolutionary Ethiopia: From Empire to People's Republic* (Bloomington: Indiana University Press, 1988), p. 20.

9   Harberson, P. 211.

10 World Bank, *World Development Report* (New York: Oxford University Press, 1992), p. 218.

11 Fred Halliday and Maxine Molyneux, *The Ethiopian Revolution* (London: Urwin Brothers, 1981), p. 115.

12 *Ibid.*

13 During the author's visit in 1988 to Ethiopia for research-related activities, interviews with non-WPE and party members showed the problems cited.

14 John Clarke, *Resettlement and Rehabilitation: Ethiopia's Campaign Against Famine*, (London: Hamey and Jones Ltd., 1986), p. 37.

15 Keller (1988), p. 200.

16 Daniel Kempton, "Africa in the Age of Perestroika," *Africa Today*, 38, 2, 1991, p. 7.

17 *Ibid.*

18 Edmond J. Keller, "Eritrean Self-determination Revisited," *Africa Today*, 38, 2, p. 10.

19 Herbert Lewis, "Beginning Again," *Africa Report*, September-October 1991, pp. 59-62.

20 "Ethiopia: From Rebels to Rulers," *Africa Confidential*, 32, 11, 13 May, 1991, p. 2.

21 "Participants and Observers at the National Conference," *EPRDF Information Center*, July 4, 1991, p. 4.

22 "Structure and Composition of the Transitional Government," *EPRDF News Bulletin*, 1, 11, 7 August 1991, p. 4.

23 "Ethiopia: Majorities and Minorities," *Africa Confidential*, 32, 14, 12, July 1991, p. 1.

24 "The Dawning of a Bright Future," *EPRDF News Bulletin*, 1, 9, July 1991, p. 4.

25 Open letter sent to the Ethiopian Embassy in Washington, D.C. by the COEDF on December 6, 1991.

26 The COED did suggest such a course in a letter written on June 14, 1991 addressed to former U.S. Under secretary of State for African Affairs.

27 The groups well-known for fighting the Derg included the OLF, EPRDF, EDU, WSLF and SLF. The rest of the political organizations at the national conference were unknown until that time.

28 "Ethiopia: Majorities and Minorities," (n. 23).

29 Makau wa Mutua, "The New Oligarchy," *Africa Report*, 38, 5, (September-October 1993), p. 28.

30   This comes from Amnesty International's "Urgent Action" letter written to Ethiopian authorities on January 5, 1993.

31   Mutua, p. 28.

32   *Zena Ethiopia*, 1, 9 (January 7, 1994), p. 3.

33   Worku Aberra, "Tribalism Rules in Ethiopia," *New Africa*, No. 311, September 1993, p. 20.

34   *Zena Ethiopia*, 1, 10, 19 January, 1994, p. 1.

35   "Ethiopia: Waiting for Justice," *Africa Watch*, IV, 7, 8 May, 1992, p. 1.

36   *Ibid.*

37   "Transitional Period Charter of Ethiopia," *EPRF News Bulletin*, 1, 11, 7 August 1991, p. 3.

38   M. Ottoway and D. Ottoway, *Ethiopia: Empire in Revolution* (New York: African Publishing Company, 1978), p. 28.

39   Patrick Gilkes, "Eritrea: Historiography and Mythology," *African Affairs*, October 1991, p. 624.

40   There is no specific figures that show Amharas have been the major beneficiaries from the policies of previous Ethiopian governments.

41   Paul Henze, "Ethiopia and the Challenge of Liberation," report given at a symposium at Arlington, Virginia, on March 10, 1990, p. 7.

42   Quoted in "Ethiopia: New Government, New Map," *Africa Confidential*, November 8, 1991, p. 7.

43   Quoted in *Ethiopian Review*, July 1992, p. 6.

44   "The Humera-Metema Corridor," *Lessane Gondar*, 2 October 1991, p. 3.

45   Faisel Robie, "Self-Determination is a Must for Ethiopia," *Ethiopian Review*, February 1992, p. 30.

46   "The Humera-Metema Corridor," p. 3.

47   Girma Bekele, "The Hidden Agenda," *Ethiopian Review*, January 1992, p. 15.

48   Quoted in Girma Bekele, n. 47.

49   A memorandum written on June 17, 1992 by the OLF explaining why it was forced to withdraw from the regional elections held in the summer of 1992 in Ethiopia.

50 *Ibid.*

51 This comes from a secret Report brought by victims of atrocities in Arsi province, where Amharas and other Christians had been massacred by members of the OLF and OPDO.

52 Keith B. Richburg, "International Observers Team Criticizes Ethiopian Elections," *The Washington Post*, June 24, 1992, p. A24.

53 See OLF memorandum above (n. 49).

54 This comes from a letter written in January 1992 by the president of the AAPO to the TGE, pleading to help halt the massacre of Amharas in southern Ethiopia; the Amharic text of the letter is found in *The Ethiopian Review*, April 1922, p. 44.

55 Quoted from a letter sent to former U S. President Jimmy Carter by the president of the AAPO, explaining the repression to which his organization is subjected under EPRDF government.

56 "Ethiopian Parliament Expels 5 Opposition Political Groups," *Arab News*, April 4, 1993, p. 3; the groups were SPLF, OPDF, HNDO, GPDM, and YPDM.

57 Makau wa Mutua, "An Oppressed Opposition," *Africa Report*, 38, 6, November-December 1993, p. 52.

58 *Africa Research Bulletin* (Political Series) 30, December 12, 1993, p. 11272.

59 *Ibid.*

60 Hailu Fullas, "An Interview with Dr. Taye Wolde Semayat," *Ethiopian Register*, 1, 1, February 1994, pp. 11-12.

61 Letter from AAPO president to Mr. Jimmy Carter, p. 5.

62 This comes from the report given by Mr. Jimmy Carter regarding his talks in Atlanta with Ethiopian opposition groups; report is published in *Ethiopian Review*, March 1994, pp. 12, 15.

63 *Ibid.*

64 *Ibid.*

65 *Lesane Gondar*, 1, 4 (Summer 1993), pp. 1-5.

66 *Zena Ethiopia*, 1, 5, 30 October 1993, p. 1.

67 Translated from an Amharic military communique that the Front released in January 1994.

68   See a military communique released by Kefagan on March 25, 1993.

69   "Crisis Brewing in Eritrea," *Ethiopian Review*, February 1994, p. 10.

70   *Ibid.*

Chapter 10

South Africa: The Long and Arduous Road to a New Dispensation

Margaret C. Lee

INTRODUCTION

The road to a new political dispensation in South Africa was long and arduous. Between political violence, the seeming inability of the major actors to come to a consensus during negotiations, and the attempt by black and white right-wing elements to destabilize the transition, it often appeared that the country was moving toward an abyss. To the credit of the people of South Africa, the April 1994 elections and the transition to democratic rule were peaceful and set an example for other countries marred by internal civil strife to follow.

As the African National Congress (ANC)-led government took over the reigns of power, the major challenge it faced was to bring about a new economic dispensation in the country. Creating a new economic dispensation in post-apartheid South Africa could prove to be more difficult than the creation of the new political dispensation. One of the major reasons that the political transition was so peaceful stemmed from the fact that during negotiations, the ANC and the National Party (NP) reached a compromise that allowed for the black majority to achieve political power as long as economic power was retained by the white minority. The ANC went to great lengths to assure the whites that their wealth would not be disturbed, and they would be able to continue enjoying the privileges they had under white domination.

Given the above, the post-election struggle is over the re-sources of the country. As the ANC-led government attempts to address the gross inequalities that are a legacy of apartheid, it is challenged with the unenviable task of attempting to bring about a new economic dispensation for the majority population without disturbing white privilege. It is the contention of this author that the ANC-led government will not be able to enhance the economic and social living conditions of the majority population without disturbing white privilege. Instead, over the next two to three years, the government will have to make a choice between upholding its compromise with the NP not to disturb white privilege, or fulfilling the promise it made to the majority population that a new economic dispensation would be forthcoming. With either decision, the democratic initiative will likely be challenged.

This chapter will examine the events leading up to the new political dispensation in South Africa and then analyze the challenge before the current government to bring about a new economic dispensation and maintain the democratic initiative. The article is divided into three parts: The State of the State February 2, 1990; The State of the State Post-February 2, 1990 to May 1994; and The Post-Election State.

THE STATE OF THE STATE, FEBRUARY 2, 1990

The decision by the two major political entities in South Africa, the ANC and the NP, to begin negotiations for a new political dispensation in the country had been long in the making. In fact, between 1986 and 1989, Mandela held at least 22 meetings with a team of government officials, and from November 1989, regular sessions were held with cabinet members.[1]

The decision by the NP to begin negotiations was influenced by the growing pragmatism of the Broederbond, a secret society of elite Afrikaners. De Klerk was admitted into the society at the age of 27. Around 1980, the Broederbond began preparing the ground for the dismantling of apartheid. Pieter de Lange, chairman of the movement since 1984, noted that, "Some of . . . [them] became convinced that Afrikaner interests had become so entwined with everyone's interests in South

Africa and internationally that you could not promote Afrikaner interests in isolation. You had to promote everyone's interests."[2]

During the latter part of the 1980's, members of the Broederbond, including F.W. de Klerk's brother, Willem, traveled abroad to hold secret discussions with the ANC.[3] Many of de Klerk's policies were later adopted from the Broederbond.[4]

In this section, the decision by the NP and the ANC to begin the negotiation process will be examined. In addition, the state of the security forces in February 1990 will be analyzed in light of the fact that certain elements within the security forces that had acquired tremendous power during the Botha era, were seemingly determined to derail the negotiations.

The Decision To Negotiate

. . . It is their mutual weakness, rather than their equal strength, that makes both longtime adversaries embrace negotiations for power-sharing. Like a forced marriage, the working arrangement lacks love but nonetheless is consummated because any alternative course would lead to a worse fate for both sides.[5]

The National Party

Even though preliminary discussions had been taking place between the ANC and the NP for several years, the ANC was surprised and caught off guard by the February 2, 1990 announcement by de Klerk that he was legalizing the ANC and other heretofore banned political organizations, and releasing Mandela from prison.

It has been well established that de Klerk's decision to negotiate grew out of an understanding that the apartheid forces did not have the capacity to rid the country of black resistance against continued white domination. Although the NP could have continued the repressive policies of the Botha era, de Klerk understood that it would be at great costs to the country both domestically and internationally.[6]

De Klerk, however, did not feel that the NP would be negotiating from a position of weakness. In fact, he determined that it was best that negotiations begin in 1990, while the government was still strong. From the beginning, the NP determined that power sharing, as opposed to black majority rule, was the only possible alternative to white domination. To this end de Klerk noted, "those who arrogantly equate the concept of a new South Africa to a takeover of power, the message needs to be transmitted loudly and clearly that the new South Africa will not fall prey to a section of the population at the expense of the rest."[7]

The NP was also very clear that white economic domination would have to remain. Therefore, de Klerk made the decision to negotiate with the idea that negotiations were "to maximize the probability of preserving the existing class structure and to minimize the probability that improvements in the welfare of blacks would come at the expense of those in the National-ist coalition. Rather than using the state to redistribute exist-ing wealth, blacks are to escape the misery of unemployment, poverty, and squatter camps through the market-place."[8]

The NP further found that it was to its advantage to unban political organizations to throw them off balance. According to Rich Mkhondo, with respect to the ANC, de Klerk "meant to exploit the differences in age, personality and ideology within the ANC leadership. His problem was how to move fast enough to thwart international pressure for tougher sanctions against his government, fast enough to entice the ANC, and yet carefully enough to keep the whites from turning against him."[9]

The African National Congress

The ANC was surprised with de Klerk's February 1990 an-nouncements, and a sense of great victory filled the ranks of the organization. As the ANC prepared for negotiations, it remained committed to black majority rule, nationalization and economic redistribution. All three of these objectives con-flicted with the NP's vision of the future.

When the ANC was unbanned and Mandela released, the organization was not as strong as it would have liked. For ex-ample, although during the 1980's the ANC was an intensely militarized organization, "It was unable to achieve its strategic aim of promoting a generalized insurrection" and "it never amounted to more than 'armed propaganda', as ANC spokes-men today readily conceded."[10] On January 18, 1990, before de Klerk's historic speech, a member of the ANC, by mistake, admitted to a group of journalists that they did "not have the capacity within . . . [their] country to intensify the armed struggle in any meaningful way."[11]

The morale of ANC members was very low on the eve of de Klerk's historic speech for several reasons. Not only had the organization been unable to wage a successful armed struggle against the apartheid regime, but during its 1980's war of regional destabilization, the South African government had forced all regional nations, except Zambia, to remove ANC guerrilla bases. This eliminated the ability of the organization to launch external attacks against the state.

The morale of the ANC was further weakened when the former Soviet Union abandoned it. In fact, it was the former Soviet Union, not the United States or Britain, which, in 1987, put more pressure on the ANC to agree to negotiations with the apartheid regime. The ANC was even implicitly threatened by Soviet diplomats who warned that aid would be discontinued if the organization became a barrier to negotiations.[12] The real shock came to the ANC, however, when the Soviets began encouraging the ANC "to work out comprehensive guarantees for the white population."[13] By 1989, a friendly relationship had developed between the former Soviet Union and the South African government. No doubt pleased with the Soviet's abandonment of the ANC, former President P.W. Botha noted "the Soviet Union had a better understanding of the situation in the South of Africa than the US."[14]

Finally, the morale of the organization was further affected by abuses that were occurring in ANC detention camps throughout the region, and allegations that there were individuals who had been placed in the organization by the apartheid regime with instructions to sow discord within the forces. One hundred such individuals were held in a detention camp in Uganda.[15] The long history of the apartheid regime successfully infiltrating the ANC had legitimately left the organization paranoid. Unfortunately, some who were not spies for the South African government were abused and even killed. This had a devastating impact on the organization. In the latter part of 1992, the ANC released a report that outlined in detail the extent of the abuse that took place in ANC detention camps.[16] Tom Lodge notes that, "Clearly, the ANC may have been unready to come home but its prospects in continued exile were darkening rapidly."[17]

On February 2, 1990, there existed political divisions within the rank and file of the ANC that were to have serious implications for the ability of the organization to unite. There were three major groups: those in exile; the underground elements; and those who had been in the forefront leading the movement to make South Africa ungovernable. The latter group posed a serious problem for the ANC because many refused to accept the suspension of the armed struggle.

Security Forces

During the three years of negotiations, one of the greatest constraints to the establishment of a new dispensation in the country were elements within the security forces, the South African Police (SAP) and the South African Defense Force (SADF), who were involved in destabilizing the South African townships. The unprofessional nature in which some of the forces operated can be traced back to the development of South Africa as a military state[18] under the administration of Prime Minister and later President P.W. Botha.

When Botha became Prime Minister in 1978, he established the National Security Management System (NSMS), which has been described as a militarized bureaucracy.[19] With himself at the top, Botha was surrounded by military-security chiefs. These "securocrats" "were empowered to intervene in every Government department in the name of national security, which became so broadly defined that it embraced everything from the state of the roads in a township to what was taught in the schools and preached in the churches."[20]

The major power within the NSMS was the State Security Council (SSC), which replaced the Cabinet as the most significant decision-making body. It was during this period, according to Herbert Howe, that sections of the SADF departed somewhat from the western professional model that calls for the military to remain subordinate to civilian control with a primary focus on external threats. By creating the "total strategy" and the military-dominated SSC, Howe further notes, President Botha politically modified the role of the SADF.[21] During the Botha era,

> the SADF provided a major backup to the South African police in many urban areas (and some rural) and conducted anti-ANC/United Democratic Front (UDF) operations. It participated in the Joint Management Centres which, inter alia, gathered extensive grassroots intel-

ligence within the townships, and provided covert financial, ordinance, and training support for such "force multipliers" as Inkatha, the Witdoeke (Western Cape vigilantes), and Uma Afrika (Eastern Cape vigilantes), and reportedly the Black Cats (an urban gang in Ermelo).[22]

The SADF was also responsible for "Operation Hammer," "a covert reaction force which could neutralize anti-apartheid activists and generally disrupt the 'enemy' in urban counter-insurgency operations."[23] In 1985, one or more of Operation Hammer's hit squads killed four United Democratic Front members, including Matthew Goniwe.[24] Allegedly, the SAP was involved with the SADF in this operation.[25]

Both the SAP and the SADF were involved in other hit squad operations to assassinate opponents of the apartheid regime.[26] In commenting on allegations of a "third force" fueling the violence in the townships, Major Nico Basson, a former military intelligence office, "alleged that the activities of the 'third force' are part of an elaborate plan, code named Operation Agree, drawn up by the SADF and the Department of Foreign Affairs in 1988 to manipulate the 1989 Namibian elections and future Democratic elections in Angola and South Africa."[27]

When de Klerk came to power, he "reclaimed civilian control of the state from the security establishment."[28] While the NP, members of parliament, senior civil servants, and cabinet ministers welcomed the changes proposed by de Klerk,[29] members of the military-security establishment were not happy.[30] In fact, Howe argues that "by initiating negotiations to prepare for an orderly transfer of formal power to a non-white majority," de Klerk "threatened the SADF's corporate (and personal) identity by reducing its power and status."[31]

Notwithstanding de Klerk's claims to reform the security establishment, on February 2, some of the security forces that had been given unlimited power during the Botha era continued to operate as a "loose cannon." Their clandestine operations strengthened, not weakened, de Klerk's control over the state. Knowing how important these security forces would be in the event negotiations failed, he did very little to curtail their operations. There was even a level of complicity in fueling the violence. This included the money given by the Foreign Ministry to the SAP, who in turn funneled it to the Inkatha Freedom Party (IFP) and its trade union, the United Workers of South Africa (Uwusa). The SAP had paid the IFP to destabilize the townships with a view to undercutting the power of the ANC.[32] In defense of the funding, which became known as Inkathagate, Foreign Minister Pik Botha noted that he had no regrets about what had happened and that, "We did it and, under similar circumstances, we will do exactly the same."[33]

THE STATE OF THE STATE, POST-FEBRUARY 2, 1990 TO MAY 1994: THE STRUGGLE FOR POWER

The struggle in South Africa prior to February 2, 1990, was to some extent, clearly defined. It mainly pitted the anti-apartheid forces against the apartheid forces. This changed drastically, however, after February 2. The struggle took on an entirely different dimension; namely, a struggle for power among many for control in the post-apartheid state, a struggle that some characterized as a war. As Jo-Anne Collinge notes:

> Analysts who foretold at the end of 1989 that constitutional negotiations would prove "another kind of war" or a new "terrain of struggle" could not have known how literally their visions would be fulfilled.[34]

Talks About Talks, May 1990—November 1991

From May 1990 through November 1991[35] (see Appendix), the foundation was laid for negotiations. Agreements were signed between the government and the ANC over the release of political prisoners, indemnity for exiles, efforts to end the violence, the easing of emergency rules and the suspension of the ANC's 30-year armed struggle against apartheid.

The first phase of the long and arduous road to a new political dispensation was marred by political violence. While both the ANC and the government accused each other of inciting the violence, the July 1991 revelation that the government had provided covert funds to Inkatha and its trade union, Uwusa, indicated that a "third force" might be operating in the townships to destabilize the movement toward negotiation.

The Inkathagate scandal raised questions about whether de Klerk was serious about negotiations, or whether he was involved in a sinister plot to destabilize the townships with a view to maintaining the white supremacist state. For example, during August 1990, de Klerk signed an amendment to the

Natal Native Code of 1887 making it legal for Zulu-speaking people to carry traditional weapons, including spears, sticks and knobkerries. Mandela responded to the amendment by contending that "it legalized the carrying of dangerous weapons" and therefore de Klerk "created the opportunity for slaughter."[36] In response to ongoing allegations of governmental involvement in the violence, de Klerk set up three separate Commissions (Harms, Hiemstra, and Goldstone) to investigate the issue.

Following a judicial commission of inquiry under Justice Harms in November 1990, it was determined that substantial evidence was presented that a death squad existed within the police and military. Also, the Civil Co-operation Bureau (CCB), a paramilitary unit within the SADF, was implicated in a series of murders.[37] Following de Klerk's order that the CCB be disbanded, a number of its personnel joined another secret SADF unit, the Directorate of Covert Collections (DCC).[38] In an effort to decrease the violence, on September 14, 1991, the ANC, anti-apartheid groups, political parties, the government and the Inkatha Freedom Party (IFP) signed a National Peace Accord designed to reduce tension and to set up mechanisms to resolve disputes.

Negotiations, December 1991-November 1993
CODESA
On December 20, 1991, 19 parties and groups met outside Johannesburg to launch the Convention for a Democratic South Africa (CODESA). This historic meeting marked the beginning of a long and arduous negotiation process to bring about a new political dispensation in South Africa. While all major actors agreed that negotiations were the only way forward for South Africa, CODESA itself was to be short-lived. In May 1992, CODESA collapsed over the inability of the ANC and the NP to agree on "how large a 'special majority' would be required for decisions on a final draft constitution."[39] On June 21, 1992, the ANC suspended bilateral talks, after accusing de Klerk and his government of complicity in the Boipatong massacre of June 17. On June 23, the ANC decided to pull out of talks with the government.

Political Violence

During this next phase of the struggle for political reform, the political violence in South Africa had several sources. These included ongoing clashes between supporters of the ANC and Inkatha as well as clashes between other rival black organizations; attacks by the military wing of the Pan Africanist Congress (PAC), the Azania's People's Liberation Army (APLA), against white civilians; attacks by right-wing paramilitary groups against blacks; revenge killings; and random attacks against black civilians in what appeared to be a sinister attempt to wreck havoc on the townships. The ANC, as well as many of the survivors of the attacks, continued to argue that a "third force" was involved in such attacks. It was believed that this force was lodged within the security services.

In an interesting dynamic to the township violence, members of the 32nd Battalion had been placed in Natal and the Reef's townships to act against urban unrest. These units proved to be extremely controversial and were accused of fueling the violence. The 32nd Battalion were veterans of Operation Zulu, which was South Africa's 1975 invasion of Angola. Although in early 1992 de Klerk announced the disbandment of this highly criticized entity, the order did not become official until April 1993.[40]

In addition to "Operation Agree" (see previous section), Major Nico Basson also "claimed that the SADF was arming Inkatha members and that the assassination of ANC activists—60 assassinations in 1991 alone—and the random killing of black train commuters—112 killed in attacks on trains on the Reef during the eighteen months ending on January 31, 1992- were part of an elaborate government plan of disruption."[41] Between 1990-1992, an estimated 119 activists were killed by assassins.[42]

By April 1992, further evidence of security force involvement in the destabilization of the townships was revealed. Specifically, two Directorate of Military Intelligence (DMI)[43] agents were arrested in London and accused of conspiring with the Royal Ulster Constabulary in an apparent effort to assassinate Dirk Coetzee, a former South African policeman. Coetzee had made public past SADF covert operations and had begun co-operating with the ANC.[44]

In August 1992, de Klerk dismissed 19 police generals reportedly in order to aid the negotiations. This purge followed a report by Peter Waddington, a British policing expert, in which he "advised that the 'high command' of the South African police should be purged as part of the country's negotiated settlement."[45]

Then, in November 1992, the Goldstone Commission of Inquiry Regarding Public Violence and Intimidation, seized documents that revealed that the SADF had employed a double-murderer (Fredi Bernard) to run a smear campaign against Umkhonto we Sizwe, the military wing of the ANC, from May to December 1991. Justice Richard Goldstone, in quoting from a DMI report, noted "that Ferdi Bernard's 48 subordinates were to use 'prostitutes, homosexuals, nightclub owners, and criminal elements' to entice Umkhonto members into compromising acts."[46]

In December 1992, de Klerk appointed Lieutenant-General Pierre Steyn, Chief of the South African Air Force, to investigate unauthorized security force actions. After hearing Steyn's report, de Klerk dismissed or suspended 23 military officers, including two generals and four brigadiers. De Klerk noted that these individuals "might have been motivated by a wish to prevent us from succeeding in our [reform] goals."[47]

The dismissals were interesting for two reasons. This first is that no charges of wrong-doing were pressed against the officers, and the second is that de Klerk did not dismiss two hardliners who indicated publicly their dislike for the ANC, Kat Liebenberg, then Chief of the SADF and Georg Meiring, then Army Commander and Liebenberg's successor.[48] General van der Westhuizen, head of Military Intelligence, was also retained despite the fact that there existed evidence suggesting he was linked to political assassinations.[49]

If de Klerk was really committed to negotiations, why did it take him so long (until late 1992) to begin reforming the security forces? De Klerk, according to Howe,

Had political, corporate, ideological, as well as structural reasons (the localized Commandos) to fear military praetorianism, and these may explain why his security reforms, both in timing and completeness, lagged behind his political initiatives. Yet de Klerk needed a strong security force to ensure that they succeeded, and apropos of de Tocqueville's warning to previously repressive but now-reformist governments, South African officials retained a "security fallback" lest the negotiations failed. If they had, political violence—which had claimed over 15,000 lives since 1986—would have surged even more and required a powerful security response.[50]

In addition, the retention of the hard-line officers forced the ANC leadership to sell several compromises to its members and supporters. They were warned not to underestimate "the regime's known counter-revolutionary capabilities" and "Mandela acknowledged the reactionary security threat from South Africa's security forces, and used this to gain acceptance for the transitional power-sharing arrangement as the only method to forestall what he termed the 'already incipient counter-revolutionary movement' with the SADF."[51] Between February 1990 and April 1994, an estimated 12,000 people died in political violence.

Negotiations Continue
Although multi-party negotiations did not resume again until April 1993, the NP and ANC began bilateral negotiations when the two signed a "Record of Understanding" on September 26, 1992. The issue that most divided the two major parties prior to February 1993 was the type of government that would be established. The ANC, until November 1992, had insisted on majority rule, and the NP on power-sharing. On February 12, 1993, the ANC and the NP agreed to a power-sharing arrangement. The ANC/NP power-sharing arrangement was a major compromise for the ANC, and many members termed it a sellout because it would leave in place both white privilege and Nationalist power. As the ANC made concessions with the NP, it entered a "shifting and dangerous political environment" where it had to recognize "white power with concessions that" would "inevitably jeopardize the unity" it had always treasured.[52]

In response to the ANC/NP agreement, Gatsha Buthelezi, leader of the Inkatha Freedom Party, in October 1992, joined forces with the right-wing to form the Concerned South Africans Group (Cosag) as an anti-ANC alliance. The members of

Cosag included the IFP, the governments of Bophuthatswana and Ciskei, the Conservative Party (CP) and the Afrikaner Volksunie (AVU). When multi-party talks resumed in April 1993, Cosag proved to be a major thorn in the side of both the ANC and the NP.

Twenty-six parties and groups gathered for the resumption of multi-party talks after an 11-month break. Between April and November, when the interim constitution was finalized, the negotiations were marred by ongoing conflicts with both black and white right-wing forces, including the Afrikaner Volksfront (AVF).[53]

On November 18, multiparty negotiators finally reached agreement on an interim constitution that would be used to govern the country for five years after April 1994 elections. There had been two major turning points in negotiations that allowed the constitution to become a reality. The first occurred during the latter part of 1992 when the ANC agreed to both include minority parties in the government and to protect the jobs of white soldiers and civil servants. The second turning point came during the final days of negotiations when the NP agreed that minority parties would not have any special power in the post-apartheid cabinet. Instead, the NP agreed that the "winners rule 'in a consensus-seeking spirit.'"[54]

Transition, December 1993-May 1994
On December 7, 1993, the multiracial Transitional Executive Council (TEC), consisting of 19 parties, met for the first time in Cape Town, giving the black majority the first say in government. The transitional phase was made difficult by civil unrest (in Bophuthatswana), ongoing political violence (including the violent clashes between ANC and Inkatha supporters and the election eve bombings by right-wing elements), and new allegations by the Goldstone Commission of the possible involvement of a so-called "third force" in the violence. The report made allegations of high level police involvement.[55] As a result of the report, de Klerk "suspended the three top generals named in the Goldstone inquiry—the deputy police commissioner, the head of counterintelligence in the SAP, and the head of the division of crime prevention and investigation."[56]

During February the ANC and NP agreed to last minute changes to the interim constitution and the Electoral Act in hopes of getting members of the right-wing Freedom Alliance[57] in the election process.[58] The transition phase was also made difficult by the threat from right-wing elements, including Inkatha, that they would not contest the elections. The newly formed Freedom Front (FF)[59] agreed to contest the elections. However, it was not until April 19 that the IFP decided to contest. This last minute decision prevented what many feared would be a major crisis in the country.

With 62.65 percent of the vote, the ANC won a major victory in the first multi-racial elections in South Africa. The NP followed with just over 20 percent and the IFP with 10.54 percent. As Nelson Mandela was sworn in as the first black president of South Africa on May 10, 1994, with all the pomp and circumstance the title bestows, perhaps the most difficult struggle of his life was before him. He was charged with the unenviable task of overseeing a government of national unity and maintaining the democratic initiative in South Africa, as well as addressing the social and economic injustices of the apartheid era without disturbing white privilege.

THE POST-ELECTION STATE: THE STRUGGLE OVER RESOURCES

The post-election struggle in South Africa is over the resources of the country. This struggle has two major dimensions. The first relates to the question of redressing the gross inequalities that exists between the white minority and the black majority. This can be classified as the black/white divide and it centered around the implementation of the Reconstruction and Development Program (RDP) and the planned redistribution of resources at the local level. The second dimension of the struggle relates to the class divide between the new non-racial elite and the masses. This struggle has been most evident within the labor movement in South Africa. Specifically, the wave of strikes that began in the country shortly after the elections has brought to the forefront the tension that exists between the new elite who have assumed power and the advantaged working class who are members of trade unions. This latter group has been challenged by the new government to compromise their current economic demands in order to enhance the prospect of increased employment for the masses of unemployed in the country. Amidst these two dimensions of the struggle over the resources of the country, the ANC-led government is challenged to maintain the democratic initiative.

The Black/White Divide

Two visions of the future have managed to coexist in the uneasy partnership between the ANC and the National party. The core of the National party leadership and its supporters, as well as the core of the largely white-run business sector, has vested its faith in the idea that nothing really will change. The good life of the "sun drenched republic" will continue to be available. This faith has been sustained partly by the ANC's embrace of pragmatic politics and economics, and by its acceptance of a "sunset clause" protecting white civil servants' jobs for several years and providing them with bonuses that may soothe their fears but will also burden the public purse for years to come. For blacks there is a definite expectation that the future will be different, that they will have vastly better prospects for housing, health, education, income, access to jobs, and control over the allocation of resources at the national level.[60]

The ANC-led government inherited an economic structure in which 70-80 percent of the wealth is in the hands of less than 10 percent of the population. An estimated 53 percent of all Africans live below the poverty line compared to only 2 percent of the white population.[61] In addition, as a result of poor education, discriminatory and repressive labor legislation, whites earn, on the average, 9.5 times more than blacks.[62]

With a view to creating a new economic dispensation in the country, the ANC-led government is committed to implementing its RDP. Also, during November 1995, local elections will be held in South Africa, at which time heretofore racially segregated local governments will be integrated and resources shared. The success of both the RDP and the plans for local governments would result in the redistribution of some of the resources in the country. Finding the funds to implement the RDP will pose a serious challenge to the government. The logistics of local elections will also be challenging.

Implementing the Reconstruction and Development Program

The RDP is designed to address the legacy of the apartheid era. There are five major policy programs in the RDF. These are: meeting basic needs; developing human resources; building the economy; democratizing the state and society; and implementing the RDP.[63]

The first priority of the government is to begin to meet the basic needs of people. This includes providing land, jobs, housing, electricity, water, transport, telecommunications, a clean and healthy environment, nutrition, health care and social welfare. Over a period of five years, the government plans to "redistribute a substantial amount of land to landless people, build over one million houses, provide clean water and sanitation to all, electrify 2,5 million new homes, and provide access for all to affordable health care and telecommunications."[64] In addition, the government plans to implement compulsory education for ten years.[65] To date, the government has taken action to implement portions of the RDP in the areas of land, housing, nutrition and health.

Cyril Ramaphosa, general secretary of the ANC and president of the Constituent Assembly, noted that "Unless we settle the land question, we do not have a country."[66] The government has made the question of land redistribution a priority. On August 17, 1994, the cabinet approved the Restitution of Land Rights Bill, which is "aimed at enabling the restoration of land to those dispossessed by apartheid." The Bill was passed by parliament and both a Commission on the Restitution of Land Rights and a specialized Land Claims Court have been established. The task of the former will be to investigate and mediate land claims, while the latter will be responsible for determining restitution and compensation to those who lost their land due to forced removals.[67] In addition, 30 percent of white agricultural land is to be redistributed to black farmers.

It is estimated that land reform could cost 10 billion Rand (approximately US $2.85 billion) over the next six years.[68] According to the bill of rights, while expropriation of land by the state is explicitly permitted, this can only occur after payment of "fair and equitable" compensation.[69]

Shortly after assuming power, Mandela implemented a program that made pregnant women and children under six years old eligible for free medical care, and in July the sod was turned on the site where the first of 747 RDP houses will be built. The government allocated $5.7 million in 1994 to help build houses.[70] In September 1994, the government announced a $135 million primary school lunch program and a $17 million plan to provide water to rural and black communities.[71]

Over a period of five years it is estimated that the RDP will cost from 26 to 30 billion dollars. According to the ANC, the largest portion of the program will be financed by more efficient use of existing resources. Other funding will come from revenues, issuing debt, and grants.[72] It is also anticipated that funding will come from foreign governments and international investment. The ANC-led government has adopted an economic policy that calls for "fiscal discipline, free enterprise, and economic growth as the engine for development."[73] Will such policies, however, lead to a new economic dispensation? For example, it has been suggested that without a growth rate of at least 4 to 6 percent, the government will have limited prospects of beginning to fulfill the promises of the RDP.

The expectation that a major part of RDP financing will come from the "apartheid dividend" (viz, savings accrued out of the elimination of overlapping programs, such as multiple departments for the several ethnic and racial groups, of the apartheid era) may also be unrealistic. Jeffrey Herbst, for example, notes that savings from the "apartheid dividend" at most would amount to 2 to 4 percent, and of this, most "will have to be invested rather than consumed in the short term, if the country is to address its structural problems."[74]

While the ANC has been lauded by many governments as well as the economic community in South Africa for its fiscal discipline, what happens if the economy does not grow sufficiently to allow for the masses to experience a new economic dispensation? The ANC-led government will have two choices. It can either continue along the path of fiscal discipline and thus appease the white minority and the business community, in which case it would be viewed as a failure by the majority population; or it can pursue a more aggressive redistribution strategy that may not be deemed fiscal responsible by the business community. This could include expropriation of unused or under-used white agricultural land and civil service retrenchments. Even the World Bank has indicated that "a short-term reduction in gross inequities is required for medium-to-long-term economic growth to reach its potential in an equitable manner. Therefore, a strategy for a significant transfer of resources during the critical transition period should be considered."[75] Such a transfer would definitely have an effect on white privilege in the country.

In the final analysis, Michael MacDonald and Wilmont James warn that:

> "Non-racial capitalism" would re-cast black inferiority in internationally acceptable terms, with blacks becoming victims of market forces instead of state racism. But large numbers would none the less feel betrayed by their continuing poverty, and by the insistence that they act as individuals in a society where whites, having used state power to establish themselves, now speak of the "privatization" of power.[76]

Redistribution of Resources Among Local Governments

In keeping with the interim Constitution, local government elections were scheduled for November 1995. These elections may prove to be a challenge to economic redistribution in South Africa since the Local Government Transition Act is "directed at the total restructuring of local government in order to phase out the existing racially based system and to replace it with a single non-racial system."[77] As Wilmont Jones, Executive Director of the Institute for Democracy in South Africa (Idasa), noted,

> It's at the local level that privileged people and white people are going to feel for the first time what it actually means to have a democracy from top to bottom. Because one of the goals of the new local government arrangements is to, for example, draw the boundaries of government in such a way that they provide the basis for the redistribution of resources from richer areas, middle class areas, to poorer areas, and from white areas to black areas, so that in the city of Cape Town, for example, the local government re-drawing the lines would contain white areas and black areas in the same local government authority.[78]

The resources available for narrowing the gap between the wealthy white suburbs and the poor townships will be limited. Nonetheless, according to Andrew Boraine, Acting Head of the Institute for Local Governance and Development, "We can't afford to maintain the standards of the old white municipalities. We have to cut down."[79] Furthermore, local government experts note that "local authorities will have to supply the service, regardless of whether communities can pay. Provision of basic services is both stipulated by the interim Constitution and promised by the Reconstruction and Development Programme."[80]

It is only inevitable that economic redistribution will be realized at the local level if these governmental structures are effectively implemented. To what extent local governmental policies will affect the black/white divide in the country will only be revealed in time.

The Growing Class Divide

"The country's maldistribution (of wealth) is increasingly shifting from being race-to class-based. Irrespective of the racial dimension of income inequality, the gap between rich and poor is so wide as to militate against long-term social stability". . . . Or, in plainer English, fresh turmoil lies ahead if the government of national unity allows a nonracial elite to take the place of the white elite of the apartheid era. . . . A new class, dependent for their wealth on the tax contributions and VAT levied even on low-paid workers, has slipped smoothly into place. Its members, black and white, Nationalist and ANC and DP, revolutionary and conservative, form a non-racial elite.[81]

After only being in power for several months, some were suggesting that Mandela had lost sight of the needs of the people. Certainly one of the greatest constraints to the development of the nation-state in Africa during the post-colonial era has been the alienation between the rulers and the ruled.[82] While it is too early to suggest that the ANC-led government of national unity has lost sight of the needs of the masses, one can clearly sense growing hostility by some at what is perceived to be the ascendancy of former liberation fighters into the comfortable and plush life of government power. Is there a growing non-racial elite in South Africa?

The growing chasm over class came to the forefront during the wave of workers' strikes that began to hit the country shortly after Mandela became president. While striking workers had numerous grievances, including continued racial discriminatory policies within the work arena, the major grievance was low wages and with it great expectations that a new economic order would be realized in the near future.

The demands of the strikers were made more poignant because of the sense of anger they felt at the fact that the new governing elite had overnight moved into high paying governmental jobs, many of whom had been leaders in the labor movement (approximately 60), including Jay Naidoo, who founded the powerful Congress of South African Trade Unions (COSATU). Naidoo, as a cabinet minister, currently has an annual salary of R470,400. The average salary of a trade union leader ranges from R1,600 to R3,500 gross per month.[83] There is indeed a huge divide between politicians who earn R20,000 to R30,000 (or more) a month and a Pick 'n Pay packer who earns R1,100 a month.[84]

Mandela has appealed to black workers to "tighten their belts and help create jobs for the 5 million unemployed."[85] Compromising their salaries and benefits for the millions of unemployed is not what the trade union members are interested in. In fact, COSATU "has specifically rejected the idea of its members making sacrifices to increase employment."[86] Perhaps more importantly within the context of the class divide in the country is the irony of the new leaders, who have acquired significant economic resources, asking workers to sacrifice for the good of the country when they themselves are obviously not willing to do the same.

This does not eliminate the problems, however, that are caused by strikes, including the negative impact on economic growth and securing foreign investment. However, if organized labor, which was a most powerful force in the anti-apartheid movement, is asked to sacrifice its economic expectations for the good of the nation, the growing non-racial elite need do the same. Just as the trade union movement was instrumental in bringing about an end to apartheid, it could also have a detrimental impact on bringing down the government of national unity.

Challenges to the Democratic Initiative
The political transition to date has been relatively smooth in South Africa for several reasons. The first has to do with Mandela and the kind of moral authority he has. He tends to be reconciliatory in terms of his approach to politics and has a powerful presence as a representative of the "nation in the making." Further, the symbolism that surrounds his personal-

ity and leadership, along with his nonpartisan approach to politics, has added enormous weight to the durability of the transition.[87]

A second factor that has contributed to the success of the transition to date is the fact that the executive as a whole has been successful. In particular, De Klerk and the NP have seemingly resigned themselves to the reality of majority rule, although Mandela noted in a July 1994 interview that it was taking the NP time to accept the new South Africa and they "still think they are the majority."[88]

A third factor contributing to the success of the transition is that the parliamentary process has been smooth as has the formation of the nine provinces and law making bodies.[89] In the case of the former, however, there has been criticism regarding the delay in the devolution of power to these entities.[90]

Finally, the security forces have also seemingly resigned themselves to the new political situation in the country. Both the South African Police Service (SAPS) and the South African National Defense Force (SANDF) have been instrumental in the transformation, and Mandela in a recent interview stated, "Whatever mistakes they have made in the past—and whatever certain elements are doing with the security forces—there is no doubt that the overwhelming majority of the security forces are behind the transformation."[91]

Notwithstanding the above, there are challenges to the maintenance of the democratic initiative in the country. These challenges can be divided into two areas. The first consists of challenges that emanate from elements within the society who feel they were marginalized and/or will be totally left out of the new dispensation. Of particular concern are the trade unions, black youth, other blacks who feel their expectations are not being met, the militant right-wing, and certain "third force" elements that remain within the security forces, especially the police.

The second challenge comes from within the government of national unity and is centered around the ability of the government to maintain the democratic initiative if political instability and/or discontentment occurs as a result of anger arising out of the inability of the government to fulfill the expectations of the masses.

The Challenge from Within Society at Large

The trade union movement, as previously indicated, has the potential to destabilize both political and economic structures in the country. As was recently noted, "An unstable workforce will sabotage the RDP more effectively than bombs."[92] With many former trade union leaders now in the government, there is a serious void in leadership. During the recent wave of strikes, critics noted that there currently exists an immature and inexperienced leadership within the trade union movement.[93] The government of national unity must develop a creative strategy to make the trade union movement an integral part of the RDP, or the movement may undermine the democratic process.

The black youth of South Africa also have the potential to challenge the democratic initiative. Having sacrificed their education to "make the townships ungovernable" between 1984 and 1986, they have great expectations that their political allegiance, especially to the ANC, will be rewarded. In addition to not being well-equipped to participate in the reconstruction and development of the country, there's a potential for the politicization of the youth in response to the slow trickling down of benefit and change.[94] The potential for politicization and political instability is heightened by the frustration they feel over the fact that select members of the liberation movement have experienced immediate economic gratification. The ANC-led government has a difficult task ahead to transform this largely uneducated and poorly skilled population into one that can contribute to the reconstruction and development of the country.

The task of transforming the culture of a society from one of protest politics to that of democracy is daunting, especially when there is a perception that there will be no economic rewards. Therefore, it is not surprising that after more than a decade of rent boycotts, residents in the black townships are reluctant to resume paying rents and service charges. It is also not surprising that squatter communities, in frustration, have begun occupying land illegally. What may be surprising is that out of frustration some activists have taken ANC officials hostage in order to high light their grievances.[95] In the final analysis, however, whether such actions are understandable or not, they tend to hinder the democratic initiative in the country.

Although fragmented and divided, the white right-wing still has the potential for creating political instability in the country. They are still heavily armed and committed to the creation of an Afrikaner Volkstaat (Afrikaner People's State). Although there does not exist a possibility that such a state will be created, in keeping with the interim Constitution, a committee has been established to look into this request.[96]

Finally, there are still elements within the SAPS that could pose a challenge to the process. Allegedly there are "scores of senior officers in the police force who were either actively involved in a campaign of assassination and terror against apartheid foes or had full knowledge of such activities." This third force is believed to still exist and continues "to exploit violence between rival taxi groups in the black townships and the violent political conflict in KwaZulu/Natal Province between Zulu supporters of the ANC and the IFP."[97]

The Challenge from Within the Government

For the ANC-led government, the ability to deliver a new economic dispensation by 1999 will be the determining measure of success. This task is daunting, and given the reality of the economic situation, the possibility exists that many expectations will not be met. How will the government respond? According to Wilmont James:

> The thing to worry about is that to the extent that social goals cannot be achieved very easily, and there's reason to think that there is going to be some difficulty in government achieving these things, the more the tendency would be to become undemocratic. Which is to say the less government can deliver, the more the temptation to become more undemocratic in terms of its means . . . The more it will experience difficulty in the things it wants to do, the more it might revert back to old ways. Old ways of patronage and placing shields between itself and the broader public. I'm not saying it will happen, but there's a danger in that happening."[98]

Hopefully the ANC-led government will remain committed to the democratic process. This does not mean that in the movement toward consolidating democracy there will not be major mistakes, such as that in July 1994 when police fired rubber bullets and set dogs on striking workers during the Pick 'n Pack strike.[99]

At times it will no doubt seem easier to resort to the past draconian policies of the apartheid regime or the ANC detention camps, or even the authoritarian and undemocratic policies of most governmental officials throughout Africa. In the finally analysis, however, hopefully the ANC-led government will stay the democratic course and even be willing to graciously relinquish power if the people decide they want new leadership.

Notes

1 Rich Mkhondo, *Reporting South Africa* (Portsmouth, New Hampshire: Heinemann, 1993), p. 24.

2 *Ibid.*, p. 20. See also Heilbert Adam and Kogila Moodley, *The Negotiated Revolution: Society and Politics in Post-Apartheid South Africa* (Johannesburg: Jonathan Ball Publishers, 1993), p. 42.

3 According to Rich Mkhondo, such meetings were also held in the early 1980's but were never made public. Mkhondo, pp. 20-21.

4 *Ibid.*, p. 21.

5 Adam and Moodley, p. 1.

6 Mkhondo, pp. 15-16; Khehla Shubane, "South Africa: A New Government in the Making?" *Current History*, May 1992, pp. 202-3; and Allister Sparks, "Transition in South Africa: Its Prospects and Implications," *PAS*, Vol. 3, Winter 1993, p. 4.

7 Adam and Moodley, p. 40.

8 Michael MacDonald and Wilmont James, "The Hand on the Tiller: The Politics of State and Class in South Africa," *The Journal of Modern African Studies*, Vol. 31, No. 3, 1993, p. 397.

9 Mkhondo, p. 22.

10 Tom Lodge, "The African National Congress in the 1990s," in *South Africa Review 6*, Glenn Moss and Ingrid Obery, eds. (Johannesburg: Ravan Press, 1992), pp. 45-46.

11 *Ibid.*, pp. 49-50.

12 Daniel R. Dempton, "Africa in the Age of Perestroika," *Africa Today*, 3rd Quarter 1991, p. 13.

13 Winrich Kuhne, "A 1988 Update on Soviet Relations with Pretoria, the ANC, and the SACP," CSIS Africa Notes, No. 89, September 1988, p. 1.

14 Boris Asoyan, "Russia and South Africa," *International Affairs*, December 1989, p. 48.

15 Lodge, p. 50.

16   See, for example, John Battersby, "ANC Admits to Abuses of Rights, *"The Christian Science Monitor,* October 21, 1992; and Patrick Laurence, "Exposing the Past," *Africa Report,* January/February, 1993, pp. 51-52. On August 23, 1993, A commission appointed by the ANC released another report on the abuses in ANC camps. See John Battersby, "ANC Goes Public on Abuses in Exile Camps," *The Christian Science Monitor,* August 25, 1993.

17   Lodge, p. 50.

18   Jacklyn Cock and Laurie Nathan, eds. *Society At War: The Militarisation of South Africa* (New York: St. Martin's Press, 1989); Jacklyn Cock, "The Dynamics of Transforming South Africa's Defense Forces," in *South Africa: The Political Economy of Transformation,* Stephen John Stedman, ed. (Boulder and London: Lynne Rienner Publishers, 1994); Gavin Cawthra, *Brutal Force: The Apartheid War Machine,* (London: International Defence and Aid Fund for Southern Africa, 1986); and Kenneth W. Grundy, *The Militarization of South African Politics* (Bloomington: Indiana University Press, 1986).

19   James Selfe, "South Africa's National Management System," in *Society at War: The Militarisation of South Africa,* Jacklyn Cock and Laurie Nathan, eds. (New York: St. Martin's Press, 1989), p. 150

20   Sparks, "Transition in South Africa," p. 4.

21   Herbert Howe, "The South African Defence Force and Political Reform," *The Journal of Modern African Studies,* Vol., 32, No. 1, 1994, p. 33.

22   *Ibid.*

23   *Ibid.*

24   *Ibid.,* and Mkhondo, pp. 73-75.

25   Mkhondo, p. 75.

26   *Ibid.,* pp. 75-80; and Gavin Cawthra, *Policing South Africa: The SAP and the Transition From Apartheid* (London and New Jersey: Zed Books Ltd., 1993), pp. 122-26.

27   Laurie Nathan and Mark Phillips, "'Cross-current': Security Developments under FW de Klerk," in *South Africa Review 6,* Glen Moss and Ingrid Obery, eds. (Johannesburg: Ravan Press, 1992), p. 121.

28   *Ibid.,* p. 114.

29   Nathan and Phillips provide a good overview and critique of de Klerk and the security establishment.

30 Sparks, p. 4.

31 Howe, p. 31.

32 Eddie Koch and Anton Harber, "Police Paid Inkatha to Block ANC," *The Weekly Mail*, July 19 to July 25, 1991.

33 John Battersby, "De Klerk Faces Test of Presidency," *The Christian Science Monitor*, July 29, 1991.

34 Jo-Anne Collinge, "Launched on a Bloody Tide: Negotiating the New South Africa," in *South African Review* 6, Glenn Moss and Ingrid Obery, eds. (Johannesburg: Ravan Press, 1992), p. 1.

35 For an excellent account of this period through July 1993, see Mkhondo.

36 *Ibid.*, p. 59 and Patrick Laurence, "Looking at the Bigger Picture," *The Star* (SA), July 1992.

37 Nathan and Phillips, pp. 120-21; and "Amnesty for the South African Government," Southern Africa Project of the Lawyers' Committee for Civil Rights Under Law, 1993, p. 4.

38 Howe, p. 37.

39 Kenneth Grundy, "South Africa's Tortuous Transition," *Current History*, May 1993, p. 229.

40 Howe, p. 37; "Buffalo Battalion Retreats from Natal Township," *SouthScan*, June 12, 1992; and "South Africa's Sinister Security Forces Have Their Tentacles Everywhere Despite De Klerk's Efforts to Reduce Their Influence," *New African*, June 1993.

41 Cock (1994), p. 144.

42 "Amnesty for the South African Government," p. 2.

43 The DMI was a covert SADF unit.

44 Howe, pp. 36-37.

45 *Ibid.*, p. 39.

46 *Ibid.*, pp. 36-37.

47 *Ibid.*, p. 40.

48 *Ibid.*

49 Cock (1994), p. 143.

50 Howe, p. 49.

51 *Ibid.*, p. 50.

52 MacDonald and James, pp. 399-400.

53 The Afrikaner Volksfront was formed by four former commanders of the SA military and police. Their major objective was to get the negotiators to agree to the formation of an Afrikaner Volkstaat (Afrikaner People's State).

54 Bill Keller, "South Africa Pact: Unlikely Partners," *The New York Times,* November 1993.

55 The findings of the Goldstone Commission as reported by the Lawyers Committee for Civil Rights Under Law included: "gun running by police to men involved in hit squads, the illegal manufacture of weapons, the issuing of false documents and passports and the orchestration of violence to destabilize the country; the provision of arms to members of Inkatha; that Inkatha Freedom Party Transvaal leader Themba Khoza was recruited as a police informer, and was supplied with arms for distribution to Inkatha supporters in hostels around Johannesburg; there is 'convincing evidence' that 'elements in the KwaZulu Police have been and are still involved in hit squad activities in Natal and also in the Transvaal'; that there is prima facie evidence that policemen and Inkatha members, carried out killings on trains (between 1990 and 1992) in which more than 300 black commuters were killed; and that evidence of the operations have been destroyed on the orders of senior police officers." Source: Lawyers' Committee for Civil Rights Under Law, Southern Africa Project, "South Africa: The Countdown to Elections," Issue 9, March 25, 1994, pp. 3-4.

56 John Battersby, "Independent Probe Links Inkatha, S. African Police," *The Christian Science Monitor*, March 21, 1994.

57 The Freedom Alliance replaced Cosag in October 7, 1993. The members included the CP, the AVF, the IFP, and the presidents of Bophuthatswana and Ciskei.

58 For a list of the concessions, see "South Africa: The Countdown to Elections," Issue 7, February 1994, The Lawyers' Committee for Civil Rights Under Law, pp. 1-2.

59 The Freedom Front split off from the Afrikaner Volksfront, which was created out of the conflict that occurred within the white right-wing after the death of the Conservative Party leader, Andries Treurnicht, in 1993.

60 Christopher Cramer, "Rebuilding South Africa" *Current History*, May 1994, p. 209.

61 Jeffrey Herbst, "South Africa: Economic Crisis and Distributional Imperative," in *South Africa: The Political Economy of Transformation,* Stephen John Stedman, ed. (Boulder and London: Lynne Rienner Publishers, 1994), p. 30.

62 Anne Shepherd, "The Task Ahead," *Africa Report,* July/August 1994, p. 40.

63 ANC, *The Reconstruction and Development Programme: A Policy Framework.* (Johannesburg: Umanyano Publications), p. 7.

64 *Ibid.,* pp. 7-8.

65 *Ibid.,* p. 64.

66 Robert I. Rotberg, "Ethnic Power Sharing: South Africa's Model," *The Christian Science Monitor,* September 14, 1994.

67 "Undoing Decades of Damage," *Negotiation News,* September 12, 1994, p. 5.

68 *Ibid.*

69 Rotberg, "Ethnic Power Sharing."

70 "New RDP Anti-Poverty Projects Announced," *SouthScan,* September 9, 1994.

71 *Ibid.*

72 ANC, pp. 142-43.

73 John Battersby, "Black Hopes, White Fears: A Balancing Act," *The Christian Science Monitor,* September 28, 1994.

74 Herbst, p. 35.

75 Cramer, p. 211.

76 MacDonald and James, "The Hands on the Tiller," p. 404.

77 I. M. Rautenbach and E. F. J. Malherbe. *What Does the Constitution Say?* (Auckland Park, South Africa: The Faculty of Law, Rand Afrikaans University, 1994), p. 53.

78 Wilmont James, "Building on Democracy in the New South Africa," Lecture at the Southern Center for International Studies (SCIS), Atlanta, Georgia, September 22, 1994.

79 "Cash Crunch Coming: Local Level Last in Line," *Negotiation News,* No. 18, September 12, 1994, p. 1.

80 *Ibid.*

81 "A New Class of Mandarins Takes Over, " *Sunday Times* (SA), July 17, 1994.

82 For an insightful critique of the nation-state in Africa see Basil Davidson, *The Black Man's Burden: Africa and the Curse of the Nation-State* (New York: Times Books, 1992).

83 "Ugly Strike Patterns," *Finance Week*, July 21-27, 1994, p. 16.

84 Ken Owen, "All Aboard the Gravy Train for Joe and Co," *Sunday Times*, July 24, 1994.

85 John Battersby, "Nelson Mandela Boldly Faces the Future," *The Christian Science Monitor*, September 12, 1994.

86 Herbst, p. 40.

87 James, "Building on Democracy in the New South Africa."

88 "Leaders May Extend Power-Sharing," *Daily Dispatch*, July 19, 1994.

89 *Ibid.*

90 *Ibid.*; and "Premiers Are 'Crying for Powers,'" *Negotiation News*, September 12, 1994, p. 11.

91 Monitor Interview with President Mandela, *The Christian Science Monitor*, September 12, 1994.

92 "Ugly Strike Patterns," p. 16.

93 James, "Building on Democracy in the New South Africa"; Drew Forrest, "Behind the R54 Strike—Black Rage on the Shop Floor," *The Weekly Mail and Guardian*, July 22 to 28, 1994; and "Ugly Strike Patterns," pp. 15-16.

94 James, "Building on Democracy in the New South Africa."

95 John Battersby, "Black Hopes, White Fears: A Balancing Act," *The Christian Science Monitor*, September 28, 1994.

96 James, "Building on Democracy in the New South Africa."

97 John Battersby, "Mandela Faces Unresolved Issue of Covert Web in Security Forces," *The Christian Science Monitor*, October 4, 1994.

98 James, "Building on Democracy in the New South Africa."

99 Forrest, "Behind the R54 Strike—Black Rage on the Shop Floor."

Appendix

South Africa: Key Events, February 1990 to May 1994

1990
February 2—President FW de Klerk legalized the ANC, the South African Communist Party (SACP), the Pan Africanist Congress (PAC), and other banned opposition movements in a prelude to all-party democracy negotiations.
February 11—Nelson Mandela, after serving 27 years in prison, was released.
May 2-4—The ANC and the government met for the first time and signed the Groote Schuur Minute in which they agreed to a framework for the release of political prisoners, indemnity for exiles and a joint commitment to end violence. The meeting took place in Cape Town at Groote Schuur.
August 6—Mandela and de Klerk met and agreed to ease emergency rules and the ANC suspended its 30-year armed struggle against apartheid.

1991
April 5—Mandela accused de Klerk in an open letter of not doing enough to end township violence and sets a one-month ultimatum for action on violence to ensure continuation of "talks about talks."
April 9—Mandela and de Klerk rescued talks in a crisis meeting that resulted in a ban on cultural weapons.
September 14—The ANC, anti-apartheid groups, political parties, government and Inkatha Freedom Party (IFP), signed a national peace accord to reduce tension and set up mechanisms to resolve disputes.
November 21—ANC, government, Inkatha and others agreed to start multiparty talks on December 20.
December 20—Nineteen parties and groups launched the Convention for a Democratic South Africa (CODESA 1), the first real attempt to negotiate a transition to democracy.

1992

March 17—White South Africans voted in a referendum to endorse de Klerk's reforms.

May 16—CODESA failed to resolve differences between the government and the ANC over minority powers and protection in a democratic South Africa.

June 16—ANC launched a mass action campaign of strikes, boycotts and rallies to force the government to speed up political reform.

June 17—At least 39 people were butchered in Boipatong. Residents accused supporters of the IFP of the massacre.

June 21—Mandela accused de Klerk and his government of complicity in the Boipatong massacre and ordered ANC negotiators to suspend bilateral talks with the government.

June 23—ANC leaders decided to pull out of the talks.

July—A special session of the United Nations was held to allow CODESA participants to express their views on the breakdown of talks and the ongoing violence. The UN decided to send a mission to SA to monitor the violence.

September 7—ANC mounted a protest march on the Ciskei bantustan in a bid to topple the leader. Security force open fire on protesters- 28 were slaughtered and 200 were hurt.

September 26—The ANC and the de Klerk government signed a "Record of Understanding" which set out a basis for the resumption of negotiations. They agreed to:

   1. Release 150 political prisoners now and 400 more by November 15.

   2. Fence and patrol 24 migrant worker hostels regarded as flash points of township violence.

   3. Ban dangerous weapons in public such as spears, axes and clubs.

   4. A single-chamber, universally-elected constituent assembly to draw up a democratic constitution within an agreed time frame.

   5. A non-racial interim government operating under an interim constitution.

September 27—Chief Buthelezi announced he was pulling out of the negotiations.

October—The Concerned South Africans Group (Cosag) was formed as an anti-ANC alliance. Members included the IFP, the governments of Bophutatswana, Ciskei and KwaZulu, and the Conservative Party (CP) and the Afrikaner Volksunie (AVU).

October 12—In a special session of parliament supposedly designed to make final plans for transitional rule and non-racial elections, de Klerk vowed to protect white minority rights in any future system. ANC protesters marched on the white parliament.

October 17—10,000 IFP members marched in Johannesburg brandishing spears and clubs to protest the ban on traditional weapons agreed by Mandela and de Klerk.

November 19—The ANC conceded to the possibility of power-sharing.

December 1—Chief Buthelezi unveiled a constitution seeking to establish Natal Province and the homeland of KwaZulu as a semiautonomous federal state. This resulted in the first public clash between de Klerk and Buthelezi.

December 2-5—The National Party and the ANC held three days of intense bilateral talks in a bid to forge an agreement on the transition to democratic rule.

December 7—Cosag met to discuss plans for multi-lateral negotiations for a federal governmental structure and to reject plans for a transitional constitution and government.

1993

January—Chris Hani, the Secretary General of the SACP, announced that the SACP would break with the ANC after the first election and form a socialist alliance with the trade unions and Winnie Mandela to fight for full rights.

February 12—The ANC and the National Party agreed to what the NP calls power-sharing and what the ANC calls a government of national unity.

March 5-6—Twenty-six parties and groups met in Johannesburg and agreed to meet on April 1 to work out details for ending white rule. All the delegates, including representatives of the PAC and the white separatists, signed a resolution declaring "unwavering rejection of all instances of political violence."

April 1—Twenty-six parties and groups, including the PAC and CP, resumed negotiations after an 11-month break.

April 10—Chris Hani was assassinated by Janusz Walus, a white Polish immigrant, who was a member of a secret right-wing cell.

April 20—The "Committee of Generals" was formed by four former commanders of the SA military and police. Their goal is to unify the right in the country and work towards an independent Afrikaner nation. The four included Constand Viljoen, the former Chief of the Defense Force, who chairs the committee; Koss Bishoff; Cobus Visser, a retired head of the CID; and Tienie Groenewald.

April 21—Dr. Andries Treurnicht, leader of the CP, died.

April 24—Oliver Tambo, ANC National Chairman, died.

May 7—The Committee of Generals, along with other right-wing elements, launched the Afrikaner Volksfront (AVF) with a view to getting de Klerk to suspend multiparty negotiations.

May 25—In the most extensive crackdown on a black opposition group since 1988, the South African Police arrested 73 senior members of the PAC and alleged members of PAC's military wing, the Azania's People's Liberation Army (APLA).

June 17—IFP delegation and other members of Cosag walked out of the multi-party negotiations because of disagreement with the ANC over the functions of regions in a decentralized government. They returned to the talks after the council agreed to consider their concerns.

June 23—Nelson Mandela and Mangosuthu Buthelezi met to discuss possible resolutions to political violence.

June 25—A crowd of 3,000 right-wingers smashed their way into the World Trade Center with an armored vehicle during multiparty negotiations.

June—A deal to establish a joint peacekeeping force was agreed to.

June 30—The multi-party negotiators reached a major compromise on the question of the principle of a strong regional government. They agreed that the boundaries, powers, and functions of semiautonomous regions will be included in a transitional constitution. The constitution will also allow for elections for regional legislatures.

July 2—The first multi-racial elections were scheduled for April 27, 1994. In protest, Cosag walked out of negotiations.

July 3—The National Union of Metalworkers announced plans to break an alliance with the ANC, trade unions and the communists following the first democratic elections.

July 26—A draft constitution was tabled at the multi-party talks.

September 8—Multi-party negotiators agreed to the establishment of a multi-racial Transitional Executive Council (TEC) to govern the country, along with Parliament, until the first multiracial elections.

September 16—De Klerk met with Buthelezi in a bid to woo him back to multi-party negotiations

September 24—The revelation was made that the ANC and the Afrikaner Volksfront had reached an agreement in which the Volksfront would participate in elections for a Constituent Assembly if their demand for a semiautonomous homeland is acknowledged in an interim constitution.

October 7—The Freedom Alliance (FA) was formed consisting of the CP, the AVF, the IFP, and the presidents of Bophuthatswana and Ciskei. It replaced Cosag.

October 18-19—Separate bilateral meetings were held between the government and the FA and the ANC and the FA.

October 21—Right-wing and conservative black leaders agreed to return to negotiations under a formula that allowed them to meet in bilateral talks with the government and the ANC.

October 29—Talks were held between the government and the FA.

November 18—Agreement was reached by multi-party negotiators on an interim constitution for South Africa.

November 18-19—The ANC and the AVF held secret talks after which the ANC agreed to consider a request for a plebiscite among Afrikaners on an Afrikaner homeland.

December 6—The multi-racial TEC, consisting of 19 parties, met for the first time in Cape Town, giving the black majority the first say in government.

December 15—The South African parliament voted to restore citizenship to residents of the four nominally independent bantustans—Transkei, Venda, Bophuthatswana and Ciskei.

December 22—The South African parliament adopted South Africa's Interim Constitution.

1994

January 17—PAC suspended APLA's armed struggle.

February 28—The old Parliament met to consider amendments to the Electoral Act and the Interim Constitution. These changes followed last-minute concessions made by the ANC and NP to bring members of the Freedom Alliance into the election process.

March 10—President Lucas Mangope of Bophuthatswana was deposed, and the South African government assumed control over the territory.

March 28—At least 53 people were killed and hundreds injured as ANC supporters clashed with tens of thousands of Zulus who converged on the city center in Johannesburg in support of King Goodwill Zwelithini.

April 5—An international mediation team that included Dr. Paul Kevenhorster of Germany, former US Secretary of State Henry Kissinger and former British Foreign Secretary Lord Carrington, arrived in South Africa in hopes of helping to re-solve the Natal/KwaZulu constitutional dispute.

April 8—A crisis summit was held between de Klerk, Mandela, Buthelezi, and King Goodwill.

April 14—The international mediation involving Kevenhorster and others ended in a deadlock.

April 19—The IFP decided to contest the elections after Pro-fessor Okumu from Kenya intervened in the mediation.

April 24—A massive bomb shook central Johannesburg, kill-ing at least nine people and wounding 92.

April 25—At least ten people were killed when a powerful car bomb exploded in central Germiston.

April 26-29—The first nonracial elections were held in South Africa.

May 6—The ANC won the election in seven of the nine re-gional provinces. The NP won in the Western Cape and the IFP in KwaZulu/Natal.

May 7—The ANC won in national elections with 62.65 percent of the votes. The NP came in second place with just over 20 percent and the IFP came in third place with 10.54 percent.

May 9—Nelson Rolihlahla Mandela was elected as the Presi-dent of the Republic of South Africa.

May 10—Mandela was sworn in as the first black President of South Africa during the Presidential Inauguration.

Chapter 11

South Africa in the African Dilemma

Akwasi Osei

INTRODUCTION

The last half of the 20th Century can arguably be referred to as the era of African political independence. Over those years, almost all the political entities gained a measure of autonomy which allowed Africans, for the first time in centuries, to reclaim political control which had been lost to various European nations. Perhaps the most intractable and therefore the most memorable of these transitions has been the situation in South Africa which has gone from crisis and conflict to reconstruction and reconciliation. As hopeful as that situation is, for the moment it shares with the rest of Africa a major characteristic of this era of African political independence (viz, political power in African hands but economic power under major external influence). In other words, just as so-called independence has been a mixed blessing for much of Africa, it will be the same for the majority of South Africans for the foreseeable future. Africans have political power but do not have economic and bureaucratic power.

In spite of this, South Africa provides the opportunity to reverse and transcend the half-century experiment in political development in Africa. Far from becoming another neocolonial dependency, the new South Africa evokes images of a genuine example of emancipation; a viable, and industrially independent state which will reflect the aspirations and hopes of the rest of the continent. South Africa has ushered in a new era of liberation which will recall the second phase of the national liberation struggle as theorized by Amilcar Cabral.[1]

Why is South Africa different? What gives it its promise? Who is Amilcar Cabral and what is his theory of national liberation? In what way does South Africa embody the promise of Cabral's theory? These are some of the questions that this chapter will attempt to answer. Like much of Africa, South Africa had been in fact a colonial settler-state. The historical account establishes beyond a doubt the usurpation of African land by foreign forces, who proceeded to legitimize their control over the peoples and the area under colonialism and neo-colonialism.

Africans in South Africa resisted European occupation of the region during the advent of European rule in Africa. They also fought against the introduction of apartheid at the turn of the century. This chapter argues that because of this rich culture of resistance, and most importantly, because of its wealth and industrial base, South Africa will blaze the trail of genuine independence to which Africa has long aspired. We have witnessed over 35 years of nominal independence in Africa however, there is a need for a genuine social revolution, and South Africa embodies this future.

Consequently, we will borrow from Amilcar Cabral his theory of National Liberation and then apply it to the South African situation in order to show what could be the most far-reaching political phenomenon in Africa in the last days of the 20th Century.

CABRAL AND NATIONAL LIBERATION

Amilcar Cabral arguably has no equal in the analysis of Africa's struggles to escape the strangling yoke of colonialism and its effects. It was in his erudite expatiation on the colonial and post-colonial situations in Africa that he imparted to posterity his theory of national liberation. To understand the African dilemma, Cabral states that the beginning point is a concrete analysis of the African condition. This should be accompanied by constant reviews of the aims and objectives of the liberation struggle in the light of any new developments.

In a concrete evaluation of his status as an assimilado,[2] Cabral discovered that he was surrounded by fellow Cape Verdians and Bissauans who were not as well off as he was.

That was the beginning of his anti-colonial journey. It led him to adopt the belief that the lot of Africans under the Portuguese oppressive rule could only improve with the latter's overthrow. He combined his work as an agronomist with his anti-colonialist fervor as he traveled around Guinea Bissau and Cape Verde assessing the impact of colonial exploitation and identifying the essential motivations for the struggle against colonial dominations.[3]

For Cabral, "domination" was the key phenomenon. To combat it, the dominated must engage in efforts to *regain* its position in a historical process which was arrested and truncated by the violence of colonialism. This was the only way towards genuine liberation. As long as the domination continued the dominated would be incapable of making their own history; they needed to free and legitimize themselves by creating their own social realities.

Foreign domination in Africa has taken two forms. One is direct domination which, according to Cabral, constitutes "political power made up by agents foreign to the dominated people (armed forces, police, administrative agents and settlers) which is conventionally called classical colonialism, or colonialism."[4] The other is indirect domination by foreign powers or the former colonial masters "by means of a political power made up mainly or completely of native agents."[5] These agents are under the pay and or control of foreign power(s). In this case the foreign oppressor continues to exploit the so-called independent country with the support of local agents who are nothing but puppets.

While classical colonialism guarantees political and economic hegemony by the dominating power, neocolonialism provides an "illusion" where increased economic and political activity among the previously dominated gives the impression of freedom and self-determination. This impression is heightened by the creation of political power structures which indicate control. However, according to Cabral, the native ruling class is subject to that of the dominating country. As long as there is some amount of outside control, Cabral notes, the dominated cannot control their own destinies. He contended that:

... freedom, and it alone, can guarantee the normal course of the historical process of a people. We can therefore conclude that national liberation exists when, and only when, the national productive forces have been completely freed from all and any kind of foreign domination.[6]

As defined by Cabral, therefore, National Liberation is the

... phenomenon in which a socio-economic whole rejects the denial of its historical process. In other words, the national liberation of a people is the regaining of the historical personality of that people, it is their return to history through the destruction of the imperialist domination to which they are subjected.[7]

This two-pronged idea is Cabral's unique contribution to African political thought. Against colonialism, the nation as a unit agitates against the physical presence of the dominant power. With the collapse of colonialism the colonial political and economic structures fall into the hands of the indigenous elite. Consequently, a new colonial phase (neocolonialism), according to Cabral, usually replaces the former colonial system. In many African countries, the neocolonial phase led to class and ethnic divisions among others, resulting in instability and political violence. In this phase, the fundamental question becomes whether the promise of freedom will be fulfilled; and if the new state could carry out a genuine social revolution in which it would rid itself totally of foreign control. Leaders at this stage are faced with a dilemma of either contributing to the perpetuation of external influence and control or adopting policies aimed at genuine independence and self-determination. If they chose the latter, they would, in Cabral's words, be "committing class suicide."[8]

THE SOUTH AFRICAN CASE

Foreign domination is what South Africa has endured since 1652 when Jan van Riebeeck landed and settled at Table Bay in the Cape of Good Hope. Gradually, through bloody wars, Riebeeck and his descendants established domination and control over the Africans. White occupation since then has led to oppression, deprivation, exploitation and dispossession of the indigenous African population in South Africa. This was accompanied by the idea of white supremacy, which was refined and codified into the policy of Apartheid in 1948. The rise to power of the Nationalist Party was the climax of the dreams, thoughts, hopes and aspirations of Afrikaaner nationalism. White privilege, white superiority, and economic exploitation of blacks have been the bedrock of the apartheid system.

It has been suggested that South Africa is a colonial settler state with a "colonial state form . . . and [the] violence and viciousness of the apartheid system" reduced the African majority to a sociological minority.[9] It was not surprising, therefore, that the disenfranchised Black majority had to engage in a protracted struggle to overthrow the apartheid system.

With the formation of the Union of South Africa in 1910, denationalization of the indigenous population was underway. The Land Act of 1913, (later revised in 1930), completely dispossessed Blacks of their land. While the rest of Africa was involved in a clear cut decolonization process, South Africans were engaged in the more pernicious struggle of regaining citizenship in their own homeland which ought to have been a birth right. Ironically it is the sophisticated nature of the South Africa struggle which evokes images of a social revolution as discussed by Cabral.

THE ECONOMIC BASE OF SOUTH AFRICA

It was South Africa's abundant wealth and resources that attracted van Riebeeck to the Cape in 1652. Today, it is still the wealth and resources of South Africa that has kept van Riebeeck's descendants in the country despite the continuous struggle against their domination of the political system and the economy.

Africans of various ethnic backgrounds had by the 16th Century organized themselves into states such as the Rolong, Venda and Sotho. Fearing the future might of these nation-states, the settlers engaged these states in skirmishes. Using force and superior weapons, the settlers were able to wrest control of the land. The availability of land to the interlopers led to a booming agricultural economy. Africans (who were land owners) were reduced to serfdom and slave labor. It was their labor that worked the increasingly prosperous farms. On the eve of what was to become the "mineral revolution," the area was self sufficient in food production.

The discovery of diamonds at Kimberley in the 1860's, and gold in the 1880's in the Witwatersrand, transformed South Africa's economy onto a higher plane. These discoveries became a catalyst for excessive migration of whites from Europe, America, and Australia to South Africa. Commenting on this, Stephen Lewis opined that "diamonds and gold transformed the country from an agricultural and trading back water to an economic resource of great value."[10] Capital flowed in large amounts and companies like Cecil Rhodes' British South Africa Company used all means at their disposal to expand their investments in South Africa.

From 1873 through the end of the 19th Century, there were many wars between the settlers of the various European nationalities as wells as between the latter and the native population. There were, among others, the Langalibalele Affair of 1873-74; the Transvaal/Pedi War of 1876; Cape Colony/Xhosa War of 1878; Anglo-Zulu War of 1879; the Gun War of 1880-81; and the Anglo-Boer Wars of 1881 and of 1899-1902.[11] New wealth and new immigrants made for serious problems. For Africans, the loss was even greater: their land was being contested for by two usurpers, the English-speaking and Afrikaans-speaking whites. With Union in 1910, the plight of Africans worsened. Africans were further destined to be nothing more than laborers who would keep the economy alive.

During much of the 20th Century, the South African economy grew and the country industrialized. The economy was further boosted with the discovery of other precious minerals such as uranium and platinum. The large profits from the export of minerals aided the apartheid government in developing transportation networks, and subsidizing local industries at a period when much of the world community isolated South Africa because of her obnoxious apartheid policies.

SOUTH AFRICA AS A REGIONAL ECONOMIC ANCHOR

Today, South Africa is undergoing political, social, and economic transformation. The apartheid system has been dismantled. South Africa is now under Black majority rule. There are speculations that an economically viable South Africa could anchor the economic revival of the Southern African region. With the end of apartheid, an independent South Africa can team up with its neighbors to create a strong regional organization. A United States of Southern Africa could be the foundation for continental unity. The creation of a viable regional organization like the one suggested has always been a motivating factor in the support of the struggle for majority rule in South Africa by her neighbors.

During the liberation struggle, South Africa retaliated against her neighbors for supporting the freedom fighters in the 1980's. She applied sanctions against Angola, Botswana, Lesotho, Malawi, Mozambique, Swaziland, Tanzania, Zambia and Zimbabwe. Consequently, these countries out of necessity, formed the Southern Africa Development Coordinating Conference (SADCC). The main objective was to decrease their dependence on apartheid South Africa which had held them hostage politically and economically. For instance, in Mozambique and Angola, apartheid South Africa collaborated with Portugal to resist anti-colonial struggles, and later financed bandits (RENAMO and UNITA) to destabilize those two nations. In the case of Namibia, South Africa occupied it against international law until 1990 when Namibia became independent. For years, the apartheid regime's defense forces attacked Botswana, Lesotho, Swaziland, Zambia and Zimbabwe for harboring anti-apartheid activists and combatants.

Economically, SADCC aimed to decrease its dependence on South Africa in the areas of transportation, security, trade and communication. SADCC members were totally dependent on a railway network which was controlled by South Africa and on which the SADCC relied to transport its exports and imports to South African seaports.

Records show that South Africa has always benefitted from trade with the members of SADCC. For instance, for the last two decades, South Africa has accounted for three quarters of regional Gross Domestic Product (GDP): the total GDP of the area (11 countries) in 1985 was $100 billion with South Africa's being $75 billion. With regard to exports, South Africa exported about $18 billion worth of goods in the region while the other ten combined exported only a total of $6.5 billion. As a result, South Africa has always continued to enjoy large trade surpluses. This dependence has been heightened by the fact that for decades South Africa relied on a substantial labor force-until 1985, 60 percent of the total miner population—from its neighbors.[12]

The death of apartheid seems to have changed the fortunes of SADCC. Indeed, the ascension to a dominant decision-making position by Nelson Mandela and the ANC offers the hope that the new South Africa will redirect its resources towards collaboration with its neighbors. In 1995, South Africa finally became a member of the reconstituted Southern Africa Development Community (SADC). Now with a membership of 12 (Namibia joined in 1990, and Mauritius in 1995), the community's main thrust is to create an economic community which would ultimately trade in one currency, eliminate trade barriers, have free movement of their peoples and goods, as well as cooperate on all matters from mining to water sharing.

The new SADC has signed a binding agreement which would require all the nations to share the water resources in the region. In an environment parched by drought over the last ten years, this is a significant achievement. The new South Africa, rather than destabilizing its neighbors, promises to provide leadership and support. The new community commands a combined $150 billion in Gross National Product (GNP) and with the removal of trade barriers, plans to trade with each other more. SADC is poised to become an economic giant on the continent, and with South Africa in the lead, the rest of Africa stands to emulate that success.

CULTURE OF RESISTANCE

Since April 1994, the overwhelming news emanating from South Africa has been the incredible magnanimity which the victorious ANC has shown as it garnered political power. What apartheid wrought for over three centuries is well-known. From birth to death, every life decision was shaped by white supremacy. For a white South African of course it was a system of privilege which for most of this century ensured the world's

highest standard of living. For Africans, and in varying de-
grees for other non-Europeans, it was the exact opposite. To
the latter, it was a bleak life. The Bantustan policy (which advocated for segregation and separate development) effectively
denationalized all Africans, and consigned millions to poverty.
Coupled with the migrant labor policy, the Bantustan policy
destroyed family life. Most Africans in the urban areas earned
less than what was officially considered poverty wages and
suffered as a result. When one considers certain basic quality
of life indices, one can only conclude that apartheid ensured
white supremacy. For instance, African infant mortality rates
were 31 times higher than those for Europeans; the doctor/
population ratio for European was 1 to 330, for Africans it
was 1 to 91,000.[13]

The legal pillars of apartheid have been torn down. The
Mixed Marriages Act, the Pass Laws, Separate Amenities Act,
the Population Registration Act, the Group Areas Act, Influx
Control Laws, and the Land Acts are now things of the past.
Nelson Mandela emerged from 27 years in political prison in
1990 to oversee the final overthrow of *statutory* apartheid.

While apartheid's legal edifice has crumbled, its concrete
legacy persists, and remains the reality for the majority of South
Africans. Most are as poor and as hungry for land in this new
dispensation as they were in the old regime. Squatter camps
and deteriorating townships are still home to millions. Walter
Sisulu captures this reality more accurately when he noted that:

> Seventeen million poor and hungry in a population of 40 million; 50
> percent unemployment [in some areas]; 7 million homeless; 9 million
> illiterate; countless millions impatient and nurtured in a culture of
> violent protests. My greatest fear is that the task is too big.[14]

In response to this, the ANC-led government of National
Unity has created the Reconstruction and Development Program (RDP). It is a social and economic rebuilding program
which will provide the needs of the first order: food, shelter,
water, health and electricity. The government has given it the
priority it deserves, making the RDP head a cabinet position.
More pointedly, the government has ensured that about 5 percent of government spending—$1.5 billion in 1995—is set aside
in the RDP Fund. An immediate RDP impact has been the

daily meal of bread and milk for four million children in the poorest areas; another is the free compulsory education and free medicine and health care for most of the poor.

For most outside observers of the new South Africa, the greatest achievement to date has been the absence of revenge on the part of the non-European population on their previous oppressors. How does one account for the extraordinary out-pouring of magnanimity on the part of ANC in taking the lead in reconciliation rather than retaliation?

A major explanation is that the long anti-apartheid struggle created a culture of resistance which has always been focused on the main objective—annihilation of white domination, and a creation of a South Africa that works for *all its* peoples. In the process, there has arisen a wise, mature political culture which allows South Africans to identify with Cabral's theory of national liberation.

Over the years, the ideological guidance and leadership that has been offered in this culture of resistance has been pro-vided by many organizations. The most successful—and endur-ing—has been the ANC, but there have been many others. For instance, there was the Industrial and Commercial Workers Union (ICU) in the 1920's, the All-African Convention in the 1930's and the Pan-African Congress (PAC) since the 1950's. Much later in the 1970's, the Black Consciousness Movement (BCM) spawned groups such as the Southern African Students Organization (SASO) the Black Peoples Convention (BPC), and the Azanian Peoples Organization (AZAPO). In the last days of apartheid, the United Democratic Front (UDF) and the Mass Democratic Movement (MDM) became the umbrella organ-izations out of which the last blows against apartheid were struck.

Through all these years, however, it was the ANC that pro-vided the most consistent leadership and direction. Founded in 1912, it is the oldest liberation organization on the African continent. It grew from largely middle-class organization of colonially educated Africans to the most disciplined, most democratic mass movement against apartheid. As its fortunes have risen and fallen in the last 83 years it has provided brains as well as the organizational acumen in giving concrete repre-sentation to millions of South Africans.

The ANC has been successful for specific reasons. First, the organization's ability to grow has allowed it to always keep ahead of its foes, and to adapt when it has had to. Its founders were Africans who seemed comfortable as leaders of their peoples within the British Empire. In the 1940's, the ANC Youth League led by leaders such and Nelson Mandela, Oliver Tambo and Walter Sisulu pushed the older leadership to adopt a more militant, politically active posture designed to rally the majority of South Africans to confront the apartheid regime. This commitment was consequently enshrined in the *Freedom Charter* adopted by the Congress of the People in Kliptown in June 1955. It embodies the fundamental principles of the struggle under the banner of the ANC.

When the apartheid government decided to entrench apartheid and became more oppressive in 1960, the ANC resorted to armed struggle. After it was banned in that year, it moved into exile to continue the struggle. As pressure became unbearable for the apartheid government in the mid-1980's, it signaled its willingness to negotiate. The ANC proceeded to negotiate. Ultimately, in 1994, the ANC became the moving force in the power-sharing, transitional government of National Unity. Its political maturity helped develop a new culture of negotiation towards change.

A second reason for the ANC's success has been its ability to keep its focus while maintaining its openness and willingness to embrace other organizations. This has been possible because the ANC has always had clear, well-identified goals and objectives and has been very successful at marshalling the various anti-apartheid groups for one ultimate purpose—a South Africa with no built-in privileges for any group, where all are equal before the law, and a South Africa where all will share in the wealth of the land.

The success of the ANC of course has been guided by a committed leadership that has been steadfast in its vision of overthrowing centuries-old white hegemony. This is what evokes Cabral's call for true emancipation from all forms of domination. This leadership has not been based on personalities, even though individuals—such as Mandela—have always been associated with it. The leadership has steered the ANC through years of struggle that have seen the highest form of political education and enlightenment for the mass of its peoples. When Walter Sisulu was released from prison (after 26 years in jail for his role in the liberation struggle), he was shocked by the high level of political consciousness exhibited by the people, including children. The votes cast for the ANC in April 1994 have to be turned into more tangible results (viz, houses, jobs, schools, and affordable health care). The ANC government has committed itself to provide 2.5 million jobs, one million new houses, another million to be provided with water, and electricity to 2.5 million more homes by 1999. South Africans believed that these are achievable goals, and so gave the ANC 252 of the 400 seats in the transitional legislature.

CONCLUSION

This paper has attempted to make the case that of the African nations, South Africa is the one best positioned to eradicate neocolonialism as described by Amilcar Cabral. After decades of independence, the continent is still grappling with the issue of neocolonialism. The spate of IMF/World Bank-inspired Structural Adjustment Programs is drawing the continent into greater reliance on external sources. Given its wealth, and industrial potential, South Africa has the capacity of becoming a regional economic power. With its culture of resistance (that has honed and sharpened the political instincts of its peoples), South Africa can create a genuine "second independence" by defeating white hegemony and finally creating better prospects for its peoples.

What are the chances for a genuine change in South Africa? The chances are good as long as the ANC continues to exhibit political maturity and magnanimity; and as long as it tackles the RDF with the same purpose and commitment it tackled the anti-apartheid struggle. For all those years, the struggle to overthrow apartheid was the overriding concern that dwarfed other concerns. In the new South Africa, creating a more equitable society in a comprehensive fashion must be the overriding concern. As the life chances of the masses of South Africans improve; as their quality of life improves; and as the legacy of apartheid is wiped out, Cabral's notion of a genuine social revolution where the aspirations of the people would be taken care of would become reality. This is the "second independence" that African nations need. The new South Africa has the capacity to lead the African continent, in the next millennium, to a true genuine social revolution as envisaged by Amilar Cabral.

Notes

1   Amilcar Cabral (1924-1973) was the leader of the Cape Verde islands during their struggle for independence. He was a very intelligent political strategist. An agronomist by training, he understood the plight of African peasants and appealed more to them in his revolutionary campaign for African liberation. For more information about Amilcar Cabral's political thoughts, read *Return to the Source: Selected Speeches of Amilcar Cabral* (New York: Monthly Review Press, 1973), and Cabral, *Unity and Struggle* (New York: Monthly Review Press, 1979).

2   An assimilado was an African under Portuguese colonial rule who was known to integrate faster and more willingly into Portuguese culture than any other colonial subject. As a reward for such wilful act of integration, an assimilado was granted a special status in the colonial system and enjoyed privileges that were denied to the majority of the native population.

3   Cabral, *Unity and Struggle*, pp. 17-27.

4   *Ibid.*, p. 128.

5   *Ibid.*

6   *Ibid.*, p. 130.

7   *Ibid.*

8   *Ibid.*, p. 136.

9   Nzongola-Ntalaja, *Revolution and Counter-Revolution in Africa; Essays in Contemporary Politics* (London: Zed Press Limited, 1987) p. 64.

10 Stephen R. Lewis, Jr., *The Economics of Apartheid* (New York: Council on Foreign Relations Press, 1990), p. 7.

11 Kevin Shillington, *History of South Africa* (London: Longman Inc., 1987) p. 31.

12 Lewis, Jr., p. 87.

13 *South African Fact Sheet*, (Washington, D.C.: Washington Office on Africa), December 1986.

14 *Emerge*, Vol. 6, #8, June, 1985, p. 28.

Chapter 12

Democratization in Africa: Challenges and Prospects*

Julius O. Ihonvbere

INTRODUCTION

People expect too much from the so-called march towards democracy in Africa. After decades of authoritarian rule and human rights abuses, largely by the same state structures, we must expect that democracy in Africa will face countless challenges. Some of these will be insurmountable for long periods. Yet, out of the new confusion, some good might emerge; a good, which will empower the people genuinely for the very first time.[1]

. . . many authoritarian oligarchic regimes in Africa (both civilian and military) . . . have been forced to accept their own illegitimacy. A central question now is how to prevent these "return to democracy" projects from becoming a new ruse for the preservation of power by the existing and entrenched ruling classes. How do we Africans prevent a repeat performance of the democratic pantomimes without democratic content that was characteristic of so many African countries in the "independence decade"?[2]

The recent literature on democratization in the developing world has tended to be rather pessimistic about the prospects for democracy under very difficult conditions.[3] This pessimism arises from the difficulty of matching the so-called preconditions of democracy with the practice of democracy in poverty-stricken, non-industrialized, debt-ridden, politically unstable, foreign-dominated, and marginal economies in an increasingly

*A version of this chapter was delivered as keynote lecture at the Twelfth Annual Meeting of the Association of Third World Studies at the College of William and Mary, Williamsburg, Virginia, October 6-8, 1994.

complex and competitive global system. Four preconditions are usually identified in the literature as necessary for not just the process of democratization, but also for democratic consolidation.

The first precondition is that some degree of capitalist development was necessary for the survival or consolidation of democracy. In the words of Samuel Huntington "economic development, industrialization, urbanization, the emergence of the bourgeoisie and of a middle class, the development of a working class and its early organization, and the gradual decrease in economic inequality all seem to have played some role in the movements toward democratization in northern European countries. . . ."[4] This was an elaboration of the 1959 postulation of Seymour Lipset that "the more well-to-do a nation, the greater the chances that it will sustain democracy."[5] Such a process of "modernization" and wealth creation was expected to promote higher literacy levels, education, a vibrant mass media, and a middle class with interest in peace, predictable politics, and political security. Can this be the case for Africa? Barrington Moore Jr. talks of the importance of having an autonomous and productive bourgeoisie as a precondition for democracy.[6] This obviously draws heavily on some experiences in Europe. Yet, it holds out little or no promise in Africa where the state plays the role of the bourgeoisie, in spite of structural adjustment programs. The largely unproductive, fractionalized, corrupt, and dependent bourgeois classes in Africa are yet to move into sectors of the economy that will reduce the tendency of using politics as a "mode of accumulation." The state remains the largest investor, employer, importer and exporter, and the struggle is to penetrate and control its institutions and resources in order to facilitate private, clan, and class accumulation to the detriment, usually, of collective or national growth and development. The state is used by the elite for accumulation rather than legitimation purposes. This erodes its tenuous legitimacy and promotes instability and the endless need to rely on the manipulation of primordial loyalties in order to dominate the political landscape.[7]

On all indicators of development, the vast majority of African states, to take a regional example, are doing so badly that most theories/models of growth and development are being called to question.[8] This would mean that democracy has no future whatsoever in Africa. We might do well therefore to accept Huntington's explanation that while "Economic factors have significant impact on democratization" they are not "determinative. An overall correlation exists between the level of economic development and democracy yet no level or pattern of economic development is in itself either necessary or sufficient to bring about democratization."[9] In fact, Robert Pinkney points out that "Countries in Eastern Europe achieved many of the other developments without democracy, while countries such as Botswana and the Gambia (sic. before the 1994 military coup), with few of the developments described, have sustained pluralist systems."[10]

The second precondition for democracy is existing political culture or traditions. This has been defined by Georg Sorensen as "the system of values and beliefs that defines the context and meaning of political action."[11] African states would do no better on this count. Whatever the legacies of a pre-colonial and pre-capitalist communalist culture and tradition might have been, the reality is that possessive individualism, the profit motive, and the atomization of the individual through direct and/or indirect incorporation into the market place have steadily eroded the traditional systems of values. The experience of Africa since the 1900's has been one of colonial capitalist brutalization, exploitation and underdevelopment; elite competition and corruption; coups and counter-coups; massive human rights violations; a political tradition of violence, intolerance, and the manipulation of primordial loyalties; religious intolerance; and the widening of the gap between the poor and the rich due to misplaced priorities and narrow vision of the dominant classes. These divisions, conflicts, contradictions, and conditions of instability and distrust have directly militated against consensual politics or the generation of a "prodemocratic consensus."[12]

The third precondition for the survival of democracy relates to what Barrington Moore Jr. describes as "a vigorous and independent class of town dwellers" which has been "an indispensable element in the growth of parliamentary democracy. No bourgeois, no democracy."[13] Although it is well known that the bourgeoisie does not always work for democracy, most developing formations, Africa in particular, have not been favored by the existence of a disciplined, creative, patriotic, productive, and rational dominant class. Many are still mired in a sea of conflict, violence, ethnic, regional and religious contradictions, and problems of leadership and succession. The experiences of Liberia, Somalia, Togo, the Sudan, Mozambique, and even Nigeria, attest clearly to the absence of the prerequisites for democracy. The elite do not engage in consensual politics; political competition is normless; and critical issues of the national question continue to mediate bourgeois and state hegemony.

Finally, the fourth set of preconditions for the survival of democracy is the "economic, political, ideological, and other elements that constitute the international context for the processes that take place in single countries."[14] These required external determinants of democratization advanced by dependency writers hold somewhat true. Their contention that the nature and context of international global capitalist domination and exploitation drained resources, encouraged the brain drain, made regimes more desperate and tied nations to the geo-strategic and other needs of the metropole remains very valid in spite of the end of the Cold War. Poverty, debt and debt-servicing, natural disasters, declining investment, closure of credit lines, falling levels of foreign aid, declining commodity prices, rising prices of imports and interest rates, and increasing powerlessness in the international system reduce possibilities for growth, accumulation, savings, and democracy in most developing formations.[15] Of course, the current global balance of power which has the United States as the dominant military power has evinced a relationship between democratization and growing United States' influence and power.

With the end of the Cold War and the apparent triumph of the market as determined by the growing influence and power of the World Bank and the International Monetary Fund, most developing nations are virtually struggling to toe the line of United States policy and become "democratic" like it in order to satisfy the new political conditionalities of Western governments, bankers, donors and nongovernmental organizations. In this instance, the democratization agenda lacks the required roots for survival and consolidation. In other instances of imposition of democracy through military threat or force as we have seen in the case of Haiti, it fails to satisfy the other pre-requisites: some appreciable degree of capitalist development; a political culture favorable to democracy; experience with re-solving major issues of politics and development in the past; and a fairly strong location and role in the international divi-sion of labor. Thus, even in Haiti, based on the preconditions above, and in spite of all the publicity and costs, there is little reason to expect democracy to thrive. The threat or use of sanctions, foreign aid, investment, support for rebel move-ments, and the granting of special privileges, do not in them-selves bring about democracy, even if they, in some instances, ease the burden on the state and its custodians and thus en-courage them to reach some accommodation with civil society and embark on political reforms as is the case in Kenya, the Gambia and Ghana. As Pinkney notes:

> Many of the lessons for the Third World arising out of the literature appear to be negative. Most Third World countries have not enjoyed the economic development cited by Lipset, or the civil cultural atti-tudes cited by Almond and Verba. The sequences in development con-ducive to democracy in the West have not generally occurred in the Third World, and the "developmental crises" have frequently crowded in on one another over a short period of time. Institutional develop-ments have generally been limited. We have seen that most Latin Ameri-can states, despite their long period of independence, have built only rudimentary links between government and governed, while the more recently independent states of Africa and Asia have had little time to develop institutions.[16]

In fact, as Terry Lynn Karl has rightly noted, "what the lit-erature has considered in the past to be the preconditions of democracy may be better conceived in the future as the out-comes of democracy. Patterns of greater economic growth and more equitable income distribution, higher levels of literacy and education, and increases in social communication and media exposure may be better treated as the products of stable democratic processes rather than prerequisites of its exist-ence."[17] It is precisely this observation that has set the new agenda for a holistic and dialectical study of the specific chal-lenges to democracy and democratization by looking at par-ticular experiences. This has the advantage of avoiding the transposition of experiences, prevents undue generalization across regions and continents, and encourages the need to pay attention to specificities and political dynamics within each social formation or region.

THE CHALLENGES OF DEMOCRACY/ DEMOCRATIZATION IN AFRICA

Democracy in Africa shares some basic features with democracy in other parts of the world—revolving around issues of personal and collective liberties, basic freedoms, rights, and obligations.[18] These rights and freedoms are often enshrined in constitutions, even under military juntas. However, the extent, expression, and enjoyment of these freedoms and rights are conditioned and determined by issues of power, politics, production, and exchange relations. They are also conditioned by the location and role of particular formations in the global division of labor, the interest of external powers in local political balances and relations, and the nature and direction of struggles in civil society. The rapid alignment and realignment of political forces in civil society, and the preparedness of ruling elites to forge a consensual political terrain to facilitate class or group projects also affect the nature of democracy and the enjoyment of basic rights and liberties. As Salim A. Salim has argued, "democracy is not a 'revelation'. How it is expressed, how it is given concrete form, of necessity, varies from society to society. Consequently, one should avoid the temptation of decreeing a so-called 'perfect' model of democracy and of exporting it wholesale or imposing it on another society."[19] It is quite true, as Martin Klein notes, that "Democracy is not an abstract ideal. People do not choose democracy because they read about it. Democracy has invariably risen out of a struggle against autocracy."[20]

Today, from the World Bank and the International Monetary Fund, to Western governments and credit clubs, the demand for democracy has become a critical aspect of their relations with the very countries they have traditionally dominated and exploited. Any serious effort at understanding the challenge or dilemmas of democracy in Africa, must, therefore, pay due attention to the region's historical experiences, the implications of that experience, and the contemporary inter-play of social and political forces. Without dwelling too much on this, the record of post-colonial African elites and the post-colonial state throughout the 1960's and 1970's was one of consolidating and legitimizing neo-colonial and unequal relations, reproducing underdevelopment, and backwardness. Since the 1960's, Africa has simply moved from one crisis to the other. Politics became warfare. Conditions of instability, corruption, waste, poverty, uncertainty, disillusionment, and violence encouraged military adventurists to hijack popular struggles in the majority of African states. Democracy was thrown out of the political terrain in virtually all African states. In countries like Senegal, Kenya, and Zambia where the military had not terminated the democratic processes, individuals, their protegees or a clique of elites simply privatized the state in the purported "interest of the nation," relying on bogus "ideologies" like Humanism, Nyayoism, Authenticity, Uhuru, and the like. This general condition of political cynicism, economic vulnerability and decay, social dislocation, and peripheralization in the global capitalist system, deepened the African crisis and made it vulnerable to dictates from the outside on political and economic matters. More importantly, the rapid economic deterioration made the elite more desperate and unwilling to tolerate opposition. This led to coups and counter-coups, civil strife, wars, and the wanton abuse of human rights.

The issues above are neglected in more popular explanations of the problems of liberal democracy in Africa, especially the role played by the West in nurturing, sustaining and reproducing despotic regimes in Africa-Uganda, Zaire, Malawi, Nigeria, the Sudan, Somalia, Liberia, and Equatorial Guinea to name a few. Explanations have tended to focus on the more superficial aspects of political change in the region. It is precisely this sort of focus that has convinced donors, lenders and Western governments that by putting pressure on governments, cutting off foreign aid, imposing sanctions, and using limited threats of sanctions, democracy could easily be encouraged in these societies. Also, it is assumed that a combination of economic and political restructuring programs, under the supervision of International Monetary Fund and World Bank officials with emphasis on the implementation of orthodox monetarist programs will create an "enabling environment" that will promote democracy, stability, growth, accountability, and development.[21] With structural adjustment and its component parts of devaluation, privatization/commercialization, deregulation, retrenchment of able-bodied workers, and the removal of subsidies from social programs especially health, education, and transportation, and a strong emphasis on debt-servicing and an international attitude designed to please the new donors and creditors, the path towards sustainable democracy and development can be guaranteed, it was assumed.

It is obvious that when the West, its lenders, creditors and elite talk of "democracy" they mean "liberal democracy": resembling, if not exactly like what prevails in the West, preferably as it prevails in the United States of America. Thus *democracy* has become another word for *capitalism*. Overall, it looks like a new *modernization* agenda: the discredited and discarded prescriptions of the 1960's which defined progress and change in terms of the extent to which non-Western societies were able to copy and reproduce Western institutions, values, ideas, ideals, tastes, and modes of governance and economic arrangements.

African leaders, afraid of the "pressures from below" and recognizing that the alignment and realignment of political forces would deprive them of the lucrative and comfortable but exploitative locations in their respective political economies, have been quick to accept political prescriptions from the West. In most cases, they have had no choice. Having bankrupted their respective countries, and manipulated primordial loyalties to the maximum as part of their divide-and-rule politics, forging an alliance with more powerful external forces has been the only option left for most of them. Pressures from unemployment, ethnic and religious upheavals, increasing bankruptcies, rising militancy among non-bourgeois constituencies, and restlessness within the military and security networks for a variety of reasons, have exposed their tenuous hold on power, and exposed these leaders to direct challenges by the people.[22]

Ironically, the structural adjustment program has helped significantly in promoting the democratization agenda in two unintended ways. First, it took away from the state and its custodians the resources, autonomy, and capacity to repress, bribe, intimidate, and manipulate non-bourgeois forces. With no money, with worthless currencies which have been badly devalued, and with investors moving to Eastern Europe and relocating capital while holding back on new investments, African leaders found themselves to be almost irrelevant in the geostrategic and economic calculations of the former cold war masters.[23] They now had to face the wrath of the people. Secondly, the proletarianization of the middle classes brought an army of bureaucrats, intellectuals, and professionals into the ranks of workers, peasants, and the unemployed. Policies of retrenchment, desubsidization, introduction of new levies, taxes and fees, as well as the repressive environment required to force orthodox adjustment on the populace increased the militancy of non-bourgeois forces, demystified the state, its institutions and custodians. This encouraged popular groups to form new organizations, revive dormant ones, ask new questions, and make new demands for accountability, participation, social justice, and basic human needs on the state. Though unintended, the impoverishment, repression, marginalization, brutalization, exploitation, and humiliation which non-bourgeois forces and vulnerable groups suffered from the structural adjustment programs and the elites in Africa contributed significantly to the renewed interests in democracy, democratization, empowerment, and the need to mount a fundamental challenge to the dictators on the African political landscape.

To be sure, elections have taken place all over the continent, even in South Africa. Military governments have been forced to make concessions to civil society and reach accommodation with or give way to popular groups (Congo and Benin); some have been forced to civilianize themselves in order to remain politically relevant (Ghana); one-party states have been transformed in less than a year into multi-party states (Zambia); presidents-for-life have been compelled to restructure their political positions and perspectives on politics and power (Malawi); dictators who were darlings of the West were pressured into holding multi-party elections through the withholding of foreign aid disbursement (Kenya and Malawi); and in a country like Nigeria, popular groups succeeded in chasing the discredited dictator from power and the remilitarization of the political landscape in November 1993 took very serious cognizance of the new power, influence, and capabilities of the pro-democracy constituencies.

Yet, these changes, important as they are, have not altered the purpose of politics, the nature of politics, the character of the elite, the nature of the repressive state, the character of society, the conditions of dependent accumulation and foreign domination, and the peripheral location and role of African formations in the international division of labor. Unfortunately for Africa, the current tendency to equate elections with democracy and give the impression that the mere existence of several political parties means that democracy exists has reduced the focus on pro-democracy and civil liberties constituencies at the grassroots. As the African situation has clearly demonstrated, elections may take place, multi-parties may dominate the political terrain, but the elitist, exploitative, violent, manipulative, and in many instances, pedestrian character of politics remains intact. If one reads Chinua Achebe's *A Man of the People* published in 1966, one will be struck with how so little has changed in the nature of the actors, the role of money in politics, the place of religion, region, and ethnicity, the diversionary politics of the elite, political opportunism and defensive radicalism, as well as the unrepentant abuse of power. These, even more than the crises of dependence, vulnerability, foreign domination, and underdevelopment, are the real challenges to democratization in Africa.[24]

EVALUATING THE DEMOCRATIZATION PROCESS

It has become necessary to take a step back from the current euphoria surrounding the democratization process in Africa. This is necessary to avoid another "false start" in the political process which might culminate in the abortion or subversion of Africa's so-called "second revolution."[25] Already we are witnessing traces of defensive radicalism; ideological and political opportunism and posturing; a concentration on aping Western models, institutions and traditions; and the politics of manipulation, violence, and diversion. Michael Bratton and Nicolas van de Walle contend that the "dynamic process of protest and reform is nascent in Africa, and the future course of regime transitions is highly uncertain."[26] They warn that "the partial liberalization of authoritarian regimes does not amount to a transition to democracy," and that "the results of elections to date" do not "provide any guarantee that competitive politics will be institutionalized."[27] Samuel Decalo is even more pessimistic about the future of liberal democracy in Africa. As he put it, "Whatever democratic advances have been attained in Africa at this stage are still largely structural and/or constitutional; certainly a strong breadth of fresh air, but likely to end up in some countries as only cosmetic and/or temporary."[28] Why are scholars so pessimistic about the democratic enterprise in Africa?

It is very clear that the prerequisites discussed earlier do not exist in Africa. Yet, any focus on those prerequisites is like condemning Africa to eternal political bondage under dictatorships which have practically ruined the continent.[29] Because a distinction is not often drawn between democracy and *democratization*, it has become rather easy for African leaders to accommodate the *features* and institutions of liberal democracy while suffocating and dividing civil society at the grassroots. Also, because the current agenda for democracy in Africa as sponsored and pursued by the neo-colonial state has been set by Western donors and Western governments, African leaders have tried as much as possible to stick to the foreign generated agenda so as to ensure that the lines for foreign aid and credit are kept open. The leaders have used democracy to give some form of legitimacy to regimes with long-standing reputations for brutality, corruption, and gross inefficiency. While the demands of donors and lenders for political pluralism were satisfied, this did not create much room for democratic deepening or economic autonomy of such governments.[30]

In the context of on-going recomposition of political, strategic, and economic relations in the emerging global order, Africa has boundless opportunities to restructure political and economic spaces with an agenda which acknowledges its historical experiences, specificities, balance of forces, and location and role in the international division of labor. Such an agenda will require leaders to reach out to their respective peoples, discard traditional patterns, structures, and institutions of politics, and reach accommodation with constituencies hitherto marginalized and repressed such as women, minorities, ethnic and religious interests. Unfortunately, even with the best of intentions, Africa's deepening economic crisis and desperate social conditions make the processes of democratization, and democratic consolidation very challenging.

The African condition today, to say the least, has very serious political, economic, and social problems. As Lance Morrow put it recently, Africa is in a "scramble for existence."[31] It is quite obvious that conditions of deepening crisis, increasing marginalization in the global system, and increasing vulnerability to external penetration, domination, manipulation, and exploitation, have had three main consequences: First, it has exploded the invincibility of the state and opened it up to challenges from disadvantaged constituencies; second, it has made the state, its agents and agencies more desperate and repressive in some instances, and willing to make concessions to civil society in other instances; and third, it has made Africa more of a pawn in the hands of international finance institutions like the IMF and the World Bank and thus created a major opening for the political and ideological manipulation of the continent. This has encouraged the imposition of models of democracy which are more often than not, out of tune with African realities and aspirations.

In the midst of the confusion, instability, conflicts, and contradictions generated and/or accentuated by the policies of the IMF and the World Bank, attention has shifted from the struggles of the people at the grassroots level; the limitations of the so-called pro-democracy movements; the required preconditions for the survival of democracy; and the urgent need for a strengthened civil society. Rather, Western governments, donors and creditors have drawn a direct link between democracy and development; sung the praises of the market; imposed political conditionalities on African states; and assumed that regimes which had spent decades suffocating civil society and oppressing their peoples during the implementation of structural adjustment can be expected to open up civil society, respect human rights, and cultivate democratic traditions. In fact,

there is not one single example in Africa where orthodox structural adjustment has led to more democracy, increased political stability, national unity, the provision of basic needs for
the masses, growth, and development. In spite of vitriolic propaganda, and the determination to pronounce Ghana as a successful case through the massive infusion of loans and other
financial support, adjustment has deepened class antagonisms
and conflicts, delegitimized the state, marginalized the masses
from the elite, and created conditions for the strengthening
of neo-colonial relations and further marginalization in the
global capitalist system. Adjustment in Ghana has more than
quadrupled the country's foreign debt, eroded its national
autonomy, and rendered the Cedi almost worthless.[32] As Georg
Sorensen has observed:

> Nowhere does the consolidation of democracy face larger obstacles
> than in sub-Saharan Africa, where the foundation on which democ-
> racy must be built, is very weak. The African state has failed both
> economically and politically: In general, Africans are as poor today as
> they were thirty years ago. At the same time, the large majority of
> African states have so far failed to institutionalize any form of effec-
> tive rule, be it authoritarianism or democracy. . . .[33]

One can now effectively make the argument that since the
on-going efforts at democracy are still conducted within the
parameters of the dictates, ideals, perceptions, and needs of
lenders and donors they would be cosmetic, tenuous, and superficial even if they cost huge amounts of money. In spite of
the widespread enthusiasm for democratization in Africa, the
current processes are informed and driven more by elite interests and struggles to survive the pressures from below and
pressures from the outside. Hence, Sorensen has argued that
such Western instigated drives for democracy would be "coun-
terproductive" because:

> The Western countries themselves are examples of the fact that de-
> mocracy cannot be installed overnight; it is a long-term process of
> gradual change. When quick fixes of imposing multiparty systems,
> for example, are substituted for the long haul of patiently paving the
> way for a democratic polity, the result may be that a thin layer of
> democratic coating is superimposed upon a system of personal rule
> without changes in the basic features of the old structure.[34]

THE NEO-COLONIAL STATE AND DEMOCRATIZATION

It is incredible that the entire world seem to be taken in by the so-called democratization processes in Africa when the brutal, unstable, non-hegemonic and grossly inefficient neo-colonial state has remained intact. The state, under the control of very conservative and corrupt political forces, has survived the "changes" in every country that has conducted so-called multiparty elections. The very survival of this state which has historically failed to meet the basic needs of the majority or guarantee basic freedoms, provides a clear pointer to the fact that "there is not much hope that the recent democratic openings will progress into consolidated democracies."[35] The current "transitions" in Africa being largely dominated, influenced, conditioned, and operated largely by the very same elite who subverted the early democratic experiments, collaborated with military juntas, and ruined African economies, there is every reason to see their new conversion to democracy as a temporary retreat strategy to remain politically relevant and to strengthen their hold on the state which is in reality a means to rapid primitive accumulation.[36] In case after case, "incumbent leaders have preempted the new winds of democracy and have succeeded in staying in power by engineering transitions from above."[37] Where they have been defeated, they have, as in Zambia with Kenneth Kaunda, continued to loom large in the political space and in other instances, they have succeeded in being part of the process of (s)electing their successors. In this way, the old political traditions, alliances, and institutions have remained intact, even if in temporary abeyance, to allow "things to cool down."

One can indeed argue that since the vast majority of the democratization agendas do not include programs aimed at dismantling and reconstructing the oppressive neo-colonial state and its institutions which have been at the heart of Africa's predicaments since the colonial days, there is no way the tenuous victories will not be easily confused, incorporated and domesticated by contradictions and coalitions arising from the distorted economic sector and negative political, even cultural attitudes largely aided by ethnic, regional, personal, and religious interests. The Zambian example where the MMD struggled to come to power only to be more faithful to the World Bank and donors, and has virtually retained all of Kenneth Kaunda's ministers and institutions, is a typical case in point.[38] Frederick Chiluba has succeeded in *changing* very little in Zambia and this has made Kenneth Kaunda's popularity to rise to the point of creating what Samuel Huntington has referred to as "authoritarian nostalgia."[39] In fact, Kaunda is already contemplating a return to power in an attempt to cash in on the crisis of democratic consolidation which has plagued the MMD government since its spectacular victory in 1991.

Finally, to the extent that Africa is unimportant in the geostrategic and political calculations of the West especially the United States, a position informed by a combination of ignorance, discrimination, fear, insecurity, and racism, democratizing nations are unlikely to receive the sort of support which Russia, to take an example, is receiving from the United States and other Western powers and institutions.[40] As well, the absence of a strong constituency for Africa in the United States or anywhere outside Africa for that matter, means that no democratization effort will receive support like Haiti did even where clear movements towards liberal democracy are terminated as has been the case in Nigeria. Sorensen points out that "no additional aid seems to be forthcoming as a result of the democratic openings. Current public opinion in the North seems to be that starvation and death are more acceptable in Africa than elsewhere or are unavoidable there. In other words, the conditions that are being imposed concerning democratization do not promise more aid if they are met; they promise less aid if they are not met."[41] This complicates the predicament of the beleaguered African state which is already under extreme pressure. This has the possibility of forcing the desperate state to return to repression, political posturing, propaganda, and the manipulation of primordial loyalties in order to retain control of the political landscape.

The reality of Africa, in spite of vitriolic propaganda from African dictators, opportunistic politicians, and so-called prodemocracy leaders is that democracy in Africa will remain a mirage as long as the current elite remain in power; in as much as the institutions, structures, and social relations with which they dominated and repressed society remain unchanged; in as much as the masses of the people are not empowered and society is not opened up for mass political action; and in as much as the economic dislocation and crisis inherited at political independence in the 1960's continues. It is impossible to carry out a viable and credible political restructuring and transformation in a political economy dominated and controlled by the very class forces and interests which ran down the various economies, accumulated huge foreign debts, repressed and tried to eliminate all popular organizations, and showed very little concern for the terrible living conditions of the masses of the people. How can leaders like Arap Moi in Kenya, Eyadema in Togo, Abacha in Nigeria, and Mobutu in Zaire, to name a few, preside over the process of democratization except at levels unlikely to challenge the enshrined traditions of corruption, repression, waste, and mismanagement?

One of the major reasons why anti-democratic forces held sway for so long in Africa is the very nature and role of the neo-colonial state. Largely a continuation of the colonial state, lacking hegemony, credibility, stability, and legitimacy; and presided over by a largely unproductive, dependent, irresponsible, corrupt, and decadent elite, the state became a direct instrument of oppression and exploitation. The state easily played the role of the capitalists. Because of the weaknesses of local dominant classes, the struggle to control the state often required the manipulation of primordial loyalties by the elite who lacked credible bases of support in civil society. Human rights abuses, wanton massacre of non-bourgeois forces, misplaced priorities, inefficiency, subservience to foreign capital and imperialism, and the general exploitation and oppression of the people became the main features and function of the state in Africa.

It is amazing that there is really not one pro-democracy movement that has the total dismantling of this state as a primary goal. Rather, what we see are struggles to *replace* the government, to *participate* in government, and to actually continue with the policies and politics of the repressive state. To be sure, some of the more established pro-democracy movements have developed some cosmetic programs for *reforming* rather than *transforming and recomposing* the state. It is even more troublesome when one critically examines the quality of the leaders of many of the pro-democracy movements. They consist of political opportunists, disgraced politicians, old and tired politicians of the first decade of independence, retired military officers, persons who have been marginalized from existing exploitative power structures, and professional politicians and petty-bourgeois lawyers. The political interests and consciousness of these persons have seriously conditioned the nature and operations of pro-democracy movements in the region. The hunger for naked power and the urge to become the head of state has fractionalized and seriously weakened the pro-democracy movements in Africa. Little wonder that in Zaire, Zambia, Ghana, Kenya, Togo, and Nigeria, their ranks are splintered, and their voices so many and conflictual that it is often difficult to discern a specific agenda beyond the clamor for a nebulous democratic agenda. Since every leader of a small pro-democracy group wants to be a presidential candidate, they refuse to reach accommodation with each other and fail to present a united front to challenge the incumbent government.[42] Hence Rawlings found it easy to win in Ghana. The boycott of the parliamentary elections did not prevent the National Democratic Congress (NDC—the PNDC without the "P"!) from securing the support of some fringe parties and giving some legitimacy to the elections.

In Zambia today, there are over 34 opposition parties all with their eyes on the presidency. The majority of the so-called opposition parties have been formed by dismissed and disgraced politicians and ministers, and they have no agenda whatsoever for economic and social reconstruction. In Nigeria, in spite of the unprecedented victory of the Campaign for Democracy (CD) over the Ibrahim Babangida junta and the ongoing struggles against General Abacha's dictatorship, new pro-democracy movements like the National Conscience (NC) and the Democratic Alternative (DEAL) are being formed by the "new" democrats everyday. This simply divides the opposition, creates diversions, and weakens the ability to present a holistic agenda for political renewal to the people.[43]

I agree with Claude Ake's position that "the self-appointed agents of democratization in Africa are implausible. They are not so much supporting democracy as using it. . . .the African elite support democracy only as a means to power, the international development agencies support it as an asset to structural adjustment and Western governments support it ambiguously torn between their growing indifference to Africa and their desire to promote their own way of life."[44] Specifically, on the hollowness of the new democratic agenda as it relates to the character of the neo-colonial state, Ake is very instructive:

> One of the most remarkable features of democratization in Africa is that it is totally indifferent to the character of the state. Democratic elections are being held to determine who will exercise the powers of the state with no questions asked about the character of the state as if it has no implications for democracy. But its implications are so serious that elections in Africa give the voter only a choice between oppressors. This is hardly surprising since Africa largely retains the colonial state structure which is inherently anti-democratic, being the repressive apparatus of an occupying power. Uncannily, this structure has survived, reproduced and rejuvenated by the legacy of military and single-party rule. So what is happening now by way of democratization is that self-appointed military or civilian leaders are being replaced by **elected dictators** (emphasis added).[45]

THE LIMITS OF ELECTIONS AS DEMOCRACY

This is where the author is of the view that the current wave of elections which are ushering in liberal democratic forms of governance in various shades are very defective. Of course, it is "utopian to expect democratic norms to be an immediate success." It is true that "Many of Africa's new leaders will fail. Some will revert to autocratic methods. Some will prove as corrupt as their predecessors. Some will prove incompetent. Some will founder on the shoals of ethnic conflict. The struggle is, alas, one that must be fought over and over again. . . ."[46] Yet, as Catherine Newbury has rightly noted, "liberal democracy (is) an important first step, providing possibilities for political organization that have been stifled under authoritarian regime."[47] However, where the on-going democratic processes seem to be focusing "mainly on political procedures and practice (liberal democracy), while excluding peasants and workers,"[48] and while actually trying to stifle pro-democracy constituencies, there is a need to examine them critically and rise beyond euphoria and the superficial, attractive as these may appear.

Of course, it is important to raise the issue of democratization under difficult conditions. The social and economic crisis makes it difficult for the people to tolerate the slow process of reform and recovery, and to be patient with some of the new leaders like Chiluba in Zambia. The people have suffered for so-long and have been exploited by local and international forces for too long. Unfortunately, the pro-democracy groups and "new" political parties all campaigned promising change, better government, human rights, and the provision of basic needs. On coming to power, they confronted empty treasuries, huge internal and foreign debts, pressures/demands from bankers and other lenders, and "political conditionalities" imposed by donors. They also had to deal with a global system where Africa was largely unimportant to global geo-strategic and economic calculations, and where foreign interests and aid were shifting to other regions of the world.

It is therefore pertinent to ask if Africa will really *democratize* when it remains the most poverty-stricken, least industrialized, most marginal, most debt-distressed, most vulnerable, and most foreign dominated and crisis-ridden region in the world? Are there any indications that the global economy will become more favorable to African participation? Will terms of trade improve to enable African economies generate more foreign exchange? Will debt relief become a serious part of global debt negotiations? Will Africa's current, almost irrelevant, but certainly marginal place in the economic and geo-strategic calculations of the developed countries, especially the United States, improve because so-called multi-party elections have been held? Will more investors and donors return to Africa? Will the international arms dealers from the East and West change their manipulative and exploitative trade relations with Africa to promote less emphasis on wars, security, and the expansion of the military? Will current patterns of resource extraction and transfer abroad be restructured to favor Africa? Finally, will the African elite accept the need for a drastic restructuring of the political terrain in such a manner as to render them powerless and accountable to the popular will?

It has been argued by several Africans and Africanists that the democratic struggles in Africa are hampered by "the implementation of structural adjustment programmes, violent ethnic upheavals, the difficulty with which new hegemonic coalitions are being forged and the resistance of the military to returning to their barracks."[49] It is clear therefore, that more than any other region in the world, and more than at any point in history, the task of successful transition to democracy, and the more challenging task of effectively sustaining and reproducing democracy in Africa could easily be subverted on its own terms.

THE MILITARY AND THE DEMOCRATIZATION PROCESS IN AFRICA

The military remains one of the major obstacles to democratization in Africa. Regardless of the positive light some may put on the leadership of people like the late Thomas Sankara of Burkina Faso, Jerry Rawlings in Ghana, and Mummar Gadaffi in Libya, the record of the African military has been one of disaster. The situation in Zaire under Mobutu Sese Seko, Togo under Gnassingbe Eyadema, Ethiopia under Mengistu Haile Mariam, Benin under Matthew Kerekou, Somalia under Said Bare, and the Sudan under Jaffer Nimeiri attest to this fact. The Nigerian case amply demonstrates that the military, as an undemocratic commandist organization is incapable of initiating, nurturing, and consolidating democracy in Africa. It has relied on brutish force, intimidation, and wanton human rights abuses to stifle civil society and reproduce its control over society. The promulgation of decrees and edicts which oust the jurisdiction of the law courts, the proscription of trade and students' unions, the subversion of the course of justice, intolerance of opposition, and general inability to appreciate or understand the meaning of accountability to civil order have made it impossible for the African military to promote the process of democratization. As every instance of military dictatorship in Africa has demonstrated, the military is as corrupt, fractionalized, and fractionalized as the political class. Discipline and professionalism have been so badly eroded that the army is at best a badly structured and badly run organization which sits on the people, suffocates civil society, destroys creativity and originality, and squanders scarce resources on the defence of the looters of the national treasury.[50]

The damage which the Generals Babangida and Abacha juntas have caused in Nigeria clearly attests to the dangers of military misrule in Africa. The singular act of terminating the march to a Third Republic cost the debt-ridden nation over 50 billion naira. The military has arrogated to itself the right to determine for the people which government is good or bad. It believes that there are two parties in Africa: the military and the people. Since it controls or monopolizes the legal control of the means of coercion, it sees itself as the senior or stronger party. It has refused to let the political process mature, get routinized and institutionalized, and has refused to allow politicians to learn from their mistakes, align and realign their loyalties and interests, and forge the required linkages with their respective constituencies to sustain democracy.

The African military refuses to believe that democracy presupposes that differences and contradictions exist and that the solution is to negotiate and reconcile these differences to the highest possible level. The African military does not believe that democracy makes room for politicians and political actors to agree to disagree, and that social pluralism is the very strength of democracy. As a largely parasitic organization, it has continued to drain scarce resources thus making it difficult if not impossible for new democratic governments to survive.

To be sure, the military has been able to intervene at will and get willing supporters in its determination to stamp out democracy from Africa because the political elite has been very opportunistic and weak when it comes to challenging military dictatorships. The political elite in Africa has not accepted democracy and talks less of democratization as a viable agenda for checking the intervention of the military in politics on a permanent basis. Their political parties have been divided along ethnic, regional, even religious lines; they have relied on propaganda, lies, and diversions in their political contestations; and they have looted the treasury like previous governments without restraint. In fact, the political elite, traditional and religious leaders, intellectuals of all ideological persuasions, and business persons rush and fall over each other to welcome the military, seek political appointments and contracts, bad-mouth the previous government, and congratulate the military for chasing away "irresponsible" politicians. This has historically been the experience of Nigeria where several leaders of the human rights and pro-democracy community defected and joined ranks with the oppressors. One good example of such betrayal of people is the case Alhaji Baba Gana Kingibe, the elected running mate of Chief M.K.O. Abiola, who quickly accepted a position with the General Abacha junta following the November 1993 coup. Such acts erode the credibility of the political elite in the eyes of the military and the people.[51] And one of the reasons why the military has hated the university system, and intellectuals in particular, is the opportunistic, subservient, and sycophantic postures of African academics.[52] Ordinary people easily become discouraged and apathetic when they see the radicals, activists, "fire eaters," marxists, and democrats of yesterday who organized "National Conferences," protest marches, even acts of sabotage, hobnobbing, and wining and dining with military officers with legendary reputations for shallow thinking, corruption, repression and other atavistic modes of behavior. As well, since the elite who are supposed to be lords in their ethnic enclaves have so openly welcomed the military, who is to stop the officers from arrogating to themselves the right to determine, condition, and structure the context and content of national politics?

The challenges and predicaments highlighted above in a global system where there is so much discrimination, inequality, poverty, exploitation, and racism should alert us all to the difficulty of building viable democratic systems based on liberal Western notions of democracy in developing formations. This is the more so when such notions are tied to foreign aid or trade: the baggage of political conditionalities imposed from the West on poverty-stricken and often desperate nations. Today, many leaders are forced to accept Western dictated political reforms because multi-party elections and the tag of "democracy" bring international recognition, and are now being used by investors as a major criterion for doing business with African states. As well, religious fundamentalism, opportunistic nationalism, ethnic conflicts, and the contradictions arising from unresolved issues in the national question pose very serious challenges to the democratic agenda in Africa. Without doubt, in Liberia, Nigeria, the Sudan, Somalia, Rwanda, Burundi, and Togo (to mention hot spots of crisis in Africa) the democratic agenda has taken a back seat to efforts to resolve the national question, reconstitute the state, and mediate contradictions and conflicts within and between political constituencies. For the weak and vulnerable, the uncertainty they face on a daily basis on the frontline of struggle or in their respective refugee camps is how to survive the hell right here on earth: a hell created by the African elite and their foreign masters and allies.

CONCLUSION: TOWARDS GENUINE DEMOCRATIZATION

While there is no doubting the fact that the current democratization agenda was foisted on African leaders by Western governments, donors, lenders, and other external sources of pressure, the real *democratization* which has been going on since the nationalists betrayed the people in the 1960's is where we must focus to discern the future of the region. Tying political pluralism to elections simplifies the entire democratic agenda. Withholding foreign aid as was done to Kenya in 1991 simply compels the incumbent government to introduce political change on its own terms to satisfy the demands of the donors. In both cases, such forms of "change" are superficial, cosmetic, and diversionary. Such democratization programs do not reach or include the supposed beneficiaries of democracy: peasants, women, workers, and young people. They are not consulted, though they are told of what has happened. They are not mobilized, educated, involved, and relied upon to generate the required environment for the sustenance and consolidation of democracy. More importantly, the democratization process foisted on Africa from above, and swallowed by the foreign aid-dependent elite does not *empower* the people in any way. This is more so since the personalities, institutions, expectations, methods, and strategies of politics remain essentially the same as the neo-colonial state and economy.

The World Bank and some donors have only recently acknowledged the need to focus on the *political* aspects of Africa's deepening crisis. There is no gainsaying the fact that on all indicators of growth and development, Africa lags far behind other developing regions. African leaders readily acknowledged this fact as far back as 1980 when they declared in the *Lagos Plan of Action* that "Africa is unable to point to any significant growth rate, or satisfactory index of general well-being, in the past 20 years."[53] Beginning with its 1989 report on Africa, the World Bank acknowledged the political aspect of the crisis and admitted the failure of its own agenda for development.

In its new position, the World Bank stressed an opening up to the forces of democracy through the creation of an enabling environment, respect for civil liberties and human rights, decentralization of power, accountability of the elites, gender equality, a check on corruption and waste, and the need for efficiency in the execution of public projects among its numerous prescriptions. These prescriptions were however aimed at the more effective implementation of structural adjustment as packaged by the Bank.[54] While African states, desperate for foreign aid and foreign exchange have been forced to implement painful orthodox adjustment programs to please the lenders and donors, the social consequences have been unprecedented in the continent. Without doubt, African economies require urgent far-reaching adjustment to recover from their economic crisis and compete effectively in an increasingly complex global economy. However, the World Bank's adjustment has consistently overlooked the nature of politics and political contestations, the credibility of the leadership, the ability of the people to resist adjustment, the depth of the pre-adjustment crisis and the nature of survival strategies already in place, the degree to which the state had been delegitimized, and prevailing ideological postures and positions, in African states. Consequently, the imposed programs have culminated in riots, violence, the massive destruction of lives and property, coups and counter-coups, and the further delegitimization of already weak and unpopular state structures.

In Zambia, the Chiluba government which was swept into power as part of the pro-democracy upsurge has not been able to carry out reform policies because of the devastating legacy of a poorly implemented adjustment program (among other reasons). Beyond dilapidated structures, inflation, a worthless

Kwacha (currency), and pressures from lenders on the government to service its debt, Chiluba has discovered that it is impossible to restructure and transform the political economy by retaining Kaunda's ministers, ministries, programs, and virtually surrendering the economy to international capitalist interests.

Yet, there is a lot of hope for democracy in Africa. Even current efforts at procedural democratization are not valueless. They open up new political spaces, affect the nature of political alignments, and create opportunities for the people to operate openly and to insist that their interests be included in the political agenda. While it is true that in most cases, in spite of the seeming enthusiasm for democracy, competition in politics has been "confined to sections of the ruling group," and we do not see "any formative role for civil society or for pressures from below for democratization," the political landscape is being gradually restructured.[55] To be sure, many of the current efforts will fail, be rolled back, or be overthrown by the military as we have seen in The Gambia and Nigeria. Many will get exhausted mid-way, and the overwhelming demands of creditors and the people will wear them out. The days of despots, presidents-for-life, and military despots are clearly numbered in Africa. The ability of the Campaign for Democracy (CD) in Nigeria to force Nigeria's strongman, General Ibrahim Babangida from power is clear evidence of the changing political landscape in the region. The fight being waged in Nigeria between the pro-democracy forces led by the CD, the National Union of Petroleum and Natural Gas Workers (NUPENG), the National Democratic Coalition (NADECO) and other popular groups and trade unions on the one hand, and the General Abacha junta on the other (in spite of the initial participation of prominent pro-democracy activists in the military arrangement), is also evidence that the forces of democracy are moving in the right direction. People (viz, market women, students, the unemployed) have learned that they must rise beyond ethnicity, region, and religion to articulate a clear agenda for struggle and to forge strong alliances in order to effectively challenge the custodians of state power. The pains and cost of structural adjustment have pushed non-bourgeois forces to the wall. These pains have forced normally docile

people, communities and groups to become highly politicized
and active.[56] They are posing new questions, rejecting old ideologies and propaganda, joining in popular protests, and demanding for the right to participate in the selection of their
own leaders. This, certainly, is a major departure from the usual
tradition in Africa. As Mohammed Halfani has rightly noted,
"More organizations have severed their ties with the state and
are seeking greater autonomy. Contemporary movements are
shrugging off state patronage in order to reconstruct the sub-
stance and direction of local-development. In some cases, their
independence has put them on a collision course with governments."[57] While many of the grassroots organizations are mere
service organizations without political programs, the services
they render contribute to strengthening civil society in a general sense but do not constitute an integral part of the direct
challenge to the neo-colonial state and imperialism, until they
become politicized.

This reinvigoration of civil society is bound to encourage a
struggle for *democratization* representing a steady process of
mobilization, education, and empowerment of the people, their
organizations, and communities in such a way as to increase
popular participation, accountability, civil liberties, and an
enabling environment for growth and development. Democratization promotes the process of empowerment and the
empowerment of the people puts them in charge of their lives
and deepens the process of democratization. As Richard
Sandbrook notes, empowerment "involves transforming the
economic, social, psychological, political and legal circumstances of the currently powerless."[58] As well, empowerment
"entails access to educational facilities and to the minimum
resources needed to sustain households. Illiterate people who
must devote all their energies to bare survival cannot empower
themselves. This process further requires that people and their
organizations have access to contending opinions and accurate information on the performance of power-holders . . . empowerment involves the difficult and hazardous task of constructing political institutions capable of mediating the
conflicting interest of classes, regions, sexes, and communal
groups, and of safeguarding the voice and rights of hitherto
oppressed groups and strata."[59] This is significantly different
from the current processes of procedural democracy which

have been reduced to mere elections and the registration of multi political parties. It is this level of democratization that the World Bank must support if it is serious about its new rhetoric. It is this process that the donors, lenders, and the United States must support if they are serious about a new global order and the restructuring of power relations in Africa. For, irrespective of ideological positions, the fact of the matter is that:

> the process of reconstituting civil society is under way. Many old and new associations are striving to enhance their capacity to direct their own affairs. They are also rejecting their traditional roles as assigned by the state and are addressing issues of empowerment and social transformation. Today, many associations attribute as much importance to the participatory mode of their activities as to the concrete outcomes they achieve. The teaching of basic and functional literacy, the performance of theatrical plays, the assistance offered in litigation, the generation of new knowledge and information through research have acquired an importance beyond the immediate material benefits to the marginalized; their emancipatory and transformational impact is equally valued. African civil associations have thus become increasingly political.[60]

Even some of the organizations I have criticized earlier are deepening their politics as they face isolation from the more politicized associations. In Ghana, younger members of the Movement for Freedom and Justice (MFJ) have challenged the leadership of Adu Boahen in an effort to separate the presidential candidate from the leadership of the Movement and to bring in new ideas which move away from the tired ideologies of the 1950's and 1960's.[61] Disagreement on issues of ideology and strategies of struggle forced some individuals out of the CD in Nigeria culminating in the formation of the Democratic Alternative (DEAL) a more ideologically orthodox organization.

The *African Charter for Popular Participation in Development* (1990), in spite of its limitations, has provided a framework for *democratization* and empowerment on which African states and popular organizations can build. Adopted in February 1990, it recognizes the "unprecedented and unacceptable proportions" of the African crisis; recognizes that the crisis is not just an economic one, but also a "human, legal, political and social crisis," and takes the position that the only way out of the present crisis is to "establish independent people's organizations at various levels that are genuinely grassroot, voluntary, democratically administered and self-reliant and that are rooted in the tradition and culture of the society so as to ensure community empowerment and self-development." The document notes that "unless the structures, pattern and political context of the process of socio-economic development are appropriately altered" Africa's crisis cannot be overcome. Among its concrete prescriptions for government, the media, youths, women, NGOs and VDOs, the international community, and organized labor is that "there must be an opening up of the political process to accommodate freedom of opinions, tolerate differences, accept consensus on issues as well as ensure the effective participation of the people and their organizations and association." Perhaps the most important part of the document is the recommendations for the establishment of national and regional monitoring bodies and the identification of ten major indicators of empowerment, participation and democratization: literacy level as an indicator of "capacity for mass participation in public debate, decision-making and the general development process"; freedom of association, especially political association; representation of the people and their organizations in national bodies; the extent of the rule of law and economic justice; environmental protection; press freedom; number and scope of grass roots organizations "with effective participation in development activities;" implementation of the 1989 Abuja Declaration on Women; political accountability of leadership at all levels; and decentralization of decision-making processes and institutions.[62]

The indicators above, go beyond the prescriptions from the West—multi-parties, elections, parliaments, constitutions, and the adoption of monetarist economic programs—which are comparatively easier for the elite to implement and manipulate as we have seen in Zaire, Kenya, and Ghana. Implementing the indicators recommended by the ECA and which have been accepted and adopted by the OAU will enthrone the power and struggles of the people and restructure the tradition of waste, corruption, decadence, and subservience which has characterized elite dominance of the political landscape since the 1960's. These pan-African prescriptions can only complement struggles for democracy *within* nation states if the process will not be encapsulated by the elites and international capital and subverted once again.

Notes

1 Interview with Hon. Samuel Miyanda, MMD Member of Parliament for Matero, Lusaka, June 1993.

2 Ayesha Imam, "Democratization Processes in Africa: Problems and Prospects," *CODESRIA Bulletin* (2) (1991), p. 5.

3 See Mohammed Alam, "Democracy in the Third World: Some Problems and Dilemmas," *Indian Journal of Politics* Vol. XX, (102) (January-June, 1986); Peter Anyang'Nyongo, Democratization Processes in Africa," *CODESRIA Bulletin* (2) (1991); Michael Bratton and Nicolas van de Walle, "Popular Protest and Political Reform in Africa," *Comparative Politics* Vol. 24, (4) (July 1992); Terry Lynn Karl, "Dilemmas of Democratization in Latin America," *Comparative Politics* (October 1990); and Robert Pinkney, *Democracy in the Third World*, (Boulder: Lynne Rienner, 1994).

4 Samuel Huntington, *The Third Wave: Democratization in the Late Twentieth Century* (Norman, Oklahoma: University of Oklahoma Press, 1991), p. 39.

5 Seymour M. Lipset, "Some Social Requisites for Democracy: Economic Development and Political Legitimacy," *American Political Science Review* Vol. 53, (1) (1959), p. 75.

6 See Barrington Moore Jr., *The Social Origins of Dictatorship and Democracy* (London: Allen Lane, 1967).

7 See Claude Ake, "Is Africa Democratizing?" *The Guardian* (Lagos) (December 12, 1993); and Peter Anyang'Nyongo, "Development and Democracy: The Debate Continues," *CODESRIA Bulletin* (2) (1991).

8 See Seymour Lipset, "Some Social Requisites. . . ," op. cit. and Terry Lynn Karl, "Dilemmas of Democratization. . . ," op. cit.

9 Samuel Huntington, *The Third Wave*, op. cit. p. 59.

10 Robert Pinkney, *Democracy in the Third World*, op. cit., p. 19.

11 Georg Sorensen, *Democracy and Democratization*, (Boulder, Colorado: Westview, 1993), p. 26.

12 See Terry Lynn Karl, "Dilemmas of Democratization in Latin America," op. cit.

13 Barrington Moore Jr., *The Social Origins of Dictatorship. . .* , op. cit. p. 418.

14 Georg Sorensen, *Democracy and Democratization*, op. cit., p. 27.

15 See Samuel Huntington, *The Third Wave*, op. cit.; and his "Will More Countries Become Democratic?" *Political Science Quarterly* Vol. 99, (2) (1984) and the contributions to J. Malloy, ed., *Authoritarianism and Corporatism in Latin America* (Pittsburgh: University of Pittsburgh Press, 1977).

16 Robert Pinkney, *Democracy in the Third World*, op. cit., p. 34.

17 Terry Lynn Karl, "Dilemmas of Democratization. . . ," op. cit., p. 5. This argument is further developed in Julius O. Ihonvbere, *Economic Crisis, Civil Society, and Democratization: The Case of Zambia* (Trenton, New Jersey: Africa World Press, 1996).

18 See Larry Diamond, J. Linz and S. M. Lipset, eds., *Democracy in Developing Countries, Vol. II, Africa* (London: Adamantine Press, 1988) and Georg Sorensen, *Democracy and Democratization*, op. cit.

19 Salim A. Salim quoted in *Africa Recovery* (November 1990), p. 29.

20 Martin Klein, "Back to Democracy," Presidential Address to the 1991 Annual Meeting of the African Studies Association.

21 See World Bank, *Sub-Saharan Africa: From Crisis to Sustainable Growth-A Long-Term Perspective Studies* (Washington, D.C.: World Bank, 1989), and World Bank, *Adjustment in Africa: Reforms, Results, and the Road Ahead*, (Oxford: Oxford University Press for the World Bank, 1994).

22 See Julius O. Ihonvbere, "The State, Human Rights, and Democratization in Africa," *Current World Leaders* Vol. 37, (4) (August 1994); and his "Is Democracy Possible in Africa?: The Elites, The People and Civil Society," *QUEST: Philosophical Discussions* Vol. VI, (2) (December 1992).

23 See Michael Chege, "Remembering Africa," *Foreign Affairs* Vol. 71, (1) (1991-92); Marguerite Michaels, "Retreat From Africa," *Foreign Affairs* Vol. 72, (1) (1993); Fantu Cheru, *The Silent Revolution in Africa: Debt, Development and Democracy*, (London and Harare: Zed and Anvil, 1989); and Michael Clough, "The United States and Africa: A Policy of Cynical Disengagement," *Current History* Vol. 91, (May 1992).

24 See Julius O. Ihonvbere, "The Kampala Declaration: Political Posturing or Collective Nationalism?" *21st Century Afro Review* Vol. 1, (1) (Fall 1994).

25 See Julius O. Ihonvbere and Terisa Turner, "Africa in the Post-Containment Era: Constraints, Pressures and Prospects for the 21st Century," *The Round Table* (328) (October 1993).

26   Michael Bratton and Nicholas van de Walle, "Popular Protest and Political Reform in Africa," op. cit., p. 419.

27   *Ibid.,* p. 438.

28   Samuel Decalo, "The Process, Prospects and Constraints of Democratization in Africa," *African Affairs* (91) (1992), p. 8.

29   See Robert Kaplan, "The Coming Anarchy," *Atlantic Monthly* (February 1994).

30   Georg Sorensen, *Democracy and Democratization,* op. cit., p. 30.

31   Lance Morrow, "Africa: The Scramble for Existence," *TIME* (September 7, 1992).

32   See Baffour Ankomah, "Ghana's Reform Programme: How Long Will It Be Before the Patient Is Cured?" *African Business* (March 1990); and Ross Hammond and Lisa McGowan, "Ghana: The World Bank's Sham Showcase," in Kevin Danaher, (ed.), *50 Years Is Enough: The Case Against the World Bank and the International Monetary Fund* (Boston: South End Press, 1994).

33   Georg Sorensen, *Democracy and Democratization,* op. cit., pp. 50-51.

34   *Ibid.,* p. 53.

35   *Ibid.*

36   See Ayesha Imam, "Democratization Processes in Africa. . . ," op. cit; Adotey Bing, "Salim A. Salim on the OAU and the African Agenda," *Review of African Political Economy* (50) (March 1991); and Claude Ake "Devaluing Democracy," *Journal of Democracy* Vol. 3, (3) (July 1992).

37   Georg Sorensen, *Democracy and Democratization,* op. cit., p. 52.

38   See Julius O. Ihonvbere, "Threats to Democratization in Sub-Saharan Africa: The Case of Zambia," *Asian and African Studies* Vol. 19, (2) (1995).

39   Samuel Huntington, *The Third Wave,* op. cit., p. 262.

40   See the contributions to William Minter, (ed.), *U. S. Foreign Policy: An Africa Agenda,* (Washington, D.C.: Africa Policy Information Center, 1994) and Michael Clough, "The United States and Africa: The Policy of Cynical Disengagement," *Current History* Vol. 91, (May 1992).

41   Georg Sorensen, *Democracy and Democratization,* op. cit., p. 54.

42   See Githu Muigai, "Kenya's Opposition and the Crisis of Governance," *Issue* Vol. XXI, (1-2) (1993); and Masipula Sithole, "Is Zimbabwe Poised on a Liberal Path? The State and Prospects of the Parties," *Issue* Vol. XXI, (1-2) (1993).

43 See Julius O. Ihonvbere, "Prodemocracy Movements and the Crisis of Democratization in Africa." Unpublished paper, The University of Texas, May 1995.

44 Claude Ake, "Is Africa Democratizing?" op. cit.

45 *Ibid.*

46 Martin Klein, "Back to Democracy," op. cit.

47 Catherine Newbury, "Introduction: Paradoxes of Democratization in Africa," *African Studies Review* Vol. 37, (1) (April 1994), pp. 2-3.

48 *Ibid.*, p. 3.

49 *CODESRIA Bulletin* (1991) cited in Martin Klein, "Back to Democracy," op. cit.

50 See Ajayi Ola-Rotimi and Julius O. Ihonvbere, "Democratic Impasse: Remilitarization in Nigeria, *Third World Quarterly* Vol. 15, (4) (1994).

51 *Ibid.*

52 See Julius O. Ihonvbere, "The State and Academic Freedom: How African Academics Subvert Academic Freedom," *Journal of Third World Studies* Vol. VI, 2 (December 1992), and Mahmood Mamdani and Mamadou Diouf (eds.), *Academic Freedom in Africa* (Dakar: CODESRIA, 1994).

53 Organization of African Unity, *Lagos Plan of Action for the Economic Development of Africa 1980-2000*, (Geneva: Institute for Labour Studies, 1981), p. 1.

54 See World Bank, *Sub-Saharan Africa. . .* , op. cit.

55 Chris Allen, Carolyn Baylies and Morris Szeftel, "Surviving Democracy?" *Review of African Political Economy* (54) (1992), p. 7.

56 "Democracy in Africa-Lighter Continent," *The Economist* (February 22, 1992).

57 Mohammed Halfani, "The Challenges Ahead," in Richard Sandbrook and Mohammed Halfani, (eds.), *Empowering People: Building Community, Civil Associations and Legality in Africa*, (Toronto: Center for Urban and Community Studies, University of Toronto, 1993), p. 201.

58 Richard Sandbrook, "Introduction," *ibid*, p. 2.

59 *Ibid.*, p. 3.

60 Mohammed Halfani, "The Challenges Ahead," op. cit., p. 201.

61 See Prosper Bani, "The Changing Character of Politics in Ghana." Unpublished paper, The University of Texas at Austin, August, 1994.

62 For a detailed discussion see Julius O. Ihonvbere, "The African Crisis, The Popular Charter and Prospects for Recovery," *Zeitschrift fur Afrikastudien* (ZAST) (11-12) (1991).

Chapter 13

Obstacles to African Development

George Ayittey

INTRODUCTION

The epistle on postcolonial Africa is perditious. On the eve of independence from colonial rule, Africans rejoiced with unbounded euphoria. "Free at last!" resonated across Africa in the 1960s. But very quickly, the hope and joy of Africans were replaced by a deep sense of disillusionment, despair and bitterness. The freedom and prosperity many Africans hoped for never materialized. By the beginning of the 1990's, it was clear that something had gone terribly wrong with African development. The continent was wracked by a never-ending cycle of civil wars, carnage, chaos and instability. Economies had collapsed. Poverty, in both absolute and relative terms, had **increased**. Malnutrition was rife. In addition, censorship, persecution, detention, arbitary seizures of property, corruption, capital flight, tyranny, and political instability continuously plagued the continent. Infrastructure had decayed and crumbled as one African country after another imploded, scattering refugees in all directions: Ethiopia (1985); Angola (1986); Mozambique (1987); Sudan (1991); Liberia (1992); Somalia (1993); Rwanda (1994). In March, 1994, the United Nations Development Program (UNDP) grimly predicted that nine more African countries were on the brink of complete social disintegration: Algeria; Burundi; Egypt; Liberia; Mozambique; Nigeria; Sierra Leone; Sudan; and Zaire.

Various hypotheses have been advanced to explain Africa's apparent economic collapse, ranging from the iniquities of slavery, the legacies of colonialism, an unjust international economic system to racial inferiority. However, most of these theories progressively fell into disrepute. An *institutional* or *systemic* approach to Africa's intractable problems is far more useful. The failure of Africa to develop in the postcolonial era has little to do with alleged racial inferiority but rather more to do with the defective economic and political *systems* established by African leaders after independence. Despite Africa's cultural diversity and the ideological predilections of its leaders, the *systems* instituted across the continent were strikingly similar. They were all characterized by a great deal of concentration of power in the hands of the state and ultimately one individual.

Politically, the authoritarian colonial state was never really dismantled after independence. In-coming black administrations rather strengthened the unitary state apparatus and expanded its scope enormously—especially the military. Even repressive colonial measures used to quell black aspirations for freedom were retained. For example, within a year of Ghana's independence in 1957, Nkrumah introduced the Preventive Detention Bill of July 1958, which gave the government sweeping powers "to imprison, without trial, any person suspected of activities prejudicial to the state's security." Nkrumah, who himself was jailed by the colonialists, proscribed opposition activities and arrested some of its leaders. Under the Preventve Detention Act, Obetsebi-Lamptey and Dr. J. B. Danquah were arrested, jailed and subsequently perished in prison. In Zambia, the state of emergency was kept for 20 years (over ten years in Zimbabwe) after independence. Rwanda even instituted a black tribal apartheid, enforced with a passbook system comparable to the one black South Africans came to hate under their apartheid in South Africa.

THE COLLAPSE OF THE POST-COLONIAL STATE

In many African countries, the political systems established became increasingly repressive. "One man, one vote" became a one-day wonder. African nationalists who waged the liberation struggle against the colonialists were hailed as "heroes" and swept into power with huge electoral majorities. But in case after case, they misused their parliamentary majority to subvert the constitution, declare their countries "one-party states" and themselves "presidents-for-life." Opposition parties were outlawed. "Dissidents" were arrested and, in some cases, "liquidated." The rationale for this burgeoning repressive system was "unity." Multi-ethnicity precluded multi-party democracy, it was argued back then. Zaire, for example, has about 200 ethnic groups and multi-party democracy would easily degenerate into "tribal politics."

African leaders argued that the "one-party state" was preferable and could accomodate all sectarian interests and "unify" the country. Further, some African leaders such as Mobutu Sese Seko of Zaire argued, rather deviously, that the "one-party state" system was derived from African tradition. In traditional Africa, there was only one chief and he ruled for life. Mobutu however failed to mention that, while it was indeed true that the African chief ruled for life, he could be removed at **any time**, if he failed to govern according to the will of the people. The modern construct ("president-for-life") was a far cry from the traditional and a meretricious ploy by autocratic African leaders to perpetuate themselves in power.

Africa's economic systems, in the postcolonial era, were similarly characterized by enormous concentration of power in the hands of the state. The preponderance of the state in the economy may be explained by two factors—ideological and situational. African nationalists, in the 1960's, were in a hurry to develop Africa. "We shall achieve in a decade what it took others a century," said Nkrumah. An economic ideology was needed but in one monumental syllogistic error, capitalism was identified with colonialism and spurned. Colonialism was evil and since the colonialists were "capitalists," it was reasoned, capitalism too was evil. Socialism, the antithesis of capitalism, therefore became the guiding ideology.

Under an imported socialist ideology, the authoritarian postcolonial state assumed the roles of economic regulator, planner, and entrepreneur. The state seized the "commanding heights of the economy" to protect the new nation against "neocolonial exploitation." A bewildering array of legislative controls and regulations was imposed on African economies. Private businesses were nationalized, foreign companies expelled and state enterprises set up haphazardly. Even centuries-old indigenous economic activities such as mining and trading were declared illegal. But in country after country—from Guinea, Mali, Ghana to Tanzania—the socialist experiment turned out to be a miserable fiasco. While the nationalists preached socialism and inveighed against colonial exploitation and Western imperialism, their ministers were living lavishly and amassing fat bank balances in Switzerland. These "Swiss bank" socialists were booted out of office in a rash of coups that swept across Africa in the 1970s.

Only a few countries—Ivory Coast, Kenya, Malawi, Nigeria, and Zaire—eschewed doctrinaire socialism however. But even in these countries, the state, for a variety of situational reasons, came to dominate the economy. Markets were either nonexistent or underdeveloped and could therefore not possibly serve as a guide to investment decisions. Even where they existed, prices were often distorted by structural rigidities and supply inelasticities, providing unreliable signals to economic actors. For example, organized capital markets have long been absent in Africa while commodity markets could be cornered by powerful commercial interests. Only the state could marshall the resources required to undertake large-scale development projects. For example, a $50 million hydroelectric project or road system could not be financed from private (African) sources—except through the state. Furthermore, structural impediments and infrastructural bottlenecks could only be removed through state planning and action. For these reasons, the state came to dominate the utilities, commercial, financial, transport, export and industrial sectors in these "capitalist" countries. But what was eventually practiced was "bastard capitalism" that enriched only the ruling elite.

Thus, beneath the ideological posturing and invective, most African countries were quite similar in terms of how they were governed and their economies managed. In virtually all cases, the state was monopolized and run as "personal fiefdoms" in the "pro-capitalist" countries (Kenya, Malawi and Zaire) or as "party property" in the "one-party socialist states" (Guinea, Ethiopia, Tanzania and Zambia). All shared one overriding characteristic: *the concentration of both political and economic power in the hands of the state.* Naturally, much of this power was abused. As Lord Acton once said, power tends to corrupt and absolute power corrupts absolutely. Political power was misused to squelch opposition and institute tyrannical reigns of terror. Economic power was misused by the ruling elite to siphon huge fortunes out of Africa.

Africa cannot survive or develop with these systems. They must be reformed. But which should be reformed first—the political or the economic system? And what type of reforms would be suitable for Africa? Would capitalism work in Africa? How about multi-party democracy?

ATTEMPTS AT POLITICAL AND ECONOMIC REFORM

Up until 1989 when communism collapsed in the former Soviet Union and the Eastern bloc countries, Western aid agencies involved in African development focused only on economic reform and paid little attention to democracy because of Cold War imperatives. It was generally believed that economic development was feasible under "authoritarian regimes." Chile and the "Asian Tigers" were frequently cited examples. Successful development, it was argued, would help create a strong middle class, which, in turn, would agitate for political reform. After the collapse of communism, however, the "winds of change" swept this argument aside and the oppressed, including Africans, began clamoring more insistently for democracy. Multi-lateral aid agencies responded by adding "aid conditionalities." In 1991, for example, the World Bank told Kenya and Malawi that it would withhold aid unless they established multi-party democracy.

The consensus now is that economic and political reform must go hand in hand. Economic reform in Africa essentially entails rolling back the pervasive influence of the state and granting greater economic freedom to the people. African economies suffer from high taxes, rampant inflation, runaway government expenditures, unstable currencies and a plethora of regulations that stifle enterprise and drive away foreign investment. From 1989 to mid-1994, over half of British manufacturing companies disinvested from their African operations. It is a fact that countries that move away from a state-controlled economy toward greater reliance on the private sector generally do better economically. Innumerable examples, from Asia to Latin America and the former Soviet bloc, can be adduced for testimony. Moreover, African leaders themselves acceded to economic reform—on their own accord.

In May 1986, they collectively admitted before the United Nation's Special Session on Africa that their own capricious and predatory management contributed to Africa's economic crisis. Subsequently, they agreed to World Bank-sponsored Structural Adjustment Programs (SAPs): to adopt a transparent management style, to dismantle the state interventionist behemoth, liberalize markets, devalue or float currencies, sell off unprofitable state-owned enterprises and remove controls on prices, interest and rents. In return, the World Bank would provide loans to ease balance of payment, debt-servicing and budgetary difficulties. In June 1987, they reaffirmed their determination to pursue the SAPs at a conference organized by the Economic Commission on Africa (ECA) at Abuja (Nigeria). But in implementing these economic reforms, wily autocrats resorted to wilful chicanery, duplicity and trenchant dishonesty to defeat the very objectives of the reform program.

A detailed assessment of the performance of 29 adjusting African countries by the World Bank in its March 1994 report found that "No African country has achieved a sound macroeconomic policy stance." Only six had arguably established an enabling environment: The Gambia; Burkina Faso; Ghana; Nigeria; Tanzania and Zimbabwe. Since then, the tiny number of "success stories" has shrunk: a July 1994 military coup in The Gambia and continuing political turmoil in Nigeria throttle economic reform. In the remaining four countries, reform is on the verge of collapse.

While African leaders were preaching belt-tightening to the masses, their own officials were exempting themselves from austerity. In 1987, while former military dictator of Nigeria, General Ibrahim Babangida, was starving the country's universities of funds because of austerity measures mandated by Structural Adjustment (economic reform), he was showering his military officers with gifts of cars worth half a billion *naira* ($120 million). In July 1992, his military regime took delivery of 12 Czechoslovakian jet trainers (Aero L-39 Albatross) in a secret deal believed to be part of a larger order made in 1991 and worth more than $90 million. Earlier in 1992, Nigeria had taken delivery of 80 British Vickers Mark 3 tanks, worth more than $225 million. In Zimbabwe in 1994, barely a month after Mugabe's government stipulated a 10-percent annual salary increases ceiling, top government officials awarded themselves increases exceeding 50 percent. In Tanzania, senior government officials and major politicians exempted themselves from taxes. In 1993, there were over 2,000 such exemptions, costing the Treasury $113 million.

Public confidence in economic reform was irrevocably shattered by the reforming regime's duplicitous posturing, shameless looting and hopeless inability to control its own budgetary expenditures. For ten years, there was no audit of public accounts in both The Gambia and Ghana. An audit in 1995 revealed an embezzlement of 535,940 *dalasis* at the Ministry of Agriculture and misuse of 60 million *dalasis* by the Gambian Farmers' Cooperative Union. In Ghana, the 1993 Auditor-General's Report detailed a catalogue of corrupt practices, administrative ineptitude and the squandering of over $200 million in public funds. A September 27, 1994 audit in Nigeria revealed that a total of $12.4 billion—more than a third of the country's foreign debt—was squandered by its military rulers between 1988 and 1994.

On political reform, a few African leaders sincerely embraced democracy and began experimenting with alternative systems: Ethiopia under President Meles Zenawi with "ethnic democracy"; South Africa under President Nelson Mandela with "government of national unity," a model copied by Angola and Mozambique; Uganda under President Yoweri Museveni with "no party politics"; and Ghana under President Jerry Rawlings with a "split party system" (viz, "no party politics" at the district level but permitted at the national level). Whether these "new" political systems will work or not is debatable. But at least the effort is being made to find a "suitable" political system for Africa.

The vast majority of African leaders, however, adamantly refused to reform their abominable political systems and resorted to tricks and manipulation of the electoral process to maintain their grip on power. Africans derisively referred to these tricks and acrobatics as the "**Babangida Boogie**": one step forward, four steps back, a sidekick and a flip to land on a fat Swiss bank account. All "much ado about nothing".

In 1990, only four out of 54 African countries (Botswana, The Gambia, Mauritius and Senegal), were democratic. Following the demise of communism, the "winds of change" toppled a few African autocrats. The number of African democracies grew to 14 in 1994: Botswana; Benin; Cape Verde Islands; Central African Republic; Madagascar; Mali; Mauritius; Namibia; Niger; Sao Tome & Principe; Senegal; Seychelles; South Africa and Zambia. (The Gambia was struck off the list after the military seized power on July 24.) But the democratization process stalled, as crafty despots quickly learned new "tricks" to beat back the democratic challenge.

Since 1990, three scenarios have emerged in the democratization process. By the "Doe scenario," African leaders who foolishly refused to accede to popular demands for democracy only did so at their own peril and the destruction of their countries: Doe of Liberia; Traore of Mali; Barre of Somalia; and Habryimana of Rwanda. (Doe was killed in September 1990; Barre fled Mogadishu in a tank in January 1991; and Mengistu to Zimbabwe in February 1991.)

In the "Kerekou scenario," those African leaders who wisely yielded to popular pressure managed to save not only their own lives but their countries as well: Kerekou of Benin; Kaunda of Zambia; Sassou-Nguesso of Central African Republic; Pereira of Cape Verde Islands; and de Klerk of South Africa. Unfortunately, they are the exceptions.

The "Babangida scenario," the third, is by far the most common. In this scenario, they yield initially after considerable domestic and international pressure but then attempt to manipulate the rules and the transition process to their advantage, believing that they could fool their people **all the time**: Burkina Faso; Burundi; Ghana; Ivory Coast; Kenya; Nigeria; Sierra Leone; Tanzania; Zaire; and Zimbabwe. Nigeria, for example, is in perpetual state of transition to democracy. Recent events in Nigeria, Togo and Zaire also show that the outcome of the Babangida scenario is highly unpredictable and its impact on economic development deleterious. The country lurches from one crisis to another, generating political uncertainty and discouraging business investment and trade.

At the present time, the greatest obstacle to Africa's development, in my view, has little to do with lack of capital or ideology. Rather, it has more to do with elite obsession with political power, coupled with the obstinate refusal to relinquish it once acquired. (There are two classes of people in Africa: the elite minority and the peasant majority.) The elite misuse this (state) power to accumulate wealth, instead of seeking their wealth in the private sector. (The richest persons in Africa are often heads of state and ministers.) Unwilling to give up or share this power, the ruling elite play one ethnic group against another (Hutus against Tutsi; Moslem against Christians—the same colonial tactic of "divide and rule"), ban or suppress opposition parties, and rig elections.

The cruel irony is that this model of governance was not that much different from the unjust system of apartheid established by whites in South Africa. There, the state was captured by whites and the instruments of state power used to advance the economic welfare and interests of only whites. All others were excluded (**politics of exclusion**). Elsewhere in Africa, *de facto* apartheid models of governance prevailed, where the state was captured by one ethnic, professional or religious group which advanced its economic interests, excluding all others from the political spoils system: In Mauritania and Sudan, the state was captured by Arabs (Arab apartheid); in Angola, Cameroon, Cote d'Ivoire, Kenya, Tanzania by one political party ("one-party state"); in Congo, Sierra Leone, Togo, Uganda by the military (stratocracy); in Nigeria and Zaire by uniformed bandits (kleptocracy).

Those excluded from the spoils systems seldom succeed in seeking a redress to their grievances because *all* the key institutions or channels of redress had been infiltrated, subverted or commandeered to serve the interests of the ruling group or elites: the judiciary, the police, the military, the press, etc. For example, in Ghana where the president, Flt. Lt. Jerry Rawlings, is from the Ewe ethnic group,

Almost all the financial institutions, major corporations and institutions in Ghana are headed by Ewes. These include the Bank of Ghana, the Social Security and National Insurance Trust (SSNIT), the Ghana Reinsurance Organization (GRO), the Home Finance Corporation. Other important public insitutions headed by Ewes are the Ghana

National Petroleum Corporation, the Ghana Ports and Harbors Authority, the Ghana Supply Commission, and the Ghana Water and Sewerage Corporation, where all seven directors are Ewes.

In the military, the General Officer Commanding the Ghana Armed Forces and the Army Commander are all Ewes. In July, over 90 percent of the more than 100 new recruits who joined the Commando Unit of the Forces Reserve Regiment were all Ewes. The C.O. of Unit 64, the FRB, is an Ewe and **the President's Presidential Guard are all Ewes.**[1] (Emphasis added).

This leaves the excluded ethnic groupswith only two options: either overthrow the ruling group and seize power themselves, or secede as was the case of Biafra (resulting in the Nigerian 1967-70 civil war) and the Republic of Somaliland (1992). Either prospect adds to the level of violence and instability that pervade Africa.

The politics of exclusion (monopolization of political power and exclusion of others from the spoils system) is the primary cause of the ruination of many African countries. Indeed, the destruction of an African country, regardless of the professed ideology of its government, **always** begins with a dispute over some aspects of the *electoral process* or power-sharing arrangements. The competition for control of the state is particularly fierce because, in Africa, the political arena serves as the stage for private wealth accumulation. And, naturally, those wield political power are loathe to give it up.

The blockage of the democratic process or the refusal to hold elections plunged Angola, Chad, Ethiopia, Mozambique, Somalia, and Sudan into civil war. The manipulation of the *electoral process* by hardliners in Rwanda (1993), Sierra Leone (1992) and Zaire (1990) ruined the future prospects of these countries. The subversion of the *electoral process* in Liberia (1985) eventually set off a civil war in 1989. The same subversion instigated civil strife in Cameroon (1991), Congo (1992), Togo (1992) and Kenya (1992). Finally, the annulment of *electoral results* by the military started Algeria's civil war (1991) and plunged Nigeria into political turmoil (1993). Even in relatively tranquil Cote d'Ivoire, five people were killed on October 7, 1995, following protest over the **electoral process**.

According to the United Nations Development Program (UNDP) *Human Development Report* (1993), 33 of the world's

43 poorest nations are in Africa. Unless drastic measures are undertaken and a stronger commitment to reform more forthcoming from the ruling elites, Africa, in the words of U.N. Secretary General, Boutros Boutros-Ghali, would be at risk of becoming the "lost continent".[2]

CONCLUSION: WHAT TO DO TO SAVE AFRICA?

Africa's unrelenting slide into the abyss of economic disintegration no longer raises eyebrows. The exceptions are distressingly few. The international and academic community is divided over the appropriate policy measures in the majority of cases where hope is fading? There are the "retreatists," who are abandoning Africa because it has lost its strategic value after the Cold War. Then there are the "Afro-pessimists," who have succumbed to "donor fatigue," after being overwhelmed by a torrent of Africa's intractable problems. And stung by costly (financial as well as human) miscues in Somalia and Rwanda, they have lost the appetite for future "African adventures."

The "optimists," on the other hand, would remain engaged to help and offer the following solutions: more aid, a "buyout" of recalcitrant rulers *a la Haiti*, and even "recolonization." Foreign aid, however, helped repressive African governments more than the people. The case for recolonization has occasionally been made in the Western media: (Robert Kaplan, in *New Republic*, Dec 28, 1992; Paul Johnson in *New York Times Magazine*, Apr. 18, 1993; Christopher Hitchens in *Vanity Fair*, Nov 1994; and William Pfaff in *Foreign Affairs*, Aug/Sept, 1995, among others). Paul Johnson, for example, argued that recolonization should be encouraged and supported on practical and moral grounds. Paul argues that:

> Many Third World countries, mostly in Africa are just not fit to govern themselves and should be recolonized. There simply is no alternative in nations where governments have crumbled and the most basic conditions for civilized life have disappeared, as is now the case in a great many Third World countries. A historic line was crossed when American marines landed in Somalia—without any request, because no government existed. It is obvious that Africa, where normal government is breaking down in a score or more states, is the most likely

theater for (more) such action. The appeals for help come not so much from Africa's political elites, who are anxious to cling to the trappings of power, as from ordinary, desperate citizens, who carry the burden of misrule. Recently in Liberia, where rival bands of heavily armed thugs have been struggling for mastery, a humble inhabitant of the capital, Monrovia, approached a marine guarding the U.S. Embassy and said, "For God's sake come and govern us."

[However] this new form of "colonialism" will differ from the old-style in that it will be done under United Nations supervision by placing countries under trusteeships. African candidates for colonialization by the "civilized world," would be Somalia, Liberia, Zaire, Angola and Mozambique.[3]

But recolonization is politically unacceptable and economically impractical. Africa did not struggle for its independence from colonial rule in the 1960s only to be recolonized in the 1990's. Even *de facto* recolonization is philosophically out of the question, assuming Europe has the resources to undertake the mammoth enterprise. It constitutes an *external* and not the *internal* solution desired since, ultimately, it is Africans who must save Africa.

The military has been the most destabilizing factor in Africa politics. Perhaps, "amnesty" *a la Haiti*, "safe passage out of the country" *a la Babangida*, a bribe or an outright buy-out may be worthwhile options to consider. To deal with the military thugs of Haiti,

> The United States agreed to release the frozen assets of Haitian military leaders and rent three properties belonging to former military commander Raoul Cedras, who left Haiti for exile in Panama early today. The actions would allow Cedras to collect millions of dollars that he reportedly amassed during his brutal three years in power as well as thousands of dollars in rental income that will further cushion his exile . . .
>
> A Treasury Department spokesman said there was $79 million in individual Haitian accounts as of Sept 15 but added that the amount was certainly larger than that because the Treasury figure came from voluntary bank declarations.
>
> US Embassy spokesman, Stan Schrager, said the United States had, in an effort to get the former generals out of the country before Aristide returns, agreed to rent the three Cedras properties . . . The agreement eased the Cedrases' immediate cash-flow problem on arrival in Panama.[4]

A similar buy-out may be considered for the military dictators in Nigeria, Togo, Zaire and other African countries. For example, a $1 billion loan can be taken to buy out the military regime and demobilize half of Nigeria's armed forces. This may sound repugnant but the alternative may be too awesome to contemplate. Consider Somalia and Rwanda which were ruined by military vagabonds.

The humanitarian mission alone in Somalia cost the international community more than $3.5 billion, not to mention the lives of 18 U.S. Marines and the cost of repairing crumbled infrastructure—schools, roads, telephones, government buildings, etc. In Rwanda, relief operations so far have cost in excess of $300 million. Had $50 million been spent to buy out the late General Siad Barre of Somalia or the Hutu-dominated regime of the late General Juvenal Habryimana of Rwanda, the savings in economic and human terms would have been incalculable.

Another possible solution is to abolish the African state altogether and then there would be no state for any group to capture. In fact, some of the so-called "primitive and backward" people of Africa did exactly that. They were called "stateless" or acephalous societies; for example, the Igbo of Nigeria, the Somali, the Kikuyu of Kenya, and the Kung of the Kalahari. These societies had no chiefs or centralized authority. It can be said with sarcasm that the Somali did indeed return to their former statelessness by thoroughly destroying their modern state through civil war. Nonetheless, the solution to Africa's political crisis can *still* be found in its indigenous institutions.[5]

When a crisis erupts in traditional Africa, the chief and the elders would call a *village meeting* and put the issue to the people. It was debated and debated until a **consensus** was reached. During the debate, the chief kept quiet and listened to the various shades of opinion aired. There were no bazooka-wielding rogues, intimidating people and instructing them on what they should say. People expressed their ideas openly and **freely**.

This village meeting was recently resurrected in a number of African countries and "modernized" to resolve political crises in what is now known as a *national conference*. This mechanism was successfully used to make peaceful transitions to democratic rule in Benin, Cape Verde Islands, Congo and South Africa.

South Africa's national conference was the Convention For A Democratic South Africa (CODESA), which drew delegates from about 25 political parties **and** various anti-apartheid groups. CODESA strove to reach a "working consensus" on an interim constitution and a date for the elections. Note that political parties were **not** excluded from CODESA. More importantly, CODESA was **sovereign** and its decisions were **binding** upon the de Klerk government. That is, President F.W. de Klerk could not abrogate any decision made by CODESA.

But when Nigeria's military regime of General Sani Abacha organized a constitutional conference in 1994, it banned all political parties from participation. In addition, it nominated 25 percent of the delegates to the conference and decreed that resolutions of the conference would not be binding on the military regime. If the white minority government of South Africa had insisted on the same stipulations, African leaders would have denounced this as palpable effontery to black people. But the same leaders accepted the perpetration of this chicanery on the Nigerian people.

It is not the backwardness of the African people but the intellectual backwardness of African leaders that keeps Africa in the economic backwater. The leadership is the *real* obstacle to Africa's development.

Notes

1   *The Ghanaian Chronicle*, Aug 7-9, 1995; p. 1.

2   *The Washington Times*, March 16, 1996; p. A9.

3   *The New York Times* Magazine, April 18, 1993; p. 22.

4   *The Washington Post*, Oct 14, 1994; p. A32.

5   See George Ayittey, *Indigenous African Institutions* (New York: Transnational Publishers, 1991).

Chapter 14

Pan-Africanism: Agenda for African Unity in the 1990's?*

Julius O. Ihonvbere

INTRODUCTION

The theme of this important conference is UNITY. This has been the theme for many of the Pan-African conferences since 1900 and has continued to be the theme of countless meetings and conferences organized by the Organization of African Unity (OAU) and other bodies. Yet, Africa and Africans seem to be very far from achieving this goal (unity) in spite of thousands of pages of adopted declarations and charters. Not only is Africa very far from unity on any front, it is today the most marginal, the most oppressed, the most exploited, the most poverty-stricken, the most debt-ridden, the most unstable, and the most denigrated continent in the world. Africa has more than half of the world's refugees, and it is the least industrialized of all the developing regions. Thus we are not just disunited, we also have nothing to show for our abundant resources.[1]

Oppression, human rights abuses, the lack of opportunities, discrimination on the basis of ethnic, racial, regional and religious considerations, ruthless exploitation of the already impoverished, wars, instability, corruption, maniacal leadership, illiteracy, dilapidated institutions, roads full of pot holes, hun-

*This is an edited version of Julius O. Ihonvbere's keynote address at The All-African Student's Conference, University of Guelph, Guelph, Ontario (Canada) on May 24, 1994.

ger, disease, and disillusionment characterize the African sociopolitical landscape.[2] This is why many of us here today, who should be contributing to the growth and development of our respective countries and to Africa are hiding in America and other parts of the developed world.

The **mark of blackness** continues to evoke and encourage all sorts of nefarious, crazy and uncouth remarks, perceptions, and conclusions about Africans and Africa. Africa is not just a **dark continent** in the eyes of the "civilized" world, but it is alleged to be the source of AIDS through some sinister cohabitation with some green monkeys in the wild jungles. Such are the stories told about Africa today in the elite media of the developed countries. If you listen to ABC's "World News Tonight" you can get a pretty good idea of where the **world** begins and ends, and it is only when some gruesome incident occurs in Africa that we see "special reports" on Africa. These infantile, pedestrian, half-baked and often ahistorical and misinformed "special" reports carefully ensure that African problems are blamed on "clans," "warlords," "tribes" or some other "black devil" which is unique to Africa.[3] At the end of the day, one is left convinced that this **AFRICA** is full of idiots, people who hate peace and democracy, AIDS infected people, animals, jungles, pathological and unheard-of human afflictions, kleptocrats who parade themselves as leaders, starving children and nations dependent on the goodwill of the UN and the West and hordes of people just seeking opportunities to escape to Europe and America by any means necessary. In fact Africa is nothing but a region where nothing good happens, where no new ideas can develop, and which is inhabited by rapacious politicians, blood-sucking generals and a people criminally addicted to blood and mayhem.[4]

I believe that there is a deliberate conspiracy, in the Western media in particular, to continue this terrible picture of Africa to satisfy the deformed entertainment demands of a generally ignorant public. The challenge before Africans, therefore, is not to deny the existence of such contradictions, conflicts, and crises in the region, but to provide historical, holistic, and dialectical explanations of how the ideals espoused by the early Pan-Africanist leaders can be mobilized in creating a new Africa.

Since the First Pan-African Congress organized by Sylvester Williams (a Trinidadian Lawyer) in 1900, six other Pan-African Congresses have been held. The Seventh Congress was held in Kampala, Uganda in April 1994. The themes in all these congresses were the same: African unity; African liberation from Western imperialism; African development; peace; and progress. The 1958 First Conference of Independent African states, held in Accra, Ghana marked the formal beginning of the Pan-African movement within the continent. Most of the ideas and declarations of the Accra meeting were to be incorporated into the Organization of African Unity (OAU) Charter in 1963. While the activities of the OAU and the politics of progressive African leaders in the 1960's saw the *political* independence of the majority of African states, they failed to alter the nature of the African economy and the region's location and role in a ruthlessly exploitative and grossly unequal international division of labor. This was largely because the struggles for political independence were struggles of limited objectives dedicated largely to winning *political* independence. Perhaps the greatest setback was the watered down OAU Charter (a compromised document reflecting the moderate views of its founders) which has made the OAU a white elephant. Consequently, African unity conceptualized and articulated as a practical cooperation at the political, social, economic and cultural levels remains more of a dream than reality. The whole spirit and ideology of Pan-Africanism has moved miles away from what people like George Padmore, Sylvester Williams, W.E.B. Du Bois, Marcus Garvey, and C.L.R. James had articulated.[5]

On June 5, 1963, leaders of East African governments met in Dar-es-Salaam and declared their unequivocal support for an East African Federation and a commitment to Pan-Africanism. As they put it:

We share a common past, and are convinced of our common destinies. We have a common history, culture and customs which make our unity both logical and natural. Our futures are inevitably bound together by the identical aspirations and hopes of our peoples, and the need for similar efforts in facing the tasks that lie ahead of each of our free nations. In the past century the hand of imperialism grasped the whole continent, and in this part of Africa our people found themselves included together in what the colonialists styled "the British sphere of influence." Now that we are once again free, or are on the point of regaining our freedom, we believe the time has come to **consolidate our unity** and provide it with a constitutional basis. (emphasis added.)[6]

In spite of their courageous declaration the East African Federation achieved very little and disintegrated without fulfilling its mission. The sub-region has witnessed wars, border closures, poverty, exploitation, and the reproduction of the decadence and inequalities of the colonial past. The record of other regions in Africa has not been better.

When George Padmore wrote his book *Pan-Africanism or Communism?* in 1956 he was reacting to his frustrations with communism. Though many of his charges against communism were baseless, his positions on Pan-Africanism were very clear. To Padmore, Pan-Africanism was an "ideological alternative" with which Africa could liberate itself from the shackles of imperialism. It would create the authentic and independent political, social, and cultural environment for creating, nurturing and reproducing what was uniquely African and thus insulate Africa from the decadence of Western imperialism. Pan-Africanism was the ideological framework for uniting All Africans in the world and for waging a struggle against "racial arrogance," "alien domination," and apartheid. Finally, Padmore argued, Pan-Africanism subscribed to a Gandhian doctrine of non-violence "as a means of attaining self-determination and racial equality." Padmore also had a message for African leaders when he noted that they "must resolve their own internal communal conflicts and tribal differences, so that, having established a democratically elected government, the imperial power will find less danger in passing power to the popularly elected leaders than in withholding it."[7] For Padmore, Pan-Africanism was a clear alternative to communism, tribalism, white racialism, black chauvinism, and reverse racism of any form. In his words:

> Pan-Africanism looks above the narrow confines of class, race, tribe and religion. In other words, it wants equal opportunity for all. Talent to be rewarded on the basis of merit. Its vision stretched beyond the limited frontiers of the nation-state. Its perspective embraces the

federation of regional self-governing countries and their ultimate amalgamation into a **United States of Africa**.[8]

We are all living witnesses to what has happened to these ideals. Some of the confusion in the early Pan-Africanist agenda weakened the whole enterprise as a revolutionary weapon. Oppressed peoples had no business preaching non-violence as a first response to a violent, illegitimate, racist, and exploitative colonial power. The ideology of non-violence was very acceptable to the colonial imperialists because it did not fundamentally challenge their control of power. However, in Mozambique, Angola, Guinea Bissau, Algeria, Zimbabwe, and South Africa, non-violence as a liberation philosophy did not work. The only response in these countries which imperialism and minority rule learned to respect was a practical violent challenge to colonial capitalist brutalization, exploitation, and dehumanization. Besides, an ideological response to challenge capitalism and imperialism was necessary to address the vestiges of the colonial experience; the termination of natural processes of state and class formation; the deformation, distortion, and disarticulation of the pre-capitalist social formations; the partial transformation of the production and accumulation patterns; the imposition of capitalist social relations; the imposition of alien tastes and values; and the incorporation of Africa into a metropolitan dominated and controlled global capitalist order.[9]

The failure to fundamentally challenge imperialism, smash it, and reconstruct the socio-political and economic landscape to reflect popular realities and aspirations betrayed the African revolution.[10] But Padmore and others were working in difficult times under very oppressive conditions in a world largely opposed to new ideas, particularly if such ideas were anti-capitalist and anti-imperialist. Consequently, in the struggle for independence, the only real source of credible support was from the socialist and communist countries of the world. Even the United States supported colonial domination and opposed the struggle for independence because it did not want to offend Europe.[11]

In 1963, African unity was given a weak and mediocre expression in the creation of a toothless, clawless lion in a deco-

rated cage in the name of the Organization of African Unity
(OAU). In place of unity, peace, nationalism, and Pan-
Africanism, the new African leaders who had taken over the
privileges and powers of the colonial imperialists came to rely
on nepotism, corruption, repression, intimidation,
depoliticization, diversions, ideological containment, pedestrian manipulation of primordial loyalties, shameless collusion
with profit and hegemony-seeking transnational corporations,
incredible subservience to Western and imperialist dictates,
and a total lack of vision for the future of Africa and
Africans.[12]

In the 1960's, Kwame Nkrumah of Ghana argued for African unity. At a rally in Accra in 1960, Nkrumah argued that
"all independent states in Africa should work together to create a Union of African States." On March 6, 1960, he gave
further support to his vision when he declared in a radio broadcast that so deep was Ghana's "faith in African unity that we
have declared our preparedness to surrender the sovereignty
of Ghana, in whole or in part, in the interest of a Union of
African States and Territories as soon as ever such a union
becomes practicable."[13] In his book *I Speak of Freedom* published
in 1961, he reminded all Africans that imperialism had so thoroughly distorted and disarticulated African social formations,
that only continental unity could save the region from further
deterioration. In *Africa Must Unite* published in 1963, he articulated a clear agenda for the establishment of an African
common market to complement the Union of African States.
As far as Nkrumah was concerned, "The unity of Africa and
the strength it would gather from continental integration of
its economic and industrial development, supported by a united
policy of non-alignment, could have a most powerful effect for
world peace."[14]

It was in the espousal of these views by the likes of Kwame
Nkrumah, Modibo Keita, and Sekou Toure, that the structural
and social obstacles to Pan-Africanist consciousness and to
African unity became evident. A country like Nigeria was in
the forefront of challenging and opposing Nkrumah's ideas
and vision for Africa. Nkrumah was called names, and his vision was reduced to a simplistic matter of personal ambition.
Unfortunately, Nkrumah, like the majority of African leaders,

was so caught in the confusion of the quest for African unity that he chose to ignore the problems of class struggle in Africa. This was to be given greater expression in the ideas of Julius Nyerere who did not admit the existence of social classes until a decade after his Ujamaa experiment ran into serious problems in Tanzania.

From this time onwards, African states jettisoned the spirit of Pan-Africanism and followed their seemingly individual ways. In reality, the ways they took were those of subservience to imperialism. Given the pressures of the Cold War, poverty, food and technology dependence, underdevelopment, foreign manipulation and intimidation, African states struggled amongst themselves to provide better concessions and conditions to imperialism even if it was generally against the well being of their peoples. Thus, not only was imperialism an obstacle to African unity, the African elite also became an obstacle to African unity.[15]

These so-called elite, creations of imperialism, openly and shamelessly betrayed the ideals of Pan-Africanism and African unity. They used inherited state power to terrorize progressive and patriotic Africans. They drove popular forces underground. They suffocated civil society. They closed all democratic options even when they ran so called "democratic" governments. They neglected the rural areas and rural producers. They strengthened the divide between the people and themselves. They came up with bogus ideological positions and so-called philosophies designed to legitimize their control of state power. They forged unequal and exploitative relations with foreign transnational corporations. They preserved the ruthless and exploitative character of the state. They "indigenized" and "Africanized" colonial institutions, taste, values and positions. They demonstrated open hatred and hostility to trade and student unions and established all sorts of criminal security services to terrorize scholars, journalists, students, professionals and activists who refused to sing their praises. They set up private estates or parastatals which they called "political parties." They wasted scarce resources on defence and the security of the "life-president" and his family. They allowed the bureaucracy, schools, hospitals, and roads to run down while they had access to similar facilities abroad and their children were safely tucked away in expensive foreign institutions. They privatized the state, its resources, and means of coercion and visited untold violence on non-bourgeois forces. They watched their peoples grow poorer, more disillusioned, more angry and more alienated as their accounts swelled in foreign banks. Their irresponsible and normless politics precipitated civil wars, ethnic and religious violence, and failed to move Africa one step away from where it found itself at *political* independence from colonial rule.[16]

The African elite, showing a total disregard for the ideals of Pan-Africanism, forged new (or strengthened old unequal and exploitative) alliances with transnational corporations, and saw nothing wrong in a shameless dependence on the West for technology, political and military support, financial aid, food aid, and you name it. Many made trips abroad to beg for foreign aid at times on their knees or on the verge of tears.[17] While they paid lip service to their opposition to apartheid in southern Africa they flirted and dined with the very same countries that kept apartheid alive. Taken together, save for a few exceptions, the African elite and African leaders did little or nothing to restructure the distorted, disarticulated, dependent, and underdeveloped structures of the African social formation. They did little to empower the peoples of Africa. They did little to challenge foreign domination and imperialist penetration and exploitation of Africa. They did almost nothing to challenge the cultural bastardization in the continent. They did little to strengthen or reconstitute the neo-colonial state. They confused the expansion of the armed forces, the importation of outdated military and security gadgets, and the establishment of violent security structures with the strengthening of the state. They foolishly confused the harassment of opposition elements, the asphyxiation of civil society, and criminal looting of the treasury with power. They did little to move Africa away from the neo-colonial cultural, social, and political traditions and world-views imposed to serve the interests of the West. In short, this opportunistic, corrupt, decadent, irresponsible, largely unproductive, shamelessly subservient, and ideologically barren class ruined Africa and mortgaged the future of the vast majority to imperialist interests. A simple look at their record in countries like Ghana,

Kenya, Zambia, Nigeria, Zaire, Uganda, Rwanda, Burundi, Somalia, Togo, and Benin, to mention a few, will suffice.[18] The case of Nigeria is probably more dramatic. One in every five Africans is a Nigerian. According to Sophie Pedder Nigerians have always believed that their country is the giant of Africa. That, "If Africa is ever going to produce a South Korea, . . . it will happen in Nigeria. Yet, each time the country has the chance to turn itself into a prosperous model for still-poor Africa, it blows it." Ironically, just 13 years ago, Nigerians "looked down their noses at poor Thais and Indonesians." Today, Nigeria resembles a 17th century village compared to either Thailand or Indonesia. The last inglorious eight years of General Babangida saw a "budget deficit amounting to 10% of GDP; an external debt the servicing of which consumes a quarter of export earnings; inflation estimated in June (1993) to have reached an annual rate of 70-100%; and real income per head a tenth of what it was (in 1985)." The country's landscape is dotted with unfinished projects, "crumbling infrastructure, unhelpful bureaucracy, capricious government policies . . ." criminal and unbridled corruption, large scale mismanagement, waste, political opportunism, and the manipulation of political power by military adventurists.[19] Today, the Nigerian government, in spite of a huge population and its oil wealth, is almost bankrupt. Yet, this same country where poverty, disease, inefficient services, crime, violence, unemployment, inflation, waste and the terrorization of popular groups have become commonplace, has sprouted more millionaires and billionaires than any other African or Third World nation in the last decade. Millionaires and billionaires without any visible means of livelihood beyond car dealerships which serve as fronts for other nefarious and criminal activities. The country has produced more military generals than any other African country: the majority of these generals have demonstrated a willingness to suffocate the civilian population as well as talents in the derailment of efforts at democratization of the political system.[20]

The story is the same for other African countries. The political and economic indiscipline and irresponsibility of Africa's dominant classes have subverted all possibilities for stability, peace, and development, thus making Africa a typical example of blown opportunities, distorted dreams, an illustration of chaos theory, and an example of gangster politics. Compared to the achievements and serenity of the old empires of Ghana, Mali, Songhai, Kanem Bornu, Benin, and the Hausa city states, today's Africa is a dirty, disorganized, dangerous jungle. Leaders like Mansa Musa, Sundiata Keita, Idris Alooma, Ewuare the Great, Shaka Zulu, Mzilikazi, Mai Ali Gaji, Gelele, and Opoku Ware to name a few, would be shocked at what the post-colonial elite have done to Africa.

The shameless dependence on the West, the unproductive disposition of the African elite, the wanton abuse of human rights, the misappropriation of state power and its resources and hostility to popular and progressive forces have not helped Africa one bit. Africa has remained a continent for denigration, racist jokes, pity, and exploitation. David Wiley has noted that "the negative stereotyping of Africa in the West is the worst among world regions and remains a durable part of Western intellectual landscape. . . . It is not surprising, therefore, to hear racists joking in some policy arenas about the continent and its political leaders."[21] It has remained the wild dark jungle largely preserved to satisfy the lecherous and erotic dreams and fantasies of foreign tourists. It has remained the huge laboratory preserved to satisfy the academic curiosity of foreign scholars. The personalities of leaders like Nguema, Idi Amin, Kamuzu Banda, Ibrahim Babangida, Arap Moi, Jean Bedel-Bokassa, and Mobutu Sese Seko provide intriguing patterns and models for research into the African personality and idiosyncracies. By and large they go to form the caricature of the African in the minds of Western scholars and tourists who see the region as one inhabited by persons of lesser mental capabilities and people completely incapable of governing themselves. This reinforces long discredited arguments in support of other forms of scientific racism and justifies forms of racism, discrimination, and denigration. It also justifies the decision by most transnational bodies to employ so-called experts on Africa rather than employ Africans. No matter how much bleeding-heart liberals wish to deny these realities, they exist in even more sophisticated forms today. And the blatant racism and discrimination have not been adequately exposed because of the failure of the African elite to distinguish themselves, map out a clear and creative agenda for reconstruction and development, mobilize their people, develop infrastructures, and generate confidence in their region, resources, economies and abilities.

In spite of very loud complaints about aid and compassion fatigue, Africa has never really featured significantly in the geo-strategic and political/economic calculations of Western powers. For one thing, the Western powers have been able to extract strong political subservience from African leaders with very limited investment and pressures. Consequently, Africa was the only region that gained nothing, absolutely nothing, from the Cold War in spite of the subservience of the majority of African states to the supposedly "generous" Western alliance. The dirty consequences of how Africa was used and discarded is now clear in countries like Somalia, the Sudan and Liberia. Military generals and corrupt elite, wearing medals and other decorations bestowed on them by colonial exploiters for visiting violence on their fellow Africans, were only too available for cooperation in the neo-colonial project. Thus the total investment of the United States in Africa is less than its investment in Brazil alone. In spite of its relatively heavy trade with South Africa and Nigeria, no African nation ranks among the top 25 locations for US investments. Exports to Africa average about two percent of total US exports: and imports, including oil, are substantially less than ten percent (mostly with Gabon, South Africa, Angola, Nigeria, and Cameroon).[22]

Total US foreign aid, contrary to popular notions, went mostly to five Africans—Arap Moi of Kenya, Samuel Doe of Liberia, Said Barre of Somalia, Gaffer Nimeiri of the Sudan, and Hosni Mubarak of Egypt. It is not an accident that these countries along with a handful of others are some of the most corruption-laden, poverty-stricken, politically unstable, highly debt-distressed, and mortgaged economies in Africa today.

What has happened in Africa, given the alignment and re-alignment of political forces at the domestic and international levels, as well as the continuing imperialist exploitation of Africa in the face of a largely unproductive and irresponsible dominant class, has been the further marginalization, exploitation, impoverishment, domination, and denigration of Africa and Africans. Some of the frightening indicators of the African predicament are as follows:

1. Africa has more than half of the world's refugees, fleeing from war, famine, drought, and repressive leaders.

2. Africa houses about three-quarters of the least developed nations in the world with the majority concretely located in the fourth world. Thirty-two of the 40 lowest ranked countries in the UN's Annual Development Index are in Africa. Africa's underdevelopment and continuing impoverishment is the direct precipitate of European colonialism, global capitalist exploitation, and the ruthless extraction of resources especially in the name of debt servicing by international finance houses.

3. Africa's economic growth rate is the lowest in the world at 1.5 per cent. With exploitation, resource transfer, the brain drain, political and military manipulation, and lack of concrete support and access to the developed world markets, growth rates were bound to be low.

4. With a population of almost 600 million, Africa's combined GNP of a little less than $150 billion is equivalent to that of Belgium (a small European country of about 10 million people). In spite of this low GNP, the developed countries have continued to extract resources from Africa. The poor continent paid out $26 billion in 1991 to creditors as debt servicing. Arrears in debt servicing obligations increased from $1 billion in 1980 to $14 billion in 1991.

5. Food production in Africa is 20 percent lower than the 1970 figure, when its population was half of its present size. Wars encouraged by the military industrial complex and traditional support for unpopular leaders have made the situation worse. One wonders how many farmers cultivated their plots in Liberia, Somalia, the Sudan, Angola, Mozambique or Rwanda in recent times.

6. Only 37 percent of sub-Saharan Africans have access to good drinking water. Yet, about 65 percent of the diseases in the region could be eliminated with the provision of good drinking water. Billions of dollars in contracts awarded to American and European companies have not resulted in improved water supply. Is it not amazing how these companies can do it in their home

countries but fail woefully in Africa? Of course, failure can be blamed on the nature of governance in Africa.

7. Africa's population, even in the face of declining productivity and food production rates, is the highest growing in the world at 3.2 percent annually. The equivalent figure for Asia and Latin America is 1.8 percent. The region's population is projected to hit 2.9 billion in 2050. This has encouraged the UN and other agencies including Western governments to divert attention by complaining about Africa's growing population. Yet, India alone is more populous than the whole of Africa. For a continent the size of Africa, is the problem one of population or one of development and social justice?

8. Average life expectancy is a mere 51 years.

9. Crime, prostitution, corruption, waste, the displacement of the poor, environmental degradation, mismanagement and the harassment of non-bourgeois forces and their organizations have all reached new proportions as regimes become desperate, after having been left high and dry at the end of the Cold War.

10. Africa, especially sub-Saharan Africa, is the most debt-distressed region in the world. At the end of 1990, Africa's foreign debt stood at almost $270 billion. Between 1980 and 1988, 25 African states rescheduled their debt 105 times. Long term debt has experienced a 19-fold increase, debt servicing is as high as 120 percent of export earnings in some countries; and debt ratios are almost double those of highly indebted middle-income countries. The real question is: how did Africa come to owe the world so much? Can we ever imagine that lending money to poor underdeveloped nations was stupid in the first instance except it was part of a grand strategy to mortgage the futures of these nations?

11. Private investments in Africa have experienced a precipitous decline in the last decade. According to Michael Chege private investment in sub-Saharan Africa declined from $2.3 billion in 1982 to a mere $900 million in 1989. Between 1979 and 1989, the British alone withdrew 31 percent of their investments from the sub-re-

gion.[23] Reasons of instability and low buying power among others, are mere rationalizations. The situations in the Middle East and more so, Eastern Europe and Russia are no better than the conditions in Africa. Yet, investments pour into these regions!

12.   The poverty-situation has not been helped by declining foreign aid in spite of vitriolic propaganda to the contrary. Russia in its few years of existence as an "independent" nation has received more investment, pledges of aid, and direct assistance from the West and Japan, than any African state since 1960 and probably more than all sub-Saharan African states put together. Russia under Yeltsin has not done better in its reform program than the majority of African states. Foreign aid to 47 nations in sub-Saharan Africa declined from 14 percent of US aid in 1984 to 11 percent in 1991. The $616 million budgeted for sub-Saharan Africa pales in comparison to $1.6 billion for Egypt, $900 million for Eastern Europe, $720 million for Panama and Nicaragua, and $3.5 billion for Israel.[24] These figures exclude special supplements to these "special" nations. Yet, it is not uncommon to hear young people and politicians complain as to how "our tax money is being sent to help these Africans."

The list of Africa's woes can go on endlessly and many scholars have made a career of frequently cataloguing these woes. They would lose their jobs or run out of ideas if Africa were to resolve these contradictions and crises. How on earth can we build a credible, popular, and viable agenda in a context of such disheartening socio-economic and political conditions? The African situation has not been helped with the imposition of misguided monetarist policies by the International Monetary Fund and the World Bank prescribing policies of desubsidization, deregulation, privatization, commercialization, devaluation and the like. These policies which neglect the region's historical experiences; the character of state and class, existing coalitions, contradictions and conflicts; the ability of non-bourgeois forces to resist; the degree of state delegitimization; the credibility of the governing/ruling classes; the room for maneuver in the global system; the resource and other material and structural differences among African states and so on, have created many problems for Africa in the last decade or so.

In country after country, stabilization and adjustment policies have culminated in or precipitated civil wars, ethnic and religious violence, coups and counter coups, demonstrations, massacre of protesting workers, peasants and women, inflation, bankruptcies, and an unprecedented deterioration in living standards and the general quality of life. There have been very destructive riots in Nigeria and Zambia to take just two examples.[25] Part of the crisis in Somalia, which the Western media has been loudly silent about, has to do with the role of the International Monetary Bank and World Bank in the country between 1985 and 1989 which effectively isolated and bankrupted the economy making an already desperate government even more brutal and insecure. As well, the failure of these monetarist prescriptions, usually conceived in purely economic terms have delegitimized the state, its institutions and agents, and at the same time ruined indigenous producers thus facilitating the recolonization of Africa.[26]

Debt-equity swap as a response to the debt crisis for instance, has made it possible for foreign interests to buy over the more lucrative sectors in African economies. The attack on the African state by the World Bank and the International Monetary Fund as well as by Western governments confuses the state vis-a-vis its role in regulating its economy. The impression is created that the West was always developed and democratic. Any student of political science would know that the development of the West was not because of hard work and savings and with limited roles for the state. Indeed, the state in the contemporary Western capitalist society is as interventionist as the African state. George Bush lost his job as president of the United States because the democrats were able to focus their campaign on the failure of the American state under the republicans to promote production, create jobs, ensure social security, welfare issues, health care and the inability of the government to open up foreign markets. The state has always been part of the process of change and accumulation.

The problem in Africa is precisely that there is no state of which to speak. What exists are ramshackle structures, presided over by political thugs and military adventurists, generals who have never been to war, and yesterday-men who lack vision, who simply pretend to be governing, talk less of ruling, a society. In no African social formation has this body, by whatever name it goes, been able to operate as a *state*. African leaders and their economies remain cheap and easy pawns in the hands of transnational corporations and Western nations with only a passing interest in the future of the region. The ease and speed with which the West found new interests and diverted aid, investment, and "compassion" to Russia and Eastern Europe, and the sort of responses by the International Monetary Fund, World Bank, donors and other lenders to Eastern European countries should encourage the emerging generation of leaders in Africa to "get real."

It is interesting to note that African leaders, having destroyed the foundations of their societies, having alienated the populace, and having mortgaged the future of their respective economies have been singing the same song: "increase foreign aid, forgive our debts, and please, don't marginalize us." If this were waxed by a rap artist like MC Hammer or Ice T, it would have been in the top ten by now—given the regularity with which African leaders and their international bureaucrats have chorused this refrain. In spite of this chorus, very little has changed in their relations to civil society or in their commitment to change. They make very limited efforts, if any, to create a new national order away from the inherited neo-colonial relations of power, production, and exchange. Having missed the way to African unity in the 1960's, and having denigrated the likes of Toure, Nkrumah and Keita, African leaders in 1991 at the OAU Summit in Lagos spent hundreds of millions of dollars to agree to an African Economic Treaty. Of course, not much has been heard about this in the Western media compared to the North American Free Trade Agreement, the Maastricht Treaty, or the crisis in the former Yugoslavia. The 1991 African Economic Treaty is not important because, after all, it is an African affair.

The OAU took three decades to return to the original dreams of Nkrumah on a **Union Government of Africa** and an **African Common Market**. Nkrumah, certainly, was so far ahead of his contemporaries. African leaders have become experts at coming up with well-written, well-worded, even sympathy-evoking documents all designed to give the impression that they are serious-minded and have embraced a new commitment to challenging the poverty and squalor in which their peoples are immersed. Some of the major declarations and charters such as *Cultural Charter for Africa* (1976), *African Charter of Human and Peoples' Rights* (1981), *The Lagos Plan of Action and the Final Act of Lagos* (LPA-FAL) (1981), *Africa's Priority Programme for Economic Recovery* (APPER) (1986), *African Alternative Framework to Structural Adjustment Programmes for Economic Recovery and Transformation* (AAF-SAP)(1989), and *The African Charter for Popular Participation in Development* (1990), though path-breaking, have never been taken seriously by the same leaders who append their signatures to the documents. The point is that if current trends continue, and the current crop of virtually useless and subservient leaders remain in power, the African condition would continue to deteriorate and the march towards total disorder would become unstoppable.[27]

WHAT IS TO BE DONE?

Africa has never been short of solutions to its numerous crises and contradictions. It is well known that Africa is one of the richest regions of the world. The Southern Africa region contains all known space age minerals. Africa, which is the most central of all continents contains a fifth of the world's landmass contrary to the misguided work of cartographers who make Africa look smaller than Europe and North America on the world map.[28] With 54 nations and a population of 600 million, why have African leaders been unable to capitalize on their advantages to change the African reality as presently constituted?

Today, Africa seems to be suffering from an overdose of solutions from America, Canada, Europe, and the Scandinavian countries. Every president, foreign minister, secretary of state or whatever, has a particular solution to the African predicament or to some aspect of the predicament. These solutions are usually advanced by politicians and bureaucrats with only a cursory understanding of African realities and whose analyses and conclusions are often based on briefings by a small bureaucrat whose closest association with Africa was a couple of courses on Africa taught by some Africanist associated with Africa after some months following some research with a grant from some conservative foundation. In fact, the insult to Africa and Africans can be seen not only in some of the pedestrian and wishy-washy books that have come out recently on democracy and change in Africa but on the fact that these "experts" and politicians actually think they have so much to teach Africa and Africans about everything under the sun. Unfortunately, in a situation where political leaders declare war on researchers and academics, where the police and secret services chase the most creative minds out of the land, where originality and creativity are loathed by ignorant and old politicians, Africa simply became a dumping ground for all sorts of ideas.

So we see African leaders rushing from one end of the political and economic spectrum to the other with such rapidity that it is difficult to keep track of development models and ideological postures. From import substitution, growth-pole development, bottom-up development, basic needs, joint ventures and indigenization, nationalization and partnerships, and most recently structural adjustment, African leaders have gone through the entire gamut of socioeconomic and political prescriptions and we can all see what they have to show for their efforts today. The World Bank in its 1989 report on Africa declared that "Overall Africans are almost as poor today as they were 30 years ago."[29] The implication here is that colonial brutalization, domination, manipulation, exploitation, and marginalization did better for Africans than three decades of swallowing hook, line, and sinker all the garbage that has come from all nooks and corners of the world since 1960 in the name of economic models for growth and development. There is no need go through these long discredited models. Let us spend some time on the current prescriptions for Africa: multi-party democracy.

As usual, African states are being forced to adopt a new model from the West as the solution to underdevelopment, dependence, poverty, and marginalization in the international division of labor. Multi-party politics was originally not part of the International Monetary Fund and World Bank package for crisis-ridden African states. In fact, it was expected that only repressive and very brutal governments could force the monetarist prescriptions on already impoverished and marginalized sections of society. African leaders and governments were still in the process of fashioning out even more sadistic ways to force adjustment programs on their peoples when *political conditionality* was added by donors as a condition for further assistance.[30] This enabled Europe, America, and Japan to call not only the economic shots in Africa but also to dictate the political tune. Corrupt and repressive governments implanted and nurtured during the Cold War like the Moi regime in Kenya and the Banda government in Malawi were forced to hold multi-party elections. True, these elections have brought about some changes. They have opened up more political spaces. They have created opportunities for deeper political work and for more organization at the grassroots level. Beyond this nothing has changed.

The West is dictating and forcing a democratic agenda on Africa and is once again putting Africa on the path to a false start: confusing democracy with elections. What Africa needs, as part of the new agenda is not multi-party politics but the total *democratization* of the political, social, and economic landscape of Africa.[31] From schools, through households to governments, there must be a new spirit of and enthusiasm for democracy, empowerment, accountability, social justice, equality, respect for human rights, popular participation, and the guarantee of freedoms and liberties. This must be done in the context of a revitalized Pan-African ideology aimed concretely at establishing a Union Government of Africa. We cannot remain oblivious to developments in North America, the Pacific Rim, and Europe.

Africa has more to gain through the rapid and drastic dismantling of presently existing oppressive, wretched, foreign dominated, debt-ridden, unstable, and dilapidated estates called "governments" and countries with artificial boundaries with only a ragged national flag and incoherent national anthems as symbols of sovereignty. African borders are already crumbling and the vast majority of governments have no legitimacy of which to speak. Let us take a few examples: what is the real legitimacy of the Rawlings government in Ghana which went ahead with a parliamentary election boycotted by all the credible opposition? How legitimate is the Chiluba government in Zambia which has failed woefully to improve living conditions to such an extent that a high degree of "authoritarian nostalgia" has become commonplace? How legitimate is the Abacha government in Nigeria which has used thieves, convicted criminals, discredited politicians, and political opportunists with little credibility in civil society to form a cabinet? In Sierra Leone the so-called government of 27-year-old Valentine Strasserr rules part of the town in daylight while armed rebels and bandits take charge for the rest of the day. Is Mobutu's kleptocracy any more legitimate when he rules the country from his yacht? How much legitimacy can other African states claim when armed bandits challenge constituted authority, and political power is maintained through lies, propaganda, violence, and thievery? It is not surprising, therefore, that people in many parts of Africa find more comfort and security in ethnic and religious organizations than in "their" government. Today, philanthropic associations and non-governmental organizations have replaced the government in providing for the basic needs of a vast number of the people. Meanwhile, pirates, smugglers, drug traffickers, and currency speculators sway in broad daylight, as international financiers sit at cabinet meetings and order finance ministers to shut up and listen to their lectures on privatization and the like.

If Africans are serious, they must now be prepared to realize Nkrumah's dream in a world which has little respect for Africa and Africans. In this new struggle and agenda, non-bourgeois forces have nothing to lose though the elites and current custodians of state power have everything to lose. African patriots must be prepared to confront domestic and international enemies of African unity by **any means necessary** (due apologies to Malcom X) to create a stronger, democratic, powerful, productive, and just AFRICA. This unfortunately, cannot be achieved without first dismantling the existing structures and institutions of the state and replacing it with a **popular national state.** In all the on-going democratization programs in Africa, there is not one in which the dismantling of the oppressive neo-colonial state is on the agenda. In country after country, the struggle by the so-called pro-democracy forces, made up mostly of disgruntled politicians, political opportunists, professional agitators, marginalized political actors and net-workers and thieves of yesterday, the struggle has been to capture the existing anti-democratic state and use it to promote liberal democracy. As the experience of Zambia has shown this is a dream that would lead to democratic decay and authoritarian nostalgia.

The current African state is inefficient, ineffective, illegitimate, unstable, violent, exploitative and completely useless as far as the aspirations of the majority of Africans are concerned. It does not reflect the interests of the people and this is why it has to be completely dismantled, in fact, destroyed and replaced by the popular national state which can guarantee peaceful co-existence, economic progress, basic freedoms, and which can challenge the unmediated domination and exploitation of Africa by foreign interests. The popular state has to be initiated at the level of social discourse and promote the collective establishment of a political environment which would enable Africans to attain the highest points of the productive and creative abilities. It is only under such an arrangement that democracy and democratization, as well as economic progress can be attained in Africa. These conditions, will, of course, be the basis for African unity by encouraging understanding, accommodation, intra-African trade, and unity.

The second item in the agenda for unity in the 1990's must be the generation of an autonomous identity and indigenous control of the content and context of African development. Frantz Fanon, Aime Cesaire, Walter Rodney, Ngugi wa Thiongo, Kwame Nkrumah, and Leopold Sedar Senghor have addressed this question of "Black Skin and White Masks" in several ways. I am not preaching reverse racism or some form of cultural autarky here.

The time has come for Africa to emerge from being an onlooker; to take charge of its own destiny; to begin to look inward; and for the misguided and arrogant African elite to begin to learn from the experiences of the people. We must stop the brain drain. Thousands of the top minds of Africa have fled the continent voluntarily or otherwise because of the corruption, repression, and mindlessness of our so-called leaders. For instance, in 1991, there were over 13,700 Nigerians seeking political asylum in Germany alone. At the end of 1993, the United States Immigration and Naturalization Service estimated that there were 23,000 illegal Nigerians in the country. Yet, there is no civil war in Nigeria. This brain and brawn drain must be reversed. The technology Africa needs to survive in order to develop may very well be found in Africans at home and abroad. What is needed to tap these rich resources is selfless leadership and a conducive social and political environment.

The third important item in the quest for continental unity is the demystification of the military. The African military is a direct obstacle to unity and progress. It has arrogated to itself the right to abrogate democratic experiments at will. As experiences in Nigeria and Zaire, have demonstrated, the military has not helped Africa move forward. Even the much praised Rawlings regime in Ghana has not significantly improved on the record of the military. The *cedi* (currency) is virtually worthless today, and the country's foreign debt has more than quadrupled. The Rawlings regime has mortgaged the prosperity of children not yet born in Ghana by its massive acquisition of dubious loans and reckless spending. Consequently, the cost of its much vaunted "success" which Kwesi Botchwey (former Ghanaian Secretary for Finance) and Rawlings have themselves questioned, is in the massive inflow of foreign support because the World Bank wanted at least one success story in Africa. Yet success in the Ghanaian economy under Rawlings is out of sight.[32]

The current military structures in Africa need to be dissolved and replaced by a popular army subject to civil society and not parasitic as is currently the case. The solution to coups beyond legal provisions which make it illegal even if it succeeds, and punishable no matter how long such military regimes stay in power must include a conscious mobilization and education of workers, women, students, young people and peasants to resist the military whenever it seizes power. Refusal to pay taxes, staying away from work and school, refusal to open markets, to operate taxi cabs and buses and so on, can make a nation ungovernable to military adventurists and force them from power. Once we tolerate them, and welcome them with dancing and singing on the streets, then, we must live with them. Countries which pretend to be democratic but embrace criminal military juntas must be forced through direct criticisms and isolation, to alter their pretentious positions. If the African military is not adequately educated, it will continue to waste resources, militarize society, and discourage all efforts at strengthening civil society.

CONCLUSION

Finally, the economic and cultural revival and restructuring must go with a strong economic agenda. Africa needs not just restructuring and adjustment but a fundamental transformation in the patterns of production and exchange. The Economic Commission for Africa (ECA) has already mapped out the process for this transformation in documents mentioned earlier. But Africans must learn to trade among themselves. A market of 600 million people is not a small market. With better economic and social programs, more stability, and democracy, the buying power of Africans will increase. Right now about 85 percent of Africa's total exports are marketed in the industrialized countries of the North compared to 75 percent for Latin America and 68 percent for South and East Asia. Only a very small fraction of officially recorded exports, of about 3 and 6 percent, goes to other African countries. This is indeed a very poor showing for all the rhetoric about continental unity, all the declarations and charters, and all the cooperation schemes which dot the continent. In 1988 intra-community trade in the Economic Community of West African States (ECOWAS) was a mere 4.9 percent. In the CEAO which was disbanded in February 1994 it was 10.5 percent; for UDEAC, it was 3.6 percent; and in CEPGL, it was only 0.7% percent.[33]

The signing of the Treaty establishing the African Economic Community (AEC) at the 27th Summit of the OAU in Abuja, Nigeria on June 3, 1991 has been described as marking a major milestone in the continent's quest for unity and development. The Treaty which contains 106 articles outlined a timetable "for the phased removal of barriers to intra-African trade, the strengthening of the existing regional economic groupings, and other steps towards African economic cooperation" which are expected to lead ultimately to the formation of an

"Africa-wide monetary union and economic community by the year 2025."[34] Article 3 of the AEC Treaty affirmed the adherence of the contracting parties to:

a) equality and interdependence of member states;
b) solidarity and collective self-reliance;
c) inter-state co-operation, harmonization of policies and integration programs;
d) promotion of harmonious development of economic activities among member states;
e) observance of the legal system of the Community;
f) peaceful settlement of disputes among member states, active cooperation between neighboring countries and promotion of a peaceful environment as a pre-requisite for economic development;
g) recognition, promotion and protection of human and peoples' rights in accordance with the provisions of the African Charter on Human and Peoples' Rights; and
h) accountability, economic justice and popular participation in development.

In Article 4, the Treaty spells out the four objectives of the AEC to be: a) the promotion of economic, social and cultural development and the integration of African economies in order to increase self-reliance and promote indigenous and self-sustained development; b) the establishment on a continental scale, a framework for the development, mobilization and utilization of the human and material resources of Africa; c) the promotion of co-operation in all fields of human endeavor in order to raise the standard of living of African peoples, and maintain and enhance economic stability, foster close and peaceful relations among member states and contribute to the progress, development and the economic integration of the continent; and d) the co-ordination and harmonization of policies among existing and future economic communities.

Article 4 lists six stages of implementation which are expected to "unfold over a period of 34 years." **Stage 1**—Strengthening regional economic communities and establishing new ones. This will take five years. **Stage 2**—Stabilizing tariffs, customs duties and other barriers to intra-community trade;

strengthening sectoral integration; coordinating and harmonizing activities of the regional organizations. This will take eight years. **Stage 3**—Setting up free trade areas within each regional community. This will take ten years. **Stage 4**—Establishing an Africa-wide customs union, with common external tariff, by harmonizing regional tariff and non-tariff systems. This will take two years. **Stage 5**—Establishing an African Common Market through the adoption of common policies in agriculture, industry, transport; the harmonization of monetary, financial and fiscal policies; and the application of the principle of the free movement of people and right of residence. This will take four years. **Stage 6**—Finalizing the African Economic Community through the consolidation of the common market structure; the establishment of an African Monetary Union, African Central Bank and single African currency; and **creation of a pan-African parliament** elected by continental universal suffrage. Implementation of the final stage for the setting up of the structure of African multi-national enterprises. This will take five years.

Such Pan-African declarations are not new to the region. The problem has always been one of political will. This is why the current crisis, difficult and costly as it has been, is very good for Africa. It has opened up the palaces, mansions, and fortresses to attack. It has reduced the room for maneuver available to African leaders. It has shown the limits of populist and diversionary modes of governance. The crisis is encouraging new questions, new alignments and realignments, new modes of struggle, and the development of holistic programs for restructuring the politics and economy of Africa. The conservative and spent character of African leaders is evidenced in the AEC Treaty. For a region which houses the largest number of cooperation and integration schemes in the world, it is ridiculous that it has mapped out 34 years to achieve an economic community. While we recognize the need to be gradual, the reality of the African condition, dictates an urgent and serious response to its deepening crisis and impoverishment. The world is not going to wait for Africa to take its time in a rapidly changing and increasingly complex global system. Africa is not Europe and the OAU should not try to emulate the European Community in addressing Africa's peculiar conditions of backwardness, dependence, domination, vulnerability, poverty and underdevelopment. Given that none of the current leaders will be in office by AD 2025, the current decision to finalize arrangements for a regional community in 34 years appears to be an attempt to buy time and give the impression that something was being done as a response to the crisis.

There is not enough time here to make a detailed critique of the Treaty. Suffice to note that the new generation of Africans must now seize the initiative. We can no longer rely on the past generation, a generation which squandered our future, mortgaged Africa to foreign creditors, and reduced our worth in the eyes of the world. When violence is necessary to resolve our contradictions we must not be afraid to employ it just because some powerful nations that thrived on violence now think that it is bad. No people are born violent. Socioeconomic and political realities, the balance of power and politics, and the character of political coalitions and contestation dictate the need to employ violence as a strategy for political action.

In conclusion, I will like to reiterate the fact that the future will look a hundred times worse than the dismal present unless we take seriously the empowerment of the people, their organizations and communities; the total democratization of socioeconomic and political relations and institutions; and the creation of a genuine African identity. For those of us who have taken permanent refuge in Canada and other parts of the world, we are being unrealistic. As Peter Tosh, the late reggae musician once said, "if you take a Jamaican banana to Toronto, it remains a Jamaican banana."[35] We must strengthen our linkages with Africa and with popular groups in Africa. We must refuse to give in to conservative and veiled efforts to denigrate or trivialize Africa. We must have the courage to reappropriate our voices and the right to speak for ourselves. Sound environmental policies are urgently required as Africa is becoming a dumping ground for the toxic garbage from the West.

The educational system needs to be decolonized and made more relevant to the needs and aspirations of the people. Universities like Legon, Ibadan, Ife, Makerere have become glorified high schools, shadows of what they once represented. Corruption, mismanagement, the illegal seizure of power via military coups, waste, and mismanagement must be punished according to laid down laws. These punishments should be severe enough to serve as a deterrent to other potential criminals. Military expenditures must be cut drastically. Emphasis must be shifted from military to **social defense.** Sound fiscal policies must be put in place and African governments must learn to collect taxes. It is an irony that debt-ridden and poverty-stricken countries of Africa do not collect taxes while the donor countries do not take tax evasion lightly. Imagine how much Africa has lost in the past three decades to this problem. The policies outlined in the *African Charter for Popular Participation in Development*[36] must be seen as guidelines for structural transformation, democratization, empowerment, accountability and a determined march towards the 21st Century. It is only under these conditions that Africa can confront its own economic crisis and create a viable basis for cooperation and unity in the context of a highly exploitative, unequal and protectionist global order. It is clear therefore that Africa needs first, credible, viable and fundamental transformation of the *national* orders, then, it will be possible to transform the continent through a continent-wide political agenda arising naturally from the national reconstruction projects. Any other approach will amount to the usual political rigmaroles, defensive radicalism, propaganda, and political posturing which the continent has witnessed thus far.

Notes

1 See Julius O. Ihonvbere, The Economic Crisis in Sub-Saharan Africa: Depth, Dimensions and Prospects for Recovery, *The Journal of International Studies* (27) (July 1991), pp. 41-69.

2 See Fantu Cheru, *The Silent Revolution in Africa: Debt, Development and Democracy* (London and Harare: Zed and Anvil, 1989).

3 For the case of Somalia see Julius O. Ihonvbere, Beyond Warlords and Clans: The African Crisis and the Somali Situation, *International Third World Studies Journal and Review* Vol. 6, (1994), pp. 7-19.

4 For a critique of this anti-African approach see Kofi Awoonor, Non-Violence: Global to Local Choices for Peace. Keynote lecture Delivered at the Annual Conference on Non-Violence held at the University of Texas at Austin, Texas October 23-24, 1993.

5 See for example George Padmore, *Panafricanism or Communism?* (London: Dennis Dobson, 1956) and Nnamdi Azikiwe, *Renascent Africa* (London: Frank Cass, 1968).

6 Declaration by the Governments of East Africa, June 1963, in Martin Minogue and Judith Molloy, (eds.), *African Aims and Attitudes: Selected Readings* (Cambridge: Cambridge University Pres, 1974), p.203.

7 George Padmore, *Panafricanism or Communism?* op cit. Reproduced in Minogue and Molloy, (eds.), *African Aims and Attitudes*, op cit., p. 210.

8 Ibid, p. 212.

9 See Claude Ake, *A Political Economy of Africa* (London: Longman, 1981).

10 See Claude Ake, *Revolutionary Pressures in Africa* (London: Zed Books, 1978); and Mohamed Babu, *African Socialism or Socialist Africa?* (London: Zed Books, 1981).

11 See Michael Clough, *Free at Last? U.S. Policy Toward Africa and the End of the Cold War* (New York: Council on Foreign Relations, 1992).

12 See George Ayittey, *Africa Betrayed* (New York: St. Martins Press, 1992).

13 Kwame Nkrumah, *I Speak of Freedom* (London: Heinemann Educational Books, 1961) reproduced in Minogue and Molloy, (eds.), *African Aims and Attitudes*, op cit., p. 214.

14 Kwame Nkrumah, *Africa Must Unite* (London: Heinemann Educational Books, 1963) in *ibid*, p. 216.

15 See Claude Ake, *Revolutionary Pressures in Africa* op. cit.; and Julius O. Ihonvbere (ed.), *Political Economy of Crisis and Underdevelopment in Africa: Selected Works of Claude Ake* (Lagos: JAD Publishers, 1990).

16 See Jennifer S. Whitaker, *How Can Africa Survive?* (New York: Council on Foreign Relations, 1988); Richard Sandbrook with Judith Barker, *The Politics of Africa's Economic Stagnation* (Cambridge: Cambridge University Press, 1985); Bade Onimode, *Imperialism and Underdevelopment in Nigeria* (London: Zed Books, 1982); and Fantu Cheru, *The Silent Revolution in Africa* op. cit.

17 See Robert Kaplan, The Coming Anarchy, *Atlantic Monthly* (February 1994) for a Sierra Leonean case.

18 See World Bank, *Sub-Saharan Africa: From Crisis to Sustainable Growth–A Long-Term Perspective Study* (Washington, DC: World Bank, 1989); and George Ayittey, *Africa Betrayed* op. cit.

19 Sophie Pedder, *The Economist* (August 21, 1993).

20 For detailed studies on Nigeria see the works of Claude Ake, Okwudiba Nnoli, Eddie Madunagu, Pita Agbese, Timothy Shaw, Larry Diamond, Terisa Turner, Segun Osoba, Bade Onimode, Yusuf Bala Usman, Iyang Eteng, Festus Iyayi, and Bayo Olukoshi.

21 See David S. Wiley, Academic Analysis and U.S. Policy Making in Africa: Reflections and Conclusions, *Issue* Vol XIX, (2) (1991), pp. 38-48.

22 See Michael Clough, *Free at Last?* Op. Cit.; Julius O. Ihonvbere, Why Africans Economies Will Not Recover, *Iranian Journal of International Affairs* (Spring-Summer 1994), pp. 146-73; and Between Debt and Disaster: The Politics of Africa's Debt Crisis, *In Depth: A Journal of Opinion and Values* Vol. 4, (1) (Winter 1994). Pp. 108-32.

23 Michael Chege, Remembering Africa, *Foreign Affairs* Vol, 7, (1) (1991-92), pp. 148-63.

24 See David Wiley, Academic Analysis and U.S. Policy Making on Africa, op. cit.

25 See Julius O. Ihonvbere, *Nigeria: The Politics of Adjustment and Democracy* (New Brunswick, New Jersey: Transaction Publishers, 1994); Fantu Cheru, *The Silent Revolution in Africa*, op. cit.; Richard Sandbrook, *The Politics of Africa's Economic Recovery* (Cambridge: Cambridge University Press, 1993); and Claude Ake, *Democracy and Development in Africa* (Washington, D.C.: The Brookings Institution, 1996).

26 See Julius O. Ihonvbere, *Africa and New World Order* (Forthcoming).

27 See Julius O. Ihonvbere, The African Crisis, Regionalism and Prospects for Recovery, in Bruce Berman and Piotor Dutkiewicz (eds.), *Africa and Eastern Europe: Crisis and Transformations* (Kingston, Ontario: Queen's University, Center for International Studies, 1993), pp. 121-32; and Olusegun Obasanjo and Felix G.N. Mosha (eds.), *Africa: Rise to Challenge* (New York: Africa Leadership Forum, 1993).

28 See African Association of Political Science, *Newsletter* (June 1993).

29 World Bank, *Sub-Saharan Africa: From Crisis to Sustainable Growth* op. cit., p. 1.

30 See Julius O. Ihonvbere, Political Conditionally and Prospects for Recovery in Sub-Saharan Africa, *International Third World Studies Journal and Review* Vol. 3, (1-2) (1991), pp. 17-26.

31 See Adebayo Adedeji, (ed.), *Africa Within the World: Beyond Dispossession and Dependence* (London: Zed Books, 1993); and Julius O. Ihonvbere, Is Democracy Possible in Africa?: The Elites, The People, and Civil Society, *QUEST: Philosophical Discussions* Vol. VI, (2) (December 1992), pp. 84-108.

32 See Ross Hammond and Lisa McGowan, Ghana: The World Bank's Sham Showcase, in Kevin Danaher (ed.), *50 Years Is Enough: The Case Against the World Bank and the International Monetary Fund* (Boston: South End Press, 1994), pp. 78-82.

33 See Olusegun Obasanjo and Felix G.N. Mosha, (eds.), *Africa: Rise to Challenge*, op. cit.; and Larry A Swatuk and Timothy M. Shaw (eds.), *The South at the End of the Twentieth Century* (New York: St. Martin's Press, 1994).

34 See *Africa Recovery* (September 1991).

35 Comments at a public performance in Toronto, Ontario, Canada, June 1980.

36 Economic Commission for Africa, *African Charter for Popular Participation in Development and Transformation* (Addis Ababa: ECA, 1990).

Contributors

George A. Agbango is Associate Professor and former Chair of the Department of Political Science at Bloomsburg University of Pennsylvania. He received his doctorate degree in Political Science from Clark Atlanta University (Atlanta, Georgia). He has held faculty positions at Spelman College (adjunct, 1987-1988) and Clark Atlanta University (1989-1990). A former Member of Parliament of Ghana (1979-1981), Agbango was the Deputy Chairman of the Parliamentary Foreign Affairs Committee as well as the First Deputy Majority Chief Whip. He was one of Ghana's chief delegates to the 1981 United Nations General Assembly (New York).

In 1987, Agbango was recognized for distinguished service to the Georgia State Senate (by a unanimous resolution of the Georgia State Senate). A year later, he received the United States Institute of Peace Scholar Award. In 1995, he was bestowed a chieftaincy title by the Paramount Chief of Kusasiland (Chief Azoka II) in Ghana. Agbango is currently the President of the African Association of Political Science (North America Chapter).

Agbango has conducted extensive research on the role of the military in Africa and has published articles on Africa in professional journals.

Baffour Agyeman-Duah is Associate Professor of Political Science and head of the Division of Social Sciences at Bennett College, Greensboro, North Carolina. He has also held teaching positions at Elon College (Elon, NC), and the University of North Carolina (Greensboro, NC). He received his doctorate degree from the University of Denver in Denver, Colorado. In 1994 he received a two-year Fulbright-Hays Fellowship and taught at the Center for International Affairs, University of

Ghana, in Legon, Ghana. Agyeman-Duah has published several articles in professional journals.

George B. N. Ayittey is Associate Professor of Economics at The American University in Washington, D.C. Since receiving his doctorate degree in Economics from the University of Manitoba in Canada, he has taught at Wayne State College (Nebraska), and Bloomsburg University (Pennsylvania). He is a former fellow of the Hoover Institute and a former Bradley Resident Scholar. He is the author of numerous articles published in professional journals in the Americas, Europe, and Africa.

Ayittey is the author of *Indigenous African Institutions* (1991), *Africa Betrayed* (1992), and *Africa's Economic Crisis: Indigenous Solutions* (1993). He is the founder and President of the Free Africa Foundation (a Washington based human rights and lobby organization).

Henry A. Elonge is Associate Professor of Public Administration at Clark Atlanta University. He received his doctorate degree in Public Administration from the Nelson Rockerfeller Graduate School of Public Affairs, State University of New York in Albany, New York. He has conducted elaborate research on civil service reform and the development of legislative institutions in Africa. He has served on Third World development programs such as the USAID Somalia Development Project, USAID Legislative Development Project in Chile, and USIA Legislative Development Project in Nigeria.

Walle Engedayehu is Assistant Professor of Political Science at Prairie View A & M University of Texas, Prairie View, Texas. He received his doctorate degree from Atlanta University, Atlanta, Georgia. Walle has published a number of articles on Ethiopia. In 1994, he travelled to Israel where he conducted research on the resettlement of Ethiopian Jews. He is the current Vice President of the International Council on Information for Sustainable Development (ICISD).

Julius O. Ihonvbere is Associate Professor of Political Science at The University of Texas at Austin where he teaches African and Third World Politics. He is currently a Program Officer with the Ford Foundation (New York) responsible for "The Governance and Civil Society Program." He previously held teaching positions at the Universities of Ife and Port Harcourt in Nigeria as well as the University of Toronto in Canada. He received his doctorate degree in Political Science from The University of Toronto in Canada. Ihonvbere has published extensively in international journals. He is the author of *Nigeria: The Politics of Adjustment and Democracy (1994)*, and *Economic Crisis, Civil Society and Democratization: The Case of Zambia* (1996). He has co-authored two books: *The Rise and Fall of Nigeria's Second Republic (1985)* and *Towards a Political Economy of Nigeria: Petroleum and Politics at the Semi-Periphery (1988)*. He co-edited *Nigeria and the International Capitalist System (1988)*. In 1994 he received the First Mario Zamora Memorial Award for "excellence in scholarship on the Third World", an award established by the Association of Third World Studies.

Margaret C. Lee is currently a Scholar in Residence at American University, Washington, DC. From 1994 to 1996, she was Associate Professor of Political Science at Spelman College in Atlanta, Georgia. Following the completion of her doctoral program at the University of Pittsburgh, Lee lectured in the department of Political Science at Tennessee Technological University in Cookeville, Tennessee, from 1986 to 1994. She was a visiting scholar at the Center for African Studies at Stanford University (1993-1994 academic year). During the summer of 1992, she was a research associate at the South African Institute of International Affairs, the University of the Witwatersrand in Johannesburg, South Africa.

Lee is the author of *SADCC: The Political Economy of Development in Southern Africa*, (1989), *The Historical Development of and Challenge to White World Hegemony*, (1995) and numerous articles on Southern Africa. She is a member of the executive committee of the African Association of Political Science.

Nchor B. Okorn is Associate Professor of Political Science at Dillard University in New Orleans, Louisiana. He earned his doctorate degree in Political Science from Atlanta University. He has held faculty positions at the University of Calabar

(Nigeria), Morris Brown College (Atlanta, Georgia), and Selma University in Alabama. He has conducted extensive research in military policies and African politics.

Akwasi Osei is Associate Professor of History and Political Science at Delaware State University, in Dover, Maryland. He received his doctorate degree from Howard University, Washington, D.C. He has held faculty positions at Oberlin College and the College of Wooster. He the author of several research papers.

Yakubu Saaka is Professor and Chair of the Department of African American Studies at Oberlin College. He received his doctorate degree in Political Science from Case Western Reserve University, Ohio. He has published numerous articles in professional journals, principally on Ghanaian politics. He is the author of *Local Government and Political Change in Northern Ghana.* Saaka is a former Member of the Ghanaian parliament. He was the Deputy Minister for Foreign Affairs in Ghana from 1979 to 1981.

Saaka is the General Editor of Peter Lang's series on Society and Politics in Africa.

Bibliography

Aberra, Worku. "Tribalism Rules in Ethiopia," *New Africa*, No. 311, September, 1993, p. 20.

Adam, Heibert and Kogila Moodley. *The Negotiated Revolution: Society and Politics in Post-Apartheid South Africa* (Johannesburg: Jonathan Ball Publishers, 1993).

Adams, Paul. "Babangida's Boondoggle," *Africa Report* (July-August, 1993).

Agbango, George A. "The Impact of Political Instability on the Economic Development Policies of Ghana (1960-1980) and Its Implications for Sub-Saharan Africa," (Ph.D. Dissertation, Clark Atlanta University, 1991).

Ahiakpor, James, C. W. "Rawlings, Economic Policy Reform and the Poor: Consistency or Betrayal?" *Journal of Modern African Studies*, 29, 4, 1991, p. 583.

Ahidjo, Ahmadou. *The Political Philosophy of Ahmadou Ahidjo* (Yaounde, Cameroun: Paul Bory Publishers, 1968).

Ake, Claude. *A Political Economy of Africa* (New York: Longman, Inc., 1981).

———. "The Case for Democracy," *African Governance in the 1990's*, Working Papers from the Second Annual Seminar of the African Governance Program, (Atlanta: The Carter University Center of Emory University, 1990), p. 2-6.

ANC, *The Reconstruction and Development Programme: A Policy Framework* (Johannesburg: Umanyano Publications, Undated).

Apter, Andrew. "Things Fall Apart? Yoruba Response to the 1983 Elections in Ondo State, Nigeria." *Journal of Modern African Studies*, 25, 3 (1987).

Apter, David E. *The Politics of Modernization* (Chicago: The University of Chicago Press, 1965).

Asoyan, Boris. "Russia and South Africa," *International Affairs,* December 1989, p. 48.

Ayittey, George B.N. *Africa Betrayed* (New York: St. Martin's Press, 1992).

————. *Indigenous African Institutions.* (New York: Transnational Publishers, 1991).

Baran, Paul A. "On the Political Economy of Backwardness," *The Manchester School,* XX (January 1952), pp. 66-84.

————. *The Political Economy of Growth* (New York: The Monthly Review Press, 1957).

Battersby, John. "ANC Goes Public on Abuses in Exile Camps," *The Christian Science Monitor,* August 25, 1993.

————. "Mandela Faces Unresolved Issue of Covert Web in Security Forces," *The Christian Science Monitor,* October 4, 1994.

————. "Black Hopes, White Fears: A Balancing Act," *The Christian Science Monitor,* September 28, 1994.

————. "ANC Admits to Abuses of Rights," *The Christian Science Monitor,* October 21, 1992.

————. "Independent Probe Links Inkatha, S. African Police," *The Christian Science Monitor,* March 21, 1994.

Bienen, Henry. *Armed Forces, Conflict, and Change in Africa* (San Francisco: Westview Press, 1989).

Biya, Paul. *The New Deal: Two Years After* (Bamenda, Cameroon: 1985).

Blomstrom, Magnus and Bjorn Hettne. *Development Theory in Transition* (London: Zed Books, Ltd., 1988).

Boley, G. E. Saigbey. *Liberia: The Rise and Fall of the First Republic* (New York: St. Martins Press, 1983).

Buell, Raymond Leslie. *The Native Problem in Africa,* Vol. II (Frank Cass & Company, Ltd., 1965).

Bwy, D.O. "Political Instability in Latin America: The Cross-Cultural Test of Causal Model," *Latin America Research Review* 3 (1968).

Cabral, Amicar. *Unity and Struggle* (New York: Monthly Review Press, 1979)

Callaghy, Thomas M. "Politics and Vision in Africa: the interplay of domination, equality and liberty." in Patrick Chabal, ed., *Political Domination in Africa: Reflection on the Limit of Power,* (Cambridge U. Press, 1986), pp. 30-51.

Cawthra, Gavin. *Brutal Force: The Apartheid War Machine.* (London: International Defence and Aid Fund for Southern Africa, 1986).
————. *Policing South Africa: The SAP and the Transition From Apartheid* (London and New Jersey: Zed Books LTD, 1993).
Cerbenka, Zednedk. *The Organization of African Unity and Its Charter* (New York: Frederick A. Praeger, 1968).
Chazan, Naomi. "The Anomalies of Continuity: Perspectives on Ghanaian Elections since Independence" in Fred M. Hayward, ed. *Elections in Independent Africa,* Westview, 1987, p. 63.
Chilcote, Ronald H. *Theories of Comparative Politics: The Search for a Paradigm* (Boulder, Colorado: Westview Press, 1981).
Chinweizu, *The West and the Rest of Us* (London: NOK Publishers, 1978).
Clarke, John. *Resettlement and Rehabilitation: Ethiopia's Campaign Against Famine* (London: Hamey and Jones Ltd., 1986).
Cock, Jacklyn. "The Dynamics of Transforming South Africa's Defense Forces," in *South Africa: The Political Economy of Transformation* by Stedman, Stephen John, ed. (London: Lynne Rienner Publishers, 1994).
Cock, Jacklyn and Laurie Nathan, eds. *Society At War: The Militarisation of South Africa* (New York: St. Martin's Press, 1989).
Cook, Chris and David Killingray, *African Political Facts Since 1945* (New York: Facts on File, Inc., 1984).
Costa, Peter da. "The Politics of `Settlement'" *Africa Report* (November-December, 1993).
Cramer, Christopher. "Rebuilding South Africa." *Current History*, May 1994, p. 209.
Daniel R. Dempton, "Africa in the Age of Perestroika," *Africa Today*, 3rd Quarter 1991, p. 13.
Davidson, Basil. *The Black Man's Burden: Africa and the Curse of the Nation-State* (New York: Times Books, 1992).
————. *Which Way Africa?* (Baltimore, Maryland: Penguin Books, Limited, 1973).
Decalo, Samuel. *Coups and Army Rule in Africa* (New Haven: Yale University Press, 1976).
Diamond, Larry. "Beyond Autocracy: Prospects for Democracy in Africa, "*Beyond Autocracy in Africa*, Working Papers for the Inaugural Seminal for Governance in Africa Program,

(Atlanta, Georgia: The Carter University Center of Emory University, 1989), p. 24-27.

Diop, Cheikh Anta. *Pre-Colonial Black Africa*, (Westport, Connecticut: Lawrence Hill and Co., 1987).

Doro, Mario E. and Newell M. Stultz, eds. *Governing in Black Africa: Perspectives in New States* (Englewood Cliffs, N.J.: Prentice-Hall, Inc., 1970).

Dos Santos, Theotonio. "The Crisis of Development Theory and the Problem of Independence in Latin America," *Siglo 21* (1969).

Dunn, D. Elwood and S. Bryon Tarr. *Liberia: A National Polity in Transition* (Metuchen, New Jersey: The Scarecrow Press, Inc., 1988), 39.

Edmond J. Keller, "Eritrean Self-determination Revisited," *Africa Today*, 38, 2, p. 10.

Ejembi, Henry I. "Science vs. Philosophy: The Search for a Relevant Political Science", in Yolamu Barongo, *Political Science in Africa*, (London: Zed Books, 1983), p.20-21.

Enahoro, Peter. "The Maturity of a Nation," *Africa Now* (London: Pan African Publisher Ltd 1981).

Enonchong, H.N.A. *Cameroon Constitutional Law in a Mixed Common Law and Civil Law System* (Yaounde, Cameroon: C.E.P.M.A.E., 1976).

Faisel Robie, "Self-Determination is a must for Ethiopia," *Ethiopian Review*, February 1992, p. 30.

Feierabend, Ivo K. *Anger, Violence and Politics* (Englewood Cliffs: Prentice Hall Inc., 1972).

Feit, Edward. "Military Coups and Political Development: Some Lessons from Ghana and Nigeria," *World Politics*, 20, 2 1968, pp.179-93.

Finer, Samuel Edward. *The Man On Horseback: The Role of the Military in Politics* (New York: Frederick A. Praeger, Inc., Publisher, 1962).

First, Ruth. *Power in Africa*, (New York: Pantheon Books, 1970).

Foltz, William J. and Henry S. Bienen, Editors. *Arms and the African*, (New Haven: Yale University Press, 1985).

Formani, Robert. *The Myth of Scientific Public Policy*, (New Brunswick, Transaction Publishers, 1990).

Fosu, Augustin K. "Political Instability and Economic Growth with Evidence from Sub-Saharan Africa"; a paper presented at the 32nd Annual Meeting of the African Studies Association in Atlanta, Georgia, November 3-5, 1989, pp. 3-4.

Frank, Andre Gundar. *Latin America: Underdevelopment or Revolution* (New York: Monthly Review Press, 1969).

Fullas, Hailu. "An Interview with Dr. Taye Wolde Semayat," *Ethiopian Register*, 1, 1, February 1994, pp. 11-12.

Gailey, Jr., Hary A. *History of Africa from 1800 to Present*, Vol. II (Huntington, New York: Robert E. Krieger Publishing Company, 1981).

Geekie, Russell. "America's Maverick Ambassador," *Africa Report* (March-April, 1993) and Binaifer Nowrojee, "Kenya: Pressure for Change," *Africa Report* (January-February, 1994).

Laski, Harold J. *The State in Theory and Practice*, (London: George Allen and Unwin, Ltd, 1936).

Ghai, Dahran and Smith, Lawrence D. *Agricultural Prices, Policy and Equity in Sub-Saharan Africa* (Boulder, Colorado: Lynne Rienner Publishers, Inc., 1987).

Giesbrecht, Martin Gerhard. *The Evolution of Economic Society* (San Francisco: W. H. Freeman and Company, 1972).

Gilkes, Patrick. "Eritrea: Historiography and Mythology," *African Affairs*, October 1991, p. 624.

Girma Bekele, "The Hidden Agenda," *Ethiopian Review*, January 1992, p. 15.

Gorbachev, Mikhail. *A Road to the Future: Complete Text of the December 7, 1988 United Nations Address* (Santa Fe, New Mexico: Ocean Tree Press, 1990).

Greene, Thomas H. *Comparative Revolutionary Movements* (Englewood Cliffs, N.J.: Prentice-Hall, Inc., 1974).

Greene, A.H.M. Kirk. *Crisis and Conflict in Nigeria: A Documentary Source Book 1966-70*, (London: Oxford University Press, 1971). 427-

Grundy, Kenneth. "South Africa's Tortuous Transition," *Current History*, May 1993, p. 229.

———. *The Militarization of South African Politics*. (Bloomington: Indiana University Press, 1986).

Gurr, Ted. *Why Men Rebel* (Princeton, N.J.: Princeton University Press, 1970), pp. 22-58, and "Psychological Factors in Civil Strife," *World Politics* (January 1968), pp. 245-278.

Halliday, Fred and Maxine Molyneux. *The Ethiopian Revolution* (London: Urwin Brothers, 1981).

Hansen, Emmanuel and Kwame Ninsin, eds., *The State, Development and Politics in Ghana* (London: CODESRIA, Books, 1989).

Hapgood, David. *Africa: From Independence to Tomorrow* (New York: Atheneum, 1970).

Harbeson, John. "The Future of the Ethiopian State After Mengistu," *Current History*, 92, May 1993, p. 211.

Heaphey, James J. "Legislative Staffing: Organizational And Philosophical Considerations," in James Heaphey and Alan P. Balutis, *Legislative Staffing: A Comparative Perspective.* (New York: Sage Publications, 1975), p. 17-20.

Heilbroner, Robert L. *The Worldly Philosophers: The Lives, Times, and Ideas of the Great Economic Thinkers* (New York: Simon and Schuster, 1953).

Herbst, Jeffrey. "South Africa: Economic Crisis and Distributional Imperative," in *South Africa: The Political Economy of Transformation*, Stephen John Stedman, ed. Boulder and London: Lynne Rienner Publishers, 1994.

Hickey, Raymond. "1982 Maitatsine Uprising in Nigeria: A Note," *African Affairs* Vol. 83 No. 331. April 1984.

Howe, Herbert. "The South African Defence Force and Political Reform," *The Journal of Modern African Studies,* Vol., 32, No. 1, 1994, p. 33.

Howitt, Kenneth. "Scientific Socialist Regimes in Africa: Political Differentiation, Avoidance and unawareness," in Carl G. Rosberg and Thomas Callaghy, eds., *Socialism in Sub-Saharan Africa: A Reassessment.* Berkeley, 1979.

Huntington, Samuel P. *Political Order in Changing Societies* (New Haven, Connecticut: Yale University Press, 1972).

―――. *The Third Wave-Democratization in the Late Twentieth Century* (Norman and London: University of Oklahoma Press, 1991).

Jackson, Robert H. and Carl G. Roseberg, *Personal Rule in Black Africa* (Los Angeles: University of California Press, 1982).

James, Wilmont. "Building on Democracy in the New South Africa," Lecture at the Southern Center for International Studies (SCIS), Atlanta, GA, September 22, 1994.

Kale, P.M. *Political Evolution in the Cameroons*, (Buea, Cameroon, August 1967).

Keller, Bill. "South Africa Pact: Unlikely Partners," *The New York Times*, November 1993.

Keller, Edmond J. *Revolutionary Ethiopia: From Empire to People's Republic*, (Bloomington: Indiana University Press, 1988).

Kempton, Daniel. "Africa in the Age of Perestroika," *Africa Today*, 38, 2, 1991, p. 7.

Keynes, John M. *Essays in Biography* (New York: Horizon Press, 1951).

Kigston, Robert J. ed., *Perestroika Papers* (Dubuque, IA: Kendall/ Hunt, 1988).

Kraus, Jon. "The Political Economy of Stability and Structural Adjustment in Ghana." In Donald Rothchild, ed., *Ghana: The Political Economy of Recovery* (Boulder, Colorado: Lynn Rienner, 1991).

Laidi, Zaki. *The Superpowers and Africa: The Constraints of a Rivalry, 1960-1990.*

Lawrence, Patrick. "Exposing the Past," *Africa Report*, January/February, 1993.

Legum, Colin. "The Coming of Africa's 2nd. Independence", *Washington Quarterly*, Winter, 1990, p. 129.

Lewis, Herbert. "Beginning Again," *Africa Report*, September-October 1991, pp. 59-62.

Lewis, Stephen R., Jr. *The Economics of Apartheid* (New York: Council on Foreign Relations Press, 1990).

Lieber, Robert J. *No Common Power: Understanding International Relations* (Boston: Scott, Foreman and Company 1988).

Lodge, Tom. "The African National Congress in the 1990s," in *South Africa Review 6*, Glenn Moss and Ingrid Obery, eds. Johannesburg: Ravan Press, 1992, pp. 45-46.

Lorenz, Knorad. *On Aggression* (New York: Bantam Books 1971).

Lowenkopf, Martin. *Politics in Liberia* (Stanford, California: Hover Institution Press, 1976).

Luttwak, Edward. *Coups d'Etat: A Practical Handbook* (New York: Alfred A. Knopf, Inc., 1969).

Machiavelli, Niccolo. *The Prince and the Discourses*, (New York: Random House, Inc., 1950).

Mahler, Gregory S. *Comparative Politics: An Institutional Cross-National Approach*, (Englewood Cliff, NJ: Prentice Hall, 1995).

Maifer, Karl. "Nigeria: Voodoo Democracy?" *Africa Report* (January-February, 1992).

Malambo, Isaac, Agnes Banda and Victor Kayira, "Three Bow Out of Presidential Race—Its Now KK vs Chiluba," *Times of Zambia* (October 2, 1991).

Marx, Karl. *Capital: A Critique of Political Economy*, edited by Frederick Engels (New York: International Publishers, 1967), 3 Vols.

Marx, Karl and Frederick Engels. *Selected Works* (Moscow: Foreign Languages Publishing House, 1958), Vol. 1 & 2.

Meisel, James H. *Counter-Revolutions: How Revolutions Die* (New York: Atherton Press, 1966).

Melinda Ham, "An Outspoken Opposition," *Africa Report* (November-December 1993).

Meredith, Martin. *The First Dance of Freedom* (New York: Harper and Row Publishers, 1984).

Michael MacDonald and Wilmont James, "The Hand on the Tiller: The Politics of State and Class in South Africa," *The Journal of Modern African Studies*, Vol. 31,No. 3,1993,p. 397.

Mkhondo, Rich. *Reporting South Africa* (Portsmouth, NH: Heinemann, 1993).

Mondlane, Eduardo. *The Struggle for Mozambique* (Baltimore, Maryland: Penguin Books Limited, 1969).

Morrison, Donald George et al. *Black Africa: A Comparative Hanbook* (New York: The Free Press, 1972).

Mulenga, Mulenga and Victor Kayora. "KK was a big liability," *Times of Zambia* (November 4, 1991).

Munoz, Heraldo, editor. *From Dependency to Development* (Boulder, Colorado: Westview Press, 1981).

Mutua, Makau wa. "The New Oligarchy," *Africa Report*, 38, 5, (September-October 1993), p. 28.

Mutua, Makau wa. "An Oppressed Opposition," *Africa Report*, 38, 6, November-December, 1993, p. 52.

Mveng, Engelbert. *Histoire du Cameroun* (Paris: Presence Africaine, 1963).

Myrdal, Gunnar. *Asian Drama: An Inquiry into the Poverty of Nations* (New York: Patheon, 1968).

Nafziger, E. Wayne. "Economic Impact of the Nigerian Civil War," *Journal of Modern African Studies*, 10.2 (1972).

———. "Economic Impact of the Nigerian Civil War," *Journal of Modern African Studies*, 10.2 (1972).

————. *The Economics of Political Instability*: *The Nigerian-Biafran War* (Boulder, Co.: Westview Press,1983).

Naomi Chazan, "Liberalization, Governance and Political Space in Ghana." In Goran Hyden and Michael Bratton, *Governance and Politics in Africa* (Boulder, CO: Lynn Rienner, 1992).

Naomi Chazan, "The New Politics of Participation in Tropical Africa." *Comparative Politics*, 14, 2, 1982, p. 169.

Nardin, Terry. "Violence and the State: A Critique of Empirical Political Theory," *Sage Professional Papers in Comparative Politics Series*, No. 01-020 (Beverly Hills, California: Sage Publications, 1971).

Nelson, Robert and Howard Hope. "Modernization and the Politics of Communalism: A Theoretical Perspective," *American Political Science Review* LXIV, pp. 1115-1118.

Nelson, Harold D. and Irvin Kaplan, eds., *Ethiopia: A Country Study* (Washington, D.C.: The U.S. Government Press, 1981).

Newagboso, Maxwell. "Religious Dimension," *West Africa*, July 18, 1988.

Boley, G. E. Saigbey. *Liberia: The Rise and Fall of the First Republic* (New York: St. Martins Press, 1983).

Ninsin, Kwame A. "Ghanaian Politics after 1981: Revolution or Evolution?" *Canadian Journal of African Studies*, 21, 1, 1987.

Nkrumah, Kwame. *Autobiography of Kwame Nkrumah* (London: Panaf Books Limited, 1973).

Nwagboso, Maxwell. "The Religious Dimension." *West Africa*, July 18, 1988.

Nzongola-Ntalaja, *Revolution and Counter-Revolution in Africa; Essays in Contemporary Politics* (London: Zed Press Limited, 1987).

O'Brien, Donald Cruise. "Modernization, Order and the Erosion of a Democratic Idea): American Political Science, 1960-1970," *The Journal of Development Studies* VIII (July 1973).

Ofori, Ruby. "Ghana: The Elections Controversy," *Africa Report* (July-August, 1993).

Onimode, Bade, Editor. *The IMF, The World Bank and the African Debt: The Social and Political Impact* (New Jersey: Zed Books Ltd., 1989).

Othman, Shehu. "Classes, Crises, and Coup: The Demise of Shagari Regime", *African Affairs*, Vol. 83 No. 333, October 1984.

Ottoway, M., and D. Ottoway, *Ethiopia: Empire in Revolution* (New York: African Publishing Company, 1978).

Owen, Ken. "All Aboard the Gravy Train for Joe and Co," *Sunday Times*, July 24, 1994.

Owusu, Maxwell. "Customs and Coups: a juridical interpretation of civil disorder." *Journal of Modern African Studies*, 22, 1, 1986.

Oyediran, Oyeleye. *Nigerian Government and Politics Under Military Rule: 1966-1979*, (London: The Macmillan Press LTD, 1979).

Palumbo, Dennis J. *Public Policy in America* (New York: Harcourt Brace Jovanovich Publishers, 1988).

Perlmutter, Amos. *The Military and Politics in Modern Times* (New Haven: Yale University Press, 1977).

Pinkney, Robert. *Democracy in the Third World* (Boulder, Colorado: Lynne Rienner, 1993).

Prebisch, Raul. *The Economic Development of Latin America and Its Problems* (New York: United Nations, Department of Social and Economic Affairs, 1950).

Rabushka, Alvin and Kenneth A. Shepsle. *Politics in Plural Societies: A Theory of Democratic Instability* (Columbus, Ohio: Charles E. Merrill, 1972).

Rautenbach, I. M. and E. F. J. Malherbe. *What Does the Constitution Say?* (Auckland Park, SA: The Faculty of Law, Rand Afrikaans University, 1994).

Richburg, Keith B. "International Observers Team Criticizes Ethiopian Elections," *The Washington Post*, 24 June 1992, p. A24.

Rodney, Walter. *How Europe Underdeveloped Africa* (Washington, D.C.: Howard University Press, 1974).

Rostow, W.W. *The Stages of Economic Growth, A Non-Communist Manifesto* (London: Cambridge University Press, 1960).

Rotberg, Robert I. "Ethnic Power Sharing: South Africa's Model," *The Christian Science Monitor*, September 14, 1994.

Rothchild, Donald and Naomi Chazan, *The Precarious Balance: State and Society in Africa* (Westview Press, 1988.)

Rudin, Harry R. *Germans in the Cameroons 1884-1914: A Case Study of Imperialism*, (New Haven, Connecticut: Yale University Press, 1938).

Saaka, Yakubu. "Recurrent Themes in Ghanaian Politics," *Journal of Black Studies*, Vol. 24 No. 3, March, 1994 p. 277.

Sabine, George and Thomas Thorson. *A History of Political Theory* (Hinsdale: Dryden Press, 1983).

Sandbrook, Richard. "Liberal Democracy in Africa: A Socialist-revisiionist Perspective." *Canadian Journal of African Studies,* 29, 4, 1991, p. 583.

Scarpitte, Krank R. *Social Problems* (New York: Holt, Rinehart and Winston Inc.).

Seers, Dudley. "The Meaning of Development, *"Eleventh World Conference of the Society for International Development,* New Delhi (1969).

Sefa Mohamed, "Questions of Democracy," *West Africa,* August 13th-19th, 1990.

Selfe, James. "South Africa's National Management System," in *Society at War: The Militarisation of South Africa,* Jacklyn Cock and Laurie Nathan, eds. (New York: St. Martin's Press, 1989), p. 150.

Shafritz, Jay M. *The Dorsey Dictionary of American Government and Politics,* (Chicago: The Dorsey Press, 1988).

Shaw, Timothy M. "Reformism, Revisionism, Radicalism in African Political Economy during the 1990's", *Journal of Modern African Studies,* 29, 2 1991, p. 194.

Shillington, Kevin *History of South Africa* (London: Longman Inc., 1987).

Sikazwe, Hicks and Davis Mulenga. "UNIP Wiped Out- Zambians Reject Kaunda's Rule as MMD Heads for Landslide," *Times of Zambia* (November 2, 1991); and Kondwani Chirambo, "Zambia Goes Agog," *Times of Zambia* (November 3, 1991).

Smith, Adam. *The Wealth of Nations* (New York: Modern Library, 1937) Book 4.

Sorensen, Georg. *Democracy and Democratization,* (Boulder, CO; Westview Press, 1993).

Tangri, Robert. *Politics in Sub-Saharan Africa,* (London: James Currey Ltd., 1985).

First, Ruth. *Power in Africa* (New York: Pantheon Books, 1970).

Tangri, Roger. "The Politics of Government-Business Relations in Ghana," *Journal of Modern African Studies,* 30, 1992, p. 103.

Tanter, Raymond. "Dimensions of Conflict Behavior Within and Between Nations: 1951-1960," *Journal of Conflict Resolution* 10 (1966).

Thompson, William. "Explanations of the Military Coup," (Ph.D. Dissertation, University of Washington, 1972).
Thompson, W. Scott, Editor. *The Third World: Premises of U.S. Policy* (San Francisco: ICS Press, 1983).
Todaro, Michael. *Economic Development in the Third World*, (London: Longman, 1985).
Tordoff, William. *Government and Politics of Africa*, (Bloomington: Indiana University Press, 1984).
World Bank. *Sub Saharan Africa: From Crisis to Sustainable Growth* (Washington, D.C.: The World Bank, 1989).
————. *World Development Report* (New York: Oxford University Press, 1992).
————. *Sub-Saharan Africa- From Crisis to Sustainable Growth* (Washington, DC: The World Bank, 1989).
Yeebo, Zaya. *Ghana: The Struggle for Popular Power* (London: New Beacon Books Ltd., 1991).
Young, Crawford. *The Politics of Cultural Pluralism* (Madison: The University of Wisconsin Press, 1976).

Periodicals and Serials Consulted
Africa Research Bulletin
Africa Watch
Africa Today
Africa Report
Africa Confidential
Africa Quarterly
African Events
African Concord (Lagos, Nigeria)
African Studies Review
African Business
Arab News
Cameroon Panorama
Colliers Year Book
Commonwealth Currents
Current History
Daily Graphic (Accra, Ghana)
Daily Dispatch
Emerge
EPRDF News Bulletin (Addis Ababa, Ethiopia)
Ethiopian Review

Finance Week
Journal of Modern African Studies
Lesane Gondar
New African
Newbreed
Newswatch
PAS, Vol. 3, Winter 1993.
Peoples Daily Graphic (Accra)
South Africa Review 6
SouthScan
Sunday Times
The Houston Chronicle
The Constitution of the 4th Republic of Ghana
The Christian Science Monitor
The Economist
The African Nationalist
The Christian Science Monitor
The Weekly Mail
The Ethiopian Review
TIME
Times of Zambia (Lusaka)
Towson Journal of International Affairs
West Africa
World Monitor
Zena Ethiopia

George Akeya Agbango is Associate Professor and former Chairman of the Department of Political Science at Bloomsburg University of Pennsylvania. He is also the current President of the African Association of Political Science (North America Chapter).

SOCIETY AND POLITICS IN AFRICA

Yakubu Saaka, General Editor

This multidisciplinary series publishes monographs and edited volumes that provide innovative approaches to the study and appreciation of contemporary African society. Although we focus mainly on subjects in the social sciences, we will consider manuscripts in the humanities that treat context as a significant aspect of discourse. Within the social sciences, we are looking for not only analytically outstanding studies but, what is more important, ones that may also have significant implications for the formulation and implementation of public policy in Africa. We are especially interested in works that challenge pre-existing hierarchies and paradigms.

For additional information about this series or for the submission of manuscripts, please contact:

Peter Lang Publishing
Acquisitions Department
275 7th Avenue, 28th floor
New York, New York 10001

To order other books in this series, please contact our Customer Service Department:

800-770-LANG (within the U.S.)
(212) 647-7706 (outside the U.S.)
(212) 647-7707 FAX

Or browse online by series at:

www.peterlangusa.com